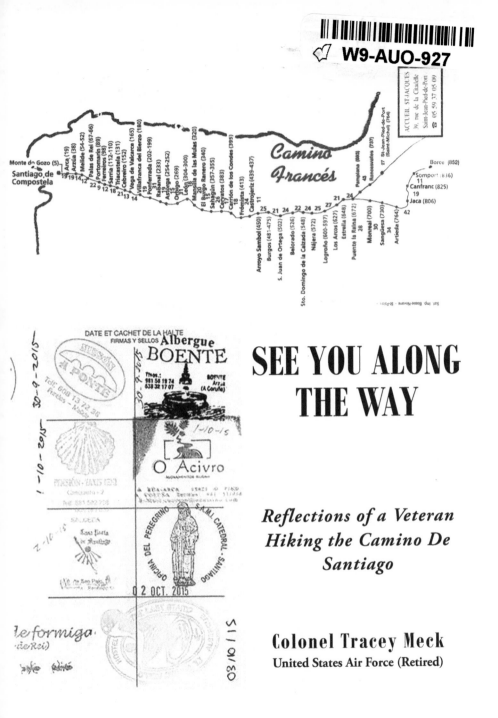

# SEE YOU ALONG THE WAY

*Reflections of a Veteran Hiking the Camino De Santiago*

## Colonel Tracey Meck
United States Air Force (Retired)

---

1 Carnet de Pèlerin de Saint-Jacques, Credencial del Peregrino, distributed by Les Amis du Chemin de Saint-Jacques, Pyrénées-Atlantiques, 39, Rue de la Citadelle, F. 64220 Saint-Jean-Pied-de-Port, France.

ISBN 978-1-64299-898-6 (paperback)
ISBN 978-1-64299-899-3 (digital)

Christian Faith Publishing, Inc.
832 Park Avenue
Meadville, PA 16335
www.christianfaithpublishing.com

Printed in the United States of America

# CHAPTER 1

## On My Way, Again
## 26 August 2015
## D-3 (D Minus Three)

The day I had been contemplating for almost two years was finally here. I boarded the afternoon Icelandair flight from Seattle to Keflavik on 26 August 2015. After a short one-hour layover, I would board another flight to Paris.

I was on my way to take a five-hundred-mile adventure of reflection and physical challenge. My goal was to complete the Camino de Santiago by hiking the popular Camino Francès (French Way) from St. Jean Pied-de-Port in the French Pyrenees, over the mountains and across the northern part of Spain to the Cathedral in Santiago de Compostela in the northwest. In English, *Camino de Santiago* is translated as "The Way of St. James." In John Brierley's guidebook, *A Pilgrim's Guide to the Camino de Santiago* (often referred to on the trail as "The Book"), he explains that the tradition of this walk has its roots around a thousand years ago as a religious pilgrimage for Europeans who could not go to Jerusalem due to the great distance. They go to pay homage to the Apostle James, who is encrypted under the altar in the cathedral.[2]

People still embark on this journey for religious reflection and renewal. Others do it for the physical challenge. Still others, for a general period of reflection. Many go during a period of transition in their lives, such as retirement or the death of a spouse; wishing to reflect on their past, sort out who they are and what they want to do with the rest of their lives. Finally many pilgrims walk the Camino

---

[2] Brierley, p. 32

for the adventure of meeting people from all over the world and sharing something special with them.

Sitting on the plane, I reflected on my reasons. Religion, transition, social interaction, and the physical challenge all played their part. This was not my first time attempting the feat. So there was also a major element of ego and the strong internal need to complete a mission that was only two-thirds complete the last time. As a type A, obsessive-compulsive, perfectionist, and retired military officer, the fact that we did not walk the entire 776 km (just short of five hundred miles) the first time had been gnawing at my soul ever since.

My original intention was to just go back and do the middle two hundred miles that we skipped in 2013. But then again, what good would it do my ego to just do what we skipped? We did just short of three hundred the last time, so knocking out two hundred would not be much of an accomplishment. The problem was that we (or more precisely, *I*) had not completed the five hundred miles. I needed to do the whole thing at one time!

To fill you in on the background of the first attempt (which, upon the advice of a fellow military colonel retiree and hiking buddy in northwest Washington, I am now calling a leaders' recon), the idea was born when a friend of my mom watched the movie *The Way*, starring Martin Sheen and Emilio Estevez.[3] Ria enjoyed the movie and decided it was something special she wanted to do to celebrate her eightieth birthday. She convinced my mom (who was seventy-two at the time) to join her. After retiring from the Air Force in 2012 at the young age of forty-seven, I moved to Washington and joined their weekly hiking group. Seeing how I enjoyed our outings, Mom asked if I wanted to go along.

At first I did not bite. "You've got to be kidding me, why would I want to walk that far? Besides, staying in hostels for over a month, I don't think so! You two are crazy."

---

[3]   *The Way* movie

Mom convinced me to sit down and watch the movie. It was intriguing. The movie illustrated one thing that Mom failed to mention. It was allowable to complete the journey on a bicycle.

"Why don't we bike it?" I asked. "It would be much faster, and we wouldn't have to stay in hostels for so long."

"No way!" Mom shot back without even thinking about it for a second. "We're walking."

Mom liked biking once in a while, but hiking was her passion.

After a couple months of pressure, I relented and agreed to go. I figured it would be an awesome thing to do with my mom. The whole reason I had moved near my parents when I retired was to do things with them while they were still young enough and healthy enough to be active. Hiking with Mom and her group down the Grand Canyon in 2011 showed me the importance of this. Until that trip, I had always assumed that I would find a second career after retiring from the military. Who knows where that would have taken me? After thoroughly enjoying the experience with Mom, I decided I did not want to put off moving near my parents for another twenty years, to a time when they would likely be in a nursing home and our contact would be limited to a couple visits a week.

I had been stationed in five foreign countries and eight states during my military career, which lasted just less than thirty years. My parents had come to visit me in almost all these locations. We had many great vacations and had seen the world together. In fact, I often explained to friends that my parents were normally more excited about my new assignments then I was because they knew they could come to visit. I treasured these times. So I made the decision to find a way to live near family for once in my adult life (Dad and Mom were now living near my sister's family, and my brother had recently moved to the same area). I wanted to be a part of their lives.

With that in mind, wasn't this just the type of thing I intended? So . . . I was in!

Later I was able to convince my niece Samantha to go along. I thought it would be good to have someone "closer to my age" on the trip. She thought that was funny since she was twenty-one and I was forty-eight, but I was young at heart. Lots of college kids hike it, so we figured Samantha would find others her age along The Way. Hence we became a foursome, and I started calling us Team Camino based on military terminology I had become used to during my four deployments to combat zones.

After a little more than a week on the trail, Samantha had to stop hiking due to very painful tendons in her feet and ankles. We discussed her condition with a fellow pilgrim who was a nurse. She advised Samantha not to push it or she could risk permanent damage and possibly even surgery. She decided to head for home. Now we were three.

Taking Samantha to the bus station—walking, of course—ate up half of our day. This threw us off the "stages" in The Book and separated us from the other hikers we had gotten to know over the previous week. Everyone, regardless of nationality, seemed to have a copy of The Book in their language. This book was our guide and broke the pilgrimage into thirty-three stages based on the author's assessment of what was a typical day's walk. Although many *peregrinos* (Spanish for *pilgrim* and the term used to refer to people walking the Camino) went further each day, others went less, the majority stuck to the stages. This meant we kept running into the same people in the hostels, cafés, bars, and restaurants. We quickly formed a "Camino family" and did not want to get separated from them, so we decided to try to make up the lost kilometers by going extra the next day. To facilitate this, we arranged for our packs to be transported to the end of stage 9, Santo Domingo.

Without the weight on our backs, we figured we could make good time. And we did. This section of the trail was marked with kilometer posts. Mom hated this, because it reminded her how far we still had to go, well over 500 km at this point.

"I don't want to know!" she said as we passed the fifteenth sign reminding us we had a long way to go.

Being a bit more analytical, I used the posts to gauge our speed. At one point we were knocking out a kilometer every eleven minutes!

We succeeded in catching up with our Camino family, but I paid a price for our aggressiveness.

I had sustained cold injuries to my feet while deployed in the mountains of Afghanistan about six years earlier. In my job as a Provincial Reconstruction Team (PRT) commander, I went on missions outside the wire several days a week. Most missions were by convoy, but some required a helicopter. In either case, there was the need to have heavy weapons mounted and ready to counter potential threats, hence huge openings. In the highly mobile multiwheeled vehicles (HMMWV, pronounced *Humvee*), it was the gun turret on top. In the helicopters, the doors on both sides or in the back were wide open with a gunner ready to engage if needed. These configurations rendered the heaters basically useless. Since we sat there for hours at a time, our feet could get very cold.

I did not have proper cold weather footwear. When we had gone through the deployment processing line at Fort Bragg, I asked for winter boots. The civilian working the line told me I was going to the desert and did not need winter boots. Having already been deployed to Bagram Airfield (BAF), Afghanistan, in 2005, I knew that it got real cold and snow was going to be plentiful. I also knew that where we would be stationed in Gardez, the capital of Paktya Province, was at an even higher elevation than Bagram—about 7,500 feet. I tried to explain this to the lady, but she wasn't buying it. She insisted I did not need cold weather boots and refused to issue them to us. When I got to Bagram, where we all flew into for in-theater training before moving to our Forward Operating Bases (FOBs), I asked the AF supply shop for winter boots. They said they did not stock them and I should have gotten them at Bragg. So frustrating.

Anyway, once winter came, I found myself with freezing feet mission after mission. Eventually, I developed cold pernio and could hardly walk. The doc gave me some pills. Those, along with trying to keep my feet warm, helped manage the condition and allowed me to remain in-country. The next time I was at Bagram, I went to the base exchange (BX) and bought an expensive pair of winter combat boots. Hopefully I could get my money back by submitting the expense as part of my travel voucher after returning to my home station. I also bought a lot of packages of toe and hand warmers and then proceeded to pass them out to everyone that boarded the helicopter for the trip back to Gardez. Once back, I instructed the guys who volunteered to run our FOB mini-BX to order the warmers and keep them stocked for everyone through the rest of the winter. People started telling me about other tricks to prevent cold injuries like putting your pack under your feet to separate them from the cold metal floors. A little late!

Anyway, the pernio caused major problems with circulation in my feet. Additionally, all the sores came back whenever the temperature drops into the fifties. I also developed arthritis in my feet in the years following my PRT deployment—potentially due to the pernio, according to one doctor. Together, these issues caused my feet to hurt when I walked, while at the same time having a numb/swollen feeling even though they didn't look swollen.

After a week of averaging fifteen miles a day, I also had plenty of blisters on my heels, the sides of my feet, and even between my toes. This all combined to create ever-increasing pain in my feet as we ticked off the kilometers.

Two days after we dropped Samantha off at the bus station, the pain in my feet was almost unbearable. I tried everything I could think of to keep going, including changing into my sandals in hopes of stopping the shoes from rubbing against my blisters. The sandals just made things worse. I could not stand it by the time we arrived at the first hostel on the edge of Belorado at the end of stage 10. I insisted we not go another step! Over dinner, I asked Mom and Ria if they would mind skipping ahead to Sarria, the last place you can start and still qualify for your Compostela, the peregrinos' prized certificate of completion. They were getting tired of staying in hostels and agreed. We decided to walk to Burgos, two stages ahead, and then catch a train to Leon. We would stay a couple of days there to sight-see and then catch another train to Sarria.

I decided I could not walk the next day. Ria was also ready for a day off, so we made our way to the end of stage 11 by bus and taxi. Mom met us there. The following day I felt a little better. Ria and I decided to hike stage 12 with Mom, just without packs.

After two days touring Leon, my feet felt much better, and I started regretting suggesting we jump forward. We sat down for another conference and decided to start back up at Ponferrada, a village with a train station near the start of another scenic mountain range. This meant we would do the first twelve days and the last nine. Although it was a hit to my ego, skipping forward ultimately turned out to be a good thing because Ria was pretty exhausted the last few days.

We prided ourselves with the idea that we were hiking with the oldest person on The Way. We discovered we were wrong in Ponferrada where we met a ninety-one-year-old man from Florida. He had not skipped any of the trail except the day prior to when we met him, and this was not his choice. He had fallen in the shower and had to get medical treatment, which meant being transported by ambulance one day further up the trail. He was intent on finishing. In fact, after he got to Santiago, he took a train back to the start of the stage he missed and did it before going home.

This certainly intensified my feelings of guilt. How could I have wimped out and skipped two hundred miles when a ninety-one-year-old made the whole thing? Thus started two years of regret and preparation to go back and do it right.

So now I found myself on the same Icelandair flight to Paris that we had taken two years earlier. This time I was alone.

"I am happy with three hundred miles," Mom said when I asked her to go. "I don't know anyone else who has done that. I don't have an ego problem. I'm good."

I was not concerned about going alone. After almost thirty years in the military, I was used to traveling around the world and often did it alone when moving to an overseas duty location. Besides, I knew I would soon start meeting members of my new Camino family.

# CHAPTER 2

Iceland to Paris
27 August 2015
D-2

After the plane change in Iceland, it was another three-hour flight to Paris. We encountered less turbulence during this leg. I really don't like turbulence. I feel completely out of control. As irrational as it may be, I fear that the plane could be shaken apart.

The guidebook suggests you leave your electronic devices behind. For me, and I imagine most people in today's electronic world, that was not realistic. Family and friends made it clear before I left that they wanted to hear from me frequently. My parents had the large map attached to a poster board that my sister's family had used to track us last time. They planned to put new pins at each place I stayed.

Fortunately, the Camino has kept up with the world's dependence on electronics. Last time there was only one night when we were not able to find Wi-Fi (pronounced *weefee* in Europe). The lack of an adequate number of electrical outlets to recharge devices had been a major problem. I hoped it would be better this time.

As we flew toward Paris, flying further in an hour than I would walk over the next five weeks, I thought about the other physical challenges I was going to have to deal with.

Typing on a computer was a central part of my job as an AF officer. Once e-mail became the most common method of communication, I spent the majority of my time at the computer. Besides reviewing and responding to e-mails, I worked on performance reports, guidance documents, letters, budget documents, PowerPoint briefings, etc. That is how we fight and win wars nowadays. We write reports and give PowerPoint briefings. In fact, this became a frequent joke when I worked as the provost marshal of Joint Task Force SHINING HOPE. The staff officers on the JTF spent so much time building briefings that we figured we should get a "PowerPoint Ranger" tab to put on the top of our uniform sleeve similar to the Ranger tabs that many soldiers wear after completing the grueling Army Special Forces training.

Over the years, all this typing took its toll. In mid-2004, I started having pain in the lower two joints of both thumbs. By the time I deployed my first time to Afghanistan in January 2005, I was wearing custom-made splints that minimized the movement of my thumbs. I also had wrist and thumb splints that immobilized them while I slept. Over time, the thumb joint pain got worse and more frequent. During my second deployment to Afghanistan in 2006 and 2007, I used Ace bandages to wrap them every day. This enabled me to take written notes during meetings with local officials and type long mission reports on the computer. After my return, I sought medical treatment. The orthopedic doctor prescribed thumb CMC restriction splints, and I have been wearing them ever since. Without them, I would not be able to type for more than about twenty minutes. I have trouble picking up small items, turning pages in books, and I routinely drop and lose control of items I try to handle.

I'll never forget the time I was having lunch with a general that had been a mentor to me. I was trying to cut large pieces of my salad down to bite-size when I lost control of my knife and it slid across my plate, sending salad all over the general's plate and lap. How embarrassing. Luckily, for some reason, she liked me and just laughed it off.

By the time I was in training for a deployment to Iraq 2011, the pain in my thumbs seriously interfered with many combat tasks, such as firing weapons at the qualification range. I knew this would be a problem if I got into a combat situation. However, I did not relay my concern to the doctor during my predeployment medical exam. Since I would spend most of my time in an office as the chief of staff for an advising and training unit, I knew the chances of being in combat were small. I also figured, pain or not, I could just gut it out and make it happen if we got into a firefight. At that point, a bit of pain wouldn't seem to matter much. It would likely be the least of my worries.

During my deployment in Iraq, I noticed the upper joints in several fingers were growing and starting to disfigure my hands. When I returned from my follow-on deployment to Djibouti, I was officially diagnosed with osteoarthritis in all my fingers. After getting an MRI of my hands the Friday before my departure for this trip, my rheumatologist told me that the erosive osteoarthritis was "aggressive." She prescribed some anti-inflammatory pills, which I picked up on the way to the Seattle airport.

I had known for some time that the hand issues would be a problem along The Way. I could not make a fist. They were painful to the touch. My fingers often locked up, and the pain could be crippling when I tried to use them to do any number of Camino-related tasks like handwashing items, conducting personal hygiene, or even gripping my hiking poles. I developed a mitigation plan during my training hikes. Putting my hands partway through the straps of the hiking poles and applying downward pressure on the strap by pushing the side of the hand below the pinky finger allowed me to achieve the benefit of the poles. The loose gripping fingers would merely stabilize and guide the direction of the pole.

Then of course, there was the feet. Arthritis in the toe joints, a bone spur on my right big toe where the shoe bends, and circulation problems stemming from the pernio worked together to cause major pain and swelling. Over the past two years I worked with a podiatrist to find mitigating measures to address this problem, including custom orthotics and ceramic plates inserted in my shoes under the orthotics that kept my arthritic toes from bending too much.

I planned other measures to capitalize on the lessons learned from the last trip regarding preventing blisters. Mom had worn toe socks commonly used by runners. She did not suffer the blisters between the toes as I had. I had four pairs this time. I also planned to cover hotspots with Band-Aids, tape, Compeed, or a second-skin product to prevent them from developing into blisters. Based on Ria's experience, I had a couple of packages of lamb's wool in the pack. I planned to put this in the front section of my shoes to protect my toes while going downhill. Finally I brought a small container of Vaseline to spread on common blister areas of each foot each morning before I put my socks on. Many people had told me that this would minimize the impact of the rubbing on the skin. Bottom line, the first line of defense is a good offense. The goal was to prevent blisters. Failing that, I had learned many methods of caring for blisters once they manifest themselves; hence I had the medical supplies to deal with it.

One other medical issue would be a problem. I've had a bad back since the early '90s. Early in my career as a security forces officer I was a flight leader, also commonly known as a shift commander. This meant that I was in charge of the on-duty shift and was the senior response official on patrol. As such, I wore the normal police equipment, including a weapon and web belt with ammunition, radios, and other equipment attached. Additionally, we wore heavy personal protective gear during daily shift exercises, combat training, and deployments. All this had taken its toll on my entire spine. The pain could be crippling when I did housework, yard work, or other activities where I needed to bend or put my head in certain positions. These joint issues caused tension in the muscles and resulted in a constant headache for twenty-plus years. After seeing numerous doctors and trying different methods to get relief, I found that weekly chiropractic adjustments were the only thing that helped me manage the pain and remain functional. There would be no chiropractor on The Way.

On the positive side, the low back had not been as big an issue as I had feared it would be the first time around. My theory was that when I'm hiking, I'm not bending over, so the low back is not strained as much as when doing various activities at home. I stood up straight. However, upper back and neck pain, and the resulting headaches, were an issue. Most likely this was due to the weight of the pack and spending a lot of time looking at the ground in order to pick smooth level ground to step on. I knew that I always had the fallback option to ship the pack if I needed to give my back a rest.

To address all this, I embarked well armed with pain pills and topical creams.

Being in better shape would also help minimize the impact of these physical issues. So instead of just counting on our weekly Wednesday hikes and workouts in my home gym to get in shape, I decided I needed to do a long hike at least twice a week. Starting in June, I cut back to volunteering just one day a week at the American Legion instead of my normal two. This freed up another day for hiking. Near the end of July, I loaded the pack that I would be taking on the Camino so it weighed as much as it would on the trail. I carried this pack on the rest of my training hikes to get my back in shape.

The final step of my preparation entailed gathering intelligence to determine the best time of year to go on this trip. Again, I relied on lessons learned from preparation for the leader's recon in 2013. According to websites about the Camino and books that I read, the best time to go would be in the fall. Temperatures in the spring are pretty good for hiking, but pilgrims are likely to walk in the rain more often than not. The problems with the summer months are high temperatures in the nineties or even the low hundreds, and huge crowds. Europeans generally vacation in August and sometimes in July. These months are also popular with college students on summer break. These two dynamics result in crowded trails, hostels, cafés, restaurants—you name it. I heard stories that some people have to sleep on the pews and floors of churches because the villages often run out of beds for the peregrinos. Some even have to camp out. One of the books that I read discussed people getting up at four o'clock in the morning to start their daily walk in order to get done before noon to avoid the heat and to be at the hostels when they opened to ensure they would get a bed. It's like a race to see who can get there first! A pilgrimage of reflection and relaxation would be impossible in these conditions. I was dealing with enough stress and anxiety in my life. This type of hectic environment on the trail would definitely be counterproductive to my purpose for going.

Therefore, fall was the best time to go. However, I had to factor in my volunteer work as an admissions liaison officer for the United States Air Force Academy. For this "job," the busiest time of the year is in the fall when seniors are applying. This is when I needed to meet with interested students and give presentations about the academy at local high schools. Additionally, I conduct the official interview that is required as part of the application process. I really needed to be home in October and November for these duties.

So I decided to go in late August. The summer crowds would be at the end of the trail when I started. This timing would get me back no later than 10 October, so I would have plenty of time to work with this year's academy candidates.

Reflecting on all this as the plane approached Paris, I felt confident that I was as prepared as I could be to tackle this challenge and be successful this time. I had done everything I could think of to prepare physically. I was also prepared mentally in that I was determined not to let the Camino and my physical problems defeat me again!

My pack was almost the last bag to come up the baggage chute. I was getting worried that they might have lost it. The good news was, my plans after the hotel in Paris were completely flexible. If I had to wait in Paris for my pack to catch up with me, it would not be a major problem. The only reservations I had prearranged were for the flight over and the hotel in Paris. Everything else was to be decided on a day-by-day basis. I was not locked into lodging or return-flight reservations. Can you imagine trying to figure out what to do with twelve extra days while you're waiting for your flight? Yes, you can change to an earlier flight, but the airlines love to charge an arm and a leg for that. Our intent in 2013, as was mine now, was to decide how far we wanted to go each day based on how we felt. We also wanted the flexibility to take time to tour various sites. Pilgrims need to have the freedom to change their mind anytime right up until they sign into a hostel. If your feet hurt, make it a short day. If you are feeling good or don't like the accommodations when you get there, no problem; just go on to the next one. Granted, not having a return plane ticket would mean purchasing one at the last minute. This would be more expensive than making the reservations months in advance, but it was worth it to have the flexibility to do what I needed to do along The Way.

To my great relief, my pack finally showed up. I grabbed it and located signs pointing me to the train station that was colocated with the airport. I followed the signs to the ticket office and purchased a ticket from Paris to Bordeaux, then to Bayonne for the following morning. From there, I would switch to a local train for a short trip to Cambo Les Bains, followed by a bus ride to St. Jean Pied de Port.

Ticket in hand, I headed out to find the hotel shuttle. Once outside, I looked up the phone number for my hotel and called them to find out when their shuttle would be by and to let them know that I was waiting for it. I had signed up for a plan with my cell phone company just prior to leaving the States, which gave me the capability to make calls in other countries without roaming charges. This was my first opportunity to test this is capability.

The hotel said that the shuttle would be by within the next twenty minutes. Too easy. Everything was falling into place nicely so far.

# CHAPTER 3

Paris to St. Jean Pied de Port
28 August 2015
D-1

The universal conspiracy against me was in full force as I embarked on the final leg to the trailhead.

My stay at the Radisson worked well, but it was expensive. The 57€ for the night was not bad. But wine, a hamburger, and the breakfast bar came to another 49€. The burger was hardly cooked; in fact, you could say the cow was still mooing. However, the fries were awesome—the closest I had had to German Pommes Frites in a long time. Those are the best fries in the world as far as I'm concerned.

My real troubles began once I arrived at the train station. The board said track 3, and even the board on the platform at track 3 said Bordeaux . . . I think.

I found car (*voiture*) 5 as the ticket said. Standing tall with pride, I relished my improvement over our experience two years earlier when we did not even realize we had assigned seats and had to be told to leave someone else's seat. Slightly embarrassed, we found our seats after somebody translated our tickets for us. Confident in my improved understanding, I started looking for my seat number. There was no 31. It went from 28 to 35. I walked up and down the car several times and could not find it. The other passengers tried to help, but they couldn't find it either. A train employee informed me that I could not find the seat because I was on the wrong train. Of course, as my luck would have it, the train started pulling out of the station, and I was stuck going to the wrong place.

The conductor was very nice about it. We sat down, and he looked up the train schedule to reschedule everything. He gave me a new schedule to Bordeaux from Lille Europe, which was this train's first stop. I would then catch a three-hour-later version of my original schedule. He said all my current tickets were good except the leg to Bordeaux. It would cost me about 20€ to get that one changed. And of course, I would need to get new seat assignments for all legs from the "train manager" (ticket office) at Lille Europe.

I would now be arriving in St. Jean about 1930. I was concerned that finding a bed would be a problem. When we arrived in late afternoon in 2013, most places were already full. It was three weeks earlier this round, so I expected more than the three hundred starters we had last time. Well, nothing I could do about it now. I would just have to see how it played out and go with the flow.

I got off the train at Lille Europe and went to the ticket office. The 0921 train from there to Bordeaux that the conductor had tried to get me on was full, so they gave me a ticket back to Paris Nord, the station I had left an hour ago. I would then need to take the subway into Paris to the Montprarmasse station. From there I'd take a train directly to Bayonne, arriving in time to catch a small local train to Cambo Les Bains, and then the bus to St. Jean at the same times that the conductor had told me. The "manager" told me that I would have to pay again since I had missed the train. I told him I understood and that the conductor had told me it would cost 20€ to make the changes. The manager looked a little confused and went to talk to his boss. I nervously waited for his return. Was he going to charge me for a whole new ticket? To my great relief, the supervisor sided in my favor, and he provided me the new tickets at no charge. I thanked him for his kindness as best I could in my extremely limited French. He pointed me to another train station across the town square where I would catch the train back to Paris.

I made triple-sure I was on the right train this time and an hour later found myself back at Paris Nord. Now the "fun" (not) started, and the "universal conspiracy against me" kicked into full swing.

Let me explain what I mean by a universal conspiracy against me. Ever since returning home from my second tour in Afghanistan, I had been battling this phenomenon. It seemed one of Murphy's

Laws of Armed Conflict had plagued me for the past ten years: "If anything can go wrong, it will, at the worst possible moment." Several things had gone wrong during the deployment, and it had left me very stressed and exhausted. Problems continued after redeployment. The first major frustration was, while I was at the temporary living facility at McDill Air Force Base, Florida, where I'd PCS'd (permanent change of station) after returning to the United States, I bit down on a peanut M&M and half a molar broke off. About a week later, the air-conditioning in my Honda CRV went out, and the whole system had to be replaced. The fact that the temperatures were in the nineties and the humidity was as well turned my car into a miserable sauna. It cost over $2,000. From then on, it was just one thing after another going wrong. Nothing was easy. Everything was harder than it should have been.

Most of the problems were just little things, but the sheer quantity and frequency was aggravating. Especially since I was fighting serious anxiety problems following the deployment. After a year running convoys and commanding the PRT while dealing with toxic US Army leaders, I was exhausted mentally and physically down to the deepest part of my being. This magnified the impact of every problem tenfold.

My theme song became a current country hit called "If You're Going Through Hell" by Rodney Atkins.[4] This song did a good job of summing up how I felt, but it also encouraged me to keep pressing forward and not let my problems defeat me.

When things went wrong, I would often tell people around me that it was because of the universal conspiracy against me. They would give me a hard time and tell me to think more positively. After all, whatever the issue was at the time, it was not really a big deal.

I remember one time during my deployment to Djibouti when I needed to travel for a few days. I decided to take our new non-commissioned officer in charge (NCOIC) of logistics with me due to the mission objective of the trip. When I asked him to go, I cautioned him that there was a universal conspiracy against me, so he

---

[4]  *If You're Going Through Hell*, Rodney Atkins

could expect our travels to be plagued with problems and delays. He laughed and said he didn't believe me. During the next three days, we encountered numerous problems, including me having to spend almost three hours on the Internet trying to purchase my return plane ticket (he got his taken care of in about ten minutes). Delays in page loading, not accepting any of my credit cards, and several other problems made me get more and more frustrated. I ended up with two tickets and then had to go through the process of contacting the airlines to cancel one of the purchases. Of course, by this time the airline ticket office was closed for the day, so I had to try to contact them in the morning while we are trying to rush off to the airport. Because of the numerous problems we dealt with, the NCO said he was never going to travel with me again! I had my first convert. He was now a believer in the universal conspiracy.

The conspiracy continued throughout the rest of my time in the Air Force, both at Central Command headquarters in Florida and later at the Pentagon. It even continued after I retired. During my short leave between my deployment in Iraq and the follow-on deployment in Djibouti, I spent two weeks at my parents' house looking at houses to purchase as my retirement home.

On the last day before I left for predeployment training on the East Coast, I found an awesome log home, on an island, in the woods, across the street from a lake. My dream home. A place that would become my sanctuary from the world. Within a year of moving in, several major things were found to be wrong that were not identified during the home inspection.

First, I noticed how cold the floor was; it seemed to suck the heat right out of the house. No matter how much the heater ran, it was always cold. This was a major problem because of the cold injuries to my feet that I had suffered in the mountains of Afghanistan. The pernio sores kept coming back, and it hurt just to put my shoes on, let alone walk, just like they had in Afghanistan. After some investigation, we determined the issue likely stemmed from the insulation under the house being installed incorrectly. Whoever had done it had built a plywood layer attached to the bottom of the crossbeams and laid the insulation between the plywood and the flooring. The problem was, there was about four inches between the insulation and the floor. Additionally, the insulation had been put in upside down. So . . . I had an insulation professional come out. He validated the assessment and quoted over $5,000 to fix the problem. Doing the math, I calculated it would take decades for the savings in energy costs to make up for the $5,000, so I decided not to have it fixed and to just wear slippers in the house. After three years of fighting cold feet and painful sores, I finally had the insulation fixed just prior to departing for the Camino. It cost me about $6,000. That's what I get for delaying a fix during a time of inflation.

Soon after learning about the insulation problem, my skylight started leaking, and water soaked my carpet in the living room. I called a roofing specialist out to fix it. He said whoever had installed it had done the flashings all wrong. I didn't know what flashings were, but it sounded bad. Of course, I had no records of who had installed it since it was done by the previous owners. Therefore, I could not call anybody to come out and fix it and had no idea if it was even under warranty. So I had him fix it.

During the next rain, the water came flowing back in. It was worse than before. I called the roofer again and told him that it had not been fixed. He said he would come out when he could. Days went by with no sign of him. I called him several times to no avail. Finally I left a message threatening to make a report to the Better Business Bureau because I was tired of having pots and pans all over my living room floor. He finally came out.

Standing on my cement patio, I called up to him on the roof, "How's it going? Have you been able to determine what is wrong?"

He copped an attitude. "I have been doing this for many years. I know what I'm doing," he insisted in an angry, condescending tone.

*Really*, I thought to myself. *Then how come it wasn't fixed the first time?*

I did not appreciate how he was talking down to me and was surprised by the hostile tone since he was a contractor getting paid to do a job and I was the "employer." Mad as I was, I kept my temper in check because there was no use arguing. I just wanted him to fix it and be done with it.

This time the fix worked. I certainly won't be asking him to come back.

While he was up there, he told me that in his opinion, my wood shake roof was at the end of its life and needed to be replaced. Not trusting him, I did not pursue that immediately. The following year, when I had another company come out and install a second skylight, they told me the same thing. I asked them for a quote. They provided options ranging between $16,000 and $25,000, depending on the type of roofing. I didn't have that kind of money, so I started putting money aside every month. I'd just have to pray that the current one held until I could afford it.

Near the end of my second full summer in the house, a strong sewage smell started coming from under the back deck. I called out the septic inspector who promptly discovered that the pump had quit working and the tank was overflowing. Further, when the pump broke, an audible alarm should have gone off. Obviously, that had not happened. We could not even find an alarm panel. The inspector went on to tell me that according to the county map of my septic system, the overflow pond was underneath the cement patio in my backyard. This violated code and did not allow the pond to breathe. The system should never have passed inspection when I bought the place. I went back to my paperwork to find out who the inspector was with the intent of holding him financially liable. This was going to be another expensive fix. I quickly discovered that he had gone out of business, and in the opinion of the person who told me that, my situation was a prime example of why. There went another couple of thousand dollars. Of course, this ate into the money I had been saving for the new roof.

The conspiracy was also taking its toll on my health. Besides the problems with the cold injuries and arthritis in my hands and toes, back problems, the constant chronic headache and anxiety, I had also been diagnosed with prediabetes and prehypertension over the past year. Would this never end?

One day I was discussing all this with my father. I whined that every time I went to the doctor, they found something else wrong.

"Then quit going to the doctor" was his insightful advice.

I could go on and on about my problems, but enough of the negative thinking for now. I needed to return my attention to today's problems.

I found the metro station easy enough by following signs pointing the way. The conductor had told me to take line 4. However, when I got to the metro station, the signs for line 4 had red tape Xs coving them. Turns out I arrived in the middle of four days of maintenance and a section of the line was shut down. I followed line 4 detour signs to another station where I assumed I could join the line after the construction. The detour signs there told me to take line 5. I took the train and got off where the signs said to, and you guessed it, line 4 was closed there too! The signs were now telling me to go to line 3. Now I was really getting worried. I was running out of time to catch my train to Bayonne. Finally I noticed other confused people talking to metro employees, so I went over and waited for my turn. One spoke English and directed me to take line 7 to a hub and then switch to 4. He showed me on the metro map. Since I had ridden subways in Europe and Washington, DC, seeing the map helped me understand.

Boy, did we make a lot of stops! Time was ticking away. By the time I got off of line 7 and found the platform for line 4, I had only about eighteen minutes before my train to Bayonne left. Trains in Europe are famous for leaving right on time, so there was no hope that it would be running late. The train station was five stops away. I feared I was not going to make it.

Amazingly, I still had about ten minutes once I got to the station, but it quickly became apparent it would not be a short walk from the metro to the train station, so myself and another guy, who was also obviously short on time, started running. We had a heck of a time getting around people who were obliviously blocking escalators and the moving sidewalks. Of course, running as fast as I could with a pack on my back was not smart due to my back problems, but I had no choice. When I got to the train station, Bayonne was not on the monitor board. There was only one train at the time mine was scheduled to depart, so I ran to that platform and asked a conductor if it was going to Bayonne. She nodded, and I boarded with a sore back, breathing heavy, and sweating profusely with about two minutes to spare . . . but I had made it—and got a good workout to boot!

While waiting in the doorway to get off at Bayonne, I met my first fellow pilgrim. She was from Germany and planned to stay at Bayonne for the night and move on to St. Jean the next morning. We agreed to watch for each other along The Way.

Once off the train, I noticed the telltale signs of other peregrinos, hiking clothes and packs with poles attached. Many already had their shells hanging off their pack. We all started exchanging information about how we planned to make the last leg of the trip. I mentioned I was supposed to take a train to Cambo Les Bains, then a bus to St. Jean. A couple ladies told me there was no train, only buses today. I looked at the monitor, and sure enough, no listing for Cambo, but there was a bus to St. Jean PP. Several of us realized we had a ticket disconnect and headed for the ticket office to get arrangements changed. Of course, there was a long line! Just one thing after another.

Eventually an employee came over and asked what we needed. I showed her the tickets and explained the problem. She said not to worry; the tickets were good, and we could just go get on the bus. She directed us where to catch it. I guess she noticed we were peregrinos and already knew about the issue. This cleared out much of the line.

Once outside we found ourselves in a sea of aspiring pilgrims. As we waited for the bus, we started to get to know each other. Everybody was energetic and excited about starting their adventure.

So starts the formation of the Camino family!

The excited friendly discussions continued throughout the hour-long bus ride to St. Jean. The Peregrino Office was closed for dinner when we arrived, so I set off in search of a place to stay for the night. The hostel across the street had a sign that read "Completo." However, just a few doors up the hill, I found one that still had a bed available. As I would find many times along The Way, there was an advantage to walking alone. It was far easier to find one empty bed rather than three or four. By the time I made up my bed and organized my things, the Peregrino Office was open. I joined my fellow pilgrims in line to register, receive my peregrino credentials, and give a five-euro donation for the shell I would attach to my pack. I then headed off to find dinner.

Memories of the town flooded my mind, and I headed to a restaurant with an outdoor porch area that overlooked the lazy river flowing through town. I remembered admiring it from the bridge two years ago.

Once seated, I asked the waitress for the Wi-Fi password, turned on my iPhone, and opened the iTranslate app. It worked great and enabled me to read the menu. Two years ago we didn't know that restaurants had Wi-Fi, nor did we have iTranslate, so we struggled to figure out the menu. Fortunately, there had been a young Frenchman at the next table who could speak English. He asked us if we needed help, and we invited him to join us. After we ordered, we discovered that he had started his Camino in Paris a month earlier. He was halfway through a thousand-mile hike. We had not realized that many people do even more than we planned to do. He explained that a thousand years ago people would walk from their doorstep to Santiago and back, so there were many "Ways" ("Caminos") that started in cities all over Europe; some even walked from as far away as Moscow.

After dinner, I returned to the hostel and spent a few minutes cutting my toenails. This would minimize the chances that they would be damaged and fall off. I then collapsed into bed. It had been a long, frustrating day, but I had made it and was looking forward to starting my trek the following morning.

# CHAPTER 4

## St. Jean Pied de Port, France, to Roncesvalles, Spain
## 29 Aug 2015
## D-Day

D-Day—the day "my Camino" commenced!

I eagerly jumped out of bed at the sound of my 0600 alarm. Enough anticipation and preparation! It was now time to make it happen.

Terrain wise, today would be the most challenging of the trek. If you take the strenuous, scenic route, the first stage is just over 25 km to Roncesvalles with 1,280 m of elevation gain to the high point at Col de Lepoeder. (Note: 1 meter equals 3.2808 feet, so the gain is 4,199 feet.) This route is known as Route de Napoléon. After the high point, there is a descent of 490 m to the old monastery, which now serves as a pilgrim hostel. There are two options for the downhill portion. The most popular is a very steep route that the volunteers at the Peregrino Office in St. Jean specifically told us not to use. Most people use it anyway. The alternative is 1.3 km longer, but more gradual. After going uphill for 21 km, people tend to choose the steeper route because it is shorter and they are tired. We went that way two years ago. Some sections were very steep, especially when your legs and ankles are tired. My memory told me it was dangerous. Therefore, it was my intention to follow the advice of the volunteers.

If the weather is bad, you do not want to take the Route de Napoléon but opt for the lower route paralleling the N-135 highway. The elevation gain is much more gradual, only 885 m spread out over 23.6 km. If the weather is decent, you want to go the steeper, longer route because the views of the Pyrenees mountains are spectacular. You see very little of the mountains on the lower route. Additionally, walking near the road is not only boring, but the noise of the traffic destroys the mood of the pilgrimage experience.

Today's weather forecast was mostly sunny and hot, in the mid-nineties. The climb would be strenuous in the heat, but as I packed

up my bedding and hygiene items, I thought of the beauty of our climb two years ago. The morning we started was foggy. We could hardly see more than a few feet in front of us. We embarked on the longer, steeper route, anyway, knowing that the forecast was for a sunny day. It wasn't long before we ascended above the clouds. From high on the mountainside, we could look down on clouds blanketing

Team Camino above the cloud-filled Pyrenees valleys on our first morning in 2013.

each of the valleys below. Tree-covered hilltops rose like islands out of a soft white ocean. Extremely beautiful.

After that experience, I would not even consider going the low route unless major storms were in the forecast. If that had been the case this time, I would have opted to stay in St. Jean for an extra night and wait for better weather. This is yet another reason not to have return plane arrangements. "Flexibility is the key to airpower." But no need to implement a fallback plan today; the weather was going to be great.

The 29€ I paid for the bed included breakfast, so I ate some bread and drank the orange juice and coffee that was left out for us. It wasn't much of a breakfast, but I wasn't too concerned because there was a café at Orisson, 7.8 km up the trail. The café was part of an *albergue* (the Spanish term for hostel). Some less-exuberant peregrinos who do not want to or don't believe they have enough stamina to do the entire climb in a day stop here for the night. It's not very big, so you have to get reservations at least six months in advance. Since I didn't know when my train would get me to St. Jean and whether or not I would have enough time to walk the first 8 km, I had decided not to make reservations at Orisson. Still there would be plenty of food to eat there. Just about every peregrino stopped in for café con leche, freshly squeezed orange juice, and a tortilla or sandwich. The views of the rolling Pyrenees from the outdoor seating area were spectacular. My intent was to get a sandwich, eat half of it, and take the other half with me to eat for lunch at the high point of the trail.

I checked e-mail and texts while I ate breakfast. The American Legion Post where I volunteered as the service officer back home had hosted a Veterans Roundtable with our local congressional representative and employees from the Department of Veterans Affairs Regional Office in Seattle the previous day. It was evening there, so the roundtable had actually only happened a few hours earlier. I sent an e-mail to the other two service officers, Mike and Leslie, asking how it had gone.

As service officers, we volunteered a couple of days a week to help local veterans apply for VA health care, service-connected disability compensation, and other VA benefits veterans had earned through their service. I helped coordinate the roundtable prior to my departure and had hoped to attend. But it was not to be. I had already bought my plane ticket when the opportunity to host the event came up. I left a list of issues with Mike for him to discuss if he got the chance. So I was anxious to hear how it had gone.

With a somewhat satisfied stomach, I strapped on my pack and headed out of the albergue about 0730. There was no ground fog this time. The sun shone brightly from the cloudless blue sky.

After about a half a kilometer, I reached the ancient city gate and asked another pilgrim if he minded taking a picture of me leaving St. Jean. He was more than happy to oblige, and I returned the favor. After bid-

Departing through the St. Jean city gate.

ding each other *Buen Camino* (the standard peregrino greeting), I followed the way-markers up the steep incline that was the start of the Route de Napoléon.

For the first 15 km, we twisted past farms and hamlets along a country road. Occasionally a local would drive past going about their daily business. As a courtesy to our gracious hosts, we stayed out of their way. It was amazing at how fast they drove on these narrow country roads with all the pilgrims making their way up the mountain. I wondered how many hikers were hit by a car each year.

Along many sections, the vegetation had been worn away by thousands of hiking boots, forming a path along the side of the road. Besides safety, walking on these paths was much easier on the feet, knees, and hip joints than was walking on pavement. One would be wise to walk on them whenever possible.

As I trudged up the steep road with my twenty-plus-pound pack on my back (I had filled the three-liter water bladder as full as I could get it, adding several pounds), I started to sweat even though the morning temperature was still in the sixties. I couldn't help but think how the organizations back home who built hiking trails all over the Cascade Mountains could teach the French a few things about the use of switchbacks when going up steep hills!

The first thing I "reflected" on was developing a "battle rhythm," better known in the civilian world as a daily routine. Based on the current time of sunrise, I decided to wake up at 0600. Besides personal hygiene, I needed to repack everything I had taken out the night before and implement my foot care Standard Operating Procedures (SOP), including preventive measures to protect my feet from blisters. Next would be a small breakfast, if available, at the albergue or at a café in the local village. If breakfast was not available where I was, normally the next village would only be a few kilometers away.

I was not in a hurry; this was not a race. I intended to take my time and enjoy the trek by stopping at least twice for breaks at cafés and an additional stop for lunch. At some point during the day, I would find a secluded place where I could do a Bible study. I brought along a thirty-day Bible study consisting of a small, very lightweight book called *Shaping Hearts, Changing Lives: 30 Days to Grow in Service.* Somebody from my church had given it to me awhile back. I wanted to include a spiritual aspect into this trek, and because this book was small and lightweight with durable waterproof pages, I figured it would be a good one to bring along.

Additionally, I planned to put a priority on getting to know other peregrinos. Once I found a bed each afternoon, I would take my shower, change into cleaner clothes, wash clothes as needed, catch up on my notes, and then seek out dinner and pilgrim fellowship. As was required at most hostels, I'd be in bed by 2200.

Sounded like a good plan to me.

A nice wind helped us fight the heat throughout the morning. Occasionally a strong gust caught me off guard. I swore the extra weight of my pack kept me from being blown off the mountain.

I arrived at Orrison about 0930. Two hours to go 7.8 km was not a bad pace, considering how steep it was. I found a table next to the railing of the outdoor seating area, overlooking a beautiful valley, and dropped my pack and poles. I wasn't concerned about anything getting stolen. There were plenty of people around, and somebody was bound to notice if a thief was on the prowl. Nothing had been stolen during the last trip, nor had we heard any discussion or stories about any incidents. It just didn't seem to be an issue on the Camino. Even so, basic precautions were in order. If I would be gone for more than just a few minutes, I took my passport and cash with me, securely tucked away in a pouch hanging around my neck.

I went inside and ordered a café con leche, a sandwich, and a *zuma natural de naranja* (natural orange juice). OJ was one of my favorite parts of the Camino. They had these machines that squeezed juice right out of multiple oranges. A large number of oranges were placed in the top compartment of the machine. When the machine was activated, orange after orange would drop down and be squeezed between several wheels. The juice was pressed out and flowed into a glass positioned below the spout. I counted five oranges squeezed for my glass. This is not something I had ever seen in the States. Glasses of natural OJ were much more expensive than coffee, but well worth it. Besides, it would be a good way to get my daily fruit.

Once back at my table, I took some pictures of the view and talked to a few of the other pilgrims who spoke English. Everyone was excited about reaching the first objective on the first day of their adventure. I took the opportunity to capitalize on the lessons learned from my leader's recon and offered my wisdom to some of the new peregrinos.

"I can already feel a blister coming on," a lady from Minnesota commented.

"Blisters were a major problem for me the first time I did this," I explained. "But I've learned several tricks. First, you should use Compeed as a sort of second skin on hotspots before blisters actually develop. It is like a clear plastic Band-Aid that will absorb the friction. You can get it at any pharmacy. You should also put Vaseline on your feet each morning, especially the places you know are susceptible to blisters such as your heels, outer toes, and the ball of each foot. Believe it or not, I even got blisters between my toes, so putting Vaseline there is probably a good idea. Stuffing lamb's wool in the toes of your shoes will help cushion your feet when going down steep hills."

"Interesting. We'll give it a try," her husband was intrigued. "Believe it or not, we haven't done much hiking, so this is definitely a learning experience."

"Have you used hiking poles before?" I asked, trying to get an idea how green they were.

"No, we purchased them just before we left the states," the lady admitted.

"Well, they certainly are vital. They really take the pressure off of your knee and hip joints. While on flat terrain, you should adjust the length so your elbow is bent at ninety degrees. Shorten the polls when going uphill, and lengthen them when going downhill to control your momentum."

"So what are the accommodations like in Roncesvalles?" the wife asked. "The old monastery hostel looks interesting, but the book is showing 183 beds in four rooms. I'm not sure I'm looking forward to that. Maybe we will put out the extra money in go to one of the hotels."

"It's not as bad as it sounds," I explained. "Each floor is a big dorm room, but they've divided it into two-person cubicles with short walls that provide a little privacy. I actually found it quite nice. It was nothing like the cramped rows of bunk beds they showed in the movie."

She looked relieved. "The entire facility is pretty nice," I continued. "There are laundry machines in the basement, and you can hang the clothes on lines to dry there or outside on a nice day. They had Wi-Fi in a dining area near a kitchen where you can make your own food. There are a couple of restaurants outside the monastery walls where you can get the pilgrims menu and meet some of the other hikers."

"Thank you! It doesn't sound so bad after all." Smiling, the couple put their packs on, adjusted their poles for going uphill, and set out with a "Buen Camino" and friendly wave.

Before moving on, I took my own advice and put a Band-Aid on a hot spot that was developing on my right heel. I had not been able to purchase any Compeed yet, so the Band-Aid would have to do until I found a pharmacy. It would still be a little while before I got to the peak and started the steep descent, but I decided, since I had my shoes off, I might as well put the lamb's wool in the toes. I then applied some more Vaseline to the feet since the downhill sections would cause more friction between my feet and shoes than the uphill sections.

Finally I checked my phone for messages and e-mails. I probably should not have done this. Leslie had responded to my e-mail asking about the veterans' roundtable. She said that ninety-eight veterans attended. This was a really great turnout for our area. She continued to explain that it had been rather frustrating. The presenters were not really listening to what the vets were saying, and the information given was surface and/or misleading. They really did not provide any substantial or helpful information. It was just an opportunity spit out the normal inaccurate and deceptive talking points we hear every day in the news and read on websites.

Additionally, one of the vets was one of our former clients. The VA had rated him 100 percent disabled due to service connected conditions. He was receiving the maximum monthly compensation and had been for the past ten years. However, he wanted a lot more than the law authorized him. Specifically, he wanted thirty years of back pay since his disability stemmed from his service in Vietnam. Leslie had worked with him and explained that the VA only paid back to the date that he applied for the disability compensation. They do not pay back to the date of injury. He did not like that answer and had become very belligerent and stormed out of the office. Now he was at this meeting, and he stood up to address the congressman. He proceeded to lambast me, by name, and a service officer from Seattle, also by name. He told the congressman we had refused to help him get what was due to him.

This kind of communication is likely why John Brierley had suggested in the *Pilgrim's Guide* that we not bring electronic communication devices. It certainly ruined my jovial mood. I became frustrated, and my anxiety level shot through the roof. Good thing the steepest part of the trek was in front of me. The exertion expended on the climb would help drain some of the hostility I was now feeling.

Fuming, I wrapped the remaining half of my sandwich in a napkin and stuffed it in an outside pocket of my pack. Putting the pack on, I grabbed my poles and started up the hill. The road started virtually straight up for a while and then became more gradual for a few clicks (kilometers). There was a van parked just before we got to

A group of pilgrims leave the road to start the ascent to the saddle where the ancient hut can be found. Note the yellow arrow on the rock in addition to the direction sign on the post. Both are common way markers that ensure peregrinos do not get lost.

the way-marker that directed us to follow a barely discernible dirt path up a steep incline to a saddle between two hills. An innovative local resident was using the van as a mobile café where we could get refreshments and snacks before the final significant uphill push. Since I still had my sandwich, I decided not to stop and instead headed up the hill.

Cresting the top, I could see a small ancient structure that had provided the pilgrims of old with shelter if a storm hit while they were in the mountains. It seemed to be a good place to do the first of my daily Bible studies. I found a couple large rocks off the side of the trail and stepped around to the far side of them. From here I had a great view of picturesque valleys and the rolling Pyrenees mountains. With the rocks isolating me somewhat from passing pilgrims, I took my pack off, set it down against the rocks, grabbed my sandwich, and sat down with my back resting against the pack.

The bottom line of the day 1 lesson was how Jesus died for us so we could have a personal relationship with Him. Because of this relationship, we can serve others on his behalf while we serve Him. In other words, one way we serve God is by serving those around us. When we accept Jesus as our Savior, He begins to shape us and the way we act and live. The scripture verse referenced was 2 Corinthians 5:14–15.[5]

So my task for today was to contemplate how I can serve others. This fit nicely into one of the purposes for my trek on the Camino. How was I going to live my post-AF life? What am I going to do? Who am I going to be? These were all questions I had been struggling with since retirement.

When I retired, I walked away from the only adult life I had ever known. I went into the academy immediately after graduating from high school. From then on, my entire life revolved around my career in the Air Force. Since I never married and never had kids, my career was my life. An instructor at the Air Base Ground Defense course I completed two years after I was commissioned asked me

---

[5]  Fryar, p. 4–5. www.CTAinc.com

why I wasn't married. My reply was that I had married the Air Force on 27 May 1987, the day I graduated from the Air Force Academy. I used the same reply many times during my career. I had been a workaholic. I took work home in the evenings and normally went into the office on Saturdays and Sundays to get caught up on things that had to be done there. This became all the more important after e-mail was instituted. I would get close to one hundred e-mails in a day and could never get through them. By Friday I was a couple hundred e-mails behind. The weekends were vital for me to get caught up. Additionally, since my troops had to guard the base and our resources twenty-four hours a day, seven days a week, 365 days a year (24/7/365), I would often go out in the evenings and on weekends to conduct post visits. This was also how I spent many holidays.

By the end of my career, I had risen to a point where I was often involved in events that were being discussed in the news. It was interesting to go home, turn on the news, and know how much of what was being reported was accurate (in my opinion, the media gets it right about 30 percent of the time). I had deployed for two humanitarian operations and four times to combat zones. I had also worked at the headquarters of Central Command in Florida, at the Pentagon, and as the DoD liaison to the Department of State's Foreign Service Institute's program to train interagency personnel preparing to deploy for reconstruction and development work in Afghanistan. During the last year of my career, I was the chief of staff for the unit helping develop the general staff at the headquarters of the Iraqi National Police in Baghdad and held a similar position with a task force on the front lines of combating terrorism in the Horn of Africa. I had often been in the middle of the major issues of the day. When I retired, all this was gone. I went from being involved in very important things, to a nobody. Lost, I no longer knew who I was.

I struggled to find things to do. I needed to feel useful, to contribute to the world around me. I could not be a "waste of air." I had to have a better reason to get out of bed in the morning than to just to walk the dog. As much as I have always loved my dogs and as important as it is to walk them, I needed to be more than that.

35

Initially, I decided to go back to school and get a degree in disaster management in hopes of making this my new career. But I had become very frustrated with the liberal indoctrination embedded in the study program. I quickly tired of reading hundreds of pages with repeated "Bush bashing" references to the "failed policies of the Bush administration" and little to no mention of the failures of local governments or the refusal of bus drivers to report for duty to evacuate the flood zones. The leading scholars in this field obviously held liberal biases, and all their teaching was clouded by them. In my opinion, college studies should be focused on facts. We should study what worked and what did not work during previous emergencies, learn from the good and the bad, and use that knowledge to do better in the future. The discussions and conclusions should be nonpartisan. The focus should be on how to effectively respond and help people during disasters. I decided that a field that taught and encouraged liberal biases with blatant political agendas was not a career I wanted to pursue. So I dropped my first class after just five weeks.

I turned to volunteer activities to keep me busy. On Mondays, I volunteered at His Pantry, the food bank at my church. On Tuesdays and Thursdays, I volunteered as the service officer (SO) at the American Legion. I also volunteered as an admissions liaison officer (ALO) for the United States Air Force Academy (USAFA) and was assigned responsibility for over forty private and public high schools along the I-5 corridor north of Seattle. In this role, I informed students about academic opportunities at the academy, what it means to be an Air Force officer, and what career opportunities are available in the Air Force. I then assisted those that decided to apply through the application process. The volunteer positions kept me so busy that I was still feeling stressed out.

Even though I spent so much time doing important volunteer work, I often beat myself up because I wasn't in a job that actually earned money. In other words, I did not have "a real job." I was living off of my colonel's retirement and disability compensation from the VA for my chronic service-connected medical conditions. Since I was single, this was actually enough to live on, but I still felt guilty. I often felt that I was mooching off of the government.

People frequently told me that I should not look at my situation as taking handouts from the government. They emphasized that I earned my military retirement through my service to my country, in peace and in war, for over twenty-nine years if you count the time I spent at the Air Force Academy (which I do since I was in uniform and was considered active duty). The disability compensation is paid to me because military service tends to wreak havoc on a person, both physically and mentally. I did not come out of the service unscathed, and I have plenty of chronic conditions, most of which were sure to plague me throughout this trip. I knew they were right, but it didn't stop my feelings of guilt.

During my Camino, I planned to work through this mentally. One of the objectives of my pilgrimage was to reflect on my career and what I had accomplished, as well as reflect on my current activities and what I was accomplishing by doing them. I needed to reflect on who I wanted to be now that I was retired, what I wanted to continue doing, and what changes I might decide to make. I also decided I wanted to use the trek to contemplate the struggles I had had with doubts about my Christian faith. This problem had haunted me for more than a decade since a major impetus for my struggle was the events of September 11, 2001.

Hopefully, by the time I was done, I would have a clearer idea of who I was now and who I wanted to be during this next stage of my life. Christian service was likely going to be a central focus.

While reflecting on these things, I decided to move on down the trail. I had already climbed 1170 of the 1280 m that we are going to climb that today. According to the book, I still had about 10.5 km and 110 m of elevation gain, not to mention the 490-m descent. The remaining elevation gain was very gradual and spread out over the next 4 km. It was almost like walking on flat ground. The section was very peaceful and passed through an area of beautiful shaded trees that served to tame the afternoon heat.

As I trudged onward, my mind became obsessed with the e-mail a had received from Leslie regarding the ex-client that took a shot me at the veterans' roundtable. His attitude boggled my mind. We are unpaid volunteers, and the services we provide them are free. We volunteer two days a week out of the kindness of our hearts, to help them navigate the frustrating, complicated, and bureaucratic VA claims system. We can't change the system. We can't change what the veteran is eligible for. All we can do is present their case as best as possible.

In military speak, this guy really needed an attitude adjustment! Maybe some wall-to-wall counseling would knock some sense into him. Where was a senior NCO when we needed one?

Thinking back to my spiritual study, the theme was, Jesus died for us so that we could serve Him through serving others. I needed to focus on that. My service should not be for the praise of man. My objective should be to do God's will and serve Him by serving His people, whether those people appreciate it or not. The real question should be, What does God think about my service?

I needed to just let it roll off my shoulders and forget about it. There are going to be a couple of idiots in every crowd. A funny fact about all of this was, it wasn't even me that was helping him that day in the office. Leslie had worked with him. I was at the other desk helping another veteran. But I am sure the same thing would have happened if I had been working with him because Leslie was right. After he left that day, Leslie talked to our main contact at the American Legion office in Seattle about the incident. He said that the same veteran had acted the same way at their office the day prior. So apparently, since he hadn't been satisfied with what the office in Seattle told him, he came into our office to see if he could convince us to do what he wanted done.

Anyway, I just need to let it go and move on, not let it bug me obsessively. I need to focus on those people who are overwhelmingly thankful for the services that we provide. As long as I do my best to remain professional and knowledgeable, then that's the best I can do. I must quit letting it stress me out.

We'll see how that goes. Executing such a mission is a totally different from deciding in your mind to do it.

It wasn't long before I crossed the border into Spain. There was a Spanish woman at the border marker when I arrived. She asked me to take a picture of her next to the signpost, and she returned the favor for me. She didn't speak much English, and I didn't speak much Spanish, so we then exchanged a hearty "Buen Camino" and continued at our own pace.

When I reached the high point for the day, there was quite a group gathered there discussing which way to descend into Roncesvalles. We saw several groups going the way that the volunteers in St. Jean had warned us not to go. I called to one of the groups to advise them that that was the dangerous way, but they decided to go anyway. This exchange got a conversation going with a group of young Americans. I explained to them that I had gone that way two years ago and it was very steep and dangerous in some sections. They were not deterred either. It had been a long day, and they did not want to do the extra 1.3 km to go the gradual route. So we bid each other "Buen Camino" and went our separate ways.

The long route had some excellent views of the rolling hills and mountains and an incredible view of the monastery-turned-albergue from high on one of the hills. On the steep route, the thick forest hid the monastery until you were almost on top of it. The views were worth the extra 1.3 km! Since almost everybody went the other way, I found myself alone for the first time that day. The solitude was another wonderful benefit. Much better.

As I approached the albergue and saw clothes hanging out to dry, I realized I had forgotten to bring clothespins. Crap!

I dropped my pack in the large entryway, grabbed my passport and pilgrim's credential, and got in line to register and get a bed. Since it was still early, about three, I got a bed on the second floor. Last time it was after five when we arrived, and we had ended up on the third floor. After the trek over the mountains, I felt privileged to only have to climb to the second floor.

Our beds on the third floor had all been single beds in two bed cubicles separated by four-foot-high half walls. This provided some privacy in the sense that you did not feel like you were in a huge dormitory. The second floor was different. Ceiling-height cubicles stretched down each aisle. As I proceeded down the aisle that contained my bed number, I noticed that each cubicle had two bunk beds in them instead of single beds. I hoped I had been assigned a bottom bunk. I had not thought to ask for one since I thought all the beds were singles. Relieved, I soon found my assigned lower bunk.

I made the bed up using the sheets they provided and spread my silk sleeping bag/sheet on top. I then unrolled my fleece blanket and tucked it in. A made-up bed is a sign to everyone that a bed is taken. That done, it was time for personal hygiene. I grabbed my shower kit, to include my small chamois backpacker's towel and my shower shoes, and headed to the showers at the end of the row of beds. By the time I got back, I had three roommates. It was the three American ladies I had talked to just before starting the descent. One of them was quick to tell me I had been right. Their descent down the challenging route was really tough and they wished that they had gone the other way. I had to laugh, noting that the longer route had been faster.

I then gathered my dirty clothes and went down to the laundry room in the basement. To my pleasant surprise, there was a man there who said that he would do the washing and drying for 2.70€. Sounded like a great deal to me. Due to the painful arthritis in my hands, washing and wringing out clothes was not something I was looking forward to. It was well worth the money to let somebody else do it in a machine. He told me to come back in a couple of hours to pick up my clean clothes.

I then retrieved my iPad from the cubicle and went into the kitchen and dining area on the ground floor to write an update e-mail for family and friends back home. This area was the only section of the monastery that had Wi-Fi. There must've been thirty people in there communicating with home.

Then it was out to the restaurant outside the monastery walls to have a drink while I waited for the pilgrims' dinner. In Europe they eat dinner late by American standards. During check-in at the albergue, I had signed up for the earliest round of dinner, which was at 1900 hours. I prefer to eat dinner between five and six, but "when in Rome . . ." I could have gotten food from the bar, but the pilgrim dinners offer a chance to meet other peregrinos and talk with them in-depth. While on the trail and in cafés, conversations are limited to "Buen Camino" greetings and maybe a five-minute conversation. While I waited for dinner, I had a glass of wine and studied the guidebook to refresh my memory about tomorrow's stage and determine where I wanted to stay the next night.

Only 751 km to go. No problem!

# CHAPTER 5

## Roncesvalles to Larrasoaña, 28.2 Kilometers
## 30 Aug 2015
## D+1

My alarm went off at 0600 in accordance with (IAW) my established battle rhythm. It took me about an hour to do my personal hygiene, get everything packed up, and prepare my feet for the day. I would look for a pharmacy or store to get Compeed today.

Once I was ready, I grabbed my pack and headed back to the restaurant where I had had dinner. When I arrived, I found a large crowd waiting to place their orders. The service was very slow. They were taking one order and making one coffee at a time. I stood in line for over thirty minutes.

This started my day off in a very frustrating way. My service in combat zones and dealing with terrorism intelligence on a daily basis while stateside resulted in anxiety whenever I found myself in crowded areas, or even areas where a handful of people crowded in around me. The other peregrinos waiting to get their breakfast did not seem to have the same sense of personal space that my heightened state of alertness was comfortable with. If I took a step in any direction to widen the space, they moved to fill in the gap. As if they would get to the bar quicker when they were closer to the person in front of them. When such situations occur, my stomach starts churning, the hair on the back of my neck stands up, and I feel flustered. I want to escape the situation. Today was no exception. However, I needed to stay in line if I wanted to have breakfast. So I fought the anxiety and forced myself to stand fast. I guess I got an exposure therapy session in.

Finally I hit the trail at 0750. It was now almost two hours since I woke up. A part of me said this was too much time and I must do better in the future. Another part of me said, Why should I be worried about it; who cares? What's the rush?

I followed the arrows out of Roncesvalles. The trail was a dirt path about three meters wide that led us through a nice forest area that paralleled a road. Thankfully, the trail was far enough from the road that it was somewhat peaceful.

I remembered that there was a small grocery store just a few kilometers up the trail. We had bought some fresh fruit there last time, and I hoped do so again. When I got there, it was closed. I was a little shocked to realize that it was Sunday. It had not occurred to me, but this meant many places would be closed. I hoped that did not mean I would have to wait another day to buy Compeed.

I entered a small village a few hundred meters further along. Sure enough, the pharmacy was closed. Well, nothing I could do about it except manage for another day. I was really getting worried about my heels because my shoelaces kept coming loose. Several times already, I had to stop and find something to prop my foot up on so I could retie my shoes without having to bend much with the pack on my back. This was important because the more I bent over, the more my low back hurt. It seemed, my every action was becoming a tactic to manage one chronic issue or another. My objective was to identify lessons learned, experiment with options, and implement mitigating techniques in order to minimize the impact.

The first café I came to was packed. I had had enough crowd exposure therapy for one day, so I kept going. It wasn't long before I came upon another café, which I immediately recognized as one we had stopped at two years ago. It stood out in my memory because there had been a dog that looked like a husky hanging around the front of the café. Every once in a while, he would decide to try to steal a meal by

getting up on an outside table next to an open window and then stick his head in, resting his legs on the windowsill or a table inside. The picture I took of him is now one of my favorites.

The dog was sleeping on cement stairs on the far side of a patio area in front of the café.

For old times' sake, I decided to stop for a break. There was only one other peregrino inside. Here was an excellent example of a "lesson learned" that could be capitalized on throughout the rest of my mission. Most people will stop at the first café going into a village, but there are normally others. So if your goal is to avoid large numbers of people, it would be beneficial to skip the first and see what else is available. If there aren't any other cafés, you can always go back.

The other customer left soon after I got my coffee and OJ. Since I was basically alone, I decided this would be a good place to do my daily spiritual study. The day 2 scripture references were 1 Samuel 3 with the key phrase being "Speak LORD for your Servant hears" and Isaiah 43:10, "You are my witness," declares the Lord, "and my servant whom I have chosen." To summarize the message, God chooses (or calls) believers to serve Him for the benefit of his people. We do not earn this right. Due to our sins, we are not worthy to serve Him. The forgiveness we receive as a result of Jesus's death on the cross opens the door for us to serve God in a manner acceptable to Him.[6]

Not quite done with my coffee, I decided to check out today's stage in the guidebook. The author recommended we go beyond the end of today's stage, Zubiri, if we did not want to spend time touring Pamplona the following day, especially if we did not want to stay there.

In 2013, we toured Pamplona and stayed at a seventeenth-century church that had been adapted into an albergue. It was called Jesús y María. It was actually pretty cool to stay in such a historical church. However, it had 114 beds in two rooms. Sure, there were plenty of other places to stay, but I had no need to spend any time in

---

[6] Fryar, p. 6–7.

a big city. I don't like crowds, traffic, noise, or any of the hustle and bustle associated with cities. Every car and every person is perceived as a threat, and all I want is to seek an escape route as soon as possible. Setting myself up to pass through Pamplona was the way to go.

A little more than 5 km past Zubiri was a village called Larrasoaña with two albergues, three pensions, and a hotel. Much better! The next day I could pass through Pamplona and stay in the next village, Cizur Menor.

I decided to do a similar thing with Logroño. It is a very big city at the end of stage 7. It was where my niece Samantha had decided to stop and go home. The night we spent there was the only one that I actually wore hearing protection. It was a Saturday, and there was some sort of a festival. About 2300, the Spaniards started partying and weren't done until 0400 or 0500. All night long, there were loud voices singing, talking, and carrying on in the street and city square outside our hostel. Even kids crying, screaming, laughing, and playing. What kids were doing up all night, I don't know! I guess this is their tradition. I could hardly sleep.

Nope, I'm not staying there again. Just like I was planning to do in Pamplona, I would walk right through Logroño and find a place on the other side. Maybe I'll just stay 5 km ahead of the stages. In the end it will even out. Today is a long day; others will be shorter. Then again, if I am ahead, I'm ahead. What did it matter? This was "my Camino." It was my choice how to do it.

It occurred to me that a potential risk of this strategy was that I might not get as much of the "Camino family" experience as we had last time. Whenever you deviate like this, you get off track with everyone you've met. But who knows, maybe there will be other peregrinos that are doing what I'm doing.

Satisfied that I had a viable plan, I put my pack on, grabbed my poles, and followed the arrows through the rest of the village. I enjoyed my trip down memory lane at the café, reflecting on how great it was to do the Camino with Mom, Ria, and my niece. We had a great time encouraging each other and sharing a challenge together.

I cherished our incredible memories. I would certainly recommend tackling this endeavor with family and friends.

Even so, I was now appreciating the benefits of doing the Camino alone. I liked having the flexibility to adjust my pace according to how my body felt and not have to worry about slowing anybody else down. My teammates had spent a lot of time waiting for me and my aching feet. I felt awful about this. As with most aspects of my personality, this likely came from my military background. It was always important to keep up with the rest of the unit during physical training challenges, to not show weakness by falling back or falling out. This is especially true for females in the male-dominated security forces career field. The last thing you wanted the other members of the unit to think was that you couldn't keep up, that you couldn't carry your part of the load, and that somebody else was going to have to pick up the slack.

The other great thing about walking alone was the extensive amount of time I could spend reflecting and relaxing. My mind wandered a lot. Other times I obsessed about a specific topic, digging deep into the underlying intricacies. Last time we talked a lot. Additionally, I felt it was my responsibility to help the group get where we were going and to plan out and track our way points. This meant I normally focused on the map, continually tracking our progress, and looking forward to our next objective—such as rest stops and water fountains. I decided that this time I was not going to dwell on those things as much. So I took the guidebook out of my cargo pocket and put it in an outside pocket of the pack. This meant I would have to take my pack off to check it. Since that meant stopping, I knew that my "drive-on" mentality would keep me from checking it too often.

Yet even without tracking every kilometer with the guidebook maps, I found myself analyzing how far I was into the adventure. I was now two days into what I calculated would be a thirty-five-day trek, factoring in two down days. If I took a down day around day 8, before my feet got real bad, I might stop the major problems before they started. The second day off should be about ten days after that. I should be in real good shape by the third section, so I should be able to complete the Camino without having to take another day off.

With travel time, the trip should take forty days. I was on the fifth day since leaving home, meaning I had completed one-eighth of the trip. Sounded like progress to me!

As I contemplated this, I recalled we did this type of calculation in the military during training exercises, remote assignments, or real-world deployments. My first indoctrination into this tradition started at the Air Force Academy. As freshmen, we were required to memorize the number of days until each class graduated. An upperclassman could stop us anytime and ask us how many days remained until he or she graduated. During active service, as you neared the end our time at a location, you were called a "short timer," and you always knew how many days you had left. A common way to express it was to say you had "$x$ days and a wake-up."

During my combat deployments, and a few times when I really wanted to leave a frustrating assignment, I would write the number of days remaining on my calendar. While in-processing to my supporting administrative AF unit on my way to Iraq in 2011, the first sergeant said something that made me stop this practice.

He said, "Don't count the days, make the days count." Wow! What a concept!

Maybe I should implement that mind-set on this trip. Just enjoy my time away from all the daily stressors.

I stopped for lunch in the village of Viskarret about 1130. It was a little early since dinner would not be until 1900, but the next possible opportunity was 6.5 km further. I guess life does not always work out exactly as one would want. "Flexibility is the key to airpower."

Leaving the village, I overtook one of the Americans I had met in Bayonne. He was older than me, maybe in his mid to upper sixties. He was slightly on the heavyset side around the stomach but otherwise appeared to be in good shape. His graying black hair was cut short around his ears in a style resembling that of someone in the military. His mustache was also cut short and would pass a military inspection.

"Buen Camino," I greeted him as I approached from behind. "Didn't I meet you at the bus station in Bayonne?"

"Yes," he smiled. "Good to see you again."

"My name is Tracey," I introduced myself. "I can tell you are American. Where are you from?"

"I'm Tom from Philadelphia," he replied.

"I live in Northwest Washington," I explained.

"I noticed your hand braces the other day," he said, nodding toward my hands that were loosely holding my poles. "Do you have carpal tunnel?"

"No, combat typing," I said, giving my routine response to this frequent question.

He replied with a questioning look.

"I am a retired military officer," I explained. "Constant typing over the years did a number on my finger joints. I now have aggressive erosive osteoarthritis and am losing the use of my fingers. You know, that's how officers fight wars nowadays—typing e-mails, making PowerPoint slides, writing reports, taking notes. Very dangerous work."

He chuckled a little. "I understand. I'm retired Army."

"Really?" I raised my eyebrow. I could feel a sense of connection starting to form. "How long ago did you retire?"

"After serving in Vietnam, I switched to the Army National Guard and retired from there as a lieutenant colonel after commanding our Battalion a couple years ago."

"Wow, you served a long time," I said, calculating in my head that it must've been around forty years since Vietnam ended in the mid-'70s. "What are you doing now?"

"I'm in charge of a nonprofit organization that supports my old unit. We reach out and help the spouses and family members when guardsmen are activated and deployed. We also hold various social functions and raise funds to help the unit."

"That's great! I'm also doing volunteer work. I help veterans and future officers." I went on to describe my activities. "I guess you can say I'm getting them coming and going."

Another chuckle.

"Between my frustrations helping veterans navigate the bureaucracy of the VA and my own struggles trying to get health care through them, I've had just about all I can take of the VA," I said, turning a bit more serious.

"I don't bother with the VA. I use TRICARE," he said, referring to the low-cost health insurance plan available for the families of active-duty personnel and military retirees.

"When I retired, they automatically enrolled me in TRICARE Standard, but I've only used it a couple of times," I explained. "I guess it's the principle of the thing. Since I'm rated over 50 percent service-connected disabled, the VA is supposed to provide my health care. So I guess I have an issue with paying the deductible and 20 percent co-pays, especially with the number and variety of appointments I tend to have. And of course, TRICARE doesn't cover chiropractors, so all they will do for my headaches and back problems is give me pain meds. I would have to pay the entire bill for my back treatments. At least the VA pays some of that."

"Only some?" he seemed confused.

"They should pay all of it since my back problems are service-connected, but it is a bureaucratic nightmare. Even though I need an adjustment weekly, they never authorize enough visits for weekly appointments, and the authorized visits are only good for a period of two or three months. An even bigger problem is that they will not accept, let alone start processing, a request for a new authorization until the period has expired on the old one, regardless of when I run out of authorized visits. Then it takes them anywhere from one to two months to process the request and provide a new authorization. This last time, they made me go back to my spine doctor at the VA to get a new referral. It took me about two months to get in to see him and then another month or so of frustrating phone calls and waiting to get the referral through the internal VA approval process and through the separate Choice program's administrative processes. In total, it took three and a half months from the time I requested the new authorization until I got the first new appointment through the Choice program. In the meantime, I have to pay for my weekly adjustments out of pocket. The whole thing is a constant frustration and major source of stress. But I am thankful that they at least pay for some of the visits.

"There are several other issues that make getting care from the VA very frustrating," I continued on my rant. "If you see VA doctors, there is no continuity of care. My primary-care provider is pretty consistent, but I tend to see a different specialty doctor each time. Another service officer told me that VA doctors have a life expectancy of about two years. I guess they can't take it any longer than that since the VA system is so bureaucratic and their treatment options are limited by countless VA policies. I don't have facts to back this up, but I know from my experience that I am constantly seeing different specialty doctors. My first primary-care doctor recently left, so I just got a new one of those too.

"The VA has a community-based clinic about twenty-five miles from my place where we can get primary care, mental health, immunizations, optometry, and hearing. Since I have a dental disability, I can see the dentist there. For everything else, I have to go to Seattle—a seventy-mile trip fighting horrendous traffic. A half-hour appointment takes most of the day. The worst part of this is, we have to go to the emergency room there if we need to be seen quickly. The only time we can go to a civilian emergency room is for things like life, limb, or eyesight. And if you do that, and they determine later that it wasn't actually a serious emergency, the VA often refuses to pay and you have to launch into a years-long appeal process. This happened to one of my clients who thought he was having a heart attack. He called an ambulance and was taken to a civilian hospital near his home. Turns out it was not a heart attack, and since he did not have preauthorization for the ambulance and the civilian emergency room visit, the VA is refusing to pay. As he put it, 'I am sorry I did not get preauthorization for my heart attack.'

"I've just about had it with all of our political leaders who constantly say that veterans deserve the best possible health care because they served their country, put their lives on the line, and made countless sacrifices. That is just empty political rhetoric. Veterans using VA health care don't have the option to go to the best physicians in their area or get cutting-edge treatment. The veteran is stuck with who the VA assigns and what experience/certifications that particular doctor has and what equipment that particular facility has available, not cutting-edge for the most part. There are just too many VA hospitals and medical centers, and veterans are spread out all over the United States. Having cutting-edge technology available at every VA facility is just not fiscally possible. Let's face it—there is not enough money in the national budget to 'fix the VA' and ensure all veterans receive the best possible care in a VA facility. It is just impossible!

"The new Choice program that all the politicians are patting themselves on the back for passing does little to help. Nor does it help most veterans get care within thirty days. Veterans must get preapproval for each appointment. For specialty care, the vet must first see a primary care doctor who must submit a referral request that goes through the VA bureaucracy before being sent to the contractor running the Choice program. Then it has to go through an internal Choice review and approval process, followed by a search for doctors near the veteran who are willing to accept Choice and arrangements made for the appointment. All this can easily take a couple of months. Not to mention the problem of getting civilian doctors to accept Choice. It is such a bureaucratic nightmare, takes forever to get their payments, and what they do get paid is below what Medicare pays. Frankly, I don't know why anybody would accept Choice except out of a sense of patriotism and desire to help vets."

"Sounds dismal," Tom said, surprised at all the hops that had to be jumped through.

"I can only think of one fix for this problem," I continued preaching from my soapbox. "Accounting for the financial problems our government is currently experiencing, I believe the only option is to eliminate the majority of VA medical facilities and replace 'in-house VA medical care' for common medical issues with a Medicare-type program. The private sector is more capable of providing accessible, high-quality, cutting-edge care for common conditions such as cancer, heart disease, diabetes, and Parkinson's disease. This system would allow veterans to obtain care in the communities where they live or select well-respected, cutting-edge specialty doctors and hospitals available in private sector, such as Cancer Centers of America. We should also be allowed to use community walk-in medical facilities for same-day care for serious illnesses or injuries that are not life-threatening "emergencies," and of course, local emergency rooms without worrying about whether or not the VA will cover the costs. The funding for this program would come from what the VA currently spends on supplies, equipment, facility construction, operation and maintenance of facilities, doctor and staff salaries, bonuses, and benefits.

"The VA facilities that remain should focus on unique military conditions, such as combat-related PTSD, TBI, multiple amputations, etc. Serious thought and planning would be needed to determine the specifics and ensure the remaining VA services are geographically accessible to all veterans and done in an efficient manner.

"Even though I feel strongly and very frustrated about all of this, I must admit that I am not sure that civilian medical insurance programs are any better or easier to manage than working with the VA. Between premiums, deductibles, and co-pays, and limited treatment authorizations, I suspect most civilians pay tens of thousands of dollars before the insurance company kicks in anything, if they can even get them to cover a particular treatment. Quite a racket if you ask me. It boggles my mind even to think about."

Saturated with the subject, we moved on to other topics. After a while, Tom perceived that I was holding back on my pace in order to talk to him.

"Don't let me hold you back any longer. Feel free to move ahead if you want to. I'm sure we will meet up again."

I took him up on his suggestion and moved on ahead after bidding him a hearty Buen Camino.

Alone again, my thoughts drifted back to contemplating how much my toes were hurting each time I took a step. I was moving pretty fast and taking large steps. In order to allow the metal plates to do their job, I found I needed to slow down and take shorter steps. The shorter the steps, the less the toes would try to bend. The other benefit was there would be less rubbing of my heels as they countered the limited bending of the toe joints due to the plates. The other major initiative to keep the heels from moving around in my shoe was to keep the laces tied tightly. This continued to be a problem.

The laces kept coming loose, causing me to have to stop frequently, bend over, and retie them. Besides the strain on my low back, the arthritis in my fingers made its objections well-known. Obviously, this was going to be a major struggle throughout my adventure.

Just after 1500, I passed through Zubiri. The official end of stage 2. I could see many pilgrims relaxing near the river and lots of clothes hanging on lines drying in the sun. Instead of going across the bridge into the village, I continued straight ahead and started stage 3. I had another 5.3 km to reach my goal for the day, Larrasoña.

I saw only a couple peregrinos after leaving Zubiri. Very peaceful. Lots of time to reflect and enjoy the solitude. My mind drifted to the broader picture. What I was doing by taking this trek actually lined up with a lot of the advice I had gotten from doctors. Physical exercise was not only good for mental health but also most of the other chronic conditions I was combating: arthritis, fibromyalgia, chronic back pain, prediabetes, prehypertension.

Over the last few years, I had read numerous articles about veterans using long-distance hiking as an avenue to help them transition to civilian life and come to terms with their physical and mental struggles. The Camino offered these benefits without the burden of a thirty-five-pound pack and camping out!

I entered Larrasoaña about 1630. The municipal albergue was already full, so I continued down the road another block to a private hostel. Initially, I thought the lady that responded to my knocking on the door was trying to tell me that they were full. However, after a few minutes of language misunderstandings, I realized that she was saying that there was a bed available. The cost was 16€—ten more than I would have paid at the municipal hostel, but there were less than ten beds in several rooms. As I signed my name in the book, I noticed that one of the names above mine was that of a person from Edmonds, Washington, I had been introduced to via e-mail prior to my departure. Her name was Teresa. She departed Seattle two days before I did, so I did not expect to see her along The Way. Yet it seemed that we would be roommates. What an amazing coincidence.

We had started two days apart, both stopped at a village other than a normal stage end, and both signed in to a very small hostel and ended up being roommates. What are the chances of that happening?

I could tell from the entryway that this was a very nice place. It was more of a *casa rural* than a hostel. The host showed me a large kitchen, dining and living area, the showers, and then took me to a room with two sets of bunk beds. One of the lower bunks was available, so I took it. Teresa was not there at the time. I started organizing my things and preparing for my shower. Another lady arrived while I was doing this. She was from Austria but spoke pretty good English. We had a good introductory conversation before I went to the shower.

When I returned, Teresa was there. I introduced myself, and she was as amazed as I was that we had run into each other under the circumstances. She said that she was only doing about a half a stage a day and had stayed the first night at the hostel in Orrison. She said it was very nice and was a great way to break up the strenuous first day's climb up the Pyrenees.

That evening at a pilgrims' dinner at a village restaurant, I met a lady in her midsixties from Ohio, and we talked for most of the meal. She was only making about 10 km a day and frequently took taxis. She figured it would take about fifty-five days for her to complete the Camino. Since she had done virtually nothing to prepare, this was not a bad pace. A friend of hers had asked her to join her on this trip and then developed a serious medical issue and was not able to come. Already looking forward to the trip, she had decided to go on her own. So far, she was really enjoying herself.

I thought about a couple of takeaways from the people I have met so far. Many people were doing it on their own and going at their own pace as I was. They were not worried about sticking to the stages in "The Book." For each individual, the Camino would be different. Pilgrims can go as far as they want, or are able to, each day. They can take taxis or buses for part of the journey if they don't buy into the "true peregrino" mentality. They can ship their packs ahead each day so they don't have to carry them. They can stay in albergues, pensions, casa rurals, or hotels. They can buy food in markets and cook it in the kitchens where they are RONing (remaining overnight) or eat in local restaurants. They can do things differently each day. It is all up to the individual and what they want to achieve. No matter what way they tackle this challenge, it's okay. It is "their Camino."

# CHAPTER 6

### Larrasoaña to Cizur Menor, 19.6 Kilometers
### 31 Aug 2015
### D+2

I departed at 0720 the next morning—a much better time to get started than yesterday. According to the weather app on my iPhone, it was supposed to rain in late afternoon. I needed to make good time IOT (in order to)be through Pamplona and settled in an Albergue before it started.

We had gotten very wet the last few days of our hike in 2013. Our wet shoes rubbed our feet raw and took days to dry out. Luckily, it had occurred at the end, so we were able to wear our sandals while souvenir-shopping in Santiago and during the trip home. Even though we put them next to an open window in every hotel, our shoes were still damp when we got home and smelled something awful. It wasn't until I put them in a washing machine that I could even stand to be near them. I did not want to deal with this situation so early in the hike, so my plan was to avoid rain whenever possible.

There was a German couple enjoying their breakfast when I arrived at the kitchen. They had stayed in the private room next to our bunk room. The wife showed me around the kitchen, and we talked for about ten minutes until they were ready to take off.

I quickly finished my breakfast and returned to the room to get my pack and poles. I bid Buen Camino to Teresa. Since she was going slower than I planned to, we likely would not see each other again. We agreed to get together when we got back to Washington and exchange stories.

After about 2 km, I approached a familiar field and had a flash-back to a significant emotional event that had occurred there. I had needed to go to the bathroom pretty bad and had taken an opportunity to depart the main trail and go behind some trees at the edge of the field, well out of sight of any peregrinos who might happen along the trail. There was no one in sight besides my teammates who would wait for me a few minutes up the trail. As soon as I started to do my business, a herd of sheep came around the corner of the field where I thought I was hidden. I immediately became very nervous, praying that I would get done before the shepherd rounded the corner. I was able to complete my task, recover, and get back to the trail with mere seconds to spare. Today I was completely alone—no peregrinos, no sheep, and no shepherds.

A little later I stopped for my morning coffee and OJ at a neat little café with unique character. The bar counter, tables, and stools were made of carved wood that still had the appearance of trees. My

new friend from Austria was just leaving, so we greeted each other in passing. I kept the break short, about twenty minutes, still intent on beating the rain.

During the next leg of the hike, I revisited why I came back. The way I explained it to people before I left was that I had an ego problem. Mom, Ria, and my niece didn't have a similar ego problem. Ronan, a retired Army colonel from our weekly hiking group, was the only one that really understood why I felt the need finish what I had started. I had not accomplished my mission, so I had to go back and do it right this time. As a fellow military officer, this made perfect sense to him. The last time we talked about it, a couple of weeks before I left, we decided that my first trip was a leader's reconnaissance— or in military abbreviated speak, "leader's recon." This is when the leader of a team goes to the operating location to gather information about the mission, the threat, what equipment and supplies will be needed, Standard Operating Procedures (SOP) in the area of operations (AO), and the challenges that the team will have to overcome.

The leader then takes this information back to the unit and uses it during their predeployment training and planning.

It was not a perfect analogy since I did not have a team coming back with me, but the general principle stands. I had learned many lessons that I successfully applied during my predeployment training and my first few days on the trip. Since I started packing, there had been a sense of familiarity, not to mention confidence in myself and my ability to achieve the mission.

The ego problem had long been my public explanation. Although there was definite truth in it, it was more of a summary, or surface explanation—a sound bite if you will, similar to what you see on the news all the time. Even though we have twenty-four-hour news stations, all they ever do is offer sound bites that have no substance, no context of the background information or contributing factors. No depth. No details. Just short often-emotional knee-jerk-reaction overview statements with no solid information but pushing normally erroneous, baseless conclusions. After all, "the devil is in the details."

So the question remains: Is there more to my desire to return than just having left the mission incomplete? Yes, it's probably more than that.

Thinking back, why did I retire when I did? One underlying factor was my numerous physical problems that were becoming a major limiting factor. Between the back, neck, spine, and hands, I started realizing that I was becoming a burden and that I would be a threat to other people's safety if I stayed in and continued to deploy.

I was also starting to see limitations at home station, mainly on the mental side, due to not being able to handle stress as easily. I had always thrived during stressful situations. The higher the stress, the more I was in the game. But now I had become way too emotional during stressful situations. This made it hard to concentrate and focus while thinking through a problem. I was tired. Mentally and physically exhausted down to deepest part of my being. I just couldn't keep up with our high operations tempo (ops tempo) anymore. My doctor even told me that if I didn't slow down and change my priorities, I could have a heart attack, stroke, or other major health problem.

I could relate. People around me were literally working themselves to death. The position I moved into at Central Command (CENTCOM) Headquarters was vacant because the person who had it before me committed suicide. At CENTCOM, I initially worked the biometrics security program. My office worked with the forward security staffs in Iraq and Afghanistan to determine requirements and manage the distribution of equipment and implementation of the biometrics program. The colonel we were working with in Iraq went back to his trailer one night and died in his sleep. No warning. Just didn't wake up in the morning. I believe he was about my age, midforties.

Later, when I was working with the Mine Resistant Armor Plated (MRAP) vehicle program, the major that worked for me had a stroke and was in the hospital for a couple weeks. He was younger than me. An NCO I had worked with in the middle of my career died a few months after retiring. Again, relatively young.

My doctor told me that if I did not change my priorities, this was the road I was on.

So I started making plans for retirement. About six months before my target date, I received deployment orders for a 365-day deployment to Iraq. I had the option to take the deployment or retire within a couple of months. If I had chosen retirement, I would have had to retire as a lieutenant colonel because I would not have had the three years' time-in-grade needed to retire as a colonel. So I accepted the deployment, and my exhaustion level and ability to handle stress continued to get worse. I remember walking across my unit's compound at my follow-on base in Djibouti after a particularly intense day and thinking to myself that I had had enough. I had done my share. It was time to move on, to rest.

So I found myself retiring at age forty-seven. It wasn't long before I started wondering, "Who am I now?" For close to thirty years I'd been a type A workaholic in a workaholic's paradise. I worked seven days a week. Twelve- to fifteen-hour workdays were fairly typical. During deployments, it was closer to fifteen to eighteen hours.

While at predeployment training for Iraq, one of the cadre was trying to get us in the deployment mind-set and told us we needed to get used to the idea that we would be working twelve-hour days. I remember thinking, "Wow, is that all? This is going to be a cakewalk!"

Now I felt so limited. There's always one physical or mental reason or another why I can't do various activities. I can't volunteer at the local dog shelter. They need people to clean cages, too much bending and use of hands. I can't clean or do projects around my house or work in my yard. I hire people to do those things. I can't join our local trail maintenance volunteer organization because I can't do the manual labor. The list kept getting longer. I started feeling a little worthless, like I was a burden on society. Just sitting around collecting two government checks: retirement and VA disability. Slowing down so severely is a very hard thing for a type A obsessive-compulsive person to accept. It bugged me, day in and day out.

I often wondered what I could do for a new career. My difficulty dealing with stress and anxiety made an executive-level job very unattractive. My back and hand problems prevented manual labor. As the aggressive, erosive arthritis in my hands got worse, typing was getting more painful. Handwriting anything more than a short note was out of the question. With the cold injuries on my feet and the sensitivity to cold that goes along with osteoarthritis in my fingers and toes, I can't be outside much in the winter. Each of these things sound minor, but when I put them together, I had a hard time imagining what kind of job I would be able to stick with.

Hence, the whole professional volunteer thing. At least in these positions, I have the flexibility to control the specific tasks I agree to do and the amount of time I donate. If I decide I can only work at a volunteer position once or twice a week to minimize the stress, so be it. If I want to take six weeks and hike the Camino, no problem. What are they going to do, fire me? Cut my pay? Even so, I often dwell on the fact that I don't actually earn a paycheck. Am I just mooching off the government?

So what does all this have to do with this trip? I guess with all the different things I've done to prepare, to overcome, to get around the disabilities and obstacles in my way, this hike is a way to prove to myself that I can still do things. That I still have determination and drive, and with them I can conquer challenges. Maybe I can even pull myself out of this slump.

Okay, so I have limitations. Deal with it. What can I do to work around them or find things that I'm still capable of doing to contribute to society? Of course, I have done a lot of that with my volunteer work. I'm busy, very busy. Is my situation really such a bad thing? So what if I'm not getting paid for these things? Am I not contributing to my community? Am I not making a difference in other people's lives? Should that be enough? Can I alter my thought processes to accept that? I sure hope so.

God didn't put us down here to earn a paycheck. He put us down here to serve Him and others, to be a blessing to our communities and a witness for Him. This should be enough.

I guess the bottom line concerning why I feel this trip is necessary is that I need to prove to myself that my limitations will not get the better of me. I can overcome them. The fact that I stopped last time because my feet hurt too bad was evidence that I was letting my limitations rule my life, to stop me from doing things. But I don't have to let them ruin my life. Conquering the Camino and making the whole five hundred miles symbolizes overcoming these limitations. I'm going to do this in spite of them!

I entered the outskirts of Pamplona at 1030. It wasn't long before I saw the lit green cross that indicated a pharmacy (*farmacia*). I purchased 17€ worth of Compeed and flexible medical tape. I had to get several types of Compeed, each shaped for a specific part of the foot. Once outside again, I found a place to sit for some long-awaited foot maintenance. I didn't have any blisters, but a couple layers of skin had been rubbed off from the outside of both of my heels. I placed a large oval-shaped Compeed the long way on each of them to cover the greatest length possible. I then took the flexible medical tape and, using the small collapsible scissors from my medical kit, cut four long pieces. I placed these along the top and bottom of the Compeed, covering the edges to prevent them from pulling up and sticking to the inside of my socks. It was almost impossible to get off of the socks, and they could become a sticky mess. I did the same with a smaller style of Compeed on the ball of my right foot under the big toe. Finally I used just the medical tape to cover the newly forming hotspot on my left small toe. Much better.

I stopped at the first café I found in search of a bathroom. Once inside, I noticed that they had chorizo (a type of sausage) and egg tortilla sandwiches. The chorizo gave the egg omelet a nice flavor, and I had not yet found one during this trip. I settled down for a late breakfast / early lunch, accompanied by a café con leche, of course. Implementing another lesson learned from our first hike, I took the top part of the bread off and discarded it. This way I would only eat half of the loaf of bread. It was only after starting this practice that I had started to lose weight the last time. You would think losing weight would not be hard when you're averaging fifteen miles a day, but it is when you eat all the bread that is presented to you. There's just too much!

Checking my phone, I was relieved to see a text from my mom. I had not heard from her for about twenty-four hours. An e-mail from a friend that I had read that morning had mentioned that there had been a major storm back home, causing widespread power outages. This was likely why mom had gone silent. Up to this point, we had been texting every morning and early evening. She seemed to be reliving the Camino via text. Then, for a while, there was nothing. I was glad to see that she was back online.

After eating, I started following the arrows and shells embedded in the sidewalks through the rest of old town. I stopped at a couple shoe stores looking for shoelaces. I was really getting tired of having to constantly stop and retie my shoes. Besides the pain that this caused in my fingers and back, it was slowing me down, and that was getting frustrating. I hoped a thinner style of shoelace might stay tied better. Neither store carried shoelaces. Apparently, in Pamplona you don't go to shoe stores to buy shoelaces.

As I got near the cathedral and all the albergues, the streets became crowded with pedestrians, bikers, and occasional cars. My anxiety level spiked. We had spent plenty of time touring the cathedral. No need to do it again. Besides, I had checked the weather app at lunch and the storm was still on the way. I needed to make it to the next village ASAP.

Finally I sighed in relief as I left the hustle and bustle of the big city. Time hack, 1247. There was a common saying at the Air Force Academy among the seniors that was normally found on the graduation week page of our cadet calendars. A picture would show the rearview mirror of a vehicle with the reflection of the cadet chapel and a caption saying "Happiness is the Academy in the rearview mirror!" As I left the city behind me, I could not help but modify this to "Happiness is Pamplona in the rearview mirror!"

A half hour later, I entered Cizur Menor. It was time to rest for the evening.

I stopped at the first albergue and was thrilled to get a bottom bunk once again. Since it was only 1315 and the sun was shining for the time being, I decided I would take advantage of the circumstances and wash some clothes. The *hospitalero* (the term used to describe the host running the albergue) informed me there was no washing machine available and directed me around the back of the building for the handwashing tub. Before proceeding there, I needed to take a shower and change into clean clothes so I could wash the ones I was wearing.

As expected, the handwashing and wringing out of the clothes was very painful for my arthritic fingers. What I didn't anticipate was that the height of the washtub was such that I had to bend over the whole time. The strain on my back was about as bad as the pain in my hands. I hoped I would not have to do it this way very often! As I hung the clothes on the line, I took note of the distant black clouds. I would need to keep my eye on the clouds and retrieve the clothes down before the rain started. They were able to hang for about an hour and a half and were almost dry when the black clouds darkened the sky overhead.

I took the clothes to my bunk and hung them wherever I could within my allotted space so they could finish drying. I then put on my rain jacket and rushed to a restaurant about a block away to sign up for the evening pilgrims' dinner, get a drink, and compose another update for family and friends.

By the time I had finished my first drink, a fierce storm had started outside. The rain came down in sheets, blowing sideways at about forty-five degrees accompanied by plenty of lightning and thunder. The storm was so fierce that everyone in the bar was fascinated and crowded the open doorway to watch. Accepting the fact that I was stranded for a while, I ordered a café con leche and continued drafting my update e-mail.

The storm was still raging outside when I finished the update, so I decided to do the day's Bible study. The reference for day 3 was Colossians 3:23–24: "And whatever you do, do it heartily, as to the Lord and not to man, knowing that from the Lord you will receive the reward of the inheritance; for you serve the Lord Christ." The bottom line message was that God has many ways for us to serve. Wherever and whatever a person does to serve others, they should do it as if for the Lord—because it is. We serve Him by serving others.[7] Intellectually, I can see the connection between this study message and my feelings of inadequacy. This mind-set should help me accept who I am now.

As dinner approached, the bar and restaurant started to fill up. I greeted many people that I had started with a few days earlier.

At the appointed time, I moved to the restaurant seating area, found an open seat next to an older woman, and introduced myself.

"It is nice to meet another American," she replied. "My name is Linda. So tell me, where are you from, and what brings you to the Camino?"

"I am from Camano Island in Washington State, and I am here to redeem myself." She looked at me quizzically. Anticipating that response, I explained my dismal first attempt. "My ego just couldn't handle it, so I'm back to try it again!"

"What a coincidence." She laughed, her eyes lighting up. "This is also my second go at this. Three years ago my son and I did 125 km. I intend to do the whole thing this time, but I am seventy-five, so I am going slow and I have no problem taking buses and taxis once in a while if I need to. I will travel the entire trail, but I will do it my way, and it really doesn't matter how long it takes."

---

[7] Fryar, p. 8–9.

"I met a lady last night that had the same plan, maybe you will run into her! Where are you from?"

"Texas," she said.

"I lived in Texas for about four years, well, sort of. I was technically assigned to Lackland Air Force Base in San Antonio for four years, but during that time, I completed two deployments to Afghanistan. Counting predeployment training and time in the country, I was gone for about a year and half of those four years."

"I live in Austin. I get down to San Antonio every once in a while."

"I must admit I've always had a little bit of a beef with Texans." After a dramatic pause, I continued, "I grew up in Alaska when there was a bit of a rivalry between the two states. At one point the governor of Texas made a comment I will never forget. He said that he didn't know why anybody would ever want to live in that frozen wasteland. That 'frozen wasteland' had been my home from the fifth grade through high school. Well, all I can say is, if Texas doesn't behave, we will cut Alaska in half, and then Texas will be the third largest state in the nation!"

Linda giggled a little, but I could not tell if she was mildly amused or was just laughing at my joke to be polite.

We then turned to discussions about current issues in the military. One of our major topics was about how military personnel were literally working themselves to death and what role that had had on my decision to retire. When she asked, I listed all the places I had been stationed around the world.

"You've had quite a life," she said, impressed by all the countries I had lived in.

"You know it amazes me how little Americans in general travel," I responded to her surprise at my world travels. "When I was in San Antonio, I was in the singles group at the church I attended. We had some sort of social function at my place one night, and they got to see all my pictures, furniture, and memorabilia from around the world. They were all amazed that I had been so many places. To my surprise, a large number of them had never even been out of the greater San Antonio area, let alone to other countries. What a shame.

People should really get out and experience other parts of the world and see how other people live. I've been to many poor places like Afghanistan, Africa, and Honduras. It really gives you an appreciation of the benefits and blessings of being American."

Linda wholeheartedly agreed. "I too have been fortunate to travel, but nowhere close to what you have done."

During dinner, one of the other pilgrims that was staying at my albergue invited me to a musical event at the church next to the albergue at 2100. By this time, the rain was merely a drizzle, so it was not a huge deal that the church was not open when we arrived about ten minutes early. I had assumed that this was going to be a village event, so I was surprised that it was not already open. It turned out that our hospitalero had the key to the church. He and one of the other pilgrims guests discovered that they were both guitar players and had decided to get together to play some songs for our group of peregrinos. By the time it got going, quite a crowd had gathered in the historic village chapel.

The hospitalero had everybody in the room introduce themselves and tell where they came from. Most people responded in English, but their accents were often pretty strong, and I struggled to understand what they said. I was able to pick up enough to know that the pilgrims came from many countries, including the Czech Republic, Wales, England, Belgium, the Netherlands, Italy, and Germany. The Austrian lady who I had shared a room with the night before was also present. Quite a diverse crowd.

Peregrinos gathered in the village church for an evening of song and fellowship.

The musicians led us in numerous songs from the various countries of those present, usually in that country's language. It was interesting that all the US songs were old country and hippie tunes from the '60s and '70s. I could tell that the young man had some trouble playing the songs from countries other than his, and even the hospitalero didn't know all the words to the tunes that he played. He often just hummed or sang "lala" to the tune. Rather humorous. We ended with everybody singing "Amazing Grace" together and then headed off to our bunks for the night. It was a really neat way to end the day with a unique Camino family experience.

# CHAPTER 7

## Cizur Menor to Cirauqui, 26.6 Kilometers
## 1 Sep 2015
## D+3

The hospitalero offered the normal continental-type breakfast for a donation instead of a set price. I decided, since he was such a great host, that I would give him a 10€ donation.

When we arrived the night before, he refused to let anyone take the single bed near the door in the closest room to the bathrooms. Everybody asked for it, but his intent was to keep it free in case an injured or sick peregrino needed it. I thought that was an outstanding policy to have. He also organized the music fellowship. This morning he inquired where everybody was hoping to spend the night and then advised us on the best places to stay there.

He even made recommendations for several days ahead, indicating that if we wanted to avoid the hustle and bustle of Logroño, we should stay at a wonderful small town called Viana a little more than 10 km prior to the city. Looking at my maps, I determined that would work well as long as I continued to stop in the middle of stages. It would set me up nicely to spend the following night in the hotel in Ventosa where Mom, Ria, and I had stayed after seeing Samantha off on the bus from Logroño. It was a very nice small hotel that seemed more like a bed-and-breakfast to me. The owner was friendly and washed and dried our clothes for no additional cost. We had private rooms with sheets and blankets on the beds and private bathrooms with showers and towels! There was a wonderful garden patio out back to relax in, as well as an outstanding communal dinner and good-sized breakfast offered as part of the price. My intent was to treat myself to a hotel once a week. This would be a great first treat.

Finally, just before we departed, he warned each of us to be careful on the steep, rugged descent after we summited and saw the windmills and famous pilgrim silhouettes about midday. He said the steep trail was always dangerous, but due to the heavy rains the night before, it would be much more treacherous today.

It was still dark when I moved out at 0655. I used the battery-operated headlamp I brought for just such occasions for about a half hour. There was a light mist in the air that danced and sparkled as my light hit it.

The rising sun revealed a layer of clouds covering windmill hill. The heavy rain had taken its toll on the dirt road we followed. Many sections were washed out; there were deep flow-ruts where a person could easily twist an ankle; and the mud was deep in places.

Per SOP, I stopped at a café in Zariquiegui for coffee and OJ after about 6.1 km and then conquered the steep ascent to the windmills and metal pilgrims of old.

After obligatory photos, I was enjoying a Kit-Kat bar from a mobile snack trailer when a tour bus pulled up and about forty tourists got off. Wearing small day packs and Camino de Santiago T-shirts and hats, they all gathered near the silhouettes for a group photo. After milling around for a while, they began hiking down the hill in a gaggle. This really rubbed me the long way.

Posing with the peregrino silhouettes

"Pretend pilgrims," if you ask me, bussed to the top of the steep hill and then hiked down with five-pound day packs. How weak!

While I waited for the gaggle to get a little ahead, I stuffed lamb's wool into the toes and heels of my shoes in preparation for the steep descent.

Slowly the sun started to break through the clouds as I started down. Besides the steep angle, the trail was washed out and rugged.

Large rocks and gravel were scattered everywhere. It was brutal. I don't think all this could be attributed solely to last night's rain. If any section of the trail needed some trail maintenance volunteers, this was it. Maybe they should pave the trail on this hillside and install steps. Carving out some switchbacks would be another option. Both options were commonly used on steep Washington trails.

As it was, I twisted my right ankle three times on the way down, and it started aching something fierce. I had brought an ankle brace along for use on my left ankle due to the chronic pain from tendon/ligament damage in 2009. To my surprise, up until now that ankle had not been much of a factor, so I switched the brace to the right for the time being.

It was amazing that the universal conspiracy had not succeeded in taking me out on the fourth day of the hike. It sure had plenty of opportunity. Maybe my luck was changing!

I guess those forty tourists had not been such wimps after all. It was no cakewalk getting down that hill. They were probably thinking that they had bitten off more than they could chew.

Another amazing positive development today was the temperature had dropped about twenty degrees compared to the first three days of the hike. It was as if the storm had blown summer away. As the calendar changed from August to September, the season had changed from summer to fall overnight.

I stopped at the next village to celebrate fracture avoidance and found a restaurant we'd eaten at before. It was where I'd had my first beer (*cerveza*) for lunch. So in tribute, I ordered one along with a plate of spaghetti. One must uphold traditions after all!

I then found a table outside and dropped my pack. That sure felt good! I oriented the pack in such a way as to allow the sun to shine on my still damp towel and socks from last night's laundry. I had hung them off the back of my pack so they could finish drying in the warm sunshine while I hiked.

The tables around me were filled with faces that were becoming more familiar each day. I talked with a group of four from Belgium and the Netherlands whom I'd first met waiting for the bus in Bayonne. The youngest in the group was the guitar player from last night. They planned to stop at the end of stage 4 today, where as I was going further. Not to worry, we seem to keep saying goodbye only to meet again further up the trail.

Most pilgrims were intently engaged in foot maintenance. Many were just airing out their feet, and some were changing socks. Others were tending to blisters.

There was still 14 km until my objective for the day, so I did not linger too long. Now that my mind was not focused on safety, I started thinking about the great news I had received when I went online and checked my bank account before leaving the hostel. Over $8,000 had been deposited on 28 August from the Veterans' Administration. This could only be the retroactive pay that they had owed me for almost two and a half years. Praise the Lord for His timing! I no longer needed to worry about how much each night's stay would cost. I could afford to take a step up from the crowded bunk rooms. I now had more freedom to take my time each day and upgrade to more expensive rooms if need be to get a lower bunk, or even treat myself to a casa rural or pension more often! This was a great weight off my mind!

The payment ended a very long and frustrating wait. The more I found out about the details factoring into the reason for delay, the more frustrated I had gotten. It not only affected me but tens of thousands of other military retirees, including many of my clients at the Legion. We all felt helpless to do anything about it.

The issue involved two policies that affect retired and combat wounded veterans, concurrent retirement and disability pay (CRDP), and combat-related special compensation (CRSC). Per current law, if rated less than 50 percent disabled for service-connected conditions, the amount of monthly tax-free VA-paid disability compensation a retiree receives is deducted dollar for dollar from their military retirement check. Therefore, the only real benefit the retiree gets for their disability is a small tax relief on the amount that the VA now pays. The tax advantage varies by individual income, but as an example at an 18 percent tax rate, this saves a 40 percent disabled veteran about $105 a month. For the 10 percent disabled veteran, the tax advantage is about $24. This "offset" does not apply to military retirees who are rated 50 percent or more. They receive the full amount of both their military retirement and their VA disability compensation.

The disability/retirement pay offset only applies to military retirees. No other type of retirement benefit (government or private) is affected by VA disability compensation. This means that the people who are dedicated enough to serve their country for twenty or more years are the only ones penalized.

Not only does this law unfairly penalize those who dedicate the majority of their working life in service of their country and willingly completed several combat and humanitarian deployments, but we continue to be penalized during the VA disability claim process. On all claims, the VA is required to pay the monthly amounts retroactively back to the date the claim was submitted. These retroactive payments are paid immediately to veterans who are not military retirees and often reach their bank before the claim decision letter even arrives in their mailbox.

For military retirees, the VA must coordinate with the DoD agency responsible for military retirement pay before the retroactive payment is made. The appropriate payment is possible at this time because the law is black and white. If the veteran is rated below 50 percent disabled, there is an offset; if 50 percent or higher, the veteran gets the full amount of both. Too easy.

But nothing is easy with the government. The VA decides the disability percentage, "closes" the initial claim, and reports it as such to Congress. After that, they open a "new claim" to determine if the veteran is authorized concurrent pay and coordinate with the DoD for potential adjustments to their retired pay. The calculations and adjustments are a little tricky for those with a disability rating below 50 percent because the retiree has already received full military retired pay for the months or years between the effective date and the decision. But it is a no-brainer for those rated 50 percent and above—no adjustment is required. As a "new claim," the claim timeline starts at zero, and it is put in to the "administrative claim" stack, which is neither reported in the VA claims backlog to Congress nor to the American people and therefore has an extremely low priority.

My original claim was decided in March 2013. DoD notified the VA in a letter dated 13 May 2013 that I was authorized concurrent receipt since I was over 50 percent. As of that date, the VA had all they needed to authorize the retroactive pay. All they had to do was go into the computer and hit Send. Now, two and a half years later, they finally got around to it.

The same inefficient, frustrating, and disrespectful process is used to process retroactive pay for veterans who endured disabling injuries during combat operations (CRSC) and now receive military medical retirement payments. So the only two categories of people who are penalized this way and forced to endure years of waiting for their retroactive pay are those that served for twenty or more years and those that were seriously injured in combat.

The American people have no knowledge of this injustice and our elected officials in Washington are doing nothing to fix it. Is it no wonder that veterans do not get too excited by all the official pats on the back they get during political statements by elected officials and the media?

A little less than halfway through the afternoon segment, I passed through the city at the end of stage 4, Puente La Reina. As I entered the town, I passed the wonderful combined hotel and hostel we had stayed at before, Hotel Jakue. Upstairs there was a very nice hotel, and in the basement was a forty-bed hostile with four-person cubicles. We had enjoyed a wonderful pilgrims' banquet with unlimited food and wine in the hotel dining room. This had been our best dinner of the trip. It would've been nice to stay there again, but I needed to go further IOT be able to pass through Logroño in a couple of days. Last night's rain left mud flowing into the street outside of the hotel. It was impossible to get around it, and my shoes sank at least an inch and a half as I passed through.

As I approached the far end of town, I saw a large crowd on the bridge. I surmised by their dress and typical tourist actions that these were once again members of the tour bus group. They must have passed me while I had lunch. I fought to suppress my anxiety and frustration as I dodged the gaggle while crossing the bridge and quickly proceeded down the sidewalk leading out of town. About a block after the bridge, my suspicions were confirmed. A large bus was sitting there waiting to take its charges to a hotel for the night. Once past the bus, the trail left the road and went down a nice secluded dirt trail away from the hustle and bustle. My anxiety dissipated, and I returned to my reflections.

I decided it would be more beneficial for me to think about the positive aspects of receiving the payment. I needed to think and pray about what to do with the money. Obviously, some of it would go to pay off my credit card bill when I got back from this trip. I was still significantly short of what I needed to replace my roof, so a chunk should go toward that.

Of course, 10 percent should go to God. There were many options for the use of these funds to be considered. I prayed for guidance regarding where God would have me donate. I could give extra to missionaries that I support monthly through my home church. There was also the church building fund which was being used to construct a large building to house additional classroom and function spaces on the campus. The church was building it phase by phase as funding allowed to avoid paying interest on a loan. We were getting close to completion, and the extra funds now would help with the electrical and other final interior details.

The Lord also brought to mind a ministry that was reaching out to Muslims around the world in an effort to introduce them to the saving truth of Jesus Christ. Having worked in Afghanistan and Iraq, and with AF and DoD anti-terrorism policy, I have come to believe that this is a very worthwhile cause. There is a lot of darkness, hatred, and violence in the Muslim world. Faith, understanding, and trust in Christ and the God of love and hope could bring light and peace to those countries. On a much deeper spiritual level, I believe that this is the only way that anyone, including Muslims, can obtain salvation and eternal life. I decided to contribute a portion of the 10 percent to that cause.

As I tackled the final stretch of the day, many parts of my body told me it was time to stop. The bone spur on my right big toe really hurt most of the afternoon. I wondered if the increased pain was because I was limping slightly from trying to twist my ankle several times coming down the hill. Additionally, my fingers hurt from gripping my poles. As I got tired, it was harder to remember to use my low-impact system, and I unconsciously started gripping instead of just resting my fingers on the poles. I was now living with the results of not sticking to the plan. Finally my back and neck were far sorer today than they had been any day so far.

It was fairly late in the afternoon when I entered the historic medieval style village of Cirauqui where I intended to stay for the evening. I immediately recognized the steep roads that weaved through the town. The climb was grueling, especially after such a long day's hike. This had happened many times in 2013. It seemed like we always

Peregrinos approach Cirauqua, a medieval village on a hill.

had to climb a steep hill at the end of the day to get to an albergue. Oh well, it was good exercise.

The albergue was worth the effort. It had a lot of medieval character. As I settled in, I greeted the young couple who had been my roommates the night before. They were from New Zealand, currently living in Australia. Apparently, we were going to be roommates again. I also met three retired Navy officers from Oregon and Idaho. Two of them were brothers, and the other was a close friend who had served multiple tours with one of the brothers. We spent about a half hour talking about our backgrounds. I could tell by his evening attire that one of the sailors was obviously a Seattle Seahawks fan.

After settling in, I went to the basement where a small bar was available and ordered a glass of wine. I spent about twenty minutes doing mission planning and then took out my service study book to read the day's lesson.

Day 4 discussed determining how God wants you to serve. The author suggested that when considering what long-term ministry you can commit to, you should contemplate three questions. What activities make my heart sing; what are my passions? What am I good at; what are my strengths? And finally, what needs to be done, and am I able and available to do it?[8] God will give you the passion, skills, and opportunity to do what he would have you to do.

These were important questions for me to consider during this pilgrimage. A major objective of my journey was to contemplate what I should do with the rest of my life. Finding a way to use my talents to serve God was central to this. My passions seem to involve keeping a connection with the military that had been my world for most of my adult life. Working as an admissions liaison officer for the Air Force Academy was definitely a positive responsibility that I enjoyed and was passionate about. I enjoyed helping veterans through my duties at the American Legion Service Office. On the other hand, this volunteer job also had many negatives that caused me extensive anxiety and stress. These polar opposite aspects of my experience there had kept me on the fence between continuing or resigning. Which direction I was leaning on any given day was a direct result of how the day had gone. Some days I was intent on staying and helping the veterans; other days I was completely fed up with many aspects of the Legion as an organization and the endless frustrating struggle with the VA's bureaucratic system. Even on positive days, by day's end I was mentally drained and feeling anxious and stressed. However, I really enjoyed helping the veterans. Coming to the personal resolution of this conflict during this pilgrimage was a must.

At 1900 hours, we gathered for the communal dinner. I was seated in a small back room with a bunch of young pilgrims. We went around the table introducing ourselves, and I asked everyone to

---

[8] Fryar, p. 10–11.

explain why they were here. They turned out to be from many different countries, and they had all met on the trail and started walking as a group. Among the group, there were two American sisters. One explained that she had just graduated from college a few months earlier and was still looking for employment. This gave her the time to do the Camino before getting tied down with a career. The younger sister had graduated from high school in June and was taking a year off before starting college.

After an enjoyable evening of good food and fellowship, we all turned in for the night.

Entryway to the communal dining
area in the albergue basement.

# CHAPTER 8

## Cirauqui to Monjardin, 23.4 Kilometers
## 2 Sep 2015
## D+4

Sections of today's trail followed the remains of an ancient Roman road made of uneven rocks that were really hard on the ankles to traverse. If this is how they constructed their roads, it is a no wonder the empire fell. As hard as it was to walk on, I could not imagine how rough it would be traveling by chariot!

By the end of the first hour, I had missed two turns and had to retrace my steps to find the arrows and get back on track. The trail is so well marked; you can't get lost unless you just aren't paying attention. My mind had been wandering and obsessing about my cold fingers and aching sore back and feet, so that may have been the issue. Of course, it may also have been the need for coffee and breakfast. The guidebook suggested if you lose your way, it is best to retrace your steps until you find an arrow, or you could be searching for a way to reconnect for hours or even get hopelessly lost. At least I followed that advice and only ended up adding about a kilometer of walking distance between the two incidents.

Once back on track, I passed through a tunnel underpass that was decorated with familiar graffiti. One of our favorite pictures from 2013 was a comic titled *I Am a True Pilgrim*. It was of a woman pilgrim with comments pointing at various pieces of clothing and gear. My favorite comment referred to her backpack which said "Too much useless stuff." The comic was faded and hardly readable.

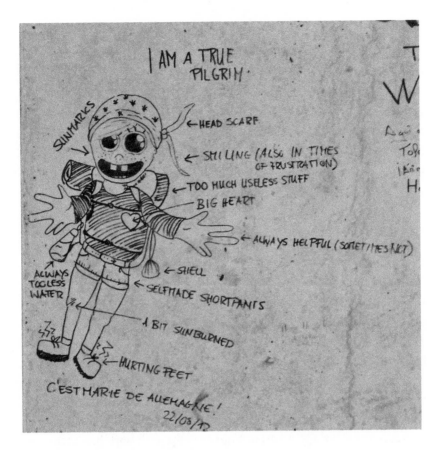

So much so that if I hadn't been looking for it, I would've missed it. Shame. We had gotten a real kick out of it.

It wasn't long before I came upon another memorable stop from the previous hike. It was an ancient bridge over a small river. We had arrived there on a hot afternoon, and the area was filled with resting pilgrims. The couple we had met from Seattle, Fred and Suzie, and their Dutch friend had been there along with several others that we had come to know. We had a restful time socializing in the afternoon heat.

By this point in our hike, the tendons in Samantha's feet were causing her a lot of pain. She took the opportunity to soak them in the cold water. She even stayed behind for a while longer when the other three of us decided to move on, catching up with us at a coffee stop in the next village.

Pilgrims rest and socialize near a river in 2013.

Today it was only about 0830 and was still cold. I actually looked a little funny at this point. The legs were zipped off of my hiking pants, and I was wearing a short-sleeved shirt. However, my arthritic fingers were still cold, so I was wearing gloves. Anyone who saw me probably thought that I was rather odd. But not to worry; no one was resting by the river this morning. Its cold waters did not seem to have as much appeal as they had on that hot afternoon! So I just paused, absorbed the memory, and pressed on to the next village where I was looking forward to getting some breakfast.

Once in a warm café, I ordered a chorizo tortilla and the normal café con leche and OJ. I had to hold the cup with both hands because one cold hand was unable to handle the weight by gripping the cup's handle, not to mention the pain involved in bending my fingers. I wrapped my hands snugly around the cup, allowing its warmth to ease the pain and relax my mind.

While waiting for my breakfast, I noticed a straggly-looking young man sitting on a stool at the counter. He had shoulder-length hair, beard, and wore a hippy-looking shirt. In a strong German accent, he offered to move over a chair to make room so our host could place my order on the counter. I told him not to worry, but he moved over, anyway, saying it would be best for the staff helping others anyway. I thanked him and then took my breakfast to a table item by item. I got caught up on my notes and texted back and forth with Mom a few times. Apparently, Jamie is calmer and not running around like a "Wild Woman" tonight.

After leaving town, I noticed the young man ahead of me. He was walking along the road, not the pilgrim path. He had bare feet and was carrying his sandals, obviously avoiding sections of the path with thick mud flow areas.

Eventually, I caught up with him and greeted him with a smile and a question about how walking in bare feet must hurt. At first I did not think he would respond. He must have been thinking about what to say.

After ten to fifteen seconds, he said, "It is better than wearing sandals. I started walking in France about a month ago. The shoes I started with were not for hiking. After about a week, my feet were torn up, so I sent my shoes home and started wearing my sandals. They were worse. They really cut into my toes and the tops of my feet. I met a Korean who wanted to use them in the shower, so I gave them to him and purchased these walking sandals. The early pilgrims walked in sandals, so I thought it would work, but they're not much better than my old ones."

This sounded familiar. "My niece said the same thing when she attempted the Camino two years ago. She had to stop in Lagroño because of serious tendon pain in both feet. We suspected that the sandals had something to do with it."

I asked him what made him go on such a long walk.

"I am from Germany. My girlfriend and I both had some time off, so we decided to travel around. We visited friends around Europe and toured several places like the Black Forest. After a while my car started having problems and broke down somewhere in France. It cost me 150€ to get it towed to a village. They didn't have the parts for a German car, so it was going to cost over 1,000€ to fix it. On the way to the village, I saw a Camino way-marker. I have been intrigued by the Camino for many years. When I saw the marker, I decided it was a sign that I was supposed to do it. But the "sign" did not speak to my girlfriend. She wanted nothing to do with it and went home. I left my car with a farmer in the village and started walking. I started out with a car, a girlfriend, and shoes. Now I have none of them."

We both chuckled.

His first week had been a time of painful lessons, but after that he often made 40 km a day. He figured that his current footwear problem was a sign that he needed to slow down and relax.

He then asked me why I was doing it, and I told him about not finishing it the first time and my need to come back and do it right this time.

Laughing, he said, "I do not have a pilgrim's credential and so have not gotten any stamps. I guess I will have to come back someday and do it right too!"

It was at this time that I began to suspect he was not the hippy he appeared to be.

About this time, we came to a road intersection but could find no way-markers. There were no other hikers in sight. Apparently, for the third time today, we had missed a turn. As we retraced our steps, I asked, "Where have you been staying?"

Pilgrim credentials were required to get a bed at a hostel, and he did not look like someone who could afford a hotel every night.

"In France, before St. Jean, there are no hostels or any other sort of support system. I have been camping out. This was okay in France. There weren't many pilgrims there, so I could sleep where I wanted and wash in rivers and creeks with no problem. Here, there are too many people. It has been much more difficult since St. Jean."

Passing under a bridge, we found no way-marker like we hoped. We looked around and saw peregrinos on the far side of a sunflower field. Apparently, the turn had been back even further, likely around where we had started talking. Continuing backward was not appealing, so he suggested we cut across the field to the trail. I hesitated, and he encouraged me to follow him. The ground appeared muddy, but not too bad, and there was actually quite a bit of space between the plants for us to walk. So I followed him.

About two-thirds of the way across, the mud started getting thicker. Our feet sank deeper and deeper. Soon my shoes and half of my soaks were caked in mud. No use turning back now. The damage had been done.

As we kept going, it kept getting worse. Finally we approached the road, but we had to first cross a small irrigation cannel with a light flow of water. No problem, we needed to clean up anyway.

"You see, it is good not to wear shoes." He laughed as the mud easily washed off of his bare feet. He sure had a point there.

As I was trying to wash my shoes off, another hiker approached us looking concerned. We looked at her, smiled, and explained that we had missed a turn. I then asked the man to take a picture of me cleaning my shoes, which he did, and then I took a picture of him to show everyone who's fault it was!

"You cannot show that to anyone!" he said as the three of us set off down The Way.

"I learned my lesson," I proclaimed. "I certainly will not be doing that again."

"Not so for me," he said, seemingly very serious. "I usually have to do things several times before I learn."

"You must be a slow learner," I joked.

The young lady who had joined us broke into a hearty laugh.

We continued talking, and he explained that he enjoyed going further than others each day because his favorite time was after everyone had found a hostel and started settling in for the night.

"It is so peaceful when I am walking alone."

I agreed with him. The last few days I had enjoyed walking past hostels with pilgrims waiting to check in or enjoying a rest while their laundry dried on a clothesline. After that, I would only see a handful of others. Those I did see ended up being hostel-mates in the next village. These midstage hostels were smaller and had a lot more character! I was also finding that my concern about missing out on the Camino family social portion of the experience was not founded. I kept running into others doing the same as me (avoiding the "normal" stage ends) at cafés and hostels. After describing this, I concluded with "I guess we are the 'I Hate

Crowds and Big Cities Camino Family.' Both of my companions laughed in agreement.

At the next village, my German friend announced he needed to find a supermarket to get some food and hopefully find a store to buy some hiking shoes. We wished each other Buen Camino and parted ways. I doubted I would see him again since he was going almost twice as far as I was each day.

The woman who had joined us after our trek through the mud had fallen behind just before we got to the village, so I found myself alone once again. This gave me time to start my reflection for the day. I decided it would be good to start at the beginning and work my way through my career step by step as I tackled each day along The Way.

* * * * *

When I was growing up, I was fascinated with science fiction and outer space adventure. I didn't like the monster films where some alien was trying to eat the crew of a spaceship or take over the earth. Instead, I was interested in the positive shows of mankind exploring space or civilized aliens visiting earth. In high school, my favorite subjects were math, science, physics, chemistry, etc. One of the papers that I enjoyed researching and writing the most was about the life cycle of a star. So naturally, I decided I wanted to be an astronaut when I grew up.

Because of my passion, early in my junior year of high school someone asked me if I was interested in going to a military academy. I quickly and adamantly replied that I was not interested at all. However, after reading the book *The Right Stuff*,[9] I realized that going to the United States Air Force Academy (USAFA) and becoming a pilot was the best way to pursue my dream. Upon further contemplation, I realized going into the military was not really contrary to who I was. I grew up as a tomboy and spent a lot of time playing cops and robbers, cowboys and Indians, and even war games. I

---

[9]   Tom Wolfe, *The Right Stuff* (Farrar, Straus and Giroux: 1979).

enjoyed military shows and movies, just not as much science fiction. I remember a time as a young teenager when I was hiking with my family near Fort Richardson, the Army base outside of Anchorage, Alaska. On a hill across a valley there was a small military unit conducting a patrolling exercise. I watched them for quite a while and was fascinated and inspired by their training. It wasn't long before I changed my mind. I started the academy application process early in my senior year of high school.

Because all the military academies are among the best colleges in the country, I knew it was very competitive to get accepted. I had always participated in sports, held leadership roles in extracurricular activities, and took the hard college preparation courses. My grades were competitive. My ACT test scores were relatively high compared to most high school students. With all of this, I had a solid application package and received several congressional nominations to both USAFA and West Point. I had no desire to go to West Point, but I had been advised to apply to multiple academies in case I did not receive an AF appointment. In the spring I was offered an appointment to USAFA and immediately quit my job at Shakey's Pizza Parlor. I no longer needed to earn money for college! I used the extra time to prepare physically and spend time with family.

I reported to the academy with the rest of the Class of 1987 for Basic Cadet Training (BCT) in early July 1983, less than two months after graduating from high school in Anchorage. The first day was a mix of excitement and shock as we adjusted to the reality that our lives were now completely different.

We got our first introduction to the cadre as we arrived at the base of the Bring Me Men ramp. They were senior and junior cadets who were our training instructors and, for most practical purposes, ran BCT as part of their own leadership training. They greeted us by getting a few inches from our faces and yelling. We were the scum of the earth, and it was their job to fix that problem. They quickly taught us how to stand at attention and how to respond to any question that started with the word *why*. The response was always "No excuse, sir/ma'am."

They then lined us up and marched us through in-processing lines where we did paperwork and were issued uniforms, bedding, and equipment we would need for basic training, to include a demilitarized M-1 rifle for drill. *Demilitarized* meant that the barrel had been filled with lead so it could not shoot; it also made them heavier than a normal weapon. We received the obligatory haircuts and room assignments in our basic training squadrons. Our first physical test came that day when, loaded down with all of our issued equipment and clothing, we had to climb the stairs to the sixth floor where Demon (D) Squadron was billeted. I thought we would never get to the top!

I was assigned to Demon Squadron's D Flight. A *flight* was our primary training formation, and the group of classmates we would spend the most time with. We did everything as a flight. Everyone in a basic cadet flight would transition together to form the fourth class (freshman) of a cadet squadron (CS) for the academic year. The basic training group contained ten squadrons with four flights each—meaning, there were forty basic cadet flights that would feed the Cadet Wing's forty cadet squadrons.

I fondly remember marching at attention back to the dormitory after dinner along the edge of the terrazzo in a long line of basic cadets in uniform for the first time. I was overcome with emotion that I was a part of this elite group, dedicated to training to serve our country as military officers. I was now part of the United States military. I was part of something bigger than myself. I had a noble life mission!

That evening we all went to the big auditorium in Arnold Hall for welcome briefings by the generals that ran the academy and other staff members. The one thing I will never forget from that briefing was that one of the speakers told us to look at the person on our right and then the one on our left.

He said, "One of you three will not be here on graduation day."

He was right. When that day came four years later, we had lost almost exactly one-third of our class.

The next morning we were rudely awakened by the cadre before the sun came up. They came down the hall pounding on the doors and screaming that we were late and we needed to get up and get ready for physical training (PT). I knew this was part of the game, but I had to chuckle and think to myself that if we were late, it was their fault, so why were they yelling at us? They had taken away our watches the previous day, and no one was allowed to have a clock in their room, let alone an alarm clock. We were not even told what time to get up. Even so, apparently we were in trouble. We quickly stumbled around the room, putting on our new physical fitness uniforms, and then lined up at attention against the wall in the hallway until the upperclassman were ready to take us out for morning PT.

Once at the terrazzo level (fourth floor), we formed up in our three-line flight formation and jogged in step as a unit to the parade field where we fell in beside the other three flights from our squadron. In typical military style, we warmed up with stretches and calisthenics as the rising sun slowly lit up the parade field. The air was chilly, and the grass was wet with dew. It wasn't long before our new white T-shirts became wet and stained with grass and mud.

The first part of PT was fairly easy for those of us who had prepared physically before arrival. However, we finished the session by jogging a couple of times around the parade field. This is where people started to separate and fall out of formation. I had run extensively prior to coming. However, Anchorage is at sea level. The academy is at 7,250 feet. There was practically no air to breathe, and I started falling behind along with countless others. As I struggled to fill my lungs with air, I recalled the medical briefing from Arnold Hall the night prior. The medic had warned us about the thin air and told us we needed to take it easy for about three weeks in order for our bodies to become accustomed. Apparently, the upperclassmen had not received this briefing!

Besides daily, progressively tougher PT, most of the first three weeks of basic was spent in the classroom learning about mili-

tary and AF history, customs and courtesies, and other important military information. We also spent a lot of time learning to
march and practicing drill. We started memorizing parts of our
class knowledge book called Contrails. Our required memorization included insightful quotes from military leaders and alphanumeric designations of aircraft from various wars. Whenever
we had a few minutes between events, the cadre would line us
up at attention against a wall and have us spit out what we had
memorized in unison.

I don't remember if it was near the end of first or beginning
of second beast (*beast* is how we referred to BCT), but one night
a couple of our classmates got a little cocky (there is a thin line
between bravery and stupidity). After the cadre had gone to bed,
a classmate proposed we order pizza from Dominoes. A couple of
the guys gathered money and went to the bottom of the stairwell to
meet the deliveryman. Returning to the sixth floor, they passed out
the pizza to everyone and then came back about twenty minutes
later to pick up the boxes. My roommate and I figured that the
guys had taken the boxes back down to ground level and disposed
of them in a large trash bin. However, when the cadre woke us up
the next morning, it was apparent that our classmates had cut corners and still had a lot to learn about special operations—namely,
avoiding detection. They disposed of the boxes in the bathroom
garbage cans. You guessed it: the cadre had found them and were
not pleased. Training that day was extra tough as we paid for breaking the rules. We were Delta Flight in Demon Squadron. Up until
this point, we had called ourselves the Demon Destroyers. Now we
were Domino's Delivers.

After three weeks, we transitioned to second beast. We got a
whole new set of cadre who introduced themselves as a far stricter
group. During first beast, our cadre were relatively kind and understanding (after the shock treatment of day one, that is) as we learned
the basics of military skills and transitioned from a civilian to military mind-set. Now it was time to be hardened into lean, mean,
fighting machines. Instead of light-blue shirts and slacks, we now

wore OD green combat fatigues. Our nice, easy lives going to briefings and practicing marching were over. It was now time to develop
ourselves mentally and physically into airman that would someday
fight our country's wars.

\* \* \* \* \*

As I reflected on my experiences in BCT, I passed through Estella
and found myself at the Fuente del Vino (wine fountain) about 1230.
Two years ago, we had arrived here about 0830. Apparently they shut
the wine off overnight and had not turned it back on by the time of
our arrival. It had been quite a disappointment. This year I timed
it much better! I took a little extra wine to make up for missing it
the first time. With my water bottle about half full, I sipped on the
wine as I continued for another kilometer until stopping for lunch
in Irache.

I lingered for about an hour and a half. The remaining mud
on my feet had started to dry, so I was able to knock a significant
amount of it off my socks and shoes. Then I applied Compeed to
a couple of new hot spots, no doubt the result of wet shoes. Since I
had my socks off, anyway, I applied more Vaseline. I left the shoes off
while eating lunch. My feet enjoyed that!

I ordered a veal lunch plate and got far more than I bargained
for. The veal cutlet was huge and the combo plate came with a large
portion of fries, sautéed red peppers, and bread. It was also much
more expensive than any other lunch I had purchased so far, 14.7€
with the tip. I decided I would be skipping dinner tonight!

As I got underway, I resumed my reflections about BCT.

\* \* \* \* \*

The central portion of second beast was the week in Jack's
Valley. This was the wooded area on the academy grounds that
we marched to for field training, including sleeping on hard cots
in large musky-smelling tents. Every day the squadrons rotated

through the various courses to include the obstacle, assault, confidence, leadership reaction, recondo, and map and compass courses. We also went to the weapons range to learn to fire the M-16 rifle and a .38-caliber pistol. On another day we did Air Base Ground Defense where we learned patrolling and setting up defenses around a base camp to include foxholes, interlocking fields of fire, and the art of just lying there for hours on end and trying to stay alert for the smallest indication of enemy activity outside the perimeter in your field of fire. Unbeknownst to me at the time, this "mission" would be a significant part of my career in security forces.

Every day was a new challenge. Successful completion of the courses normally required teamwork, or at least each member of the team helping to motivate and encourage the others. We learned that there is no "I" in team. It was counterproductive to mission accomplishment for one person to attempt to outshine everybody else. The goal was always team success, not individual success. However, it was also clear that if each individual did not do their best and pull their own weight, the team would fail. The last thing anyone wanted was to be the person pulling the rest of the team down. This was especially important for the females.

The first women to be allowed to attend the military academies reported in the summer of 1976, graduating just three years before I arrived. Although significant progress had been made during the previous seven years, male prejudice against female cadets was still an obstacle for us to overcome. There was an average of only four women per flight of approximately thirty cadets. Our male counterparts and the cadre expected us to be weak. Some of us were (as were some of the male basics), but all the women were determined to show the male cadets that we could be productive members of the team. We did not want the standards to be lowered in order for us to succeed; we wanted to prove that we could achieve the established standards and be successful.

There are three specific events that stand out in my memory about second beast. The first was a base newspaper article about our class in Jack's Valley that showed me sitting on a cot in the medical tent soaking my feet because of significant blisters. For some reason, this picture has become one of my mother's favorites. I am not so sure that it is the most becoming photo ever taken of me.

*Ohhh my foot!*

Basic Cadet Tracey Meck soaks her foot in the Orthopedic tent at Jacks Valley. The Cadet Clinic and Academy Hospital have set up a field clinic to treat minor injuries that may occur during training in the valley. (U.S. Air Force photo by SSgt. Guido Locati)

They say that "significant emotional events" stand out best in a person's memory. My experience on the confidence course definitely fell into that category. I have never been too thrilled with heights. Many of the obstacles that we needed to conquer on the course were high off of the ground. Two in particular caused me problems. One was an obstacle that had two logs that went straight up with crossbeams that were spaced at ever-increasing gaps as they got further from the ground. We had to climb from one crossbeam to the next and then down the other side. To my horror, the gap to the final crossbeam was greater than I was tall. I could not imagine how I would be able to pull myself up and over that beam to start my descent down the other side. I'm not sure how I did it, but I remember being scared to death.

On another obstacle, we climbed the ladder to the top platform and then we were supposed to flip ourselves off one platform, by wrapping our arms around the beam supporting the platform while lowering our feet to the next one down. The top platform was sixty to seventy feet up. I remember lying there with my head hanging over the edge and staring down at the ground. I froze. There was no way I felt I could trust myself to flip over and lower my feet to the next level. I lay there paralyzed for ten to fifteen minutes, trying to convince myself to try. My teammates relentlessly shouted their encouragement. Somehow that motivated me to find the courage to do as I was instructed. It turned out to be much easier than I could ever imagine. Flipping from one level to the next the rest of the way down was easy, but I will never forget lying at the top, looking at the ground so far below, and trying to convince myself to try.

The third significant memory from second beast was our flight marching back to camp after a long day at one of the courses. It was already dark, so we carried our flashlights in our right hands. While we marched, we sang "America the Beautiful" and other patriotic songs. The strongest wave of patriotism you could imagine engulfed me as we made our way through the dark, singing as a team with our individual points of light swinging back and forth in unison.

After we completed BCT and the rest of the upperclassmen returned from their summer programs, the entire wing marched out to the parade field for the acceptance day ceremony. The basics stood in our forty basic cadet flights facing the forty cadet squadrons. We were going into CS-40, so we were at the far end. During the ceremony, epaulets with the freshman insignia were attached to the shoulders of our light-blue shirts by the second beast cadre. This reflected our promotion to "the lowest rank in the wing." That sounds terrible, but it was actually a proud day. We were no longer basics. We were now officially part of the Air Force Academy Cadet Wing. Proudly, each flight marched forward and fell in at the back of their new squadron.

* * * * *

By the time I got to Monjardin, both the association and the private albergue were full. The person before me took the last bed. It was my friend from Austria that I kept running into. I had seen her earlier in the day and had jokingly asked her to save a bed for me at the albergue. She felt really bad to take the last one. I tried to reassure her that she had no need to be concerned. The hospitalero offered to let me sleep on a mattress on the floor in the entryway. I was not real keen on this idea because of my back issues. I told him I appreciated his offer but I would check to see if there was any room at the casa rural.

The casa rural was about two blocks away. For 35€, I was able to secure one of the three private rooms they still had available. The room came with sheets and towels. It even included the host washing and drying my clothes and a continental breakfast. Factoring all that in, it wasn't such a bad deal. I enjoyed another night of treating myself!

Between several conversations with other pilgrims while enjoying a light snack at the restaurant next to the association albergue, I dove into day 5 of my study on spiritual service. Today's study was about how easy it is to get caught up in the details, "politics," and personality issues revolving around your volunteer duties. This can lead to stress and a loss of focus on what you are really trying to do through your service. The study cautioned the servant to take the time to step back and look at the mission. What impact is it having on the community, and how you are assisting God by serving His kingdom? You must look at the big picture once in a while.

We were also cautioned not to serve in order to earn the approval of God or out of a feeling of obligation as part of a community. The servant's focus should be on his or her relationship with God. The desire to do tasks should be the result of your relationship and faith, not as a way to earn God's approval or because you feel you need to as part of the community. [10]

I could easily apply this concept to my volunteering at the Legion. I often got stressed out by the constant flow of clients, the endless ringing of the phone, and the feelings that we were beating our heads against the bureaucratic VA wall. Instead getting stressed, I should focus on helping veterans who could not hope to navigate themselves through the absurd and bureaucratic processes. I should not get upset about the few disgruntled clients who were not able to get what they wanted. Rather, I should focus on how many we helped get what they were authorized. I also shouldn't let the daily frustrations cause me to lose sight of my purpose. The vast majority of our clients truly understood and appreciated the value of our service. I also believe that God recognizes and appreciates it when His servants volunteer to assist others.

After the service study, I turned to mission planning for tomorrow's hike. I was currently about halfway through stage 6. In order to position myself to pass through Logroño the following day, I needed to get at least halfway through stage 7 tomorrow. I recalled the hospitalero from Cizur Menor had recommended we stay in Viana. I added up the kilometers and realized that I would need to complete 30.6 clicks to get there. This was very ambitious, 2.5 more than my longest day so far. I looked for a shorter option. The closest town with lodging prior to Viana was Torres del Rio. If I were to stop there, I would only be going about 19.4, requiring me to go 32.7 clicks the following day to skip Logroño.

---

[10] Fryar, p. 12–13.

That was definitely too much. It looked like I had no option but to go the 30.

I turned in early so I could get started at a reasonable time in the morning.

# CHAPTER 9

Monjardin to Viana, 30.6 Kilometers
3 Sep 2015
D+5

A couple from New Zealand gave me a tour of the continental break-fast bar area. We exchanged the normal introductory pleasantries: names, nationality, and where we started the Camino. As we discussed our objectives for the day, they showed me their plan using an app on their phone. I was surprised. Since every ounce is significant, the advantage of having a Camino app is clear. I was doing a similar thing with my Bible and a couple of e-books. It had not occurred to me to look for a Camino app. Similar to the hiking app that I used in Washington, a pulsating blue dot depicted where you were on the map. That function would have been quite useful yesterday when I kept missing the way-markers. With that information, you could easily find the most direct route to rejoin The Way without having to backtrack. The app also showed what percentage of the Camino you had completed. We were currently about 15 percent through. At first that felt good, then I thought, "Only 85 percent left to go."

After they left, I considered locating and downloading the app the next time I had Wi-Fi. Knowing my type A personality and how absorbed I had been with my maps in 2013, I decided I did not want to watch the "percentage completed" that closely. If I had the app, I would likely check the percentage several times a day. It would be similar to counting down the days until the end of a deployment. I decided to take the first sergeant's advice again and "not count the days" (or the percent complete) but "make the days count." The best CoA was to not download it. As for the need to retrace steps when

I miss a way-marker, I would think a little more attention to detail should eliminate that problem.

Four times during my first hour on the trail, I had to find something to prop my feet up on in order to attempt to tighten my shoelaces. The limited range of motion and pain in my arthritic finger joints and back made this a chore. Although somewhat frustrating, it was better than dealing with my heels rubbing raw. Slowing down my pace also reduced the rubbing, as did the addition of lamb's wool in the heels of the shoes.

By 0840 I had covered an incredible 6 clicks and arrived at a mobile snack trailer set up in a field a couple hundred feet off the trail along an intersecting country road. The owner was just opening up and prepping his stove and ingredients. He said it would be about fifteen minutes before he was ready to take orders. Since breakfast at the casa rural had been so basic and I had a long day ahead, I decided it would be worthwhile to wait. My patience was rewarded with a hot, freshly cooked breakfast sandwich and freshly squeezed OJ. Was there any other type of juice in Spain? After about forty-five minutes at the mobile café, I was back on my Way and started reflecting on memories from my fourth-class year at the academy.

Mobile snack trailer where I stopped for breakfast about six clicks into the day's walk.

\* \* \* \* \*

After the acceptance ceremony, my flight was officially the fourth class of cadet squadron 40: Ali Baba's 40 Thieves. The academic year was a mix of courses similar to a normal college, Professional Military Education, and intramural sports for those not on intercollegiate teams. Freshmen were required to walk at attention along the walls of hallways and along the white strips on the terrazzo. Once we got on the bridge leading to the academic building, Fairchild Hall, we were at rest. This meant we could walk normally and talk to each other. We were also at rest in our rooms.

When not in class or engaged in sports, the upperclassmen could conduct individual and group training. We were required to continue the memorization we started in BCT, including military and Air Force history, aircraft alphanumeric designations, and silhouette identification for aircraft from previous wars and currently in the inventory. We learned all verses of the national anthem and Air Force song and quotes by national and military leaders meant to inspire us and teach us key leadership lessons. Additionally, each day we were required to read the newspaper and be prepared to discuss current events and recite the menu for each meal. Upperclassmen could stop us in the hallways or on the terrazzo and ask us questions about any of this. Imperfection often resulted in loud, harsh words and push-ups. If one of our classmates was involved in one of these training sessions, other freshmen in the area were expected to rush to his or her side and provide support and assistance to take some of the pressure off their classmate. This sort of activity could go on until 1900 hours when academic call to quarters started.

Many of the quotes we had to memorize stuck with me and guided me throughout my career. They built the character expected of officers and taught us how to lead troops. I found myself thinking about many of them often over the years. They helped guide me through professional and leadership challenges. On many occasions I found myself wishing that some of my coworkers and supervisors, especially those serving in the US Army that I worked with during joint operations, had internalized these words of wisdom. A few of the most useful quotes from our Contrails knowledge book included the following:

> Never tell people how to do things, tell them what to do, and they will surprise you with their ingenuity. (General George S. Patton Jr., *War as I Knew It*)

Ask not what your country can do for you—but what you can do for your country. (President John F. Kennedy) [Note: This is one that I believe the general US public should contemplate in contemporary times.]

Be an example to your men, in your duty and in private life. Never spare yourself, and let the troops see that you don't in your endurance of fatigue and privation. Always be tactful and well-mannered, and teach your subordinates to be the same. Avoid excessive sharpness or harshness of voice, which usually indicates the man who has shortcomings of his own to hide. (Field Marshal Erwin Rommel)

War is an ugly thing, but not the ugliest of things. The decayed and degraded state of moral and patriotic feeling which thinks that nothing is worth war is much worse. The person who has nothing for which he is willing to fight, nothing which is more important than his own personal safety, is a miserable creature and has no chance of being free unless made and kept so by the exertions of better men than himself. (John Stuart Mill)

There is no limit to the goal you can do if you don't care who gets the credit. (General George C. Marshall)

A leader is a man who has the ability to get other people to do what they don't want to do, and like it. (Major General James C. Fry)

The discipline which makes the soldiers of a free country reliable in battle is not to be gained by harsh or tyrannical treatment. On the contrary, such treatment is far more likely to destroy than to make an army. It is possible to impart instruction and give commands in such a manner and such a tone of voice as to inspire in the soldier no feeling but an intense desire to obey, while the opposite manner and tone of voice cannot fail to excite strong resentment and a desire to disobey. The one mode or the other of dealing with subordinates springs from a corresponding spirit in the breast of the commander. He who feels the respect which is due to others cannot fail to inspire in them respect for himself. While he who feels, and hence manifests disrespect toward others, especially his subordinates, cannot fail to inspire hatred against himself. (Maj. Gen. John M. Scofield's graduation address to the graduating class of 1879 at West Point)[11]

The academic load was greater than at most institutions of higher learning in the United States. The first semester I took fifteen credit hours, twenty-one during second semester. These were all core courses that every freshman took. Cadets did not take classes in their selected major until their second class year, and we only took a total of eleven courses in our major. The core curriculum was broad and introduced us to many areas of study but was heavy on engineering, science, and math. We took such a variety of courses that we often commented that we knew a little about a whole lot, but not a whole lot about anything. During our fourth-class year, we took psychology, chemistry, a foreign language, world history, calculus, biology, English composition, and engineering fundamentals.

Probably the most "emotionally significant" academic memory from freshman year was our chemistry final at the end of the first

---

[11] Contrails, volume 29, 1983, United States Air Force Academy, Colorado, p. 254–258.

semester. It was my last final before I was authorized to go home for Christmas break. The instructor had told us the questions would get progressively harder. The first question would be the easiest. I will never forget the moans and general sense of despair that permeated the room after everybody read the first question. I guess I was not the only one who was surprised by its difficulty and what this meant for the rest of the test.

By the way, "test" is not the proper way to describe this activity. At the academy, we did not have tests, finals, or exams. Instead we had graded reviews.

Reflecting on that idiosyncrasy made me remember some of the other odd truths about life at the academy. Our rooms had to be in inspection order before we left for class in the morning. During the day, squadron leadership often inspected our rooms, and the results impacted our military performance average. The standards were tough. To pass we followed a few rules: don't sleep under the covers (we used safety pins under the mattress to hold the sheets and covers tight with perfect folds); there could be no water in the sink; and by no means was there to be garbage in the garbage can!

One reality that really hit home quickly regarding academics was that the cadets were selected from among the top 10 percent of high school students in the country. The academy graded on a bell curve around the "mean." The top of the curve, or average, was the B/C cutoff. Most of us had received mostly As in high school. That meant if you were rated around 95 percent of high school students, that put you at the B/C cut off at the academy. In high school I was very upset the two times I got Bs. Here, I was sometimes relieved to get a C. Bs made me very happy. I was ecstatic to earn one A during my fourth-class year. Being dyslexic, I had to work extra hard to achieve even these grades in the academy's tough academic environment. I normally continued studying long after Taps sounded to end our day. I managed to do this by drinking several cups of coffee and a six-pack of Coke every day. Weekends were filled with study when we did not have Saturday morning inspections (SAMIs) or "mandatory fun," like going to football games. On many occasions, my roommate and I brought our homework to the football game. The camaraderie of the games could be fun, but when struggling with classes, it seemed that my time could have been better used with my nose in the books.

A few other short memories came to mind. We were not allowed to have refrigerators in our rooms. When the temperatures dropped outside for the winter, I took advantage of the cold air by placing my Cokes outside on the windowsill. Normally this got them cold enough to be a refreshing drink; occasionally they froze hard as a rock; and a couple times they exploded.

Another memory was a long line of cadets in black hooded parkas marching in single file along the terrazzo strips from the chow hall to the chapel for morning services at sunrise on cold winter mornings. Cadets had the option of going to an early breakfast and then attending chapel services before the academic day began. I found this to be a great way to start a stressful day.

When not studying at football games, we found humor cheering on our team. Our football team was not very good during my freshman year. So it wasn't long before a cheer was developed that identified how our team played.

"Up the middle, up the middle, up the middle, punt."

As the players repeated these plays on the field, we repeated this cheer in the stands. Fortunately, our team did much better the following years.

Our fourth-class training continued until late spring 1984. The goal of four class training was to teach us not only to be followers but also how to think calmly and logically under great pressure and stress. The training also taught us the value of working as a team and capitalizing on each other's strengths, as well as the need to put the good of the team above our own individual needs and desires.

After enduring a long march and a couple of hours of borderline "unauthorized" intense training by upperclassmen who were upset that our recognition day was so much easier than theirs had been, we received our Prop and Wing insignia that proved we had completed training requirements for our fourth-class year. We were no longer at attention when outside of our rooms, and there was no further training by the upperclassmen. We were treated like everybody else in the wing.

In late May, the first class graduated and were commissioned as second lieutenants. At this time, my class was officially promoted to cadets third class. We cleaned out our rooms and put all of our personal items that we would not need over the summer into storage. Then we all headed off for our summer programs.

* * * * *

Officially completing stage 6, I took a coffee break in the Los Arcos town square. The three retired sailors were there, and we talked for a while.

As I left the small village, it started to drizzle. I wasn't too concerned at first because the rain was so light, but as I approached a tunnel under the N-111, the rain started coming down harder. I took advantage of the tunnel's shelter to dig out my raincoat and the pack's rain cover. After putting them on, I proceeded across the river to Torres del Rio. By the time I got to the village's first intersection, the rain was coming down fairly heavy. There was a hotel on the corner with a café. It was lunchtime, so I decided to stop for lunch and get out of the rain. Maybe I could wait it out.

My friend from Austria was seated at one of the tables reading a book. It was amazing how we kept running into each other. Our selection of lodging and eating establishments were almost identical. She looked like she was enjoying her book, so I decided to give her privacy and settled at a nearby table.

A few minutes later, an American pilgrim I had not met came in seeking shelter from the rain. We discussed our fortune of being so close to this village when the rain started. We exchanged some small talk, ordered sandwiches and coffee, and then retreated to individual tables to log onto our electronic devices.

I checked text messages and e-mail and responded to several. I then checked the weather app and was pleased to see that the rain was not projected to last more than an hour.

By the time I had finished my meal and got caught up on e-mail, the rain had stopped. I returned my rain jacket and the pack cover to the top pocket, making note to myself that I needed to remember to pull them out and hang them up to dry once I settled in for the night. My luck was holding out as far as rain avoidance was concerned. Maybe the universal conspiracy against me was taking a holiday!

I headed out into the partly sunny afternoon to get started on the final 10.6 clicks to Viana. The yellow arrows directed me up a hill. After about a block, I noticed a small store and café on the right that looked very familiar.

In 2013, we had spent a couple hours there. Samantha's tendons hurt so much at this point she decided it would be in her best interest to stop walking. Earlier in the day we had ran into a pilgrim at a pharmacy who was a nurse that dealt with sports injuries. She told us that Samantha needed to rest several days and that if she kept pushing it, she may end up needing surgery. Samantha decided to stop totally and head for Scotland to search for family history information from her father's side. After walking another 8 km, we had decided to stop at Torres del Rio and take a bus the other twenty to Logroño where there was an train station. We enjoyed coffee and then lunch after being told the bus came at 1500. We were at the bus stop before 1500 but on the wrong side of the road. It passed us by. So . . . we went back to the café, and they called us a taxi.

As I passed the café, it occurred to me that for the first time, I was now walking a part of The Way that I had not done previously. I found this rather exciting.

After a while, I saw the American woman I had met at lunch ahead of me. She was putting her pack on after taking a break. I reached her before she was ready to go and formally introduced myself. As we started walking, she told me her name was Leslie and she was from California. We then commenced with the obligatory conversation about my hand braces and how I attributed the condition to "combat typing" from my time in the Air Force.

"So what was it like being a woman military officer?" she inquired.

"There were a few occasions when being a female seemed to cause problems for me, but for the most part it wasn't much of an issue," I explained. "The integration of women has made a lot of progress since the '70s, especially in the Air Force. I did have a couple of major issues with senior Army officers when I was working in a joint environment in Afghanistan and Iraq."

"Oh," she said quizzically.

"It might sound funny, but I was more accepted by the Afghans than I was by some in the US Army. As far as Afghan government officials were concerned, foreign military women and members of international aid organizations are a sort of third sex. They don't treat us like their women, but we are not men either. As the Provincial Reconstruction Team (PRT) commander, I had control of the money for the provinces that I was responsible for. They either had to work with me, or not get the projects they wanted. They were more than happy to work with me. In fact, during my year in-country, only one Afghan refused to shake my hand, a provincial *iman*, but this only happened the first time we met. After that, he offered his hand to shake each time we greeted each other. On the other hand, there were a couple of Army colonels I worked for who did not seem to think that a woman ought to be a PRT commander."

"What is a PRT?"

"Sorry, I should know by now that most people have no idea what a PRT does, nor even that they exist." I took a step back in my explanation. "The majority of provinces in Afghanistan and Iraq were assigned a reconstruction and development team. My team was responsible for Paktya and Logar provinces south of Kabul. Our mission was to work on infrastructure development, economic development, security capacity building, and mentoring government officials. These operations were considered nonkinetic, as opposed to kinetic operations, which included kicking down doors and going after the bad guys. The kinetic guys blew things up and killed people; we built things and hugged people. Our mission was to win the hearts and minds of the public, encourage their support for the Afghan government and the international coalition, and to improve their economic opportunities. The idea was that if they had a sense of a bright future, they would not become or support the terrorists, hence security and quality of life would increase. I found this a very rewarding mission."

"Sounds great. I had no idea we were doing that over there."

"Yeah, most people don't have a clue because the media only reports on things that go *boom*! So much is going on that the public never hears about it. There could be a thousand off-base missions in a day. And 999 will do great things with no problems. The news reports on the one that gets hit, so as far as most Americans are concerned, attacks on us are all that is going on over there."

"Was this what you did throughout your career?" she asked.

"No. My primary career field was security forces. In other words, I was a cop—or military police, as most civilians would understand. My assignment to the PRT was a career-broadening assignment. It fell into a category that we called Stability Operations. I was on the PRT from April 2006 to April 2007. After that I rotated between security forces and Stability Operations for the remainder of my career."

"Stability Operations," she said inquisitively.

"The media commonly refers to it as 'nation building.' In the military, Stability Operations is what we do during what is referred to as phase 0 operations. That is when it is relatively peaceful before or after hostilities. The goal in this phase is to assist a country stabilize itself politically and economically so that their population feels secure and able to pursue economic stability for their families. The idea is that creating such an environment will decrease the chances of future hostilities. If the population feels safe, secure, and confident that they can meet their family's needs, and they believe that they can trust their government, there should be less need for violence, and the young will not to turn to terrorism. Objectives we pursue during phase 0 are normally done in conjunction with the State Department, the United States Agency for International Development (USAID), the UN, and nongovernmental organizations (NGOs). Together we help the country build roads, medical clinics, schools, water, electrical systems, and other infrastructure needed for a successful society. Economic, political, law enforcement, and military capacity building is done through training and advising missions.

"I honestly believed this was the way for us to win the war in Afghanistan—or rather, to win the peace. We were taught that our reconstruction projects would bring hope for a brighter future to the people of Afghanistan. It was important to defeat and eliminate Al Qaeda and the Taliban, but we could not kill our way to victory.

"Intelligence indicated that many Afghans supported the terrorists, not because they agreed with their ideology and vision of the future, but rather out of fear. The villagers knew that if the coalition and government were not always present and failed to maintain control, the terrorists would return and kill all those who had supported the coalition or the government, including their family members. The common villager often believed that the only way to survive was to project neutrality or even oppose the government and outwardly support the terrorists. It was a basic matter of survival.

"Although I believed in the overall theory, over time I began to realize that some of the methods we were using and the projects we were selecting were doing more harm than good."

"What do you mean?" Leslie seemed generally interested. "How can making life better for the people be harmful?"

"As an example, we did numerous projects to clean out irrigation canals. For the first six months or so, every time we visited a village and held a Shara with its elders, they requested a project to have their irrigation canals cleaned. They explained that the rains and melting snow caused debris to clog the canals so they couldn't irrigate their fields. They needed reliable irrigation for a productive crop. This made sense to me, so we submitted several project proposals to request funding for the projects. Once funding was approved, we put a contract out for bid, evaluated the submissions from local companies, and then selected one to do the project. We never did the work ourselves; we always contracted it out. The idea was to not only to get the project done but to employ the locals, build their job skills, and put money into their economy. The Afghans would not only receive a completed project but the people would gain employment and job skills that would enable them to sustain economic development and earn a livelihood for their families long-term.

"After about six months of responding to these requests, I started to become a little frustrated. It had been raining, snowing, and melting since the dawn of time. I became curious as to what they did prior to our arrival after 9/11. So I asked Shabir, my lead inter-preter, what they had done prior to the coalition's arrival. He told me that the village would come together as a community and take care of it. It was similar to the barn-raising events from America's frontier days. I asked him why they didn't do that anymore. I will never forget his answer: 'Because you will pay them to do it.'

"I was stunned. It may be true that the Afghans had not had a lot of schooling, which limited their knowledge, but they were far from stupid. They had found a way to manipulate us and our genuine concern for their well-being. I immediately put out the word to my team that we wouldn't do any more canal-cleaning projects. Instead we would only pursue projects that addressed issues that the local villagers and government were not capable of doing themselves. I also submitted a report to higher headquarters and copied the other PRT commanders, encouraging everybody to stop these projects because they were undermining the historical way of life in the villages.

"Through this experience, I realized that what we were actually doing was building a welfare state and a culture of dependency. The Afghan villagers had come to a point where they were going to sit back and do nothing until the government or the coalition stepped in to do it for them, or at least pay them to do what they had always done in the past as a community.

"The lesson was short-lived. Two years later, I returned to Kabul for a PRT conference. Almost every province had a PRT by this time. The United States still operated twelve of them, the rest were split between various other countries in the coalition. The coa-lition headquarters had teamed up with the embassies to bring the military, governance, and development leadership from each of the PRTs to Kabul to exchange ideas and lessons learned, and to receive guidance. During a session about the budget and project funding, a USAID representative explained how each year the PRTs had to sub-mit project requests to clean the irrigation canals. He recommended that since it was an annual requirement, the funding for the proj-ects should be included in the budget so that the PRTs would not need to submit requests every year. 'Just make it Standard Operating Procedure,' he said.

"I couldn't believe what I was hearing. This was a 'development expert'! He should've known better. He supposedly had been trained and had development experience. He should have understood how to build a sustainable, self-supporting society. Instead he was advocating institutionalizing the projects that were undermining the villagers' self-sufficiency!

"I couldn't contain myself! I stood up and related my experience and what we had determined two years earlier. I emphatically explained that we needed to concentrate on building a self-sustaining, Afghan-centered environment and economy. I told them that if we continued doing everything for them, or even paying them to do what they should be doing for themselves, then our children would be deploying to Afghanistan and doing the same things twenty years from now. Our objective needed to be to work ourselves out of a job. To help them build the tools and capacity to do it themselves without the international community giving them handouts. Loud applause indicated that I was not the only one in the room that had become frustrated. This seems to be a common problem with international development efforts around the world."

"How so?" she said, obviously not making the connection.

"For decades the US and other governments in the international community, not to mention NGOs, have been flooding third world countries with aid and assistance," I continued on my soapbox. "I've sponsored children in third world countries for many years, hoping to help them receive a proper education so that they have the tools they need to lift their families out of poverty. Yet the plight of these countries has changed very little, although several generations have passed. Why is this?

"It may not be politically correct to say, but these are my perceptions based on my observations, travels, and limited experiences interacting with the local people and governments. A common trend in these countries seems to be that they are ruled by corrupt governments and their people lack an effective work ethic and have no desire for self-sufficiency or improvement, let alone a desire to achieve excellence and progress. They are focused on day-to-day tasks to get by. In Turkey, if you order an item from a merchant, he will likely tell you something along the lines of 'It will be ready next Tuesday—*inshala*.' *Inshala* means 'God willing.' Normally when you show up on Tuesday to pick up the item, it will not be ready. You ask when it will be ready, and the merchant says '*dopu demani*,' or 'the day after tomorrow,' and then adds the standard escape phrase *inshala*.

"In many countries in the Middle East and Horn of Africa, the men halfheartedly work in the morning and by noon they are chewing a local drug called Khot and spend the rest of the day high. You can tell that they are chewing Khot because of the huge bulge in their cheeks.

"Corruption at all levels of society seems to be a cultural standard in most of these countries. Take Haiti and the Dominican Republic as an example. They share an island in the Caribbean Sea. The terrain and environment are the same, but one is doing okay and the other is engulfed in poverty. What is the difference? One major difference is that the government of Haiti is corrupt.

"After all of these decades of kindhearted aid and assistance and countless mission trips to these countries, little has changed. I think we need to ask ourselves why all the aid has not succeeded in improving these impoverished societies. Instead of helping them, are we actually fostering a culture of dependency and building welfare states? Are our heartfelt efforts actually counterproductive and doing more harm than good? Are we addressing the root cause of the problems, or are we just putting a Band-Aid on the symptoms? You know, I cannot help but think that these concepts can be applied to America today."

"How so?" she seemed surprised.

"I really wonder if our welfare, unemployment, free medical, and other benefits for the poor actually motivate them not to work or improve themselves. If they can get all of these benefits by not working, where is their motivation get a job and improve their situation?"

"They may have disabilities, or just not the right skills to get a job, we can't blame them for that," she replied, exposing her liberal biases.

"It may be true that many unemployed do not have the right skills to get a job, but should that mean we give them handouts for the rest of their lives, or should we offer programs that help them develop employable work skills so that in the long run, they can be self-sustaining and productive? The age-old 'Give them a fish or teach them to fish' saying," I countered. "While touring in southern Arizona, I found out about the Civilian Conservation Corps (CCC) that helped America to get back on its feet after the depression. Unemployed people were given jobs on government projects that improved the national infrastructure. These projects taught them job skills, built work ethic, and they earned enough in wages to meet their basic needs. The pay was low enough that participants were not motivated to stay in these jobs. Once they had gained job skills and experience, they would seek private-sector jobs where they could get higher wages and move up the economic ladder. As their skills increased in the private sector, so did their wages and their ability to care for their families. Wouldn't a program such as this be more effective than paying people welfare and other benefits and not requiring any contribution to the community or labor in return for those benefits? We can't afford to pay people to do nothing their entire lives. Where is the pride of self-accomplishment and taking care of your family? It used to be shameful to take handouts. I agree that these programs are great for the short-term, to help people get through a tough time and get them back on their feet, but we now have a culture of dependency being handed down from generation to generation."

After we beat that horse to death, she asked me what I thought about our involvement in Afghanistan and Iraq.

"Considering what you have said, should we have gone into those countries? What advantages did we gain by being there? Was it worth the money and lives expended? Those resources should be used to take care of our own people."

I took a moment to think through my answer now that I knew she was liberal. I guessed she was anti-war. I decided to tread lightly but still try to make my point.

"In my opinion, the lessons from the wars in Afghanistan and Iraq are similar to a major lessons we learned from our involvement in Vietnam. If we are going to send US troops somewhere to fight an enemy, then we need to be 'all-in,' like we were in World War II. We need to be willing to dedicate overwhelming force and do what it takes to achieve our objectives within the bounds of international agreements and decency concerning the conduct of war, all while maintaining high moral standards."

As we entered the town of Viana, Leslie asked if I saw a difference between how Republican and Democratic administrations handled overseas conflicts in light of my "all-in" theory.

I replied, "I'd say President Bush was about 75 percent in, while President Obama is only about 25 percent. In both cases, I believe our actions and policies are driven far too much by politics at the expense of American lives and money. Because of this, we have not actually achieved our objectives in either country. Terrorism is still rampant, and quality of life has not improved for their people. They are no more stable now than they were when we started."

I was surprised, but appreciative, that she was open to my opinions.

About this time I realized we had passed right through old town where the albergues were located. I pointed this fact out to Leslie, and she stated that she planned to go on to Logroño and spend the night there. Since I had already gone over 30 km, I was not interested in walking another ten. We agreed that we had enjoyed our conversation and hoped to meet again. Bidding each other Buen Camino, I turned around and passed back through the city gate into old town.

Fortunately, I found that the albergue where I was planning to stay was only a block back. It was mere minutes before I had secured a bed.

The albergue was a converted historic monastery. I enjoyed the ancient atmosphere, but similar to the old monastery we stayed at in Roncesvalles, Wi-Fi was only available in the dining area on the first floor. On the positive side, this was a good place to interact with other pilgrims who were checking their e-mail and doing other things online. They had several vending machines with food and drink, to include beer. Beer in a vending machine. Wow!

After I was settled and had my shower, I went out to explore the town and look for a pilgrim's dinner. Instead of going to one of the crowded restaurants I had passed on the main street, I decided to check out the side streets. I found a nice-looking place a couple of blocks off of the main street, ordered some food, and then started mission planning for the next day.

About twenty minutes later, my friend from Austria walked through the door. Amazing, I sought an out-of-the-way restaurant, and we had still ended up at the same place. This time she joined me, and we spent a good hour enjoying a nice conversation. Per our emerging SOP, we were staying at the same hostel, so we walked back together.

# CHAPTER 10

### Viana to Navarrete, 22.1 Kilometers
### 4 Sep 2015
### D+6

Since I planned to go a significantly shorter distance, there was no hurry getting out of the albergue in the morning. I went to the Internet room and got a coffee from the vending machine. Poor quality, but it would do for now.

I found an electrical outlet near the table where I could recharge my phone. I had not been able to charge it the night before because someone had tied up the outlet all night. There ought to be a hostel etiquette rule against that. I guess I could have unplugged it. He would likely have gotten the hint.

My Austrian friend soon arrived with another woman and introduced us. Turns out her friend was a retired senior chief from the US Navy. The Austrian thought it was interesting that the two female Americans she had befriended were both retired military. I pointed out that she was the fifth US veteran that I had met on the Camino so far. That led to a discussion about why the Camino is a good fit for veterans.

Through conversations, I found it common for pilgrims to use the Camino to process significant life transitions. For some it is the death of or divorce from a spouse; for others, retirement. Similarly, veterans, especially those who deployed for combat tours, face challenges transitioning to the alien civilian world. The long hike offers plenty of time to reflect on their military careers, while contemplating the options they are considering pursuing and who they want to be as they move forward with their life.

The trek itself offers familiarity. As a peregrino, you have a mission—a desired "end state" you are trying to achieve. Prior to departing home station to deploy to the area of operations (AO), you do predeployment training and planning. You must develop a packing list and acquire the items needed. You plan out the logistics of deploying to the trailhead. Once on the trail, each evening you do tactical mission planning for the next day. You gather intelligence by talking to other peregrinos and studying the guidebook, to include a map reconnaissance. Hospitaleros are another good source to develop. You determine your potential courses of action (CoAs) and do a cost-benefit analysis and risk assessment for each. Armed with all this information, you then select a CoA to execute the following day. You identify waypoints and the objective for the day, thus developing a Concept of Operation or CONOP. The next day you execute your CONOP. For each task in your daily battle rhythm, you establish Standard Operating Procedures (SOPs).

You meet people from all over the world and bond as a team with a common purpose; in other words, you form a coalition. Everyone helps each other, and a spirit of camaraderie permeates the group. It is not a competition. There is no stabbing each other in the back or clawing your way ahead of the other guy like in the corporate world. Instead, you form quick friendships, and you become a team—Combined Joint Task Force Camino. You exchange information about lessons learned and best practices when you see a fellow pilgrim in need. Everybody wants to see everybody else succeed. There is even a team rally cry: "Buen Camino!"

It is physically challenging: a five-hundred-mile ruck march. You are going to have feet and, likely, back problems, so you plan as best you can and implement preventive and mitigating measures. You learn when to take a down day to heal, always keeping your eye on the strategic objective—arrival in Santiago. You want to achieve daily objectives but must understand that by pushing yourself too hard, you risk not achieving your ultimate goal. You must make tactical as well as strategic decisions.

Finally it is mentally challenging. It takes a lot of determination to keep going when your feet or back hurt and you know you still have hundreds of kilometers to cover. Sometimes it takes mind over body. Other times it is wise to take a strategic pause, or recovery day, to consolidate your gains so you can "live to fight another day."

Before we knew it, time had flown by and there was just a few minutes before 0800 when we needed to be out of the albergue so that the staff could prepare for the next group coming in. We bid each other Buen Camino and returned to our bunks to grab our packs and poles.

I decided to get some breakfast before departing town because Logroño was almost 10 km away, and the guidebook map did not show any cafés during this stretch. I found a café that sold small ham-and-egg sandwiches. Our sandwiches were normally made on a half French loaf at least a foot long. These were about four inches long and about half the width as normal. Just the right size! I did not even have to take the top half of the bread off. It was starting out to be a really good day.

Passing through the old city gate, I resumed my reflections of my USAFA days.

\* \* \* \* \*

Summers at the academy consisted of three three-week periods. Cadets get to take one of these periods as leave and the other two are used for summer training programs. During my third-class summer, my first period was Survival Evasion Resistance and Escape (SERE) training.

The first ten days were lectures on the international laws of war and how to survive if you were shot down behind enemy lines, including how to evade capture and return to friendly lines. And then, in case you are captured, we learned about the Code of Conduct for prisoners of war (POW), how to resist interrogation, and how to survive captivity.

We then entered the practical phase, the trek. We spent a few days navigating through the woods using map and compass techniques. We learned to set up camp using our ponchos and parachute cord to make shelters, find and prepare edible plants and animals to eat, and how to keep out of sight to evade capture by "enemy" patrols.

On trek day one, we made a cold soup with vegetation and bugs for protein. When I saw an ant swimming on the top of the water in my cup, I could not bring myself to drink it. I just was not yet hungry enough.

A couple days later was the infamous session on preparing a rabbit to eat. We learned how to build a trap, and once we had the rabbit (which was actually provided by the cadre), we had to kill it and prepare it for cooking. Tradition was to get someone to eat the eyeballs. After all, they provide much-needed salt for your diet. I was quite a bit hungrier at this point but still was not able to bring myself to eat the eyeballs. One of the other members of the team was more than happy to show how manly he was, and he downed them. More power to him!

We then cut up the meat, found some edible vegetation, and made rabbit stew. The cadre provided pepper (not very realistic—where would we get pepper if we ejected out of our airplane behind enemy lines?). One of the guys who obviously had no cooking experience poured an excessive amount of it into the stew. It was ruined, but we ate it, anyway, because by this time we were quite hungry and we were really looking forward to the protein.

During the last evening of the trek, we arrived at the coordinates where we were supposed to meet up with an underground representative that would arrange our return to friendly lines. Our class had been split into small groups of five or six people, and all the groups had been directed to coordinates close to each other. Most groups arrived hours before the planned rendezvous. My group decided that this would be a likely place to encounter the enemy, so we decided not to camp anywhere in the woods. Instead we climbed into a large rock formation and found a semiflat, well-hidden ledge to wait. As the sun began to rise in the morning, we heard a lot of yelling on the forest floor below. We crawled over to the edge of the rocks and looked down. As we had suspected, opposition forces (OPFOR) were sweeping through the area and capturing the teams that had set up camp in the woods. We were quite proud of ourselves as we gazed down on the turmoil below from the safety of our perch. They never found us, and we were able to make our rendezvous with the underground on schedule.

However, our cunning did not get us out of the POW camp learning objectives. After being congratulated for not getting caught, my team was loaded onto the bus with everybody else and taken to the POW camp. These were definitely challenging days. We were crammed into barracks, endured interrogations, and were even put in tiny boxes that we barely fit in when we pulled our knees tight against our bodies and tucked our head as much as we could. The box was probably the worst. This activity mirrored what the Viet Cong had done to US prisoners ten to twenty years earlier. Imagine being cramped in a seated fetal position for hours or even days. By the time they let you out, every muscle in your body was cramped and some joints just did not want to move.

One of the most emotionally moving events of my career occurred at sunrise on the morning we were "liberated" from the POW camp. All the prisoners were formed up for morning roll call. However, instead of the OPFOR flag being raised to their national anthem as we expected, the stars and stripes were raised to "The Star-Spangled Banner." I don't think there was a dry eye in the class.

For me, the second period of the summer was leave, so I went home to Alaska. During the third summer period, I joined several other three degrees working on the yearbook staff for BCT. By this time, the new class was in second beast. Jack's Valley was much more fun in this capacity!

We moved back into academic squadrons at the end of second beast. The class of '87 changed squadrons at this time. The idea was to start fresh in a new squadron as an upperclassman. I was assigned to CS 35, Wild Weasels, and would remain there until graduation. So while attending one of the most prestigious institutions of higher learning in the country, I started out as a demon, then became a thief, and now I was a weasel. I found this rather humorous.

Inspiring wall art on the wall of CS 35

We continued taking primarily core courses, including behavioral science, economics, differential equations, mechanical engineering, management, physics, political science, computer science, composition and speech, and American government. Additionally, all the third classmen participated in the "Soar for All" program. Each of us got eleven sessions where we learned to fly gliders. We were taught how to control the glider when it was connected by cable to a powered Cessna aircraft for takeoff. Once we reached the appropriate altitude, we disconnected the cable and completed the flight without power. The first ten sessions were with an instructor pilot; the last one was our solo.

Because my goal was to be an astronaut, my intended major was physics. I took the sophomore core physics course the first semester and the junior core course the second semester. I really struggled both semesters and was actually relieved to get Cs after many hours of extra instruction in my professor's office. This made me wonder if I was really cut out to be an astronaut. I found myself far more interested in my political science courses. In fact, if I didn't have time to do all the homework for every class (which was standard), I was far more motivated to do the political science (poli sci) lesson, hence earning As and Bs. Before the end of the spring semester, I had officially changed my major to international affairs with a specialty in national security. So much for being an astronaut.

\* \* \* \* \*

By late morning, I entered the historic section of Logroño. I recognized the parking lot where the taxi had dropped us off back in 2013. A block later, I passed the Albergue Santiago where we had stayed. It was the former parish staff quarters connected to a centuries-old village church. As mentioned earlier, the noise of a local festival had kept us awake all night, but the albergue itself was something special.

The parish priest was the hospitalero. After getting bunks in the crowded thirty-two-bed overflow room, we walked to the train station, hoping to get a ticket for my injured niece to travel to Scotland. The men at the counter spoke little English, and we had major trouble trying to explain what we wanted. It sounded like she would have to take a train somewhere then get another ticket to somewhere else. None of us felt comfortable with the difficulty, so we decided to go back to the hostel and try to make plane arrangements online. Back in the bunk room, we met a man named Gary. He turned out to be a priest from Seattle and had walked the Camino the previous year. He was walking a few days of the trail on his way to volunteer as a hospitalero for a couple weeks. He was very familiar with the transport options and helped us make a plan. In the end, it was decided she would take a bus to Madrid and then fly on a European discount airline, Easy Jet, to Edinburgh.

The communal dinner there was in a true family atmosphere. There was no charge, but the staff gladly accepted donations. Peregrinos helped cook the meal. Mom and Ria stepped up and assisted with the cleanup after the meal. Samantha and I sought out the place in the hostel where the Wi-Fi was the strongest and placed a landline call through my iPad's Skype app to her parents stateside. She explained her situation and plan to them, and they gave their blessing.

After the kitchen was cleaned, the priest took interested peregrinos through an underground passageway to the old church next door. He held a devotion, explained a little history of the church, and we sang some religious songs in various languages. Very nice.

* * * * *

Returning to the present, I found a café to stop at for an early lunch. As I enjoyed my coffee and another small sandwich, I took time to complete day 6 of the service study. Today's lesson cautioned us not to get so busy and caught up in the tasks associated with our service that we ran on fumes and didn't have the time or energy to develop and grow our spiritual relationship with God.[12] My exhaustion and frustrations emanating from my work at the Legion was a perfect testament to the truth of this teaching.

After lunch, I followed the way-markers out of the old city and into the hustle and bustle of modern Logroño, officially starting stage 8. As anticipated, city life caused a bit of anxiety. Capitalizing on my gains and the lessons learned from Pamplona, I focused on greeting the locals I passed with a hearty "Buenos Días" and a smile. It worked again, and my transit through Logroño was manageable. Before I knew it, I was in a nice, relaxing park area outside of town. Once again, The Way was looking very familiar. I was back on a section that we had covered in 2013. With about 10 km to go, I returned to my academy reflections.

* * * * *

My first summer program during my two-degree year (also known as second class year and equivalent to the junior year at a civilian college) was Operation Air Force. I was fortunate to get Elmendorf Air Force Base in Anchorage, Alaska, along with about ten other C2Cs. We spent three weeks visiting various units and

---

[12] Fryar, p. 14–15.

career fields on the base. The idea was to get a taste of what the active Air Force was like and experience some career fields that we may be interested in after commissioning.

One day we flew in a C-130 to several Forward Operating Bases in the Alaskan frontier. It was a resupply mission to these outposts. One in particular had a rather short runway with a downhill slant and a steep hill at the end. To take off, we accelerated down the runway and then had to pull up sharply to avoid hitting the hill. A bit nerve-racking if you ask me.

We accompanied another C-130 crew on a logistics support mission to one of our bases in Japan and then on to South Korea. Due to crew rest requirements for the pilots, we stayed the night in each country. Besides visiting operational units and seeing how overseas units operated, we were given the opportunity to explore the communities outside the base gates. This gave us some great insights into what it would be like to be stationed overseas and explore the local culture.

Just before returning to the academy, we received incentive rides in helicopters and T-38 training jet aircraft. This experience reinforced my decision to abandon hopes of being an astronaut. I did not like the jet aircraft and told the pilot not to do any loops or rolls or anything fancy. My path to being an astronaut had revolved around becoming a jet pilot, advancing to test pilot, and then eventually to astronaut as the space pioneers in the book *The Right Stuff* had done. To be a test pilot, you had to be the best of the best. I now knew for sure that would not be me. However, I was intrigued by the helicopter incentive flight and opened my mind to this being an alternative career path.

At the end of the first summer period, we returned to the academy, and I served three weeks as a member of the cadre for first BCT. This was my first exposure to leading, motivating, and training troops. I relished these duties. This represented another significant data point in my career field decision process.

During my second-class academic year, I took five political science classes as part of my international affairs major, along with normal core courses such as aeronautical engineering, probability and statistics, introduction to law, thermodynamics, leadership in small groups, electrical engineering, advanced composition and speech, and US history. I really enjoyed the political science classes and discovered that I enjoyed law even more. My grades improved significantly, and I found myself on the superintendent's list. This meant that I made both the dean's list for academics and the commandant's list for achievement in the military training regimen. It only lasted one semester, but it was great while it lasted.

During the summer of my first class year, I was once again part of the BCT cadre. The other period, I worked logistical support for SERE. This was another eye-opening experience. It is amazing how complicated the logistical support of such a training program can be. During my final academic year, my classes included astronautical engineering; world literature; science, technology, and warfare history; law for commanders; ethics; aviation fundamentals; engineering systems design; another law class; modern physics in the Air Force; and five more political science classes focusing on the politics of national defense.

It was during my senior year when I got my first experience dealing with male prejudice against females in the military. The first women admitted to the military academies started their freshman year in 1976. We were the seventh class with females. The integration had gone extremely well, considering the significance of the change and the short period of time that had elapsed. However, there were still a few male cadets with bad attitudes. One of these holdouts was a classmate in my squadron.

He made it clear to my roommate and myself that he did not believe that we should be at the academy. He frequently made disparaging comments about female cadets. He even flat out told my roommate and me that the mere presence of women at the academy diminished the prestige of him being there. His perspective was that if a woman could do this, then it's no big deal that a man was doing it.

After putting up with his comments for several months, we eventually had had enough and decided to bring it to the chain of command. A week before graduation, a disciplinary board decided that his actions were not acceptable for an AF officer. Classes were

USAFA graduation photo.

complete, so the board decided to award him his degree but not allow him to be commissioned. Because he had received a four-year college education at government expense, he had the same five-year service commitment as any other academy graduate. The board decided that he would serve his commitment in the enlisted force.

For the rest of us, graduation day was very exciting. My parents, sisters, brother, grandparents, and some aunts and uncles flew down for the festivities. The football stadium was packed to capacity as the senior class marched proudly onto the field where a stage had been set up for the guest speakers with 964 chairs lined up in front of it. After the speeches and the long procession of the individual cadets crossing the stage to get their diploma, the signature roar of jet aircraft speeding low over the stadium was our signal to throw our hats into the air. As the white parade caps ascended, the four-ship formation took a sharp turn straight up and then separated in four directions. As the graduates hugged, high-fived, and congratulated each other, kids swarmed the field, seeking to secure a cap as a souvenir. I kept an eye on mine and retrieved it as quickly as possible after tossing it in the air. My intent was to give it to my brother.

It is impossible to describe the feelings of pride and elation that floods over a person at a time such as this! We had conquered the academy challenge and received our commissions. We were now second lieutenants, ready to embark on meaningful adventures where we would be able to make a difference in the lives of those under our command and for people around the world whom we would be tasked to help during humanitarian and combat missions that we knew would eventually would come our way.

That night my family and I went out for a steak dinner at a local western-themed restaurant. Sporting my dress blue uniform with gold lieutenant bars glistening on my shoulders, I finally found the courage to ask my mother something that had been bugging me most of my life. I asked her what good it did for the starving children in Africa for me to clean up my plate. I told her that if she wanted to help them, she should "pack up it and ship it to them." She laughed heartily and asked why it had taken an academy education for me to realize that. She has never forgotten that exchange and reminds me of it every chance she gets. It is one of her favorite stories to tell new friends.

\* \* \* \* \*

I arrived at my objective for the day, Navarrete, about 1330. Most of the path today had been on pavement. My feet and back took a terrible beating. The balls of my feet were getting that all-too-familiar wincing pain that stopped me the last time. I tried to walk on dirt beside the pavement, but the terrain and vegetation made this impossible most of the time. Looking back in my journal from stage 6 in 2013, pain in my feet had already started to plague me. My entry for the day stated . . .

> Boy do my feet hurt!!! The balls hurt most. When I step on rocks incorrectly, it is excruciating! At the same time, the toes have a numb/swollen feeling. Weird contrast. They feel numb, but are hypersensitive to pain at the same time. Its been like this since about mid day yesterday. It's pretty bad when the 80 and 72 year olds leave me in their dust and have to keep waiting for me. I'm not sure if the problem is the arthritis, poor circulation due to the cold injuries, or something totally different. Even the 21 year old with tendon problems is putting me to shame. Well, I knew my physical issues would be a problem, but I expected the problem to be the back, not the feet. My feet feel like lead bricks. I liken them to Frankenstein's. Each foot fall seems to crash into

the ground. I wonder if each step could cause an earthquake.

I guess I should take solace in the knowledge that my foot problems had reached this level later this time. I was now halfway into stage 8 and just starting to have problems.

Mission planning for tomorrow was pretty basic as it would be my first down day. My plan was to stay at the hotel in Ventosa were Mom, Ria, and I stayed in 2013. I looked the phone number up in the guidebook and called to make a reservation. To my extreme disappointment, they had no rooms available the next night. I'd been looking forward to this all week. Lesson learned, if you want to stay somewhere and it's a nice place, make reservations two to three days in advance instead of waiting until the night before.

So I consulted the guidebook and found another place slightly closer to Navarrete, only 5.7 km away. I called the Albergue San Martin in Sotés and reserved the room. Sotés was 2.1 km off the main trail up a steep asphalt road. The main challenge for tomorrow would be needing to be out of the current albergue no later than eight but not being able to check in until twelve. This meant I had four hours to go 5.7 clicks.

While checking e-mail on my iPad, I noticed a book I had downloaded prior to departure. It was called *Seeking Allah, Finding Jesus*, by Nabeel Qureshi. I read the foreword, introduction, and prologue sections. It sounded very interesting. The book is the testimony of the author who was born in America to Pakistani immigrants. He was raised in the Muslim faith and, while seeking a stronger, more personal faith with Allah, he befriended a Christian at college. They had many discussions about the two religions, each man trying to convince the other of the truth from their perspective and the beliefs they had been raised with. After several years of discussion and study of both religions, Nabeel converted to Christianity. This book is about that process, including internal struggles and family conflicts involved in the conversion process.

I was interested in this topic because of my work in Afghanistan and Iraq, and my friendship with *Mark*, who worked as an interpreter for my PRT in Afghanistan. He converted to Christianity and later immigrated to the United States as part of the Afghan Special Immigration Visa program. Our friendship and his conversion journey sparked my interest in understanding how to help Muslims see the truth of Christianity—a very difficult and dangerous thing to do because in Islam, conversion to Christianity is punishable by death.

I was also very interested in what facts and information Nabeel came across that convinced him of the truth of Christianity and the falsehood of Islam. Understanding what convinced him to convert could be very helpful in strengthening my own faith.

# CHAPTER 11

Navarrete to Sotés, 5.7 Kilometers
5 Sep 2015
D+7
Maintenance Down Day

Keeping to the theme of prevention, I planned today for maintenance and to rest my feet, back, and legs. The "experts" always say the
body needs some downtime to maintain itself and develop muscle.
I planned this for a long time, but as I got closer, the need became
apparent.

I took my time getting ready, packing, and having the continental breakfast downstairs. I vacated the albergue just before the 0800
deadline and found a café to relax at for a while. With four hours to
kill before check-in, I was in no hurry.

I took advantage of the extra time and did day 7 of my Bible
study on *Growing in Service*. Today's premise was that humans tend
to imitate the people that they hang out with. When we spend a lot
of time with someone, we eventually start taking on some of their
characteristics and beliefs. The reverse is also true. Therefore, we
need to hang out with other believers who base their actions on the
Word of God. This way we will support each other and help each
other grow in our relationships with Christ and our ability to keep
our focus on His ways. We need to ensure that our conduct is honorable and godly. We don't want to be an ungodly influence on those
around us, thus hindering their spiritual growth.[13]

---

[13] Fryar, p. 16–17.

The morning air was chilly, and I was seated at an outside table, so by 0830, I decided to get moving. Besides the gloves I wore the last couple days, I had my jacket on for the first time. Good thing I brought it. I considered leaving it at home since I was walking three weeks earlier this time and we had not needed jackets until October.

I entered Sotés about 1000 and followed small stickers on light poles pointing me to Albergue San Martin. They were a little harder to find than the usual yellow arrows that marked the Camino. I was still rather early, but since the hostel was off the beaten path, I wondered if they would let me in early. Couldn't hurt to ask, anyway. Maybe they would at least let me drop my pack and go back to a café to wait.

The stickers led me to a house with a fenced yard and a sign with a capital *A* indicating that it was an albergue. It appeared to be more of a casa rural. Definitely a pleasant surprise, especially considering a bed only cost 10€ for a night.

There were two dogs in the fenced yard. The brown one stuck his head through the fence, obviously asking for attention. The black one stood back and barked. As I approached and started petting Browny, Blacky ran into the doghouse and continued barking from his protected refuge. Pretty cute.

I rang the bell on the fenced gate, and a teenage girl came out to let me in. The place was clean and ready to receive new pilgrims. She was not at all concerned that I was early. She spoke a little English so was able to show me the ropes since her mom was out. There were two rooms with a total of eight beds, some in the bunk bed configuration and some single beds. She said I could have a single bed since I had made a reservation. There was also a kitchen with a long dining table. Snacks were in the middle of the table for sale. Drinks were available for purchase in the refrigerator. A clothes washing machine was built into the cabinet area, and she explained that it would cost 3€ a load. Finally she showed me the common sitting area and bathroom with a shower. All the comforts of home. She gave me clean towels and left me to get settled. I took a shower even though I had not worked up a sweat. Dirty or not, I could not pass up the opportunity to use a real towel!

Once out of my dirty clothes, I used their washing machine, throwing in my sleeping clothes to make a larger load. I found an outside water outlet and washed off the mud that still clung to my shoes from the tromp through the sunflower field. The warm, bright sun quickly dried the shoes and laundry.

Through all this, no one else arrived, and I began thinking I just might have the place to myself. All the advantages of a hotel, but way cheaper. The hotel in Ventosa would have cost me 65€. I guess it was not so bad that the hotel had been booked solid!

I then headed back into the main village for lunch. I could not believe it; there were actually people, young and old, out and about. Seeing people in the villages we passed was an oddity with the exception of proprietors with businesses that supported peregrinos. Here, there were adults gathered to talk, kids playing, and a few cars working their way through the narrow medieval streets. I'd been told the seemingly empty villages were because people had to go to the big cities for jobs. I guess on one level it made sense, but on another level I was confused. Spain had been around for a very long time. However, the "big cities" were not large when compared to big cities in the United States. So far I had walked through two: Pamplona and Logroño. It only took a couple hours to transit each. Most of the Camino passed through sparse farmland and tiny villages. There had been a couple with life, but I had to wonder what is going on with the population. Surely this ancient country in the middle of Europe should have a lot more people than this.

After lunch, I went back to the albergue and read the first three chapters of *Seeking Allah, Finding Jesus*. In these chapters, Nabeel explained his heritage and the lives of his parents and grandparents, as well as his family life and earliest introduction to Islam up to the age of four. His story gives great insights into Muslim family life and its interwoven, inseparable connection to their religion.

I then took a nap for a couple hours. About 1630, Dad and Mom rang me up on FaceTime, and we talked for about forty-five minutes. My mom put my toy poodle Jamie on her lap so that I could see her. I greeted her with some of the common phrases that I usually say to her in the way that I normally articulate them. She recognized my voice and the phrases and started looking around and sniffing, trying to find out where I was. She apparently missed me as much as I missed her.

By the time we finished talking, the hostess was ready to serve dinner, so I settled in to catch up on some of my notes while I ate. Since there was no one else staying here to talk to, I took the opportunity to listen to music on my iPhone.

Today marked the end of the first week of my Camino. So far I had traveled 181.3 km, or 112.4 miles. I often joked that the one gripe I had with the movie *The Way* was the lack of even the briefest mention of the physical (especially feet) challenges that pilgrims must deal with. Therefore, I believe it is only fair for me to be honest about my suffering so far.

The metal plates, custom orthotics, and larger, stiffer shoes are definitely helping! The balls of my feet and toes still got that pesky numb/tingly feeling, but it was worse when I wear normal hiking soaks with liners. Together, I guess, they are just too thick, making my shoes too tight and likely impacting circulation. The stand-alone toe socks were thicker than the liners, but only about half the thickness of hiking socks. Alone, they seemed to work much better. Even with the plates and orthotics, the area around the bone spur below my right big toe often experienced intense stabbing pain. All toes ached to some extent, and the more I walked on pavement, the more the balls of my feet hurt.

I knew these sensations were going to be my constant companion throughout my Camino. I planned to walk on dirt as much as possible and considered the constant pain the price I must pay to prove to myself that I had not become weak. I was not going to let the "victim" mind-set overwhelm my life. As a T-shirt I bought while at the academy said, "No Pain, No Gain!" This proved to be a bit of a rally call for me throughout many challenging times of my career. Every challenge and every pain was another chance to prove to myself that I had what it took to endure and succeed, no matter the physical and mental pain I had to overcome. In this manner, The Way was similar to those training and combat zone experiences.

Back and neck pain were also constant companions. Since my headaches are secondary to my back and neck issues, their intensity increased with the spine problems.

The other major issue that impacted me all day every day was the arthritis in my hands. Whether it is holding on to my poles, trying to get something out of my pocket, doing personal hygiene, tying my shoes or adjusting my pack, I dealt with frustrating pain in my fingers. As planned, I relied on the sides of my hands pressing against the straps of my hiking poles in order to get the advantage of less stress on my knees and feet. Showers, dressing, or packing often brought extreme pain when I absentmindedly bent my left pinky finger.

To my dismay, the pain in the hands just keeps getting worse! Why? I often wondered. I was only fifty and had been struggling with this increasingly since my early forties. In my opinion, I had the hands of an eighty-year-old. Was it the smoke from the burn pits, the predeployment vaccinations (anthrax, small pox, etc.), the anti-malaria medication, the dirty air I breathed day-to-day in Afghanistan and Baghdad, or something else I was exposed to over the years that led to the early onset of all these problems? Or was it the countless hours typing on a computer keyboard—combat typing!

Whatever the cause, I aggressively searched for alternate ways to do the things I needed to do just to live day-to-day. I had considered waiting another year to come back to the Camino when a couple friends could join me, but I feared the aggressive progress of the arthritis in both my feet and hands might make it impossible. So here I was, alone but enjoying the balance between solitude during my daily trek and the social interaction I got with fellow peregrinos at rest stops and during the evenings in the villages.

I don't know if it was a ligament or tendons, but on and off today I experienced stabbing pain in the arch of my right foot when walking. Was this another evolution of my ongoing foot issues? Who knows. For now I would continue to try to take it easy when the pain attacks.

Before turning in for the night, I did the mission planning for Sunday. I decided to do 26.7 km and RON in Cirueña. This would be another long day, and I was concerned about my feet. However, the next best lodging opportunity was 8.1 km closer, only about 18.6 km. Too short, especially since I had done so little today. On the positive side, the majority of the day would be on earthen trail. It looked like the only pavement would be as I passed through the town of Nájera at the end of stage 8.

# CHAPTER 12

## Sotés to Cirueña, 26.7 Kilometers
## 6 Sep 2015
## D+8

Taking advantage of the solitude, I read day 8 of the service study over breakfast. The essence of the message was that if you know and follow God's Word and are sensitive to the leading of the Holy Spirit, you can be confident that your service is in line with God's intent. You should look at your spiritual leaders as examples for shaping your own faith and life of service, just as others may notice the way you serve and pattern their own service accordingly. The author referenced three scriptures: 2 Timothy 1:13–14, Hebrews 13:7, and Acts 20:17–38.[14]

Following the "leading of the Holy Spirit" has always been something that I found difficult. As a military person, following orders was not the problem. But since the Holy Spirit does not speak audibly and clearly, nor does He issue written mission orders, I have always found it difficult to figure out what the "leading of the Holy Spirit" is and what my own personal ideas and intentions are, not to mention deceptive leading by the devil. Sometimes I wish the Holy Spirit would burn a bush in front of me and speak to me through it, then I would clearly understand what God wants me to do and could confidently be "all-in" to make it happen.

Turning to the east on the main road through the village, I was soon in Ventosa, where I had hoped to stay last night and stopped for a coffee break. It was here that I saw the first other pilgrims since this

---

[14] Fryar, p. 18–19.

time yesterday. It was nice to take the night off from the socializing and enjoy some solitude, but now I was excited to be back among the group.

The warm café and hot coffee were a welcome relief. The weather app said that it was in the low forties, and it certainly felt like it. The chill easily penetrated my jacket and gloves. I had not zipped the legs back on my hiking pants before departing, and my bare skin was not happy. I considered attaching them while at the café, but the hourly forecast indicated it would be warming up soon, so I decided to gut it out. I figured I would just have to take them back off within an hour, so it wasn't worth the effort.

Upon exiting Ventosa, the trail veered off on a dirt road through farm fields. Finally, some relief from walking on pavement! There was a car parked on the right side of the road next to the field. Over the next hundred meters or so, I saw three different people with expensive-looking large cameras taking pictures of pilgrims as they walked by. There was no obvious indication of who these people were or why they were taking pictures of us. I just smiled at them and continued walking.

The situation was reminiscent of a similar circumstance at the academy. Every day tourists would look down on the terrazzo from the chapel wall, watching the cadet wing march into Mitchell Hall during the noon meal formation or going about their daily routine to and from class or other activities. It was an odd feeling to be a tourist attraction. We often jokingly referred to the academy as "the zoo" because of this. A comic in an annual academy calendar showed tourists looking down on cadets on the terrazzo from the chapel wall. Next to them was a big sign that read "Do Not Feed the Cadets."

\* \* \* \* \*

Considering the similarities of these events eased me back into my career reflections.

After graduation from USAFA, we had approximately a month to take some leave before reporting to our career training (tech school) locations. For me, that meant joining five of my classmates and about fifteen others at Lackland Air Force Base, Texas, for the Air Force Security Police Academy's Basic Officer Course.

When I had come to the realization that being an astronaut wasn't going to happen, I had to consider other options. During a career day, I went to a briefing on being a helicopter pilot, since I had enjoyed my flight at Elmendorf. The briefer said that the number of helicopter pilots was very limited and the AF was seriously considering contracting out the requirements. If that were to happen, active-duty helicopter pilots would be cross-trained into fixed wing. He said that they would not have the option to go to a nonflying career field. Since I had already decided I did not want to fly fixed wing, this briefing convinced me not to pursue helicopters either.

So I turned my attention to another passion I had growing up—law enforcement. This old interest, combined with my passion for my law courses at the academy, led me to look into security police as a fallback career field option (plan C, if you will). I was intrigued by the information that I found and decided to select it as my first choice. Since most academy graduates wanted to fly, there was not much competition for the available slots, and I was easily selected for this opportunity.

Since I was pilot qualified and had selected a nonflying career field, I had to report to the commandant of cadets and explain why I was turning down the opportunity to fly. The Air Force didn't have many female pilots at the time, so I only had to go see the one-star commandant. If I had been male, I would have had to explain it to the three-star superintendent. My point to the commandant was that I was not interested in flying and therefore felt I lacked the motivation to get through pilot training. If I washed out, then I would have wasted a pilot slot that could have gone to another officer who really wanted it and might have become an outstanding pilot; hence the slot would have been wasted. The commandant agreed to approve my request.

My career selection meant my chances of making general was almost nil. The majority of generals in the Air Force are pilots. In the security police (SP) career field, there was only one one-star general authorized. Disappointing, but I decided not to worry about it.

Potential promotion to general was decades away, and how my career path would go between now and then, well, there was no way to know. Besides, being a general had never been a priority for me, and I didn't see the point of going into a career field I was not interested in just to make general.

Besides my interest in law enforcement, I had discovered during my time as a cadre member during BCT that I enjoyed leading people. SP officers normally started out as a shift commander in charge of an entire flight of enlisted cops from day one. Pilots sometimes get to supervise a couple lieutenants when they are senior captains. They are lieutenant colonels before they get any real leadership positions. The decision, therefore, was easy. Who knows, maybe they will need a chief of police on a moon base one day!

At the basic officers' course, they introduced us to the major components of the SP mission. Enlisted SPs had three distinctly different career fields: law enforcement (LE), security, and combat arms training and maintenance (CATM). There was no differentiation in the officer corps; we led all three.

LE is responsible for entry control at the base gates, traffic control, and basic base patrols. Their priority was to respond to alarms at funds storage facilities, stores, pharmacies, low-priority munitions storage areas, and armories. What we called "funds and guns." Additionally, they responded to domestic disputes, fights at the clubs, issued traffic citations, made DUI arrests, and responded to base emergencies or other criminal activity. Basically what most civilian police do.

Security troops are responsible for priority resources such as planes, critical communication facilities, selected Command and Control facilities, and high-priority munitions storage areas.

CATM is responsible for the base firing range and ensuring all personnel who need to be qualified on weapons receive the training and hands-on firing experience they needed to qualify and stay proficient.

The last major area of responsibility for the SPs is Air Base Ground Defense (ABGD), our primary responsibility in combat zones. We were responsible for defending the Air Bases from enemy attack so that operational units could conduct their missions and had a place to land when they got back. Besides perimeter defenses, we patrolled outside the wire to protect the base from attacks and ensured no one fired a surface to air missile (SAM) at aircraft taking off or landing. Off-base convoy security also fell under the ABGD mission. Essentially, we were the "Army of the Air Force," as I liked to describe it.

My classmates turned out to be people that I would work with and run into at conferences throughout my career. The SP officer corps was a small tight-knit group. Those that were commissioned in the same year progressed along similar career paths and, therefore, would see each other frequently. Friendships that were made there lasted until retirement and beyond.

In September 1987, we graduated from the SP Academy and headed off to our individual assignments. Mine was Malmstrom AFB in Montana where I was assigned as a flight security officer in the missile field. While on duty, my flight was responsible for the security of dispersed missile sites. Since Ronald Reagan was the president at the time, we affectionately referred to the missile field as Ronnie's rocket ranch.

I asked for this assignment because Malmstrom's Security Police Group had been awarded the best in the Air Force in 1986. I figured it would be smart to start out at a top-rated base and learn the trade from the best of the best.

\* \* \* \* \*

By 0900 hours it was warm enough to take off my jacket. My legs were no longer cold. Just after 1000 hours, I removed the last of my snivel gear, the gloves, as I entered Nájera and officially completed stage 8.

The Way out of town followed a dirt road up a hill. Towering rock formations lined each side. The people of this area must be very supportive of pilgrims walking the Camino. They had placed tall wooden stakes every kilometer. The familiar Camino yellow arrow was permanently placed on top with the shell symbol underneath.

Below that was the number of kilometers remaining. Vertically from the bottom were the words "A Santiago," which means in English "To Santiago." Two years ago the kilometer markers appeared fairly new. After we had passed about ten of these, Mom made it clear that she did not want to keep being reminded how far we had to go. It might have been motivating if we were nearing the end. However, this section of trail was still over 550 km from Santiago. Apparently, many people agreed with her, and few of the kilometer plates were intact in 2015. On pole 571, the plate was covered with graffiti that read "We don't want this, OK? Stop telling us! Take off!"

* * * * *

After a couple weeks of localized training, I was assigned to a flight of about forty people ranging in rank from airmen basics (E-1) fresh out of their own tech school, to two master sergeants (E-8) nearing retirement after over twenty years of service. As the only officer on the flight, 2Lt Tracey Meck was technically in charge on day one. I learned quickly that the SP Academy had merely scratched the surface of what I needed to know to do the job right. As I had been advised to do, I looked to the master sergeants to teach me the ropes. Instead of looking at them as subordinates, I considered them more as partners and mentors. They'd been doing this for their whole career. They knew the rules and procedures and, more importantly, how to lead, train, and motivate the young troops. They not only taught me administrative tasks but more importantly how to develop the enlisted force and grow new leaders.

We worked a nine-day cycle. During our three days in the field, the flight staged out of various control facilities near the missile sites and responded to alarms, conducted patrols, and participated in response exercises to train for various security scenarios. Meals, a day room, and sleeping quarters were available at the control facilities. On the morning of the fourth day, the oncoming flight (our replacements) traveled out to do changeover in the field. This was called recovery day. It was often mid to late afternoon before we got back to the base; turned in our weapons, equipment, and mandatory paperwork; and were ready to start our time off.

The next three days were what we called protected time off (PTO). Since supervisors were often needed to come in and process paperwork, and the flight security officer (FSO) and flight security supervisor (FSS) were required to attend meetings and coordinate with the back-office staff, we sarcastically referred to PTO as "pretend time off." One day I made a reference to the fact that I was working on a PTO day to my supervisor, the operations officer. His reply was that since I was in civilian clothes at the time, it was actually a day off. I think he was trying to be funny. Just the same, I was learning that being a security police officer was a 24/7/365 job (meaning, you are on duty twenty-four hours a day, seven days a week, 365 days a year).

After PTO, we had a day to take care of appointments we couldn't do while posted in the field. The final day was a training day.

I liked Malmstrom, and the area where the base was in Montana. I was born in Bozeman and had also lived in Billings, Helena, and Butte before moving to Alaska when I was in the fifth grade. In a way, it was like going home. I definitely liked the Rocky Mountains. Most of the missile field was on the planes, but we were never out of sight of the Rockies.

The other thing I liked about the area was, it was a small town where ten cars stopped at a traffic light constituted a traffic jam. I remember a time when I took a drive south of town and stopped at a souvenir shop. When I got out of the car, I instinctively turned around and locked the doors. The shop owner was standing in the store's doorway and was obviously dismayed.

When I approached, he said in a slightly frustrated tone, "You don't need to do that here." He was actually offended that I felt the need to lock my car in front of his establishment!

I really enjoyed working in the field with the troops. I learned a lot about "boots on the ground," front-line leadership that could not be learned in an academy environment. These were not overachieving cadets living in an academic environment. These were a mix of airmen—some as young as eighteen away from home for the first time, others seasoned supervisors with families, and countless other responsibilities competing for their time. I learned how important it was for a leader to take care of his or her people. If the leader takes care of the troops; the troops will take care of the mission. Leaders do not get respect from their subordinates simply because of their rank. They must earn it. This did not mean that you make friends with your subordinates—rather that you demonstrate that you care about them personally and about their career development. They also wanted to know that you had their back if something negative happens and they were not being treated justly by the higher-ups. I knew I had earned their respect when they started calling me LT (pronounced *El Tee*).

Another sign of respect was when they started playing practical jokes on me. Since we were in the field for three and a half days at a time and seldom had any real security incidents to deal with, the troops had plenty of time to find ways to entertain themselves. Practical jokes were at the top of their list.

I will never forget one particular prank they played on me on a hot summer day. While I slept in a back bedroom, I made the mistake of leaving my beret in the common area. Somebody smeared Icy Hot along the leather rim. Once I was up, showered, and had eaten, it was time to head off to another control center to visit with one of the other crews under my command. I grabbed my beret, bid everyone farewell, climbed into my official patrol SUV, and headed down the dirt road. It wasn't long before my forehead started to sweat under my beret. The sweat interacted with the Icy Hot along the entire line where the brim of the hat touched my forehead. The burning sensation became overwhelming. Realizing what they had done, I tried to wipe the Icy Hot off of both my forehead and the brim, but to no avail. Once applied, Icy Hot is not something that can be wiped off. It was about an hour before the burning sensation started to subside.

There was one dynamic of working at a missile base that caused me (and most of the airmen) a lot of frustration. Ours was a no-fail mission, and procedures had to be followed precisely. There was no leeway for halfhearted efforts or stupid mistakes. Being "stupid-on-station" could often lead to stiff discipline. Article 15 Nonjudicial Punishment, sometimes with demotions, was often imposed for infractions that would normally be handled with additional training, a stiff talking to (often referred to as wall-to-wall counseling), or a letter of counseling or reprimand if they had occurred at lower-priority missions.

Article 15s were sometimes handed out unjustly as a knee-jerk reaction, seemingly without a clear understanding or concern about the background and circumstances of the incident. If the squadron or group leadership detected a general trend they thought was becoming a problem, they often came down very hard on a scapegoat to send a message to the rest of the group. We called this being SACamsized. SAC stood for Strategic Air Command. It was the Major Command (MAJCOM) that oversaw all strategic missile and bomber wings. SAC was very strict on discipline. It was often said that the easiest way to make staff sergeant (E-5) at a SAC base was to get there as a tech (technical sergeant, E-6), meaning it was easier to get demoted than promoted.

A prime example of being SACamsized happened to one of my super troops. He was highly motivated, excelling in his Air Force career, and very intelligent. He had all the makings of a future chief master sergeant or even potentially earning a bachelor's degree and a commission as an officer.

One day a civilian came up to the gate of the control facility and said that his car had run out of gas. He was wondering if the crew could give him some gas from the on-site pump. The airman refused because the gas belonged to the government and was strictly for official use. However, he and his partner said that they would take a gas can to a local gas station, purchase a gallon, and bring it back to him. On the way to the gas station, there was a long, steep hill. As their vehicle went down the hill, it sped up, and soon they were going well over the speed limit. The local police pulled them over and issued a ticket.

Since the driver was such an excellent troop, had never had any sort of negative paperwork in his entire career, and had earned the highest possible ratings in the last couple performance reports, I recommended a letter of reprimand (LOR) as punishment. Normally, you would start with the letter of counseling (LOC) for a first-time offense, but since the police had clocked him going eighty-five in a fifty-five, I felt it was advisable to go directly to the next level. Our commander disagreed. He felt he should get an Article 15. Whereas LORs did not follow you to other assignments and could be pulled out of your records anytime, Article 15s followed you for the rest of your career and normally meant you would not get promoted for quite a while. This was serious action.

I do not remember exactly what the punishment was that was associated with this particular Article 15, but I clearly remember the impact on my super troop. He lost all motivation for his Air Force career, and for the rest of the time I knew him, he talked of nothing but getting out of the military as soon as his enlistment period was up.

I was becoming more and more frustrated with the leadership practices of my superiors. Talking it over with my senior NCOs, they assured me that it was not like this at most bases in the Air Force. Therefore, I looked forward to the two-year point when I would be eligible to transfer to another unit. One thing was for sure: I needed to try to get an assignment in a MAJCOM other than SAC.

* * * * *

I struck up a conversation with a Dutch couple while enjoying a tortilla for lunch in Azofra.

"This is a great experience," the male peregrino said beaming. "Our only regret is we have only three weeks to walk the Camino. We will get as far as we can, but we will have to come back next year to finish."

"You are lucky that you live in Europe. I imagine traveling down here is not too expensive," I replied. "I met a couple on the Camino a couple years ago with the same problem, they were from Ohio. They could only get two weeks off work at a time, that plus travel time meant they were going to have to do the Camino over a three-year period. Considering the cost of airfare, this would be a very expensive way of doing it!"

"Oh yes," his wife said in solid agreement. "We just have to get on a train and we are here in a day. It does not cost much."

"I wonder if the couple from Ohio is on the trail again," I said thoughtfully. "If they followed their plan, they should be finishing up the last section this year. Maybe I will run into them near Santiago. It would be great to get caught up and see how things turned out for them!"

Once finished with my lunch, I set out for the last 9 km of the day.

\* \* \* \* \*

After working rotations to the field for about a year and a half, I was switched to another squadron and given a slightly higher position. Instead of being in charge of an on-duty flight, I supervised the convoy and maintenance security section. No longer working in the field with my troops on a daily basis, I provided oversight from a back-office management level. Fortunately, I was trained and certified as a convoy commander, so this frequently got me out of the office and back into the field.

I really enjoyed convoy duty. Since I was the officer-in-charge (OIC) of the section, I assumed the traditional Joker One call sign. Our emblem was based on the joker from a card deck. I felt honored to be given such an important and critical responsibility. I liked the higher-level management, but missed the day-to-day interaction with troops in the field. Going on convoys gave me some opportunity to be with the troops. There were a couple of other certified convoy commanders in the squadron, so I did not go on every mission. When I was not out with a team, there was plenty to do in the office.

One day our convoy was caught in a blizzard that hit earlier than forecast. As the convoy commander, I became very nervous, as did my driver. It was vital that we got back to base safely. While discussing the situation, I commented that I could barely see the front of our vehicle's hood, let alone the trucks carrying the rest of the team. My driver chuckled and said situations like this built character. I told him I thought I already had enough character.

Even though I enjoyed this new position in a different squadron, I still had to deal with what I felt were typical SAC knee-jerk overreactions from above. As soon as the timing was right, I requested reassignment. It was not long before I had orders to Comiso Air Station in Sicily. Instead of SAC, I would be assigned to United States Air Forces Europe (USAFE, pronounced *You-Safe-EE*). Since the Cold War was in high gear, USAFE was focused on preparing to confront the USSR in the event they invaded Europe by crossing the Fulda Gap or challenged NATO in any way. USAFE units were focused on base-wide exercises and training to prepare for their wartime mission. They expected to be at the tip of the spear. My senior NCOs told me there was a lot less micromanagement and knee-jerk responses to events there. USAFE was a command on the brink of war, and that's where the focus was. I could not be happier about the assignment.

* * * * *

Upon entering Cirueña, where I intended to RON, I immediately recognized it as a place we had had lunch in 2013. Excruciating foot pain was my companion that day. I could not wait to get into the café, get my shoes off, and rest my feet for a while. Every step had been a battle. Today there was pain in the feet, but nothing close to that day. Yesterday's rest had obviously been a good idea!

I decided to check out an albergue called Virgen de Guadalupe. It had twenty-three beds split between five rooms and was only 7€. After the privilege of having a casa rural to myself the previous night, I decided tonight I would go into a hostel. Besides, since yesterday had been a down day, the people I had gotten to know over the last week were now a day ahead of me. It was time to start meeting a new Camino family.

The hostel was a couple of blocks off trail. As I approached the building, I was discouraged by its old and run-down condition. It definitely needed a few coats of paint. I hesitated for a moment but then decided to go ahead and check it out. They had beds available, and the host assured me I could get a bottom bunk. I decided to stay; it was only one night after all. The village only had a population of one hundred people, so what did I expect?

The hospitalero asked if I wanted to partake of the communal dinner. I asked him what was being served and was told it was some sort of a bean soup dish that was typical in the area.

"I really do not like beans," I explained. "I will go to the café in town and get something there."

"No, this is impossible," he cautioned. "It is Sunday. Nothing else is open. If you are hungry, you will have to eat here."

Reluctantly, I signed up and paid the extra 7€. I turned down the breakfast, however. A town of 6,600 was only 5.8 km up the trail. If nothing was open in this village before I left, my plan was to wait and eat a big breakfast in Santo Domingo de la Calzada.

After he stamped my pilgrim's credential, he showed me a large living room area where we could get tea and coffee. A couple couches were set against the wall to the left, and a dining room table was in the larger area to the right. This was the area where the Wi-Fi was strongest, although even here it was weak and slow. He then took me upstairs to my room. There were three sets of bunk beds. Two of the lower bunks were already taken. I claimed the third, unpacked, and made up my bed. One of my roommates was asleep on the other side of the small room, so I did my best to keep the noise down.

By the time I got back from the shower, two more ladies had arrived. The host intended to keep the room all-female if possible. I certainly appreciated that, though I was getting used to having males in the same room. So far there had not been any problems, and everybody had behaved themselves and respected everybody else's privacy. Neither two years ago, nor during this trip, had I heard of any problems resulting from coed rooms. The Europeans often commented about how the "sensitive Americans" needed to get over their privacy and gender-segregation concerns. Still it was nice that the host was trying to keep our room all-female.

The five of us in the room spent about a half hour introducing ourselves and telling stories from our adventure so far. One of the ladies was from New Zealand, one from Spain, and another was an American from Maine.

I do not remember where the other lady was from, but based on her command of English, I was sure she was from America. She was older than me, probably in her mid to upper sixties, and had short, straight white hair. Like the rest of us in the room, she was walking alone. She told us about a couple of times when she had experienced extreme acts of kindness while on The Way.

"By the time I hit the top of the hill in the Pyrenees on the first day, I had run out of water," she explained her first major crisis. "It was ninety-five degrees, and I was very thirsty. I had no idea what I was going to do. All I could do was pray and ask God for help. To my amazement, a few minutes after I prayed, a car pulled over to the side of the road just in front of me. I called to the two men in the vehicle and asked if they had any water they could give me. I could not believe it! Not only did they give me water, but one of them even massaged my sore feet. I was so thankful!"

"Sounds like you were not the first pilgrim in distress that they had come upon," I lightly joked, intrigued by their kindness.

"My good fortune did not stop there," she continued. "I spent last night in Ventosa. When I arrived, I had only 5€ in my pocket. The albergue cost ten. Dinner was extra. The town was so small there was no ATM. I had no idea what to do. The next town big enough to even possibly have an ATM was 10.5 km away. There is no way I could go that far! I was tired and had had enough for the day. But the hospitalero was so kind! When I explained my problem, he took pity on me and allowed me to stay for five euro. He even signed me up for the dinner. Simply amazing!"

After a few more minutes of the group discussion, a couple of us decided to walk back to the main road and see if any of the bars were open so we could get a drink while we awaited dinner. We entered the restaurant/bar where we had had lunch back in 2013 and found that not only could we get a drink there but they were serving plenty of food. Many of the items on the menu looked very appetizing. We decided that we'd much rather eat here than what was being offered at the communal dinner at the albergue. I looked up the phone number in my pilgrim's guide and called our hospitalero.

"This is Tracey Meck," I explained. "The café has food. JoAnn and I want to cancel our dinner reservations."

"*Como*," he replied in a questioning tone. "Cancel reservation? You do not want to stay here?"

"Yes, we want to sleep there, just no dinner," I tried to explain in as simple English as I could.

"*No comprendo*," he said. "Reservation?"

"No, we have *camas* already," I tried to explain again. "We just want to cancel dinner."

Frustrated that he suddenly could not speak English, I tried to explain it several more times, throwing in the little Spanish that I knew to get the point across. He even acted like he did not recognize our names when I repeated them a couple more times. After several minutes of seemingly getting nowhere, I gave up and decided we would just have to talk to him when we got back. We both suspected that he was playing ignorant so that he would not have to refund our money.

Knowing that I did not like what was being served for dinner at the albergue, I went ahead and ordered a chicken dinner at the bar. I would try to get my money back, but even if I did not get a refund, at least I would have a full stomach.

When we got back to the albergue, we approached the hospitalero and requested a refund for the dinner. He had regained his command of the English language and said it was impossible to give the money back because he had already made the dinner based on the number of people who had made reservations. Resigning to the loss of the money, I decided I would go to the dinner and at least drink some wine. Since a glass of wine at a bar cost between 1 and 1.5€, I decided I had better enjoy the wine because it would be the most expensive of the trip. At least this way I would get something for the money I had given him.

About twenty minutes before dinner was scheduled to be served, the hospitalero stopped by the room to remind us.

"You need to take your shower now before dinner," he said, looking directly at one of my roommates.

We looked at each other in shock as he turned and walked away.

"That was weird," the lady from New Zealand said bewildered.

"Yeah, I think it's a little creepy that he knows who has taken a shower and who hasn't," I said, raising my left eyebrow. "I'm getting more and more concerned about this guy. I don't trust him. First he told us nobody was serving food in town because it was Sunday, then suddenly he couldn't speak English when we tried to cancel our dinner reservations, and then when we got back he said it was too late get our money back because he had already made the meal. Now this."

My roommates agreed.

"I don't like how he is ordering us around," the lady from Maine added. "It's just weird!"

At the appointed time we all walked down the hall to the small dining room and kitchen. There was a long table with bench seating on both sides and one seat at the end near the door. I sat next to a girl who appeared to be in her early twenties. We introduced ourselves and were surprised to discover that we were both from the greater Seattle area. I was also pleasantly surprised to see the three Navy retirees I had met a few days before. They had not taken the day off as I had, but they were not walking as far as I was each day; hence our paths crossed again.

Everyone had a great time getting to know each other and talking about our adventures, and we saw a different side of the hospitalero. He was actually very kind and had made the traditional Spanish meal by hand from scratch and served it to us family-style. Sitting down with his own bowl of soup, he explained the history of the local area's support to the ancient pilgrims. I came away with a much more positive opinion of this little albergue in a tiny village.

# CHAPTER 13

Cirueña to Belorado, 28.5 Kilometers
7 Sep 2015
D+9

At 0715, I set out with my roommates—Kay, from New Zealand, and JoAnn, from Maine—for Santo Domingo de la Calzada where we planned to eat breakfast together. We used our headlights to navigate our way through the narrow streets. As we cleared the closely clumped buildings and exited town, we were treated to a beautiful sunrise. In the middle of a large traffic circle stood a couple large, flat metal silhouette statues. One of an ancient peregrino made an awesome photo with the beautiful sunrise backdrop.

My friends set a fairly brisk pace. My feet were hurting again, the worst being the top of my right foot near the toes. Hotspots on both heels flared as my shoe rubbed against them with each step. I struggled to keep up.

Kay and JoAnn were curious how my deployments to the Middle East had affected me. They'd heard so much in the news about the mental and physical struggles of veterans returning from the wars. They were interested in getting a firsthand report. We spent most of the nearly 6 km to Santa Domingo talking about how physically and mentally exhausted I had become during my four deployments and tours at CENTCOM and the Pentagon. I explained how others had literally worked themselves to death and my doctors had cautioned that I was on that trajectory. We also went into some detail about the toxic leaders that I worked for in both Afghanistan and Iraq who had so drastically affected my mental condition.

\* \* \* \* \*

A joint PRT and Afghan National Police convoy prepares to leave FOB Gardez Jan 2007.

As a lieutenant colonel and the commander of Provincial Reconstruction Team (PRT) Gardez during my second tour in Afghanistan, myself and the other Air Force members of my team fell under an Air Force's 755th Expeditionary Support Group at Bagram Airfield (BAF) for all administrative and personnel issues (known as ADCON or Administrative Control). However, for Tactical and Operational Control (TACON and OPCON), we reported to the brigade commander in charge of Regional Command-East (RC-E), an Army colonel with whom I butted heads almost from the beginning.

He seemed far more interested in the kinetic portion of the fight than the nonkinetic operations the PRTs were doing, even though he had briefed the PRT commanders during in-processing that the reconstruction and development mission was what was actually going to bring long-term stability to Afghanistan. He said we could not kill our way to stability and prosperity for the Afghan people. However, his words were not reflected in his actions. When he came to visit Forward Operating Base (FOB) Gardez, I was normally not notified in advance. All coordination was done with my counterpart who commanded the two hundred–plus soldiers dedicated to kinetic operations (the term used for traditional combat operations) in Paktya and Logar provinces. This unit was colocated with us on the FOB, and their commander was dual-hatted as the FOB commander. On numerous occasions, the first I knew the brigade commander was visiting was when I saw him walking across the courtyard or in the dining facility (DFAC) better known as the chow hall. He spent a lot of time talking to the kinetic commander and his troops. He never visited with the PRT airmen or soldiers (PRTs were "joint" teams—meaning, we were made up of personnel more than one US military service). The only time he visited with me was when I had done something that he didn't like, and his intent was to chew me out.

We arrived in early April 2006, and the first major incident that caused friction was in May when a soldier from our security platoon was caught sleeping while posted on the security perimeter at an off-base project site. In the AF, a guard sleeping on post was one of the worst infractions he could commit, even in peacetime. In my mind, it was much worse when it happened in a combat environment. SF SOP was to immediately relieve the individual of duty, suspend his authorization to carry a weapon, and start preparing administrative discipline, normally an Article 15. In this case, the soldier was allowed to continue his job at the time because they still needed to convoy back to the FOB through hostile territory. The team needed him and his weapon. When they returned to base (RTB), the AF major who was the mission commander briefed me on the incident.

I was flabbergasted that someone providing perimeter security in a combat environment would fall asleep while the rest of the team was counting on him. They thought he had their backs. What was even more egregious was that there were three other people in the vehicle from which he was performing his gunner duties. His team leader and the two other members of the fire team were seated inside the vehicle. They should have ensured that the gunner stayed alert.

I relieved both the gunner and the team leader of duty. They became extremely angry, and the irate feelings spread throughout the security platoon. They were a very close-knit team, and they did not take kindly to an AF officer taking disciplinary action against one of their own. Although I was not comfortable with disarming soldiers in a combat zone, their hostility reached such a level that I became concerned and saw no other choice. I did not want irrational, angry people carrying loaded weapons. I certainly could not trust them to perform security duties.

The platoon leader and sergeant complained to their home station battalion commander who was in-country and maintained a certain level of ADCON for the soldiers. The battalion commander and I shared ADCON, which was very odd. Anyway, I contacted their commander myself and explained what had happened. We discussed proceeding with Article 15 punishment. I found out later that behind-the-scenes, the battalion leadership was not as supportive of my actions as the commander had let on when we talked on the phone. A few days later the commander and the unit's sergeant major visited our FOB and spent time with their platoon. Word got to me that the sergeant major had told the team not to worry. It did not matter what negative action I took against members of the platoon. It would all be purged from their records as soon as they got back stateside and would have no impact on their careers.

Most likely through the sergeant major's channels, word got to the brigade commander. I doubt the colonel got the full story since it was filtered through the unit's home station leadership. He did not seem to understand the seriousness of the incident, nor how angry the individuals and platoon as a whole had become. Without prior notification to me, the brigade commander took a helicopter to our FOB and came directly to my office for the first time since we had arrived. He proceeded to chew me out for about a half hour. He really wasn't interested in hearing the other side of the story. He ordered me to return them to duty and give them their weapons and ammunition back.

Clearly the actions of the Army chain completely undermined my authority as the PRT commander. For the rest of our year in-country, I struggled to earn the platoon's respect and to make them feel a part of the team. They decided they were going to be separate, and that caused a lot of tension.

In early June, I was tasked with answering a congressional inquiry in response to a letter one of them had submitted to his congressman. The complainant wrote in his letter that he could not believe that his platoon was put under the command of the "non-combat Air Force." He made it clear that he felt the team's AF officers didn't know what they were doing and were going to get everybody killed.

In my official response, I explained the Air Staff at the Pentagon selected me for the position. I explained that as a security forces officer with twenty years of experience in security operations and convoys, I was more than qualified to direct security operations. I also explained that the mission commander on the day in question was an AF intelligence major on his third or fourth combat tour who had previously led numerous convoys in Iraq. Together we had far more experience than anyone in the security platoon, most of whom had never deployed before. I was frustrated that I was the one who had to answer the inquiry, but considering how negative the Army chain was to me personally, it was likely best that I did.

In early fall, there was another incident where I butted heads with the colonel. The soldier who fell asleep on perimeter security reported that he had seen an AF captain taking a photo of a female Army Civil Affairs lieutenant going to the bathroom under a poncho during a convoy stop. (Women could not go off road to find a secluded place because the fields were often littered with buried mines left over from the Russian occupation. There were no McDonalds or gas stations to stop at, so women had to squat next to the HMMWV and use a poncho for concealment.)

Upon hearing the complaint, I tasked my SF personnel on the PRT to investigate. They confiscated the camera and found no evidence of the alleged picture. The officer in question denied taking the picture, and the investigators could find no other witnesses. So it came down to the story of a young disgruntled soldier against an AF captain who had consistently demonstrated high moral standards. In my opinion, there was not enough evidence to support the allegation, and therefore taking disciplinary action against the captain was not justified.

Again the brigade commander visited my office to ream me out for not taking decisive action, relieving the captain of duty and sending him back to his home station for disciplinary action that would have certainly ended his career. I stood my ground. Because the AF maintained complete ADCON over airmen, the colonel had no authority to override my decision. My AF boss supported me. In fact, it was situations like this that led the AF to dig in its heels about the ADCON issue. This angered the colonel, and in my opinion, he took it very personally.

In the midst of all this turmoil, the senior enlisted member of my team, an AF senior master sergeant, told me he thought the tension between me and the brigade commander had its roots in the fact that I was female. In his discussions with senior NCOs from other PRTs, he found there was no tension between him and the five male PRT commanders in RC-E. The brigade commander often visited with the other PRTs and had periodic sit-down discussions with their commanders about mission objectives and potential projects. These discussions never happened at PRT Gardez. It was the senior's contention that the colonel was not a fan of females in the military, let alone as an unit commander in a combat zone, even if the unit in question was nonkinetic.

His theory was hard for me to believe since it had been over ten years since I had experienced this sort of discrimination. But the more I contemplated the incidents, I realized there might have been some truth in the senior's speculation.

People often ask me what it was like to be a female in a military leadership position working directly with Muslim Afghan government officials. I tell them that I had great working relationships with the Afghans. They were not opposed to working with females from another country, the whole third-sex theory. In fact, during the change of command ceremony at the end of my tour, the governor of Paktya Province spoke about how much he appreciated what I had done for his people and how I differed from other commanders in that I had "the heart of a mother" for the Afghan people. Several years later, one of the interpreters who worked for the PRT and with whom I had maintained contact told me that the people of Paktya and Logar still talked about me and how much they appreciated my caring attitude and all that I had done for them. To this day, I remain honored to have had such a positive and lasting impact.

If only my dealings with the US Army had been so positive. Instead it seemed to be a constant battle. I called it "friendly fire." Whether dealing with superiors or subordinates, I struggled to earn respect and accomplish the mission without undue stress. It was as if I had to start six feet under and dig myself out before I could start earning respect through my actions, achievements, and sound decisions. When combined with the typical stressors of command in a combat zone—such as the constant threat of potential attacks on the FOB, sending your people out on daily convoys with the full knowledge that they could be hit by an improvised explosive device (IED) or suicide bomber or even ambushed by the enemy at any moment, dealing with the aftermath of such attacks, eighteen-hour workdays with no days off, etc.—one can easily imagine how the totality could push a commander to the limits of their stress-toleration capacity. I felt I handled the combat stressors fairly well, but the friendly fire was a different story. It is pretty bad when you go on a convoy in a combat zone to get stress relief!

\* \* \* \* \*

We found a wonderful café in Santo Domingo that served American-style breakfasts, to include a couple of eggs made to order, bacon, and toast. I never was a fan of European-style breakfasts, so I welcomed the taste of home.

As we prepared to leave, an American peregrino at another table greeted us.

"Looks like it's going to be a nice day for a walk," I opened a small-talk session.

"Yes, it does," he said in a depressed tone, his eyes looking toward the floor. "Buen Camino, I am afraid I will not be able to enjoy it today.

"Are you taking a day off?" I asked, a bit concerned about his tone.

"Oh, how I wish that was all it was. I'm afraid I have developed severe blisters on both feet. They are very deep, open sores," he explained as he took the sock off his right foot to show us.

One glance made me wish he had not exposed his sores. They were pretty disgusting—deep, bright red, with puss.

"I went to the doctor yesterday. He said under no circumstances should I continue the hike. I need to take four or five days off to let them heal. But I don't have time for that. I have to get home on schedule due to commitments. I don't see the point of taking several days off and then continuing if I'm not going to be able to finish. I am just going to fly home."

"I am so sorry! You should consider coming back next year and pick up where you left off," I encouraged him. "There is nothing wrong with splitting it up into two sessions. Everyone's Camino experience is their own. You can do it in any way that works for you!"

For the first time, I saw a little bit of light in his eyes. "I will certainly consider that!"

A couple blocks after leaving the café, we saw a sign pointing to the town's cathedral. My walking partners said they would like to tour it.

The thought of a delay and extra walking around town did not appeal to me.

"I really need to continue on. I hope to go 28 km, and my feet are already killing me. I had trouble keeping up with you this morning. I think it best that I continue on at my own pace so I can slow down and take smaller steps."

We bid each other "Buen Camino," and they headed off to the church.

\* \* \* \* \*

My mind was stilled locked on our earlier discussion and drifted to two other run-ins I had with the Army chain of command in the latter half of my PRT tour.

In late October 2006, I was visiting my parents for my fifteen-day midtour R&R. A couple days before starting my journey back to Gardez, I received an e-mail from my executive officer asking me to call him as soon as I had the opportunity. He said it was very important. A knot formed in my stomach. He would not have reached out to me back in the States to tell me about a positive development. Obviously, something bad had happened.

When I called, he informed me that one of our convoys had been ambushed. Several people had been seriously injured, but to my great relief, none of our troops had been killed. Two had been medically evacuated (MEDEVAC'ed) to Germany for advanced care. To make matters worse, the brigade had opened an investigation into the incident, and it wasn't going well. He couldn't give me many details over an unsecure phone line, but at least I had the opportunity to get into the right mind-set before returning to base.

I received the full briefing as soon as I arrived. Our convoy team had been up near the border with Pakistan in northeast Paktia. Our Police Training and Advisory Team (PTAT), made up of AF SF, had been doing assessments at several border guard posts. On their way back to an American outpost where they were scheduled to stay the night, the front vehicle in the convoy was hit by a rocket-propelled grenade (RPG). Several occupants were seriously injured, and the vehicle was rendered useless. As the rest of the team worked to rescue the occupants from the burning vehicle, the enemy opened fire from three directions. While some members of the team returned fire, others extracted the wounded and loaded them into other vehicles. Before the ambush, one of the other HMMWVs had broken down and was being towed. Unable to be burdened with two disabled vehicles, the team destroyed them.

Four vehicles worth of people crammed into two and sped out of the kill zone as quickly as they could, returning fire with the heavy weapons mounted in the gun turrets. Several people risked their lives under fire to extract the wounded and provide exceptional field care, stabilizing them until they could get to a medical facility. Our medical technician stopped serious bleeding for one of the injured, saving his life. An Army NCO could not cram himself into either vehicle. There just wasn't room for one more. He climbed onto the back hood of a HMMWV, grasped a tie-down hook with all he had, while firing at the enemy with his other hand. The fact that nobody was killed was attributed to the skill and professionalism of the entire joint team that made up the convoy that day. Eventually, several received valor awards for their actions; the NCO who clung to the back of the HMMWV received a Bronze Star with Valor.

As bad as that day was, our pain was only beginning. The brigade commander opened an investigation and was intent on finding somebody to blame and make an example of. Because of our previous disagreements over discipline issues, the colonel maintained responsibility for the investigation and would not allow me to be a part of the process. Of course, this made me furious, but there was nothing I could do.

Ultimately, the biased investigators who worked for the brigade commander, blamed the incident on the mission commander who was an Army Civil Affairs major. They relieved him of duty and initiated Article 15 proceedings. The commander's justification was that the major had deviated from the approved convoy route and should not have been on that road at the time. The commander said that this demonstrated a lack of discipline on the PRT and ultimately blamed me for the incident because he said that I had created a command environment that allowed such an event to happen. I will never know how he reached these conclusions because I was never allowed access to any investigation details.

Additionally, the commander said that the PRT had no business checking on the border posts. He said it was not part of our responsibility. This assertion was confusing. Training and advising the Afghan police was the central aspect of the PTAT's job description, and we had an operations order (OPORD) from the brigade commander's staff directing the PTATs to do border post assessments. Not to mention that he personally had approved the convoy's Concept of Operations (CONOP) and, therefore, the mission. Apparently all this was irrelevant.

There were other facets about the incident that were not fully investigated, nor factored into the resulting recommendations for disciplinary action. The convoy in question was not just made up of PRT personnel. There were also US Army personnel from the nearby outpost and a couple Afghan policemen who were working with the soldiers. When the fighting started, the soldiers from the outpost immediately fled the area, leaving the two Afghan policemen behind. Since they had not been riding in PRT vehicles, my troops assumed they had left with the soldiers. Besides the PRT had their hands full taking care of the wounded, destroying the crippled vehicles, and fighting off the enemy.

After the PRT escaped the kill zone, the Taliban executed the Afghan policemen. The investigation report held the PRT mission commander liable for their deaths and put none of the blame on the outpost personnel even though they had left the PRT and the Afghan police in the middle of a serious firefight.

I have often wondered if the enemy's motivation for the attack stemmed from an incident that happened in the area in September when a combined United States–Afghan kinetic operation had killed a Taliban leader in the same general area. The locals had refused to believe (or at least put on a good show about not believing) that the man who had been killed was Taliban. The incident set off a major tit-for-tat feud between the United States and Afghan government forces operating in the area on one side and the local villagers and insurgents on the other. Could the attack on our convoy have been a target of opportunity in this mini war? Were the kinetic troops from the outpost the real target?

In spite of all these mitigating factors, somehow the colonel determined it was my poor leadership that created an environment where such an attack was bound to happen.

The final incident started after our replacement PRT arrived in April 2007 and we were in the changeover process. For our S4 staff (logistics), this included a complete inventory and inspection of assigned equipment. During this process, it was discovered that a set of night vision goggles (NVG) was missing. Every square inch of the FOB was searched to no avail. These were considered sensitive equipment because, obviously, we did not want them to get into the hands of the enemy.

By this time, the colonel that I had butted heads with had rotated back to the States. Initially the new colonel and I got along fairly well. My main complaint was that he could not say a single sentence without at least three curse words. In my world, this was considered unprofessional. He had actually been very supportive, including reversing the first colonel's decision to downgrade my end of tour medal from a Bronze Star to a Meritorious Service Medal. After looking into the facts of the ambush incident, he disagreed with the first colonel's conclusion that the root cause was the command environment.

Our good working relationship ended when I notified him about the missing NVGs. Another stressful investigation was opened. This time the targets of the investigation were myself and my policies, my first sergeant, and our S4, a second lieutenant the Army had taken from a different career field. In my opinion, the Army chain of command failed to provide him adequate training and experience before assigning him to the PRT as the senior supply officer. The first sergeant also had no prior experience or training in his job. As a result, we were not well versed in standard Army accountability procedures, and therefore we did not follow some procedures that the chain of command assumed we knew. Apparently this contributed to losing the NVGs. I will never know for sure since we never figured out what happened to the NVGs. The procedure that we missed was not standard in the Air Force, and the PRT commanders were not trained on it, yet the Army expected us to follow it. Since I had not implemented it, the Army said I was at fault.

This line of reasoning was very frustrating. The Army chain should not have assumed that AF and Navy commanders were aware of Army policy. Even more puzzling, the policy not only required monthly inspections for sensitive items but paperwork documenting the inspections was required to be forwarded to the brigade S4. Since we hadn't done the inspections over the past year, the paperwork had not been submitted monthly as required. However, nobody from the brigade staff inquired about the missing documentation. A simple phone call from the brigade S4 informing us of the requirement the first month would have fixed the oversight, as would a document directing monthly inspection and reporting suspenses. These facts were ignored in the investigation report. Nobody on the brigade staff was found even partially liable.

When the changeover was completed and my team went to Bagram to await transportation out of country, I met with the AF general who held ADCON for the PRT airmen and explained the whole situation. He said he would meet with the Army and consider their investigation results before making a decision regarding what to do. I had worked with this general throughout my tour and trusted him implicitly to do the right thing. My fate was in his hands.

The process was not complete by the time my team departed for the United States. Myself, the first sergeant, and the S4 were ordered to remain in-country until it was resolved. The day before the rest of the PRT left, the brigade commander had a member of his staff call me at the Air Force group headquarters to remind me that I did not have the authorization to leave with the team. This really upset me. The Army didn't trust me to follow orders and felt that it was necessary to harass me about it. I told him I no longer worked for the Army and if they didn't trust me, they needed to talk to my general.

The next day I went to the passenger terminal to see my team off. Refusing to back down, the Army brigade commander sent a private over with orders to make sure that I, a lieutenant colonel, did not get on the plane. It was humiliating. I was furious and snapped angrily at the poor private who was only following orders. Very upset, I tried to call the general after returning to the support group tent, but he was in a meeting and could not be disturbed. I talked to his chief of staff and completely broke down when I asked him to tell the Army to leave me alone.

Ultimately the general agreed that mistakes had been made but that there were mitigating circumstances, including the different procedures and cultures of the AF and Army, the lack of adequate training on Army procedures, and the failure of the Army to notify us when the appropriate documents had not been submitted on a monthly basis. It was his judgment that all these circumstances had contributed to the mistakes. He told me that the Army wanted to disapprove my medal and recommended an Article 15. This would have completely ended my career. The general said he disagreed with them and issued a "local" letter of counseling, which was purged from my file as soon as I departed Bagram a couple days later. The primary purpose of the letter of counseling was to take official action in order to prevent the Army from pushing for stiffer punishment.

The general had saved my career. He also went to bat for me and got my Bronze Star reinstated.

Needless to say, I was a bit of a basket case mentally and have been struggling with this issue ever since. My career was my entire life and identity. Threatening it was as traumatic to me as a serious injury during battle would have been. Probably worse, since a battle injury carried some honor in the eyes of a warrior. Losing a career because of mistakes is far from honorable; it is disgraceful.

When I reported to a new assignment at Headquarters Central Command (HQ CENTCOM), a month after arriving back in the States, I found myself working for an Army colonel at the Joint Security Office. I quickly discovered I had developed a phobia against Army colonels. It is a good thing that my direct supervisor was an Air Force colonel; his boss was the Army colonel. At least I had an intermediary, supportive supervisor. In fact, my direct supervisor had been the officer in charge (OIC) of the Ground Combat Skills Level IV training course that I took en route to my assignment in Sicily back in 1989. We already knew and respected each other. He proved to be a great supporter over the next year while I struggled with my mental issues.

\* \* \* \* \*

Just before 1300 I stopped for lunch in Castildelgado. So far I had covered eighteen clicks. My right foot really hurt, particularly at the base of the big toe and along the top of the foot behind the toes. The pain was significantly worse than any other day so far. I removed the laces from my right shoe and replaced it using a different pattern. Instead of crisscrossing the laces back and forth, I wove the laces through the holes straight up both sides until I got to the top holes where I crisscrossed them. Someone had shown us this trick at the end of our trek in 2013. The idea was to give the foot more space. I was pretty sure my foot was swelling, so this should help relieve the pressure.

I was now halfway through stage 10. My memory has always been best regarding "significant emotional events." Stage 10 was one of those memories. It was during this stage when both of my feet had hurt so bad that I had talked Mom and Ria into jumping ahead. I recognized each location where I had tried something new with my foot gear in an attempt to ease the pain. I had tried taking my shoes off and wearing my TiVo sandals but found them worse than shoes. I kept checking my feet to see if there was anything I could do with the Band-Aids and the Compeed to ease the pressure. Nothing had helped.

Considering the right foot was the only one that was giving me a major problem today, I counted my blessings. Trying to think positively, I told myself that pain was weakness leaving my body. Maybe if I told myself that enough times, I would believe it.

IOT give my feet a little more time to rest, I opened my service study to day 9. The premise of today's study was that when Jesus said "follow me," He meant that we were to believe in Him and imitate His life and the lives of strong Christians. Conversely, we must not forget that other Christians may be watching and using us as an example to shape their own lives in service to Christ. We want to ensure that our life is worthy of that imitation. The following verses were used to substantiate the lesson: Phil. 3:17; 1 Cor. 11:1; 2 Tim. 1:13–14; Phil. 4.9; and 1 Thes. 1:6.[15]

\* \* \* \* \*

Back on the trail, my mind wondered to another toxic boss I worked for in Iraq in 2011. This time the problem had nothing to do with my gender or branch of service. He was an equal-opportunity abuser!

By early 2011, I was working at the Pentagon and had managed to improve my mental state significantly. I felt capable of handling another deployment and had a deep desire to do so. Part of my struggles since Afghanistan were because I felt I had failed by becoming so stressed out and emotional by the end of the tour. The tension

---

[15] Fryar, p. 20–21.

and investigations left a cloud hanging over the whole tour. Since I was feeling better, it became important to go on another deployment to prove to myself that I was capable of successfully completing a deployment and serving my country with honor.

I told my boss that I felt ready to go. A week later I got an e-mail informing me I had been selected for a 365-day tour in Baghdad. I was shocked. Even though I had told him that I thought I was ready, he had not mentioned there was a pending O-6 (colonel) tasking. Besides, a year in Baghdad was not exactly what I had in mind. A standard four-month AF deployment in a less hostile place would have met my purpose just fine.

I had seven days to turn down the orders and request retirement instead, but my retirement date would have to be no later than 1 June of that year. This was not a viable option because I could not retire as a colonel until I had the rank on for three years. June was the two-and-a-half-year point. If I retired then, my rank would revert to lieutenant colonel. I had worked too hard and too long to let that happen.

I prayed to God for guidance, but as normal, I could not discern His response. God did not burn a brush in front of me and talk to me through it. It is much easier to follow His will when you are absolutely sure of what He is telling you to do! So I sided with my ego, and not wanting to lose my colonel's rank, I accepted the deployment.

My position was chief of staff (CoS) for the Iraqi Training and Advising Mission to the Ministry of Interior (ITAM-MoI) at Joint Security Station (JSS) Shield. Our mission was to advise the Iraqi police generals and assist them in developing the capacity of their national headquarters. As CoS, I was second in charge of the unit. My boss was a civilian Department of the Army senior executive service 2 (SES-2). SESes are civilians employed by either a military service or the DoD. Their rank is equivalent to general officers. The two meant my boss was equivalent to a two-star general.

I had a bad feeling about him from the moment we met. I flew into the primary US base in Baghdad, Camp Victory, and spent a couple hours with our logistics section who arranged for our supplies to be transported to JSS Shield. My new boss was there meeting with the Operation NEW DAWN general staff who were working out of one of Saddam Hussein's palaces. It had been arranged for me to fly to Shield with him in a helicopter.

View from a helicopter over Baghdad, Iraq, 2011.

Our logistics troops delivered me to the landing zone (LZ) about fifteen minutes before the scheduled departure. As the boss's vehicle pulled up, the helicopters started their engines and the crew indicated they were ready to load us. Weighted down by my helmet and IBA, with my M9 pistol strapped to my leg, M4 rifle slung over my shoulder, and a web belt loaded with equipment and ammunition—I walked over to him as the logistics troops loaded my bags into the helicopter. I introduced myself, and he basically just grunted and headed for the helicopter. He barely even looked at me. I wasn't quite sure what to make of it, but it was not a positive sign. I hoped he was just in a hurry and had a lot on his mind. Otherwise, this was going to be a very long year.

Upon arrival at Shield, the AF Security Forces colonel I was replacing picked me up at the LZ and took me to the small containerized housing unit (CHU) I would call home. CHUs were basically trailers that could be transported by semitrucks or cargo aircraft. Obviously, I had moved up in the world since pinning on colonel. When I was in Afghanistan as a lieutenant colonel, I had no indoor plumbing. For all personal hygiene activities, we had to walk across the compound to the shower and bathroom trailers—or, in the case of Gardez, the small primitive room inside the mud walls of the Qalat that the PRT operated out of. In Iraq I had a "wet" CHU. At the front of the trailer there was a desk and refrigerator and then a closet and bed with a tiny bathroom and shower at the far end. I guess the trailer was about fifteen to eighteen feet long and six feet wide, but size didn't matter. In a combat zone, having a sink and shower in my living quarters was practically equivalent to being in heaven.

After dropping my bags in the CHU, we went to my new office and started discussing the unit and my duties. We talked for a while and then went to the boss's office for an introductory meeting. It was my perception during this meeting that my predecessor was basically a "whipped puppy." His demeanor was very submissive, and he pretty much just agreed with everything the boss said when they discussed current issues. I did not detect any independent thought or reasoning. I found this interesting. It was atypical for an SF colonel. They are normally strong and confident in discussing their viewpoints and providing recommendations to the chain of command. Previously, I had replaced the same officer at Soto Cano Air Base, Honduras, in 2002. He definitely projected himself in a much stronger manner there. Something was obviously wrong here. I did find a ray of hope in that the boss was slightly more friendly during this meeting.

Over the next few months, I had to deal with a very negative command environment established by the boss's attitude. He made it clear that he was the center of the mission, and what he was doing and his priorities took precedence over everything and everyone else. For instance, myself and one of our division chiefs had the conference room reserved for one of our weekly meetings via video teleconference. Just prior to the start of the meeting, the boss came in and said he needed the conference room to meet with two individuals who had stopped by to talk. I explained that we needed the video teleconference equipment and it would be hard to arrange for the use of another room with the meeting starting in just a few minutes. His reply was very directive and harsh: "This mission is about what I am doing. That is all that matters. You will just have to figure something out."

He and his guests could easily have met in his office, allowing the staff to use the video teleconference equipment. I hid my frustration as much as I could, and we set out to search for another place, hoping we would be able to join the meeting before it ended.

On another occasion, five or six of us went to the Green Zone for various meetings along with the boss's security detail who provided security for the convoy. We arranged to meet at the front of the main building at a certain time to convoy back to Shield. I finished my meetings and coordination early, so I enjoyed a mocha from the Green Bean Coffee shop just inside the building entrance. About ten minutes before the established time, the boss arrived and told us to load up because we were leaving. The problem was one of the captains had not yet arrived. I pointed this out, noting that we still had about ten minutes before the established time. Most leaders I knew would have waited for the captain, at least until the established convoy time. The boss said that he was ready and we were going now. The captain would just have to figure out how to get himself back to Shield. Considering this required either another convoy through Baghdad or a helicopter mission, there was no telling how long it would take him to find a way back. You don't just generate a convoy or helicopter mission to transport a young captain who missed his ride.

The next day I was talking to a member of the boss's personal security detail, and the subject came up. The security contractor was obviously as frustrated as I was with the boss's decision. He said this type of thing happened all the time. He was sure that sooner or later somebody would be killed because of the boss's self-centeredness. In his opinion, the boss was not at all concerned about the well-being of his security detail or members of his unit. He mentioned a few other examples of the boss putting others' lives at risk.

Our discussion prompted me to seek out the Navy O-6 (captain) who had the additional duty of Inspector General (IG) for JSS Shield. He enlightened me of other issues involving the boss. The CoS before my predecessor had been relieved of duty because she had a nervous breakdown caused by the stress of working with him. She had submitted an official IG complaint about his inappropriate conduct, which was still pending with no action taken nine months later. He explained the boss was a West Point graduate who had been forced to retire from active duty as a LTC because he was passed over for promotion to colonel. He was incredibly bitter about this but somehow had managed to get hired as an SES. In his mind he was an Army major general, even if he wore a suit instead of a uniform.

Since the Navy captain was the senior naval officer on Shield, he was particularly concerned about the Navy lieutenant that worked as the boss's aide-de-camp. The boss had taken him from the slot the Navy had deployed him to fill and drafted him unwillingly, and against Navy wishes, to be the aide. The boss was constantly on his back, cussing at him, pressuring him to do things that were not appropriate, etc. The lieutenant was getting more and more stressed out, and the captain was seeking help from the Navy to force the boss to return the lieutenant to the position that he was deployed to fill. So far, there had been no progress on this.

As time went on, more problems came to light. Even though he had a wife back in the States, he was overly friendly with a civilian lady he had hired to be his public affairs officer and to advise the Iraqi generals on public affairs issues. (He created the unneeded position specifically for her and skipped the required official DoD hiring protocols—no job advertisement, no résumé review, no interviews.) He was frequently with her during the day, and they always spent several hours together in the evening in one of their offices or CHUs.

This last part was frustrating to me because I could not go to bed until he approved the day's situation report (SITREP). I was often done with it between 1800 and 2000 but would have to wait until 2300 to get his okay and/or guidance because he was socializing with his girlfriend. It should be noted that adultery is illegal in the military and men and women being alone together in the housing units was strictly forbidden by General Order 1 (GO1).

He was also known to order helicopter missions to transport himself and the lady when he actually had no purpose in going. Rather, she would want to work on a project (which was often not in her job description, nor associated with any guidance from above), and he would order a helicopter mission to take the two of them even though he had no role. There was a high demand for the limited number of helicopters, so they were normally allocated for high-priority operations and VIP transport. He used his rank to get the helicopter missions approved. The deception was blatantly obvious on one mission. When they got to the destination, he did not even get out of the helicopter. She left for a while, and when she returned, he instructed the pilots to RTB.

The biggest headache for me was that she wore his rank and went around nastily ordering people to do things, saying that the boss was supportive. She was extremely abrasive and directive when she had no authority to give orders to people who did not work for her. I was the one the troops complained to and had to find ways to ease the tension.

As mentioned, the boss was an equal-opportunity abuser. There was an Army LTC who worked for the boss stationed at a geographically separated location with the Kurdish leadership in the northern part of Iraq. It was quite apparent that the boss did not like him. The boss was constantly undermining his authority by coordinating with Kurdish officials without the involvement of the LTC whose duty description made him responsible for the coordination. Based on comments the boss made to me, it was obvious he was looking for any opportunity he could find to fire him, which of course meant ruining his career.

By the time I had been there for a little over two months, I had enough data and submitted an IG complaint outlining all the boss's inappropriate and illegal activities. Within days, the Navy LT aide and the Army LTC in Kurdistan independently submitted their own IG complaints. That made four open IG complaints against him.

It seemed that my primary function in the unit was to run interference and protect unit personnel from the boss's abusive demeanor. I also endured him publicly chewing me out and harshly opposing my inputs during staff meetings. The members of the unit were shocked that he would rebuke his second-in-command in front of them. Most people surmised that he felt threatened by me because I had been a PRT commander and, therefore, had experience advising government officials. Added to this, the division chiefs often came to me for advice. He felt that they should go to him because he knew all. What he didn't seem to realize is that the staff did whatever they could to avoid talking to him (or maybe he did realize it, and that was why he was so angry).

One day the Navy captain told me he was simply amazed at how professional and calm I remained each time the boss undermined my authority and chewed me out in front of our subordinates. What was not apparent to him at the time was that the abuse was wearing me down and my stress and anxiety levels were peeking. Inside, my mental stability was approaching where it had been when I returned from Afghanistan in 2007. I was just hiding it fairly well.

It all came to a head one day when there was an IED attack against State Department personnel who were conducting advising duties at the national prison adjacent to our base. The blast shook the whole base. SOP during such incidents was to conduct accountability of all personnel to determine who was involved and the impact of the event. The aide implemented the procedures, and after about fifteen minutes, I went to his office and asked how it was going. He said that everyone was accounted for except the boss's girlfriend. He had called her office and sent e-mails, but she had not responded to either. The boss was not in his office, and the aide did not know where he was. Knowing that no one wanted to go look for the girlfriend because of her abusive attitude, I told him that I would go check her office personally.

She opened the door when I knocked, and I immediately noticed the boss sitting in a chair behind her. With as much cheer as I could muster, I stated that I just wanted to see if she was okay, and since she was, I would be on my way.

Surprisingly, the boss became very angry, stomped to the door, and harshly exclaimed, "My aide is doing accountability. It's not your job. Go back to your office, and mind your own business."

Anger welled up in me. Fighting to hide it, I simply replied, "Yes, sir," and closed the door while turning to leave.

His hand flew out and pushed the door back open, exclaiming, "Don't you dare slam the door on me!"

Startled, I whirled around to look at him.

"Go to your office," he angrily continued! "We are going to discuss this."

Once in my office, I sat down and just glared at him.

"That was purely insubordinate," he said, clearly irate. "If you want to go home, well, I can make that happen. You are fired. Pack your stuff, and get off my base before the end of the day."

I just glared at him, trying my best to check my emotions in until he left.

After three months of dealing with his abusive actions toward me and trying to protect the unit from him, I had reached my limit. This was the final straw that broke the camel's back. I had a private breakdown for a few minutes and then worked hard to pull myself together. Once at an acceptable level of composure, I walked across the base to the office of the Army one-star general that commanded the base and the police advisory unit that worked with the lower levels of the Iraqi National Police. He was not in my chain of command, but he was the base commander and the only one I could think of to talk to. He had always been kind and very supportive when we had talked in the past. He was already aware of the IG complaints and some of the inappropriate activities that my boss was engaged in. As hard as I tried, I was unable to hold back the tears as I related what happened. Military colonels do not cry, but I had once again been pushed past my emotional limit and was unable to stop the flow of tears.

After I finished the story and regained some control, the general advised me to go to the medical clinic while he called the three-star commanding general (CG) who was both his and my boss's supervisor.

The doc and I had talked previously about how mine and the unit's interaction with the boss was causing me extreme stress. The last time I had seen her about my stress battle, the boss's aide had come in physically sick. He was violently throwing up and was very weak. The doc assessed it was a physical reaction to the stress. As the aide, he had to be near the boss for twelve to fifteen hours a day. As much as he harassed me, at least I could escape to my office. For the LT, there was no escape.

After I was at the clinic for about a half hour, the general's CoS and the other O-6 on the general's staff came to visit. The three of us had become friends, and they were there to show their support. They were well aware of my boss's activities and had been the recipients of his wrath many times themselves. We talked and even joked a little for a while. My heart rate started to come down, and my attitude improved little by little.

Eventually the general called us all to his office. He told me that the CG had said my boss had no authority to fire an O-6 and kick her off the base.

"He said you are to remain here until he reviews the situation and decides what to do. The CG is on the phone with your boss right now, telling him as much. For now, steer clear of him."

It was obvious to all that I would not be able to work with the boss anymore.

"I have been ordered to take your weapon and ammunition for the time being."

"I understand," I said, my eyes staring at the floor. "It is SOP in my career field in circumstances such as this."

I could not help but reflect back to May 2006 in Afghanistan when the Army O-6 had chewed me out for taking weapons from the two irate soldiers, insisting that it was inappropriate to take a soldier's weapon away from him in a combat zone. Now an Army three-star was ordering an Army one-star to take my weapon because of my emotional state even though we were in the heart of Baghdad.

After a few days, the CG decided to bring me to the Green Zone. He said he would have his deputy work with me to find a position where I could work and complete my deployment. However, before assuming a new position, he wanted me to go to Camp Victory for a mental health evaluation at the American hospital there. The outcome of that assessment was that I was having a "normal reaction to an abnormal situation." The doctor told the CG that I should not go back to my previous job, but I would be just fine working in a more positive environment.

The boss was allowed to continue performing his duties during the investigation, which dragged on seemly endlessly, so much so that he completed his deployment at Shield and returned to the Pentagon.

The IG notified me a year later, while I was on terminal leave, they had finally completed the investigations and all our allegations were substantiated. However, by this time the boss had transferred to an SES position in another federal agency. They forwarded the report, but the other agency had no obligation to do anything with it. Three years later, as I walked the Camino, the boss's name still appeared in his prominent job on the agency's website.

Still, there was a silver lining around the situation: ultimately it led to my forward deployment to augment a Joint Special Ops Task Force at Camp Lemonnier in Djibouti. This would turn out to be a very positive, rewarding assignment where I worked with some of the most dedicated and professional members of the US Armed Forces. I cannot fathom a better position to take me to my intended retirement date. If I had not been removed from my ITAM duties, I would not have been able to apply for this incredible position!

* * * * *

As I approached Belorado, my right foot could not be happier that today's trek was almost over.

The first building I reached on the edge of town was the albergue where we stayed in 2013. When we had arrived, my feet hurt so bad that I did not think I could take another step. Fortunately, this was the hostel that Ria had shipped her pack to. What a relief. I didn't even unpack when we got to our room. I just lay down and put my feet up in the air. Both were throbbing so hard I thought the pressure might break the skin. Later that evening we made the decision to skip ahead.

In defiance, I merely paused to take a picture in remembrance and then proceeded toward the heart of town with the goal of making it to the last albergue. This was my way of conquering the weakness I had allowed to control my attitude that evening. By passing by this point, I was telling the Camino I was not going to let it defeat me this time!

After cleaning up and turning my laundry in, I went to the dining area to relax. A lady was reading a book at the table next to mine.

I struck up a conversation. To my surprise, she was a civilian who worked for the AF at the headquarters of Air Mobility Command. With this common basis, we became immediate friends and had a great discussion about our careers.

After dinner I returned to my bunk and finished the night by reading chapters 4 through 7 of *Seeking Allah, Finding Jesus*. In these chapters, the author described how he was raised and educated in the Islamic faith. Practice of the faith, memorization of Koran verses, and learning about Islamic history was a daily focus in his parents' household. His father was in the US Navy stationed in Scotland. Similar to Muslims living in America, they were a minority in Scotland. He described how important attending the mosque was during his childhood development. There they were a part of a like-minded community, something that was not possible where they lived near the Navy base.[16]

It struck me as interesting that Islamic instruction was so fundamental and basic to every daily activity. No wonder Muslims are so dedicated to their faith.

I as lay in bed, I reminded myself that the situations I reflected on earlier in the day were anomalies. I loved 90 percent of my career. I had wonderful leadership experiences and worked for many outstanding supervisors that I still consider friends. I was routinely rewarded for my dedication and achievements and given the opportunity to do incredible things that most people can only dream about or watch in the movies. I was a part of something bigger than myself for almost thirty years. Since I never married and did not have children, my career and who I was as an AF officer was almost my complete identity. For most of my career, I told people that I had no plans to get out because "I have no idea what I want to be when I grow up." I was a workaholic in a workaholic's paradise. This is why the transition to civilian life was so difficult. In a way, I lost my identity, and now I must figure out who I am.

---

[16] Qureshi, chapters 4–7.

People are people. Some are kind and focused on the team; others would stab their own mother in the back to get ahead. I'm sure there are great people, and there are jerks in every line of work. From what I hear, the corporate world is a dog-eat-dog world with everybody scrambling over each other to move up the ladder. I doubt if I could have had any other career without occasional stressful situations and personality conflicts. Some things are just a part of life.

With these more positive thoughts, I drifted off to sleep.

# CHAPTER 14

## Belorado to Villafranca Montes de Oca, 12 Kilometers
## 8 Sep 2015
## D+10

Awaking to my phone alarm at 0700, I swung my legs around to the floor and stood up. An intense, stabbing pain erupted in the front portion of my right foot. Quickly transferring my weight to my left foot, I clenched my teeth to suppress a surprised scream so as not to wake up other pilgrims. Apparently, this was not going to be a good day on the Camino.

I limped through my morning routine, putting weight only on the heel of my right foot and avoiding the ball and toes as much as possible. The skinned area on the outside of the heel caused some pain and discomfort, but it was nothing compared to putting weight on the front part of the foot. Thankfully, when I put my shoes on, I noticed that the pain was reduced significantly; in fact it was now bearable. I did not understand what difference the shoes make, but I was very thankful.

As I limped out of Belorado, it occurred to me that this was virgin trail. Because both of my feet hurt so bad in 2013, I had decided to take the day off. Ria said she also needed a break. Several peregrinos had told us that stage 11 was challenging, so Mom wanted to conquer it. Ria and I decided to catch the bus to San Juan de Ortega at the end of the stage. We would meet Mom there. As it turned out, the bus only ran along highway N–120, so we could only go as far as Villafranca Montes de Oca. We took a taxi from there. Since today's trek would cover this skipped section, I guess there was some poetic justice in needing to both conquer the pain and cover the territory today.

My mission objective for the day was to cover the entire 24.2 km we had skipped in 2013. However, it soon became apparent that I would have to fall back on a saying inscribed on a statue on the USAFA's terrazzo: "Flexibility is the key to Air Power." Today pain was going to win the battle against my determination. I decided it would be best to accept my physical limitations and take it slow in hopes of allowing my foot to heal somewhat. My focus needed to be on winning the war—i.e., the ultimate objective, Santiago. Arrival was all that mattered; timing meant nothing.

As I hobbled along, countless people of all ages passed by. Grimacing in pain with every step, I found this very humbling. During the first week of this trek, I was the one passing everyone else. The tables had certainly turned.

After about forty-five minutes, my friend Kay from New Zealand came up beside me and walked with me for about fifteen minutes. She was concerned about my limping, so I explained how my foot was feeling. I also mentioned that it was rather humiliating to have so many people pass me, especially all the older people.

By profession, she was a mental health therapist, and this part of her took over the conversation. She encouraged me to keep going and not give up.

"You can make it, and it doesn't matter how long it takes. All these other pilgrims are not dealing with the same physical conditions you are, so it really doesn't matter if you take longer than they do. They don't have arthritis in their feet, nor are they dealing with the impacts of the cold injuries. In fact, I am inspired by your determination to complete this hike and what you have accomplished so far in spite of your physical problems."

Uplifted by her speech, we agreed that stopping early today was likely my best CoA.

After 4.8 clicks, I stopped for coffee and a tortilla. While resting my aching foot, I studied the guidebook to determine what options were available for plan B. Villafranca Montes de Oca was about 7.2 km out. I decided that this would be a realistic goal.

Intellectually, I was sure that this was the best course of action. My ego, on the other hand, felt it was too soon for another break.

After all, I had only walked two days since my down day. I told my ego to knock it off. I needed to focus on the strategic objective.

The pain in my right foot dominated my thoughts, yet I managed to chuckle as I passed several fields of sunflowers. Pilgrims had made faces by pulling out carefully selected seeds. I found it quite hilarious.

I entered Villafranca about 1130. The first building I came to was a bar and pension. I decided to pass it by and check availability at the Albergue San Antón. The book said it was a private albergue attached to a hotel. While passing the bar, I took note of the sign in front advertising massages. Smiling at the prospect, I decided to come back and get one after I secured a bed for the night.

Even though it was before noon, San Antón was accepting pilgrims. They had numerous options for rooms at 5€, 8€, and 10€. I asked to see the 8€ and 10€ options. The 10€ option was in a room of single beds in cubicles with half privacy walls. Since I was so early and would be there for a while, I thought this would be a nice configuration. Most of the cubicles had lockers. I chose one with no locker in order to get a private electrical outlet to charge my iPad and iPhone. We must have priorities!

After completing my SOP, I hobbled back to the bar where I had seen the sign advertising massages. The therapist started at 1600. I signed up for the first half-hour slot. It looked like this was going to be a good day after all!

Back in my cubicle, I rolled my feet over my foot massager and then elevated my aching right foot on a pillow. It was now time to plan for tomorrow's mission. Just over twenty-four clicks, about halfway through stage 12, there was a village called Cardeñuela Riopico. It boasted three albergues and a casa rural. Plenty of options in case my foot made me go slow and I arrived late. Another good reason to make it that far tomorrow was that it would position me perfectly to pass through Burgos the following day and continue on to a small, quiet village on the other side.

I then turned to day 10 of my service study. Today's teaching emphasized the importance of reading your Bible and spending time with Christ each day. Only in this way can a believer grow in their relationship with Christ. One suggestion was to find a Bible reading plan online to follow. You can also choose a short book in the New Testament and read just a couple of verses a day and then spend time contemplating its meaning in general and for you in particular. Another effective method is to select one of the Bible's shorter books and read it from start to finish each day for a week or two, while setting aside time to think, pray, and write about what you discover. Whichever method, it was recommended that you write in a journal about what you've read each day, pray about it, develop a routine, and follow through.[17]

This is an area where I could certainly improve. I've never been disciplined enough to make the time for daily Bible study. Many of my Christian friends would likely say that this could be a reason I have trouble discerning God's will for my life.

I then pulled up *Seeking Allah, Finding Jesus* on my iPad and read chapters 8 and 9. The chapters continued to explain his childhood Islamic training and described many of the basic tenants of the faith as an introduction to Christians who were most likely to read the book.

Up until this point, I had the big room to myself. To my surprise, the first roommates to arrive were my three retired Navy friends. Since I had traveled such a short distance today, I figured that most of my friends would be far ahead and I had just seen these guys at lunch yesterday. They explained that they had only gone a few more kilometers after I saw them.

I offered my foot massager, and they gladly accepted. I also let them know that there was an electrical outlet in my cubicle if they

---

[17] Fryar, p. 22–23.

needed to use it. One of them produced a plug-in charging device that had multiple USB connections available so several devices could be recharged from one outlet. This was an outstanding device to have since just about everybody wanted to charge devices each evening. Bringing a device such as this is a good way to help out your fellow peregrinos while ensuring that you always had the opportunity to charge your own devices.

While I marveled at this innovation, Debbie, the lady I met last night who worked for the Air Force in Illinois, arrived along with two other women that I had met at breakfast this morning. We shared highlights from our day as everyone got settled. A common theme was the need to slow down and rest our tired bodies.

Even though where I had my massage appointment was only about two hundred meters away, I left about 1540 because I knew that it would be very slow going. My back really appreciated the massage, but the pain was excruciating when she massaged both feet, especially the balls and arches. The toe area was only slightly more bearable. As I endured the torture, I kept thinking about the T-shirt I had at the academy that read "No pain, No gain." In the end, my back definitely felt better, but I don't think my feet made much progress. There was just about as much pain going back to my albergue as there was coming down.

Debbie and another American were sitting at a patio table when I returned, so I ordered a drink and joined them. We discussed how cursing was a typical part of a military male's standard vocabulary.

"I liked to set the foundation and groundwork right away when I was in charge," I explained. "During the first meeting I had with the primary leaders on my team, I told them that how they talk was their concern, but that I did not want to hear a lot of cuss words when we were conversing."

I went on to describe how I handled a major from another section that we met with frequently while I was at CENTCOM headquarters.

"No matter what he was talking about, there were always several curse words in every sentence. After a while I got tired of this, and one day I looked him in the eyes and asked, 'Is it possible for you to say just one sentence, just one, without a curse word in it?' He looked a bit embarrassed, and after that he worked hard to limit the number he used when I was around and normally apologized for the ones that slipped out."

Debbie said she had had similar experiences and had also asked her coworkers to tone it down with quite a bit of success.

A waitress approached us and called our attention to a table closer to the main building where there was half of a drink, half a sandwich, and an open diary. A dog seemed very interested in the sandwich. The waitress asked if we knew who had been sitting there and if they were done. It was approaching the busy time of the evening, and she could use the table for somebody else. I walked over and found a name on the diary that I recognized. It belonged to the Californian woman that I had walked with the afternoon after waiting out the rainstorm over lunch. I told everyone that I had seen her sitting near the registration desk at the entrance to the main hotel where the Wi-Fi was the strongest.

Debbie's friend went inside, found her, and informed her of the waitress's concerns. When they both returned, Debbie and I were quite surprised to see that the lady from California was very upset. By this time, the dog had succeeded in eating the sandwich.

"I have no idea why you felt the need to interfere," the Californian said sharply as she glared at my new friend. "I don't know why you think it is your business, but no, I was not finished with my meal!"

Noticing that the dog had eaten the sandwich, the lady switched her attention to the waitress.

"I can't believe you let the dog eat my food! And what difference does it make to you if I am not finished at this table? I am a paying guest!"

She obviously failed to understand why the waitress was interested in clearing the table.

The waitress's English was pretty basic, but she's definitely understood the tone. The Californian took her drink and stormed back into the building.

Debbie's friend was visibly upset that she had been yelled at.

"Don't worry about her," Debbie tried to reassure her. "You did the right thing."

"I agree!" I weighed in. "She's the one with the problem."

Our encouragement seemed to help somewhat, but she said she was going to go back to her bed for a while. This was the first time that either Debbie or I had seen somebody get ugly with others on the Camino.

I joined the three Navy retirees for dinner in the hotel's fancy dining room. They were really enjoying conquering the Camino together.

It wasn't long before the discussion turned to my service in combat zones. They were particularly interested in the PRT experience and wanted to know what I thought of our "nation building" efforts.

"I was very motivated at first because I was convinced that reconstruction and development was the long-term solution to bringing stability to Afghanistan," I explained. "The idea was to give the people hope and work skills so that they could establish productive lives and earn a living to support their families. By doing this, the theory was the young men would not be motivated to join terrorist organizations. The people of Afghanistan are similar to people all around the world. They just want safety and security so that they can support their families in peace."

However, I qualified my comments by relaying my later concerns about how the projects and money that were flowing into the Afghan provinces and villages were not having the desired effect due to the culture of the country. Once again, I found myself relating my favorite stories about the irrigation canals, building a welfare state and culture of dependency, and examples of unintended consequences.

"The majority of Afghans may not have formal education, but they were far from stupid," I continued. "They knew how to work us." I then launched into another example to illustrate my point.

"By the time I arrived in 2006, a PRT had been operating in Paktya and Logar provinces for four years. They knew full well that the PRTs rotated in and out as complete teams and little institutional knowledge survived the transition. So if they did not get their way with one PRT, all they had to do was wait until the next team arrived and start their lobbying efforts again. They made a mistake by doing this too quickly with the arrival of my team. The outgoing PRT was still showing us the ropes when we went together to a ribbon-cutting ceremony at a medical clinic in Zurmot, one of the most unstable districts in Paktya. USAID had funded the construction of the clinic with the hope that a project in the area would help win support for the Afghan government and the coalition.

Lt. Col. Meck talks to Afghan leaders before the clinic ribbon cutting ceremony.

"During the ceremony, there were a lot of speeches, including the provincial governor, Governor Taniwal, the district commissioner, and several Afghans from the village. Shams, our USAID rep, spoke for the PRT. The outgoing commander and I sat up front and observed.

"As the Afghans spoke, an interpreter sat between me and my predecessor and quietly translated. They all thanked America for the funding and managing the project. However, they said that we really needed to better understand their culture because the project did not include a security wall and this was essential for any government building, especially one that treated women. The wall needed separate gates so males and females could enter and access their segregated portions of the building without ever seeing each other. Every Afghan speaker insisted that such a wall would need to be built before the clinic could be put into operation.

"I was really puzzled. If this was such a basic concept, how could the PRT have made such an error? Would this not have been a major topic of conversation during project planning? Countless clinics had been built around Afghanistan over the years. Wouldn't such a standard part of the culture be included in standard construction templates already in place for new teams to use so mistakes such as this would not happen?

"After the speeches, we toured the clinic and sat down to enjoy snacks and tea. Governor Taniwal made another speech, and then separate discussions broke out around the table. Both during those discussions and later as I made my way back to my vehicle, several Afghans requested I initiate a new project to build the security wall. A major point that had been pounded into our heads during pre-deployment training was that we should never make promises. So I took notes and told them I would consider their request.

"Once back in the office, I asked my predecessor what was going on with the wall. He chuckled and said that the Afghans were trying to manipulate me and take advantage of the fact that I had just arrived and did not know the history of the project. He said a major facet of their project planning was trying to ensure that the Afghans felt they had ownership of the project. This meant not only did our project need to be something they requested, but they also had to have some meat in the game. If they had ownership, they would ensure the security of the project during construction and later during operation. The standard way the team had ensured Afghan ownership was to make them responsible for 10 percent of the project. In the case of the clinic project, the agreed-upon 10 percent was the security wall. Since they knew that I most likely did not have that piece of background information, they hoped to convince me to do their part of the project. Their mistake was that they brought this up before my predecessor had left.

"To prevent such a situation in the future, we discussed that a better way to handle the 10 percent issue would be to make their part an integral part of the basic project. This way the project could not be completed without them doing their part."

Continuing to dominate the discussion, I explained how this incident highlighted another major problem that haunted the US efforts in Afghanistan throughout operations there. Because the Army was primarily in charge of this joint operation, unless a particular action was strictly one service-oriented, most things were done the Army way.

"You know how to spell *joint*, don't you?" I said to emphasize my point. "A-R-M-Y."

This triggered a chuckle from my Navy friends who obviously agreed with my assessment.

I then went on to explain that the Army insisted units "train as a team and deploy as a team." Hence, the entire new PRT came together at Fort Bragg and went through training as a team. The idea was that all the diverse personnel belonging to different services and different career fields would meld together as a unified team during training so when they got to into country, operations could commence seamlessly. This sounded very good except when you consider that all the institutional experiences and lessons learned through the school of hard knocks redeployed with the outgoing team.

"We had a ten-day changeover period that we called 'Right Seat, Left Seat.' During the first five days, the new team shadowed the old team. Roles were reversed the second five days. The new team took the lead on mission planning and execution, while the outgoing team observed and mentored as needed. A firehose of information was exchanged during this time. Simultaneously, the new team was trying to get settled in, and the outgoing team was packing up and preparing to depart. Each section was also doing equipment accountability and inventories. It was an extremely busy time, and in our case, 80 percent of the outgoing team actually departed the FOB as their replacements arrived. Only key personnel and team leaders remained for the changeover. This was necessary because there weren't enough beds for both teams.

"I estimate we retained about 10 percent of the information passed on. The majority of the background, cultural issues, perceptions of personalities of Afghans we would work with, policies and procedures, and lessons learned left with the outgoing team. We were basically starting from scratch and making things up as we went along, relearning through the school of hard knocks all the lessons the previous team had learned. This scenario was repeated constantly throughout the country and to some extent even adversely affected kinetic units.

"A couple years later, I had a discussion about this issue with the deputy commander at CENTCOM. I proposed a new rotation system for PRTs. Based on a one-year tour for PRT members, the vision was that 50 percent of each functional area on the PRT would rotate out every six months. The PRT commander and the XO would be offset so that one of them always had the institutional knowledge. My intent was to meet the Army halfway by ensuring at least half of the team trained together and deployed together. I felt that this was a good balance. The deputy was intrigued with the concept but pointed out that the 'train together, deploy together' procedure was being used by kinetic Army units all over the country, it was Army SOP.

"I took a deep breath and asked, 'So how's that working out for you?' I can't believe I actually said that to a two-star!

"To my surprise, he chuckled and said, 'Not so well.' He then signed off on the staff package and returned it to me for further processing."

By this time, we were almost the last ones remaining in the dining room. We decided it would be best to depart so the staff could finish cleaning up.

# CHAPTER 15

## Villafranca Montes de Oca to Cardeñuela Riopico, 24.1 Kilometers
## 9 Sep 2015
## D+11

I had removed the Compeed from my heels to let the skin dry out overnight. The rubbed areas and former blisters were looking fairly good today, but I applied new Compeed, anyway, to protect the areas from further damage. An ounce of prevention is worth a pound of cure, so "they" say. So far my antiblister techniques were working very effectively.

Many people, including last night's massage therapist, told me I needed to lighten my load. I was lightening it slightly each day by mixing my vitamin and mineral powder packets with a bottle of water. Each packet weighed a couple of ounces at least. Using my expendable toiletries also chipped away at the weight. For someone who has not done a long-distance trek with a pack, this may not seem like much. To a Camino peregrino, every ounce saved is sacred. Still, I needed to cut back more. I had gone through my pack several times but couldn't find any additional items I was willing to dispose of.

I decided to reduce the amount of weight that my feet and back had to carry by not filling the water bladder in my pack. Instead, I would carry a half-liter bottle of water in the cargo pocket of my hiking pants—left leg, of course. With all the villages and fountains with potable water along the way, there should be no problem running out if I just make sure to refill it each time I have a chance. This will easily save two to four pounds of weight. Maybe it would relieve some of the explosive pain I endured with each step.

I was limping down the trail by 0810, taking great care to put my weight on the heel of my right foot and not the ball. The Way went straight up a steep hill this morning, and by 0830, I was sweating and took my jacket off. My pace was a little better today. People were still passing me, but I was passing others from time to time. I kept telling myself it was okay if people passed. It is best not to push too hard yet, after all the foot is still swollen. Give it a break. The trek is a marathon, not a sprint.

This train of thought led me to think of a military phrase I heard many times during combat training and deployments: making a "tactical withdrawal." The phrase made *retreat* sound positive. Sometimes it was actually the best course of action to take in light of certain tactical situations IOT achieve strategic objectives. A similar comical term that describes this type of tactical move is "advancing to the rear."

The phrase "tactical withdrawal" could easily be modified to apply to my situation on the Camino in light of the half day that my aches and pains had forced me to take yesterday. Every day is like a battle within a much grander campaign. Some days we are victorious and make progress against the enemy. Other days it doesn't go in our favor and it's smarter to do a tactical withdrawal so you can regroup, resupply, rest, do some maintenance, and then try pressing forward again from a stronger situation. All with the end state in mind—winning the campaign! You don't have to win every day. Some days will go better than others. The key is keeping your mind on the end state and focusing on what needs to be done to achieve that goal.

Don't worry about the calendar; nothing says I have to do the thirty-three stages and thirty-three days. I can go slow. I can go fast. It doesn't matter. This is "my Camino"!

Who cares if people pass me? It is better they get on ahead, anyway, and then I can have some peace. As usual, I experienced anxiety when I heard people approach my six. I was weaving back and forth looking for the smoothest turf. So was everybody else, so they would get right up behind me before breaking out to go around—unnerving, to say the least. When I heard their poles clinking, the hair stood up on the back of my neck. If I slowed down or even stopped, it forced them to go around, and then life was good again.

Anyway, the moral of the story is to keep your eye on the end state. Sometimes that means you have to do a tactical withdrawal from a day's battle. In the end, you must win the war.

A little after 0900, I reached a monument to Spain's civil war. The Monumento de los Caídos is not only a monument to the war but marks the shallow mass grave site of a large group who were executed during the turmoil. Nearby there were several picnic tables in the shade of some trees. Even though it was still early, the shade was welcome because it was getting warm quickly this morning. I took the opportunity to remove my remaining snivel gear—i.e., gloves and pant legs—before embarking on the next 8.6 km to San Juan de Ortega and reflecting on training for my first overseas tour of duty.

\* \* \* \* \*

There could not have been a hotter time to attend Ground Combat Skills Level 4 training at Fort Dix, New Jersey, than August 1989. Yet I suspected it was much better than going in the winter when you would have to deal with the freezing temperatures during the field events.

A common saying at the academy with regard to interservice rivalries was that West Point had two hundred years of tradition unhampered by progress, and the Air Force Academy had twenty-nine years (at the time) of progress unhampered by tradition. It appeared the "real" Air Force was similar. For some reason, someone at the Air Staff had decided to change Air Base Ground Defense (ABGD) to Ground Combat Skills. I guess they felt that this title better described the course content, but even for those of us who had only been in the career field for two years, the change never clicked, and we continued to call it ABGD until separation.

Anyway, myself and a small group of company-grade security police officers spent a few hot, humid weeks learning and practicing the ABGD skills I had been introduced to during BCT. Several in the class were old friends, having been in my Security Police Basic Officers Course a couple years earlier. There was another young officer, Keith, who was heading to the same base I was, Comiso Air Station, Sicily. With a common future, Keith and I became quick and lasting friends.

This course developed us into officers of what I like to describe as the "Army of the Air Force." We learned everything from map and compass land navigation, to convoy operations, foot patrols, and perimeter defense. After studying the basics in the classroom environment, we took to the woods for hands-on practice.

We spent several days on weapons firing ranges. For most of us, this was our first opportunity to try our aim on the pop-up target ranges that are common throughout the Army, but rare in the Air Force. The silhouettes, shaped and painted like the upper half of an enemy soldier, popped up sporadically at distances ranging from fifty to five hundred meters. Each silhouette was only up for a few

A group of us all cammied up at Ground Combat Skills Level IV. I am the one on the right.

seconds. In that time the shooter needed to detect the threat, aim, and fire one or more shots. If the shot hit the target, it would immediately fall back down. If the target was missed, it would go down on its own after a few seconds. To be successful, the shooter needed to be observant, levelheaded, and careful to take enough time to aim and breathe effectively in order to hit the target in the short time that it presented itself. It did not take long for me to realize that my aim was really bad at five hundred meters. Since we were only allowed a limited number of rounds of ammunition, I decided to spend more effort and bullets on the closer targets. Tactically, this was sound, anyway. It is very hard to accurately identify targets over hundred meters away, and even if you do identify it as the enemy, it is very difficult to accurately engage it. Additionally, at that far out, the target was not likely an immediate threat to you or your team. It is always wise to engage the closest targets first and worry about the others after you eliminate the greatest threats. Overall my score was not so great, but I did manage to eliminate the majority of the fifty- to one-hundred-meter threats.

The land navigation course was memorable but not really "fun." We were split into small teams of three or four people, and each team started from a different point spread out about one hundred meters apart. We were provided azimuths and distances to a series of waypoints along a route to our ultimate objective point. If you were off by even a portion of a degree on the azimuth or your distance estimation, you could easily miss a waypoint or even find one meant for another team. If that happened, it would be nearly impossible to get back on track for your later points.

Only a small number of the teams actually arrived at their specific objective point. It was very hard to walk in a straight line over rugged terrain with a lot of underbrush and obstacles such as ponds, marshes, and dense vegetation. We had to learn how to dog-leg, or box, around these obstacles and somehow get back on the right trajectory on the other side.

Additionally, we discovered that a very frustrating type of vegetation flourished in the thick New Jersey underbrush. We called it wait-a-minute vines. They were hiding everywhere in the brush, and as you focused on staying on course, they would reach out and grab your boot, stopping your forward momentum as if they were saying "Whoa! Wait a minute. Where do you think you're going?"

I'm not sure how we got onto the topic, but one evening while we were preparing for a night training event, we started talking about my marital status. The guys came to a consensus that while I was at Comiso I would most likely find that special someone. I adamantly told them that I did not expect that to be the case. I had married the Air Force on 27 May 1987. Unbeknownst to me at the time, this would become a common topic throughout my career, and this became my standard response.

The grand finale was a several-days field training exercise (FTX). The scenario was that our class was a security flight assigned to one sector of the defensive perimeter around a dirt airfield near the front lines in a war against the Soviets (our anticipated enemy at the time). The mission of the airfield operation was to receive and unload C-130 aircraft tasked with resupplying Army forces operating in the area. The C-130 was a small cargo aircraft with four props that could land on short, rugged dirt runways, and therefore its primary mission was resupplying forces in remote forward areas. The job of the SPs was to provide security for the runway and the airman executing and supporting the operation.

The officers in my class rotated through the various roles the flight was responsible for, both enlisted and officer. For likely the only time in our careers, we actually dug and manned foxholes 24/7 (the lowest-ranking airmen always get this job), conducted reconnaissance patrols outside our perimeter, and set up sensory devices to detect enemy forces trying to sneak up on us. We also implemented the senior enlisted and officer duties by coordinating interlocking fields of fire on the perimeter with the sectors to our right and left, establishing hardline communication with our Sector Command Post (CP), manning the CP, providing supervision to the fire teams on the perimeter, and providing Command and Control from the CP in the event of an enemy attack.

Of course, we had the opportunity to fight off numerous attacks by the opposition forces (OPFOR) using blank ammunition and a laser system that could detect the accuracy of the fire. A laser emitter was attached to the end of our M-16 rifles and sited-in so the laser went where the rifle was aimed. The percussion from firing a blank round caused a laser beam to be emitted. Each individual had a harness with sensors on their body and more sensors attached to their helmet. The sensors would either indicate a near miss with a couple short beeps or a hit with a constant, irritating whine that the individual could not shut off without what we called a god key. The instructors strictly controlled the god keys so that individuals could not hide the fact that they had been hit. We each carried a card sealed in an envelope in our pockets. When our sensor system indicated a hit, the envelope was opened to find out if we were killed in action (KIA) or wounded in action (WIA). If wounded, the card would tell us what our wound was and give some specifics so that we and our teammates could practice self aid/ buddy care (SABC).

There was a lot of hard work, and because of the frequency of attacks and the need to provide security 24/7, we got very little sleep.

By the end we were all extremely dirty and very tired, but motivated and proud of our success.

I did very well on all the academic tests and even earned 100 percent on the Army physical fitness test (PFT) by exceeding the high end of the scoring range for all events, earning the coveted Army PFT patch—a rarity for an airman. I was especially proud of this because not only did I exceed the standards for females, but I also exceeded the maximum standards for men. This was important to me because I did not feel that there should be different standards for men and women. I believed that in combat situations, women needed to perform to the same standard as men, and therefore such things as PFTs should have the same standards. My objective was to prove to my male counterparts that I could succeed by achieving the same standards that they were measured by.

I did not feel that I was as successful in the field events as in academics and PT. It was my assessment that I was in the middle of the pack. I held my own but did not feel that I stood out from the crowd. So it was a complete surprise to me when I was recognized as the overall distinguished graduate (DG) during the graduation ceremony. This was a great honor for me since it was fairly early in the era of women being allowed in such roles as leading defense forces protecting forward-operating bases.

\* \* \* \* \*

I arrived in San Jaun de Ortega about 1115. It was a tiny village marking the end of stage 11 with a population of about twenty people. There was an albergue, a bar/restaurant, a casa rural, and of course, a small, old, yet elaborate village church. In 2013 we had stayed here and made many memories—most outstanding but one in particular was not so good.

\* \* \* \* \*

Ortega was our destination the day that Ria and I took the bus and taxi while Mom walked stage 11. We arrived before 11 and had to wait in the restaurant until the albergue was ready to accept new peregrinos for the night. We ordered lunch and met a young couple from Israel. They were spending their honeymoon walking the Camino.

Once the doors of the albergue opened, we registered ourselves and Mom. Normally they don't let you register someone who is not physically there; however we had her pilgrim's credential and had retrieved her pack, which she had decided to ship ahead that day, so they made an exception. After making our beds, Ria decided to walk down the trail in the hopes of meeting up with Mom and walking into town with her.

On my way out of the shower, I slipped on the wet floor and hit my head fairly hard against the wall. I was rather dazed for several minutes. Fortunately, there was a nurse nearby. She checked me for signs of a concussion, which didn't appear to be present, but she found a nice bump forming on the back of my head. She said that was a good thing because if it didn't swell out, it would probably swell inward. She cautioned me to take it easy the rest of the day and ship my pack tomorrow. No strenuous or quick movements and as much rest as possible. I decided to take a nap.

Around 1400 Mom and Ria arrived and told me that Mom had seen the couple from Seattle and their Dutch sidekick, Roy, several times during the day and they had asked about Ria and I. Fred and Susie were enjoying a drink at the bar and wanted us to join them. Roy had fallen back some, and Fred and Susie were waiting for him to arrive to decide if they were going to stay there or move on.

Once Roy arrived, they discussed the situation and decided to stay with us. It turned out that it was Roy's birthday. We agreed to meet later for dinner to celebrate. Since it was such a festive event, we decided to dress up. Accordingly, before heading down for dinner, we zipped the legs onto our hiking pants.

\* \* \* \* \*

After lunch I commenced stage 12, once again traveling on conquered trail. After Ria and I had taken stage 11 off, we decided to walk stage 12 to Burgos before taking the train to Leon from there. Both for the sake of my feet and the bump on my head, I had taken the nurse's advice and shipped my pack that day. Today I carried my pack.

As I walked, I noticed that the intensity of the pain in my right foot varied significantly. On a scale of 1 to 10, there were times when the pain was a three or four, and other times it peaked around eight. I started wondering if, during the times when it did not hurt too much, maybe my nerves were just numb so I could not feel it as much?

Historic café in Agés.

I arrived at the next village, Agés, about 1300. My plan was to pass right through, but I saw the café we'd eaten breakfast at in 2013. It looked like it was straight out of the mid 1800s, outstanding atmosphere and lots of character. For old times' sake, I stopped for OJ and decided to do the day's service study. The restaurant in Ortega had been very crowded and noisy. Not the best place to do the study. This café was relatively quiet and peaceful. Much better.

Day 11 emphasized the importance of praying for those we serve, referencing Colossians 1:9–12, in which Paul talks about praying that those he is serving develop a close, personal relationship with Christ and that their faith would produce fruitful service to others.[18] This was a concept that had never occurred to me. I would have to try to remember it!

After the study, I topped off my water bottle and set out once again. A couple blocks later, I came upon Debbie from Scott AFB. She was at the intersection studying her guidebook and the street signs. It appeared she was trying to find an albergue. After exchang-

---

[18] Fryar, p. 24–25.

ing greetings, she explained she planned to stay here, but she first needed to find an ATM as she was out of euros.

I pointed out that the chances of there being an ATM in a village this small were next to nil. There would be plenty in Burgos, but finding one before that was highly unlikely. I sold her about $40 worthwhile explaining I was planning to go on another 9 km before stopping. There was a small village that had several lodging options that sounded inviting. She decided to join me, and we continued on together, talking the whole way. She explained she was generally a slow walker, so she did not mind matching my limping pace.

We stopped to check out an ancient, yet still functioning, Roman well about 2 km from Cardeñuela Riopico and then arrived about 1530. There were no lower beds remaining in the big bunk room, so we opted for a slightly more expensive room with only six beds in it. I took the lower bunk closest to the bathroom in anticipation of another night of very painful walks to the restroom; the closer I was, the better.

After getting settled, we purchased a bottle of wine to share and found a table in front of the albergue in the cool shade of a couple trees. We were soon joined by the couple from Austria and then numerous other familiar faces. The incredible communal dinner served family style was attended by approximately thirty peregrinos. The atmosphere was festive, and we all had a great time socializing and exchanging stories about our Camino experiences and aches and pains with those sitting near us.

Communal peregrino dinner.

A perfect textbook Camino evening!

# CHAPTER 16

## Cardeñuela Riopico to Tardajos, 25.7 Kilometers
## 10 Sep 2015
## D+12

What a special treat to have only two of us taking turns in our private bathroom this morning! Similarly, we were blessed with the ability to decide between us what time we would get up and to have the somewhat rare privilege of light while preparing our feet and packs for the day's hike. It is funny how you learn to really appreciate basic activities such as turning on the light in the morning.

Debbie and I decided to start our trek together. We had shared drinks and dinner with a friend of Debbie's from Sweden last night, and we ran into her again while having our basic European continental breakfast and coffee from the vending machine in the dining building. She decided to join us, and the three of us were on our way toward Burgos by 0820.

The dismal state of my right foot was the primary topic of conversation throughout the morning. As usual, I had to get up several times during the night. Each time my foot touched the ground, it exploded in excruciating pain. I decided to count myself as blessed that, at least for the time being, only my right foot was affected, enabling me to hop to the restroom. Everyone agreed it was quite odd that my foot hurt so much less with my shoe on. We theorized that the compression may have something to do with it, but in reality none of us had a clue.

As we approached Burgos, there were three options. One went to the right around the airport and passed by the train station, following the N-1 highway all the way into the center of town. The second option went to the left of the airport on an isolated dirt road, but then followed the N-120 highway into Burgos. Our selection was to take the third, scenic route across the N-120 and through a long park that followed the Rio Arlanzón. Pilgrims not wanting to stop in Burgos at all could follow this "green" river trail all the way to the far side of town where it intersected once again with the primary route. We could hear the traffic in the distance from the N-120, but it was far more peaceful and scenic than the other two routes.

While in the park, a couple on horseback passed us. They wore small daypacks with Camino shells attached. Additional gear was stored in saddle packs. We all knew that traveling by horseback was one of the three options for completing the Camino, but this was the first time any of us had seen peregrinos riding horses.

Just before the entrance to old town, we crossed a bridge and entered the hustle and bustle of Burgos. Our first order of business was to find an ATM for Debbie. I also seized the opportunity since it would be some time before we came to another big city. Resupplied with euros, we then sought out a restaurant to have lunch and discuss the rest of the day.

Both of my friends were eager to tour the sites of Burgos and planned to stay for the night and maybe even through the following day. Per SOP, I had no intention of staying in Burgos. However, we had not toured the inside of the extravagant cathedral last time, and I wanted to visit before heading another 10 km out the other side of town. I gave my friends a heads-up that they needed to be sure to bring their pilgrim's credential for a significant discount from the cathedral entrance fee. Of course, they would also want the cathedral stamp!

Once done with lunch, we parted ways, and I made a beeline for the cathedral. Along the way I observed a long line outside the main albergue waiting for the doors to open. There must have been a couple hundred people stretching out for about a block. Our lunch waiter had mentioned there was a big bicycling competition going on.

Nope, not even going to think about staying here! The sight almost made me want to run out of the city as fast as possible. I just might have done it if only my foot didn't hurt so bad.

I spent about a half hour gawking at the elaborate decorations and tributes to the Christian faith inside the cathedral. The immense structure was laid out in the standard cross shape typical of most historic European churches. Besides the main altar in the top section of the cross, there were numerous small chapels in side rooms, each one adorned in gold-coated structures holding elaborate statues representing the founders of the faith and depicting various important events. Numerous crypts along the walls held the entombed remains of church leaders that spanned centuries.

After retrieving my pack from the locker at the entrance to the cathedral, I started following the familiar Camino trail markers, pausing for a few moments as I passed the restaurant where we had an ad hoc "going-away dinner" with our Camino friends in 2013. The three of us were jumping forward, and a couple from Ohio was returning to America. They were both young and had jobs that only allowed them a little more than two weeks off at a time. They had completed one-third this year and planned to come back the next two years in order to complete the rest. It occurred to me that if they had followed through with their plan, they could be back on the trail, completing the final leg of their journey.

As I left the popular and crowded town square where the cathedral was, I was overwhelmed with a feeling of accomplishment and avid determination as I realized that I was now embarking on the twelve stages we had covered by train. Skipping these stages had bugged me for two years and were the reason I felt compelled to return to the Camino.

I stopped at a farmacia and explained as best as I could the problem I was having with my foot. I even took my shoe and sock off to show the pharmacist how it was swollen. She recommended an anti-inflammatory cream. I purchased the extra-strength version.

As I approached the far side of town, I entered a beautiful tree-lined path through a garden area. I immediately recognized it as the path from the movie *The Way* where the Gypsy boy was forced by his father to carry Tom's pack to the edge of town as punishment for stealing it the  previous day. This was a very memorable part of the movie and a location we had missed in 2013.

I guess my "when I was here two years ago . . ." stories will have to stop for a couple weeks! Everything will be new for the next twelve stages.

Since most peregrinos were staying to tour Burgos, there were only a couple of us on the trail heading out of town on this warm and sunny afternoon. One I encountered was searching for a place to stay at the edge of town. Another had arrived in Burgos from America that morning and was just starting her Camino. She planned to go to the same village I was heading to for the evening. We talked for a few minutes and then each settled into our own pace, often playing leap-frog as one of us decided to stop and rest, look at the guidebook, or check something out; of course, I stopped a few times to tighten my shoelaces. My mind quickly settled into an afternoon of reflection.

\* \* \* \* \*

The Air Force scheduled Keith and me to fly to Sicily in September 1989 on a military-chartered airline flight. This was a welcome relief. When I was first told that we would be flying over on a "military flight," I automatically thought it was going to be in a jump seat of a cargo aircraft like the one that we had flown on from Alaska to Japan and Korea during Operation Air Force between my third and second class years at the academy. This was not like that at all. It was my first exposure to what service members affectionately call the Freedom Flight—a normal airliner with regular seats and stewardesses, just like any civilian would fly on internationally. The only difference was that it was chartered by the military and filled with service members and their families moving to bases throughout Europe. As we dropped troops off at the various stops, others bordered who were rotating back stateside after completing their European tour or going home on their midtour leave. Keith and I got off at Naval Air Station Sigonella on Sicily. From there, the Air Force bussed our group of newcomers two to three hours to Comiso Air Station in the southeast section of the island.

Gazing intently out the window of the bus as we approached the front gate, I had an overwhelming feeling of "welcome to reality." The guard building at the entry control point (ECP) was made of thick cement that reminded me of a bunker. There was a double fence extending in each direction and, I assumed, circling the entire base. Loops of razor wire were affixed on top of both fences, and sensors could be seen monitoring the dead zone between. About one hundred feet inside the gate stood a two-story building with bullet holes and shrapnel chips that had never been fixed.

I gulped and wondered what I had gotten myself into.

As we traveled around to the back side of the historic Wing Headquarters, a modern base emerged. In fact, at the time, it was the newest base in the AF inventory. Family housing had not been completed, so it was an unaccompanied tour. In a way, this meant everyone was "single." Hence, the social aspects of our off-duty time were much different than at a regular base. Normally, married service members spend their off-duty time with their family. Here, there were no families. So everybody came together and formed close-knit groups. We spent our time together bowling, having barbecues, touring the island, playing cards, or just hanging out at the officers' club. This was the environment that was the foundation of exceptional friendships between comrades in arms.

Our in-processing briefings included information about the history of the base. It had been built just prior to World War II and had been a key Air Base where the German Luftwaffe had been stationed initially as part of their role in the Axis Alliance. On July 11, 1943, the Allies captured the base and then used it for Allied air operations for the remainder of the war. The battle damage on the side of the Wing Headquarters building remained as a tribute to the battle to capture the base.

After the war, the base was not used much. In 1981, the North Atlantic Treaty Organization (NATO) decided to use the base to house a combined (in military speak, *combined* refers to more than one country's forces being involved) US and Italian Ground Launched Cruise Missile (GLCM) unit as a critical element of our Cold War strategy in response to the Soviet Union's deployment of new intermediate-range missiles. Several other bases in Europe were also selected to house these critical missiles. Between war damage and the devastating effects of time, very little of the old base could be salvaged. The vast majority of it was demolished, and construction started anew.[19]

Although a central part of life in both the civilian and military communities today, GPS was an amazing technological jump forward at the time. We marveled at the fact that a missile could be launched from Sicily and hit a specific building in Moscow. The capability was threatening enough that the Soviet Union entered into disarmament negotiations. In December 1987, presidents Ronald Reagan and Mikhail Gorbachev signed the Intermediate-Ranged Nuclear Forces (INF) Treaty, agreeing to eliminate the entire class of weapon systems. When we arrived in 1989, four of the originally planned seven GLCM flights were operational. Activation of the other three had been canceled, and plans were being made to deactivate the four existing flights.

Many of the base's new homes would never have a family living in them.

At the end of a couple weeks of localized training with the 487th Missile Defense Squadron (487 MDS), Keith and I were taken to the off-base field training area where one of the flights was going through a six-day "dispersal" exercise. The squadron training officer stopped our vehicle on the side of a hill overlooking a dense wooded

---

[19] "Comiso Airport," Wikipedia, February 7, 2018, https://en.wikipedia.org/wiki/Comiso_Airport

valley. He said he wanted to show us something, so we dismounted. Looking downward, he asked us what we saw. Our eyes scanned the valley back and forth several times, but we could not see anything out of the ordinary. He chuckled and pointed to an area apparently thick with vegetation, stating that there was an entire missile flight hiding down there. Our eyes followed an imaginary line from his pointing finger into the valley and closely studied the area he indicated. Eventually we noticed that some of the vegetation lines seemed a little too smooth and straight. As we looked a little harder, we were able to make out some of the camouflage netting that hid the flight's large vehicles, tents, and personnel. We were simply amazed by how well the camouflage netting hid all the vehicles and people.

Once down in the valley, we entered the flight's area through the entry control point (ECP) to see firsthand how flights set up while they were dispersed in the field. Keith and I would be defense force commanders (DFC) for one of these flights (Keith for A flight and me for C), so we spent a significant amount of time touring the defensive perimeter to observe how the defensive fighting positions (DFPs, or more commonly known as foxholes) were positioned to ensure interlocking fields of fire and the placement of heavy weapons that ensured a ring of bullets could be sent downrange along a final denial line circling the flight. Most of the DFPs were manned by US Air Force Security Police, and some were manned by Italian paramilitary police called Carabinieri. Outside the DFPs were sensor fields that would detect enemy forces trying to sneak up on the perimeter. In a central location inside, we observed how the defense force's Tactical Operations Center (TOC) was set up and operated. The TOC was very similar to the Sector Command Posts we had trained in at Fort Dix. It had the same function and most of the same equipment. As DFCs, this was where we would execute our Command and Control duties.

The doctrine behind dispersing missile flights was to get the missiles away from known bases when tensions got too high and hide them around the island of Sicily. Packing up and moving the entire flight whenever the situation required was not a problem. These attributes made our weapons systems hard for Soviet GPS guided missiles to target in preemptive strikes. Being in charge of the defense of one of these dispersed missile flights was a dream job for a young security police officer during the Cold War. Basically on the front lines! I was honored to have been selected for the position.

My flight, Cobra Flight, did an exceptional job throughout the year I was there. The troops were highly motivated and skilled at their jobs. The Launch Control Centers (LCCs) and transporter erector launchers (TELs) were considered "critical vehicles" (CV), and the defense force's top priority was to protect them and the resources they carried from enemy attack. Protecting people was a secondary concern. During our first four field dispersals, Cobra Flight lost no CVs to enemy attack. This was an exceptional accomplishment for us. No other flight made it through even one dispersal without losing a CV. They had one disadvantage that did not apply when my flight was in the field. Flights who were not currently on dispersal provided volunteers to play the role of the OPFOR against the flight in training status. Several of my troops volunteered to be OPFOR for the other disposals and brought their skills and motivation with them. They frequently wiped out the exercising flight's CVs.

I joined my troops on OPFOR duties two or three times and loved it. Being on the defense had some advantages—such as, site selection; planning your defense to ensure there are no gaps in observation and fields of fire; layering the defenses so if the enemy penetrated one line of defense, they would quickly run into another and another after that; employing sensors to detect people approaching; and being familiar with the terrain. The OPFOR also had significant advantages. We could sleep whenever we needed to because we choose when and how to attack. We did not have to be vigilant 24-7 like the defenders did, waiting for an attack that they knew was coming but not knowing when or how. With just a little intelligence about the target's SOPs, we could observe and identify weaknesses and exploit them during our well-planned attacks. We knew where they were. We had a much smaller footprint, just four to five people. Finally we had flexibility. If things weren't going our way or the situation was not optimal, we could execute a tactical withdraw, regroup, and try again when conditions were more advantageous. The defenders had to defend whenever we attacked. No flexibility. They were almost completely in reaction mode.

It was surprising to me how easily our small team was able to routinely penetrate another flight's defenses and wreak havoc. Once past the DFPs, we found that moving around without trying to hide was to our advantage. When we were not trying to be stealthy in the darkness, the defenders would normally assume that we were members of their team. There were so many people at every layer of the camp that it was hard for anybody to know who was friendly and who was foe. Since there were only a handful of us, we could assume that most of the people that we encountered were our enemy. All we needed to do was to confuse them enough to get close enough to a CV to throw an explosive device at it.

It gave us a great feeling of exultation when we would get inside the perimeter and start drawing fire from the defenders. We could then withdraw and laugh as they continued to fire at each other in the confusion. On occasion, the firefight lasted thirty to forty minutes after we had departed the area.

Although I felt a great sense of accomplishment when we successfully incapacitated a flight, it also scared me to realize that our little group of OPFOR was not actually trained nor experienced in these types of offensive sabotage operations. If we could do this much damage, how much more could an elite unit of Soviet Spetznaz do?

As mentioned earlier, Cobra Flight was much better at defending our CVs than the other flights. I credit much of this success to the effectiveness of our Reconnaissance and Surveillance (R&S) team who patrolled the avenues of approach outside our sensor fields. The troops on our R&S team were generally the same ones who performed OPFOR duties against the other flights.

After successfully defending our CVs for four dispersals, we adopted the rally cry "Strive for Five" as we prepared for and executed Cobra flight's final dispersal exercise. Due to the implementation schedule of the INF treaty, Cobra and Delta flights were scheduled to be deactivated a few weeks after we returned from the field. That was also when I was scheduled to PCS to Germany. In fact, most of my flight was set to rotate out within a couple months. This was our last chance to work together, and we were very motivated to uphold our reputation. However, our past success, pride, and yes, a tad bit of arrogance, served as a rallying point for the other flights. Some of their best people volunteered to be the OPFOR, and their primary objective was to prevent us from achieving our goal of five dispersals without losing a CV. It was all-out war.

The first few days were successful as usual. Then one night all hell broke loose when the OPFOR managed to penetrate our perimeter and started wreaking havoc on the interior. I don't remember a lot about the attack because I had been working so hard that I had not slept in over three days. I was sitting in the Alternate Tactical Operations Center (ATOC), our backup control center for security operations, when the first *rat-a-tat-tat* of gunfire broke out. I tried to ascertain the situation from the reports coming in, but because of my exhaustion, I struggled to get a clear understanding and effectively order responsive action. Fortunately, one of my staff sergeants (SSgt) had set up an observation post (OP) on the top of the cab of one of our large cargo trucks. When the fighting broke out, he climbed into the OP with a set of NVGs and got a bird's-eye view of what was going on. From this strategic position that we had affectionately named the Eagle's Nest, the SSgt was able to pick up the slack for me and provide effective Command and Control to counter the OPFOR attack. Still, the OPFOR managed to get close enough to one of our CVs to throw a simulated explosive device that landed close to it. The observer/controllers (O/Cs) credited them with a CV kill.

As the report of the CV's destruction came over the radio, a stunned silence set in. Nobody said anything for about forty-five seconds. The time passed so slowly it felt like an eternity. How could this have happened to Cobra Flight?

Finally the silence was broken by the SSgt in the Eagle's Nest. He located the retreating OPFOR using his NVGs and guided our quick-response force (QRF) to intercept them and eliminate the threat. Still, the damage had been done. Our egos had been deflated.

The O/Cs had taken note of my lack of involvement in the response. Quickly assessing my state of exhaustion, they designated me as WIA, and I was "treated" by the aide and litter team and then taken to our camp's medical aid station. I slept for eight hours on a stretcher next to the ambulance truck. My wounds miraculously healed themselves, and I returned to duty after my nap, but the time and nap could not heal my bruised ego.

I had learned a valuable lesson that would follow me the rest of my career, even though I often forgot its importance and had to relearn it. If an officer does not take care of him or herself, he/she cannot effectively lead the troops, and this could get people killed and compromise the mission. An officer must be dedicated and work hard to accomplish the mission, but this focused effort must be balanced with the rest and proper self-care essential to maintaining a clear mind that can effectively process situational information and direct appropriate responses. An officer who cannot think straight is worthless to the unit.

We were able to shake off the shock of the loss of the CV by the next day, and the rest of the dispersal went fairly well. However, during the admin overnight before returning to base, we experienced a far worse shock: the death of a unit member.

By the end of a six-day dispersal FTX, everyone was exhausted, and it was not safe to drive a couple of hours back to the base. Therefore, after filling in the DFPs and breaking down all the defensive and operational equipment and packing it away for the trip home, we staged the convoy in a large open area for the night. The base's senior NCOs brought out grills, hamburgers, and hot links, and everybody enjoyed a barbecue before getting a good night's sleep. After the first round of food, we decided commemorate the last Cobra dispersal with a flight photo. We erected the TEL, and everyone climbed on

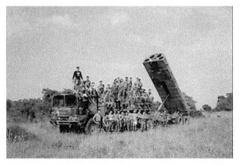 various parts of the vehicle to pose for the picture. It was an exciting time, but we had no idea that it would be the last photo ever taken of a member of our team.

Soon after the photo, a group of airmen took a couple of HMMWVs and

started driving around the hills of the training area. They went off-road and attempted to drive horizontally along the side of a steep hill. They found themselves on a raised portion of land that increased the angle of the vehicle just enough that it rolled over and down the hill. The vehicle doors were easily removable, and as the HMMWV rolled upside down the first time, one of the doors fell off. During this early period of HMMWV use, there were only lap restraints for seat belts. So the next time the vehicle rolled on its side, the upper portion of the airman's body was flung out the side of the vehicle through the now-missing door, and as the vehicle continued to roll onto its top, the airman's neck was broken. He died instantly.

One of the other airmen called for help over the radio, finishing his radio message with the gut-piercing words "I think he's dead."

The flight commander, a missileer captain in charge of the entire multifunctional flight and my direct superior during disposals, tracked me down and informed me what happened. He asked me to stay at the camp to explain the situation and console the other members of the team while he went to the scene of the accident to find out what had happened and the condition of all involved. I think he was trying to protect me from the emotional trauma associated with responding to a gruesome accident site. If the victim had been one of my cops, I would not have agreed to this, but the airman was a maintenance troop and therefore not under my direct supervision, so I agreed.

The following day we dispensed of the traditional victory lap around base upon our return. Instead, we solemnly returned our vehicles and equipment to the various staging locations and returned to our dorm rooms to process the events individually and with small groups of friends.

We held a formal military memorial service a few days later. The airman's photo was placed on a stand next to an inverted M-16 with a helmet balanced on top and a set of combat boots at the base in the traditional configuration. Cobra Flight formed up in front, and other members of the base population gathered to the sides. Several members of the wing's leadership team and a couple of the airman's close friends spoke in tribute, and then we came to attention and saluted while taps was played. One by one we filed past the memorial display, and each gave our fallen comrade a final salute.

This was my first solemn military memorial ceremony, but it was far from my last.

* * * * *

The pain in my right foot continually intruded on my reflections. As I approached Tardajos where I hoped to stay, I saw many signs advertising a private hostel called La Fábrica. The signs showed it to be very nice with small rooms, Wi-Fi, washer and dryer, a restaurant—pretty much everything that you would want. The guidebook said that it had fourteen beds spread between four rooms, plus some more expensive private rooms. It looked very appealing.

As I approached the intersection where a side road took you to the hostel, I had to make a choice. It was about 1530, so I knew that most people would be settled in for the night. The hostel was three hundred meters off trail. That meant an extra six hundred meters if I got there only to find there were no vacancies. My right foot did not think that this was a good risk to take. However, I was intrigued by the advertisements. I decided to take the chance. I should have listened to my foot.

My luck was no better at the municipal hostel on the far side of the village, and I found myself retracing more painful steps to return to a pension in the village center. To my delight, I was able to get a private room for only 15€, significantly less than I would have paid at La Fábrica who advertised their private rooms for 35€. I shared a bathroom with several other rooms, but that was not a big deal. I had my own room, complete with sheets and towels!

As I was eating dinner at the restaurant on the ground level, the Austrian couple with whom we'd spent happy hour the previous night joined me. It continued to amaze me how I kept running into the same people over and over. Obviously, we had similar views on staying in cities and how far we liked to hike in a day. In fact, they intended to go to the same town as I did the following day, Hontanas, in the middle of stage 14.

* * * * *

Back in the luxury of my private room, I read chapter 10 of *Seeking Allah, Finding Jesus*. The chapter revolved around his experiences with Ramadhan while his dad was stationed in Scotland with the US Navy. The major disadvantage of celebrating this Islamic holy month so far north during the summer was that they had to fast for as long as eighteen hours a day. The author describes that Ramadhan was not just about fasting but improving relationships, building community, and strengthening one's faith and purity. I was surprised how excited he described this time being for Muslims. He said it was like having Christmas for an entire month. Although it was difficult to go from sunrise to sunset without eating or even drinking water, the author describes the morning and evening feasts as times of great celebration and indulgence. In fact, he notes that many people actually gained weight.[20] Very interesting.

In my observations of Muslims during my overseas to tours, I had perceived it as a month of suffering due to the fast. I guess this is tainted by my experiences with hunger. I can have a real negative attitude when I am hungry and thirsty.

---

[20] Qureshi, chapter 10.

# CHAPTER 17

## Tardajos to Hontanas, 21.1 Kilometers
## 11 Sep 2015
## D+13

I embarked on my trek across the Meseta at 0800. This is the part of the trail that most people consider boring. The area consists of endless farm fields with only modest and gradual elevation gain through rolling hills. The villages and hamlets are further apart, and there is very little to shade you from the heat of the sun. A hike through this area would be brutal in July or August.

As I passed the village albergue on my way out of town, the horse pilgrims that we had seen in Burgos yesterday were loading up for the day's journey. It would be interesting to research how the journey is usually done on horse. Obviously, only certain albergues would be set up to host them. I wondered if there was a special guidebook for this type of pilgrimage?

I spent some time talking with Lori from Los Angeles during my first coffee break. She was having serious tendon problems and had decided to take the day off after only walking the 2.4 km from Tardajos. She felt a little guilty about this and wondered what she would do all day, especially during the wait for the albergue to open. The guidebook mentioned a museum in the village; she could kill some time there.

"I've been shipping my pack the last couple of days to relieve the pressure on my tendons. It's helped, but I guess I need to let them rest entirely for a day," she explained. "You should consider shipping your back and give your feet a break."

"I have seriously thought about it, but the one day that I did it in 2013, I really regretted not having my stuff with me. My friend shipped hers every day, and we found that it really cuts into your flexibility because you have to go to the village where you shipped it. You can't stop early if you need to," I replied.

"I guess that's a good point. Maybe you could consider forwarding some of your pack's contents to the post office in Santiago," she suggested. "I did that the other day, and it turned out to be very easy. Just take your 'nice to haves' to the post office, and they will box it up, address it, and ship it all for you. It only cost about 15€, and they will hold it for up to thirty days on the other end."

"Someone told me the Spanish mail system is unreliable," I said leerily.

"Now you tell me! Well, I guess it is too late now," she chuckled.

Similar to me, she had decided filling her water bladder made the pack too heavy and now just carried a water bottle. Her water bladder was in the box she sent to Santiago.

At 2.6 km further down the trail, there was a nice, cool natural fountain where I refilled my bottle once again. Away from the trail slightly was a clump of trees standing like an oasis in the middle of the brown fields that surrounded us. Several picnic tables were scattered among the trees, offering a shaded rest area for weary pilgrims. The perfect setting for my daily Bible study.

Day 12's message tells us that not only does the crucifixion of Jesus make salvation possible, but His sacrifice also enables us to pray and serve in His name. In this way our actions are the method that God uses to accomplish His purposes. Because we are adopted into God's family when we accept the gift of salvation based on Jesus's sacrifice, we now have the honor of being a channel through which His love can reach others. The scriptures referenced included John 14:13, Luke 9:48, and John 17:9.[21]

Contemplating this message made me think of His Pantry where I volunteer on Mondays. Local grocery stores donate items that need to be rotated off of their shelves but are still consumable. Additionally, members of the church and community frequently

---

[21] Fryar, p. 26–27.

donate items which they have purchased for this purpose or produce they grow in their gardens. Well over fifty members of Camano Chapel volunteer in this ministry. Some pick up items at the grocery stores. Others, like myself, work in various capacities to set up, organize, and help the clients that come through.

Volunteering in this capacity gives us the opportunity to help members of our community who are struggling financially. However, it is not just the physical needs that are addressed. Quite often the circumstances that have resulted in their financial difficulty also wreak havoc with their emotional and spiritual health. One of the pastors is always available for any of the clients who want to speak to him. Many are spiritually uplifted merely by the acts of kindness bestowed upon them. Some have come to know Christ as their Savior, and others have started attending outreach ministries that focus on addressing the roots of their problems. Most enjoy the socializing while there.

Besides the satisfaction I get from helping others while serving God, I have found this to be an excellent opportunity to get to know the chapel staff and the other volunteers while engaging in Christian fellowship.

As I endeavor to determine who I am and what I should do with my life, I must keep the importance of getting involved in church activities in mind. I must convince myself that although I once served my country, now that I am retired, I have the opportunity to serve God and members of my community more directly. This had always been very difficult because of the long hours that I worked, stress and exhaustion, the constant moving, and deployments and other military-related trips. Seldom was I really able to connect with my church. Very few people in the congregation even knew who I was, and I certainly had no time to contribute to a ministry. Now I have that opportunity. I must convince myself that this is an honorable purpose.

By engaging in service, I cannot be considered a "waste of air" even if I don't get paid for what I do.

\* \* \* \* \*

As I walked, it occurred to me that it was 9/11, the fourteenth anniversary of the terror attacks on America. I spent the next 11 km reflecting on my experiences on that horrible day and the days that followed.

Prior to the terrorist attacks, my career was on a standard progression for security forces officers. I had worked my way up from leading on-duty cops at the flight level; through back-office staff positions, such as resource officer and operations officer; to assuming command of a squadron about fifteen months prior to that fateful day.

Regardless of the level, Security Forces Squadrons focused on resource security, law enforcement, and training for potential contingency deployments. This was all very routine and seldom eventful in a peacetime environment, even at our overseas bases. For most of the base, cops were the guys on the gates and a bit of a nuisance when we insisted on adhering to inconvenient security procedures.

After the 9/11 attacks, the focus of wing leadership on our operations was much more intense, and anti-terrorism became the top priority at all bases, stateside and overseas. Antiterrorism involves policies and procedures aimed at defending a base, resources and personnel through infrastructure design, active security and deterrence, as well as responding to and recovering from terrorist attacks. Key elements included hardening the base using barriers, substantial construction, blast-proof windows, and executing aggressive security procedures that would cause anyone conducting surveillance to think twice about striking the base. A common phrase that we used to help us frame our planning mind-set was "Why attack a lion when there are so many sheep available?" We wanted our base to be the "lion."

On September 11, 2001, I was a major and the commander of the 56th Security Forces Squadron at Luke Air Force Base (AFB) near Phoenix, Arizona, known as the "sheriff."

Breakfast in hand, I sat down at the coffee table in my living room to watch the news before going to work. As the TV tuned in, my hand stopped halfway to my mouth with a fork full of omelet. The twin towers in New York were on fire. They were replaying a video of the second plane hitting and a street full of people running for their lives with falling debris and smoke everywhere. I could not believe what I was seeing. I knew instantly it was a terrorist attack.

After a few moments, I recovered from my shock, grabbed my phone, and called the Wing Command Post.

"This is Major Meck. I'm watching the news and see the terrorist attack in New York. Does the wing commander know, and is he recalling the Battle Staff?"

"Not yet," the controller replied.

"I recommend that you notify him immediately and let him know that my recommendation is that we recall the Battle Staff. I'll call the support group commander myself."

Hanging up, I placed a call to my boss. He was watching the news as well and agreed with the Battle Staff recall.

"Command Post is calling the general. I will start a squadron recall and then stop by to meet with the chief and my ops officer for a few minutes to give them some general guidance. Then I'll meet you at the Command Post."

"Very good. I'll see you there," the colonel replied.

Next, I called the Law Enforcement Desk (LED) to initiate our squadron recall and let the dogs into the backyard for a few minutes while I shoveled the rest of my breakfast into my mouth. There was no way to know when I would get back home. Fortunately, I had a dog door insert in my sliding glass door so at least the dogs would be able to go in and out as needed if I was gone for an extended period of time.

When I arrived at the LED, they were watching the news on TV and informed me that a third plane had crashed into the Pentagon and another one was suspected to be hijacked. The base's higher headquarters, Air Education and Training Command (AETC), had notified us to implement THREATCON Delta.

Thus started three weeks of nonstop work with little sleep.

Luke AFB was unique in that it was divided in half by a civilian road. The side with the flight line and most squadron offices was secured by a fence and several entry control points (ECPs, or "gates") manned by my cops. The other side of the base contained family housing, the hospital, commissary, and base exchange. There was no entry control. The first thing we had to do was close down the civilian road that split the base and establish ECPs on either end and at various locations on the unsecured side, thus bringing the entire base into the security perimeter. Of course, we had no jurisdiction on the civilian road, so the Glendale Police Department sent officers to jointly man those ECPs.

Besides activating several new gates, we had to double the manning on all gates, increase the number of interior patrols, and add a quick-response force (QRF). Our unit manpower could not handle this level of commitment for more than a couple days even by using all personnel (thus canceling all days off) and splitting the squadron in half, working twelve-hour shifts. All back-office functions ceased except for those involving Command and Control and the placement of physical security barriers that predesignated locations.

We earned manpower slots based on our required posts, manned in eight-hour shifts, in a completely peacetime, no- to low-threat environment. As the day progressed, it became apparent that our new level of manning would be required for an extended period of time. Therefore, my first task at the Battle Staff was to inform the wing commander what our manning requirements were and explain our limitations.

"Sir, we are going to need augmentees from the rest of the wing," I informed him.

To my pleasant surprise, he agreed without hesitation. Up to this point in my career, it had always been my perception that the rest of the wing saw security as an impediment to normal operations. I was constantly on the defense, trying to convince the operators that security procedures were directed by higher headquarters and we had no choice but to follow them. We could not cut a lot of corners. Today I seemed to be everybody's best friend, and they were all bending over backward to help.

For the first week or so, the businesses outside our new ECPs on the civilian road were very supportive. The restaurants even brought over large quantities of food for on-duty security personnel. However, it was not long before the closure of the road and the diversion of normal traffic around the base started impacting their customer base.

They started losing money and initiated pressure on the Glendale city government to find a way to get the road opened. This meant the establishment of four more ECPs, and thus more augmentees. Further crippling us, we received a tasking to deploy a thirteen-person squad and a five-person flight headquarters element, including a lieutenant, to Southwest Asia to help secure a new base that was standing up to support the initiation of combat operations. It was around this time that the local Air Force Reserve Security Forces Squadron was activated and ordered to join our unit and help with the increased requirements. They also received deployment taskings, but the remaining personnel relieved some pressure and allowed us to release some of the augmentees back to their assigned units.

Although every permanent military base in the United States and overseas was increasing their security posture, several indicators in our area piqued our concern about the local threat and compelled us to harden our base more than others, so much so that the security forces staff at AETC started calling us Lukesan. This was a pun referring to Osan and Kunsan Air Bases in Korea. Because the Korean War had never officially ended and tensions there remained high, these bases were always at a level of security expected in a combat zone. Luke had started looking a lot like them.

In the squadron, we preferred to call ourselves Lukenstan. With the war on terrorism kicking off in Southwest and Central Asia, we all wanted to be a part of it. Our country was at war, and we were trained to protect it. Most of us wanted to be in the thick of the action. I even went so far as to ask the support group commander if I could put my name in the hat as a volunteer for a deployment.

His response was quite clear: "You are the squadron commander, and you are needed here."

The homeland had been attacked, and the threat was high stateside. Most of the bases that we wanted to be at in Central Asia were in countries that ended in "stan." By calling our base Lukenstan, at least we could say that we were in a "stan."

The first indicator contributing to our heightened level of concern were reports that some of the hijackers had received flight training in the Phoenix area and support from the local mosque.

Additionally, one of the senior NCOs from my unit worked part-time as a pizza deliveryman. His supervisors there informed him that a couple days after 9/11, two men with dark complexion, potentially of Middle Eastern descent, applied to be deliverymen. During management discussions with the applicants, changes to procedures on Luke were discussed. Prior to 9/11, food delivery personnel only needed to show an order form indicating that somebody on the base had ordered the food and requested it be delivered to a dormitory room, family housing, or an office building. After 9/11, we changed the policy, and the deliverymen could only go as far as a gate. Once informed of this change, the two men pulled their applications and were no longer interested in the job.

Finally an airman reported to the Office of Special Investigations (OSI) that he was trying to sell his truck. A couple of men with dark complexion offered to give him $10,000 cash with the condition that he leave the DoD sticker on the windshield of the vehicle. This was suspicious because prior to the attacks, vehicles with a DoD sticker on them were normally just waved onto base. Of course, starting on 9/11, this policy changed DoD-wide, and there were now 100 percent ID checks. Our deduction was that these men were trying to gain access to the base without being checked.

Throughout the remaining nine months of my command at Luke, our focus was on managing all the enhanced security procedures and manning, equipment, and facility requirements while also rotating squads of cops through back-to-back deployments to Southwest Asia in support of the building Global War on Terrorism (GWOT). The activated reserve security squadron and remaining augmentees became part of our squadron family as the enhanced security procedures transitioned to the "new normal." It was not long before it was apparent that we would never return to the pre-9/11 security posture, and we started requesting additional permanent manpower. Of course, all bases in the AF needed additional manpower. The problem was, there was a congressional limit on the total number of AF personnel. For one career field to receive increased manning meant other career fields had to give up positions. Of course, the other career fields also had increased deployment responsibilities in support of the GWOT. This issue became an ongoing battle throughout the rest of my career as the entire AF's operational tempo, and associated manpower requirements, continued to increase while politicians cut military manpower to save money.

\* \* \* \* \*

I stopped for a late lunch at an isolated albergue about 100 meters off of the trail and about 4.8 km before today's objective, Hontanas. I fought with myself a bit about taking the detour because my foot was hurting; as was the emerging trend, it seemed to feel a bit better this afternoon than it had this morning. The signs for the albergue advertised lunch, and it looked intriguing because of its isolation and the rustic atmosphere. Everyone else was just passing it by and heading for Hontanas, so there was some concern that they might take all the beds. Checking the guidebook, I saw that there were several hostels and a casa rural with well over one hundred available beds. It should not be a problem to stop.

I ordered a meal and found a table outside where I felt comfortable taking off my shoes. I just didn't feel right doing foot maintenance inside for some reason. I had been experiencing the pain of a hot spot on my right heel and was happy to see that there was not yet a blister. I took out my medical kit and applied a Compeed surrounded by medical tape per SOP. Taking advantage of my bare feet, I applied another dose of anti-inflammatory and pain creams to both feet before getting underway again.

As I entered Hontanas, I saw a sign advertising a newly opened albergue on the left side of The Way called Juan de Yepes Albergue de Peregrinos. I decided to give it a try and was able to get a lower bunk in a back room downstairs. Where we signed in was a little café with drinks, snacks, and personal items for resupply. There was plenty of seating inside and on the patio outside the entrance. After setting up my bed and getting a shower, this would be a very relaxing place to write an e-mail update for family and friends back home.

The room was almost empty, so I was able to take my bunk choice. When I got back from the shower, Tom from Philadelphia, with whom I had spent time the first few days, was unpacking at the bed next to me. It was great to see him again! I really hadn't expected to since I had had so many problems with my feet and taken some downtime.

"I spent an entire day and two nights in Burgos," he explained. "It was an incredible city, and the cathedral was very inspiring."

"I passed through as quickly as I could," I replied. "With that bicycle competition going on, it was way too crowded for me. Besides, I saw much of the city last time, so I only stopped long enough to see the cathedral, which we didn't tour in 2013."

"I have been nursing some blisters, but they are getting better," he said.

"I've had plenty of problems with my feet, including swelling, because of my circulation issues from the cold injuries, but I've been pretty successful in preventing blisters," I replied. "Between the toe socks, keeping my shoes tied tightly, and using Vaseline, Band-Aids, and Compeed on hot spots in at-risk areas, I have been able to get away with only a couple blisters."

Remembering that I planned to write a book, he laughed and said, "That alone is worthy of being published!"

Taking my leave, I returned to the café area, requested the Wi-Fi password, and composed the following e-mail to send home—complete with a few pictures, of course.

Subject: Update 11 Sep

I will start by reminding you that today is another anniversary of the 9/11 attacks. May we never forget! I know that day changed the course of my career. Do you remember what you were doing when you heard the news? What was your response?

I have currently completed 198 miles! I am half way through stage 14.

I'll start by saying F2BNH struggles and pain still applies. However, I must say that my biggest challenge at this point is my right foot. It is swollen top and bottom. Fortunately, it is far worse at night when I have sandals or just socks on. Crippling when I get up to use the restroom at night! However, for some reason it feels a little better when I put my hiking shoes on. Instead of getting worse as I tackle my daily walk, it gets better as the day goes on. Pretty weird if you ask me, opposite of logic.

I am not the only one dealing with foot issues. Very few are walking without a limp for one reason or another. For some it is tendons, some ligaments, some blisters. Many are dropping out. Others take one or two days off. Some are shipping their packs each day to reduce the pressure on their feet. I have shortened my average distance to about 20 km; some are stopping at 10. Tomorrow I will ship my pack and see how that feels.

Yesterday I passed another milestone in my journey. I limped into Burgos about midday. There were just too many people in that big city. The line to get into the main Albergue was VERY long due to some big bicycle competition going on. I could not get out of town fast enough. 10 kms later I checked into a relaxing pension where I had my own room for only 15€! What a deal for quite privacy!

It was from Burgos that we took the train to jump forward two years ago. So everything I have seen since about 2pm yesterday is all new. I guess my "when I was here two years ago" stories will have to stop for a couple weeks!

I am now passing through the Meseta area. It is rolling hills with farm land. All the fields I have seen so far have been harvested and are now brown. Almost like a desert. When I come to trees or a village, it is like an oasis.

Meseta landscape

I am really enjoying the time I hike alone. Hiking with Mom, Ria and Samantha last time was VERY SPECIAL! However, hiking this alone is an entirely new experience. I highly recommend both!

I would like to thank everyone for their prayers and encouraging notes. I will make it this time!

I then returned to my bed and read *Seeking Allah, Finding Jesus*. In chapters 11–12, the author gave an enlightening perspective on the culture clash that second-generation immigrants experience in America, especially Muslims. He explained that from the Muslim perspective, people's religion is more of a cultural identity than an actual belief and faith. If you were from the West, you were Christian, and the Western culture was a result of the Christian culture, regardless of an individual's belief in God. Between this embedded mind-set and their comfort with others of their own culture, those that immigrate from Muslim countries tend to associate only with other immigrants that share their culture.

The children are a different story since they attend schools and associate more with Americans. Being raised as Muslims at home and exposed to American culture at school means that they do not fit in either; it is as if they have a third culture. However, depending on each child's experiences both in the home and in the American community, the development of their individual "culture" varies. Therefore, none of the children actually fit in with either community, nor even other members of their generation in the Muslim community.[22]

The explanation explained a few things that had perplexed me for a couple of years. Mark, one of the interpreters who worked for my PRT in Afghanistan immigrated to the United States. Initially, I tried to help him settle near where I lived, but it was not long before he found a community of Muslim immigrants about an hour and a half south and moved in with them even though they were part of the culture he had come to America to escape.

The members of this immigrant community did everything together, to include all gravitating toward the same place of employment so that they would work together with other immigrants of like culture. This meant that they were stuck bouncing from one near-minimum-wage job to another as a group. They always talked about trying to get educated in a trade and find better jobs, but in the end they followed each other from one job to another.

I found it hard to understand why there is such a tight bond between the Afghans in the community and why they were not trying to assimilate into our society. There are so many things that they could do to make their lives here more comfortable, successful (from our perspective, anyway), and prosperous, but they don't seem willing to seriously work in that direction. Thanks to this book, I am beginning to understand a little better.

However, I do wonder why so many Muslims are immigrating to the United States if they are so deeply indoctrinated into believing that everything American—and Western in general—is immoral and that we are all strongly anti-Muslim. Why immigrate to such a decrepit and hostile place and then isolate themselves from the society? Why not immigrate to a Muslim-dominated country with religious beliefs and culture similar to their own?

Additionally, the book's cultural lessons do not help me understand why my friend in particular has been unwilling to break away

---

[22] Qureshi, chapters 11–12.

from the Afghan immigrant community or take serious steps to assimilate into the American society. He is unique in that he converted to
Christianity while living as a refugee in England and then furthered
his faith while working with the US military in Afghanistan. He
was severely beaten by family members due to his conversion. Word
spread, and the Taliban sent him a "night letter," informing him that
he had been sentenced to death for working with the US military,
converting to Christianity, and talking about his new faith with other
Afghans. Under the threat of death, he was successfully able to secure
a Special Immigration Visa (SIV) designed for our interpreters and
escaped to the United States.

When he arrived, he was adamant that Allah was actually Satan
and his home country was living in complete spiritual darkness. He
was extremely thankful to be in the United States where he could
practice his faith because of our religious freedom. At the time, his
intent was to go to Bible college and look for opportunities to serve
God, such as translating the Bible into Pashtun and spreading the
Good News of the Gospel to Muslims.

However, once involved with the Afghan community, he did
nothing to pursue his dreams, nor did he attend Christians church services or fellowships. He did not want his friends in that community to
find out that he was a Christian because he was afraid that they would
harm him. I found this perplexing because he was not concerned about
this while he was living with Afghans on US military bases in-country.
He attended the base chapel services and their Bible studies.

Hopefully, continued reading of this book will help me understand.

At the appointed time, Tom and I joined a relatively small group
of pilgrims at the albergue's communal dinner. As usual, the dinner was
an outstanding opportunity to meet others. At our end of the table sat
two young German ladies, a South African couple, Tara and Al from
Canada, and a woman from Vancouver, Canada, by the name of Joy.

We all enjoyed lighthearted conversation while consuming
exceptional chicken, a rice dish, and salad served family-style. Even
with ten hungry pilgrims eating, we were unable to finish the massive
platter of food.

# CHAPTER 18

## Hontanas to Itero de la Vega, 20.2 Kilometers
## 12 Sep 2015
## D+14

I awoke to the sound of my four roommates getting dressed and packing before 0600. Since they were all men and it would be a long time before the sun came up, I decided to snooze until they left the room. This way I could get ready in private and didn't have to wait for the availability of the bathroom, making for a relaxing and easy prep period. A small luxury, and highly appreciated.

By 0730 my feet were prepped and gear packed, and I headed out for breakfast where they were cooking made-to-order tortillas. Before ordering I inquired where to put my pack, which was prepared for shipping. The night before I had obtained a shipping envelope and studied the guidebook to determine my objective for the day. I decided to try to stay at the Albergue San Nicolás on the outskirts of Itero de la Vega. It was about 20 km and sounded like a very unique place with a lot of historical character. The guidebook said that it had no electricity, phones, or any other modern conveniences, except a fairly new bathroom and shower facility in the backyard. The main building was originally a pilgrim hospice from the twelfth century, and the owners wanted to keep it in its original state. They even offered the washing of feet as was common for early pilgrims. Of course, there was a communal dinner for those lucky enough to get one of the twelve beds available. It sounded like an adventure to stay there while getting a good feel of what it was like for pilgrims in the Middle Ages.

I wrote "Albergue San Nicholás" and my name on the envelope, inserted the required 5€, sealed it, and attached it securely to my

227

pack, then placed it in the designated room with several other packs awaiting shipment. The weather forecast called for sun all day, so the only items I took with me were my jacket, gloves, water bottle, poles, and a packet with my identification, credit cards, passport, and money. I was a little leery about going without "my stuff," but I figured I might as well give it another try. My feet could use the break.

It was 0740 when I found Tom in the dining area and asked to join him for breakfast. The sun was just starting to lighten the sky outside. My timing was just about right; this would likely become the new normal: aim for an 0800 departure time.

After sharing our intentions for the day, Tom stated, "A couple guys I was talking to this morning told me that there was a volunteer medical team here yesterday afternoon checking on pilgrims and seeing if anybody needed assistance. I heard they gave one guy an injection because he had an infected blister. Another young man passed out while his blister was being treated. They ended up taking him to the hospital."

"Wow! Any idea how he's doing?" I asked.

"I guess he came back last night and is doing well now. They think he was just exhausted."

"Too bad I didn't hear about the team while they were here. Maybe they could have given me some advice and checked my foot. Then again, maybe that wouldn't have been such a good idea. I don't want any medical people telling me I should drop out of the hike. One way or another, I'm going to finish this."

Tom laughed. "You'll make it! Your determination is inspiring." Standing up and slinging his pack onto his back, he continued, "Well, I'm gonna hit the trail."

"Okay, see you along The Way! I'll be heading out shortly."

About ten minutes later, I grabbed my poles, stuck the water bottle into my cargo pocket, and headed out into dimly lit village street. The sun wasn't high enough to light the

streets, so they were still in the shadows of the buildings. The road through town was illuminated by small lights on the sides of a few buildings. As I walked down the narrow street, I marveled at the medieval European construction and atmosphere of this small village. They had done a great job of preserving the history of the village and its support of pilgrims.

* * * * *

Reaching the bottom of the hill, I headed out across the brown, fairly flat farmland and started reflecting on my two years stationed at Hahn Air Base in Germany starting in September 1990.

As a senior first lieutenant and starting my third assignment, I was assigned to the day shift. The 650th Security Police Squadron (SPS) was a standard base-focused unit. There were three flights that rotated through what we called the "swings and mids" schedule. These flights would work three swing shifts, have a twenty-four-hour break, work three midnight (mids) shifts, and then have three days off.

Alpha Flight (days) was broken into three squads that worked day shift only. The squads rotated through the "six and three" schedule with two squads working at any given time and one squad on break. Because the flight was self-relieving, we had 50 percent more people than the "swings and mids" flights, hence the assignment of a senior-ranking first lieutenant. With about seventy people it was the largest flight I had led yet.

The mission of the 650 SPS was to provide security for the 50th Tactical Fighter Wing's (TFW) fleet of F-16 aircraft, the flight line, a priority A weapon storage area, and a geographically separated priority C munitions storage area located about twenty miles from the base called Morbach. Priority A was the highest-security priority and required an extensive amount of security posting, sensors, and heavy weapons. Similar to Comiso, our mission was central to NATO's Cold War objective of deterring Russian aggression into Europe. If the Cold War turned hot, we had the resources to not only defend Europe from air attack and strike advancing enemy ground units, but we also had the capability to strike devastating blows deep inside the Soviet Union itself.

The chances of the Cold War turning hot were diminishing. The INF treaty that was closing Comiso AS was a part of this reduction in tensions. The fall of the Berlin Wall the previous November was another obvious sign in this northern part of Europe.

I had been fortunate to take a quick trip to Berlin in December 1989. Several of us from Comiso had taken the train to Austria to ski. I decided to give up a day of skiing and take an overnight train to Berlin. I had not been able to convince anyone to go with me, so I had set out on this adventure alone. The train arrived early in the morning, and I proceeded to find my way around Berlin's subway system to the Wall. I was amazed at the crowds. People were coming and going through a gate in the Wall. Others lined up along the Wall and appeared to be taking pieces of it off. I moved closer to observe the activity and saw that this was precisely what was happening.

The Wall did not have to be demolished with a high-cost contract. Souvenir hunters were doing a great job. A gentleman who spoke a little English offered to let me use his crowbar so I could get a piece myself. I jumped at the chance and secured two large chunks. I have heard rumors that in the years since the Wall came down, about three times the actual mass had been sold in pieces as souvenirs. I have never had to wonder if my pieces were genuine. I know they are because I pried them off myself.

After securing my souvenirs, I found a head-sized hole in the Wall and peered into East Berlin. As far as I could see into the city, there was a line of people waiting to cross into the west. In stark contrast to the modern city of West Berlin, everything I saw on the other side was dirty and extremely run down. The dark, dull, dreary pictures that we see depicting the Soviet Union and East Germany were right on target. For the thousands of people standing in that

long line at the gate, most likely for hours on end, crossing the border was an obvious privilege and gave them hope for a better life. The train back to Austria didn't leave until late afternoon, so I wandered around the streets of West Berlin and discovered the most popular destination for those who had crossed through the gate: McDonald's. I have never seen such a crowded McDonald's. I must've stood in line for forty-five minutes to get a burger and fries.

Now, ten months later, I was moving to Germany only a couple of weeks before the official reunification of East and West Germany. I felt it was an extreme honor to be here at this historic time.

A little more than a month before I departed Comiso, Iraq invaded Kuwait on 2 August 1990. Since we were getting ready to deactivate two GLCM flights, we joked that a good way to dispose of the missiles would be to use them to turn Iraq into a glass parking lot. Of course, we weren't serious, but when the military is faced with potential combat operations, jokes about ways to beat the enemy help relieve some of the tension.

While I was home on leave, I had contact with Keith, who was still at Comiso. He informed me that the remaining members of Cobra Flight had been tasked with deploying in support of Operation DESERT SHIELD. He was deploying with them as their flight commander.

It is hard to describe how this news hit me. I was in shock. I felt deep disappointed and rather guilty. I was their flight commander, or at least I had been less than ten days earlier. I should have been going with them on this deployment. My team was going to war without me while I enjoyed a visit with family in Alaska. This did not sit well with me.

The formation of a coalition to oppose Iraq and the buildup of forces from thirty-four coalition countries in the Middle East had little impact our operations at Hahn. At least not until we all received the "O-Dark-30" phone call initiating a squadron recall on the morning 17 January 1991. Once I had signed into the unit, I was told that the officers needed to report to the commander's conference room. I hurried over while my flight sergeant oversaw the accountability of our personnel.

While we awaited the arrival of the commander, our small group of lieutenants speculated on what was going on. Was this the kickoff of another base exercise? We had these periodically to ensure our readiness to generate aircraft to protect Europe in the event of hostilities with the Soviet Union. Others suggested that it might have something to do with the Middle East. It was all speculation until the commander entered the room decked out in combat gear. He was wearing a flat jacket and helmet, and had a loaded M9 pistol in a holster attached to his fully equipped web gear. He had never done this during an exercise. We immediately knew that something serious was going on.

Sitting nervously around the table, we listened intently as he informed us that the coalition had initiated combat operations and crossed the border into Kuwait in an effort to push the Iraqi troops out. A knot formed in my stomach, and the hair on the back of my neck stood up. Our military was now involved in a full-fledged shooting war for the first time since I rose my right hand and pledged to support and defend the United States against all enemies, foreign and domestic.

He went on to describe how we were ramping up security. As the largest conventional munitions storage area in Europe, Morbach was tasked to play a vital role in the war effort. Our unit was tasked with establishing security operations at a completely unprotected railhead in a wooded area about five miles from Morbach, allowing logistics personnel to load trains

1Lt Tracey Meck securing the Operation DESERT STORM munitions supply line in Germany, Feb 1991.

with munitions bound for the Middle East. It wasn't the same as being in theater on the front lines, but at least we were going to play an important part in the war effort.

Although it was exciting at first, the twelve-hour shifts required to man all the extra security posting, and the monotony of daily operations with no real local threat started to wear on us after a week or two. Then the rumors started that our unit was going to be tasked to send a flight into the operational theater to help secure an Air Base launching missions against Iraqi forces. Hoping for another chance to get into the fight, I rushed to the office of my boss, the operations officer, and volunteered to lead the deploying flight.

"I appreciate your desire to go, but we are sending our mobility flight. Lt. Knight will lead them. Even if we had not made that decision yet, we're not sending females. The flight is going to war, and we don't send women to combat," the captain explained.

"They're not going to fight the enemy on the front lines," I exclaimed. "They're going to secure an airfield in a different country than where the fighting is."

"It's close enough," he replied.

I was very disappointed and somewhat angry. There was no law against females providing security at a base in the rear. This was merely a male chauvinistic attitude. After being selected as the honor graduate of my GCS class and spending a year as a DFC training to defend our resources in a combat field environment, I felt I was more qualified to deploy to a war zone than any of my male peers. What was the point of training females for these duties and assigning them to the positions if they were not going to be able to do their jobs when the situation turned hostile?

They would not have sent me instead of the lieutenant they had already decided on, anyway, because he was the mobility flight commander. I wish my boss had just left it with that explanation instead of expanding on the whole female thing. He didn't have to go there. Anyway, now I knew where I stood.

Talking to Lt. Knight after he returned, he confirmed my suspicions. Hahn's flight was the only security police flight at the forward base that had no females.

\* \* \* \* \*

It was only about 1000 hours when I entered Castrojeriz. Way too early for lunch, so I just stopped for coffee and a croissant to tide me over. Although the trail was flat, a new battle presented itself. Flies were constantly buzzing around my head; they seemed attracted to me for some reason. They were really getting on my nerves.

Another issue was how fast cars whizzed by us as we walked along the edge of a narrow country road. I was shocked that many did not even bother to move toward the middle when they sped by. Once again, I wondered how many peregrinos got hit by such careless drivers each year.

Upon leaving the café, I hiked up the steep hill on the street through town. About halfway up, two dogs raced by me and headed straight for a bush in the front yard of a house on the next corner. They both peed on the bush, then turned around, and raced each other back down the hill where they had come from. That was one of the funniest things I had seen in a long time!

As I neared the end of town, it occurred to me that the next opportunity to purchase food would be at the Albergue San Nicolás. Due to its rustic description, I theorized that there probably would be no food available until they served dinner around 1900 at the earliest. I decided to play it safe and stopped for an ice cream bar at the last café before leaving town.

Ouch, 2€ for an ice cream bar! That was almost $3! More than twice what it normally cost for a glass of wine. This reminded me of a similar ice cream bar I had purchased in an airport in Africa while I was traveling around as part of my duties while deployed to Camp Lemonnier. After purchasing it with local currency, I sat at a table calculating how much it had actually cost. It had been more than $6. Considering that, I guess this was not such a bad deal. The cost of the ice cream bars in Africa had perplexed me at the time because Africa was such a poor continent. Most likely they were targeting rich tourists transiting the airport. I had noticed in my world travels that there was often a price for foreigners and a much cheaper price for locals.

I decided the best course of action was to sit at an outside café table and savor every last bite!

\* \* \* \* \*

As I departed town, my thoughts drifted back to Hahn.

After about three months of heightened security and shipping munitions to the combat theater, things started to return to normal. On 27 May 1991, I was honored to have the Security Police Group (SPG) commander promote me to captain. Along with the promotion came a job change. I moved over to the 50 SPS as the operations officer. For the first time I was now working the law enforcement (LE) side of our career field. It was a much smaller unit than the 650th, and I actually had less people under me than I had had on Alpha Flight, but I had moved up to management in the "back office." Instead of supervising day-to-day patrol operations, I was now in a policy-making and oversight position.

As with my leadership in the 650th, I got along great with my new commander and learned a lot from the operations superintendent about LE operations. However, it did not last long.

Over the summer we received word that the base had been selected to close, an early victim of the "peace dividend" as the Soviet Union crumbled. For us, the first step was the consolidation of the SPG into one squadron, redesignated as the 583 SPS. The majority of the officers I had worked with the first year rotated out that summer, and a smaller officer corps moved in.

The new squadron commander was Lieutenant Colonel (LtCol) Jones. Whereas the former group commander had been well respected by everybody in the unit because of his dynamic, strong, demanding, but obviously caring leadership style—the new commander's leadership style was short, abrupt, and demanding in a negative way. The change was very difficult to adjust to, completely different from the units I had previously been assigned to.

My ops position was a casualty of the consolidation, and I was reassigned to Delta Flight even though I was a captain and still the ranking flight leader. The "demotion" was justified by saying that they did not want to move the lieutenant that had taken over Alpha Flight when I moved to the 50th. I wasn't too excited about leading a smaller flight and working swings and mids, but it was what it was. I really didn't understand why I couldn't go back to Alpha Flight since I had been their leader just a few months before. But looking back from a big-picture perspective, I can see that there were positive aspects to the change.

For one, firsthand experience working a schedule where you changed your sleep cycle by eight hours every three days served me well when considering potential new shift schedules later in my career.

As time went on, I started suspecting that there was more to the assignment than just not wanting to move the current Alpha Flight leader.

Almost from the beginning, Lt Col Jones started coming down hard on me. He found fault in almost everything that I did and never missed the opportunity to chew me out about something. One particular issue that stands out clearly in my memory was the quality of our daily security and law enforcement blotters.

A major part of my duties at the end of the shift was to review the blotters; identify grammar, spelling, and content errors; and then have the security controller and LE desk sergeant make the corrections before turning it into the back office. One morning, a month or so after he arrived, he called me into his office, obviously irate. He shook the blotter at me, slammed it down on his desk, and told me it was a piece of crap.

"Did you even read this?" he growled. "I want this fixed before you go home."

I had just finished a mid shift and was ready to head home for bed. Instead I got a cup of coffee and sat down to find and fix the errors. Between the two blotters, which encompassed about ten pages total, I found three or four typos I had missed.

During my next shift, I read several blotters from other flights to compare. I found several errors on every page. In many cases the grammar was dismal, to say the least. In my obviously biased opinion, our blotters were far superior to the others that I read. Based on this and numerous other incidents over the coming weeks, I started suspecting that I was being singled out for harassment.

After a few months, a pattern became apparent. The colonel was constantly praising the work of all the white male officers. However, myself, the other female officer, our new Hispanic operations officer, and the two black officers could do nothing right. He even tried to court-martial one of the black officers, who was later acquitted and reassigned. It was our assessment that Lt Col Jones was trying to end the careers of the minority officers.

Myself and the ops officer submitted complaints to the base's IG, detailing what we felt was inappropriate harassment and inconsistencies between how he treated and evaluated us versus the white males. We were very disappointed to get the response delivered by the support group commander. The basic summary was that the IG agreed that the colonel's leadership style was inappropriate and discriminatory. However, since he had been credited with our unit receiving an "Excellent" rating in a recent higher headquarters inspection, no action would be taken. Extremely frustrated, I was happy that it was time for me to rotate to a new assignment.

About a year later, my commander at Little Rock AFB informed me Jones had been forced to retire after yet another IG investigation found he had discriminated against his female operations officer at the base he had moved to after Hahn closed. I felt somewhat vindicated, but I was still mad that I had had to go through such a stressful period. I was very career-oriented and could not imagine doing anything besides being an AF SP officer. Watching my career fall apart in front of my eyes because I was being unfairly evaluated because of my sex, as confirmed by the outcome of the IG investigation, had torn me apart. I had felt totally out of control and unable to do anything to improve the situation until I moved to a new assignment and was able to start fresh with new supervisors.

But new supervisors could not solve the entire problem. Lt Col Jones wrote most of my second officer performance report (OPR) from Hahn. It said I met standards, but the wording was extremely bland and weak. In the AF, officers really have to mess up bad to get a block marked down to "Does Not Meet Standards." The "rating" is really dependent on the strength of the wording in the narrative sections. The final narrative section, written by the group commander, was very strong, but he could not force Lt Col Jones to change his wording, and his two sections remained very weak. There is no way that this would be overlooked by future promotion boards, and the OPR would be in my records forever. For all practical purposes, this disqualified me from consideration for a below-the-zone (BTZ) promotion to major seven years down the road. With the way the Air Force worked, once you were promoted BTZ once, it was likely you would get promoted early to later ranks. Without early promotion to major, you were almost guaranteed "on-time" promotions for the rest of your career, and you would never make general.

Fortunately for the young black lieutenant that Jones tried to court-martial, he was able to impress his next supervisors so much that he received an Air Force level award for superior performance that enabled him to be selected for major two years BTZ. An incredible comeback for him, and well deserved. He was a strong, intelligent, people-oriented leader.

The ultimate benefit that I received from persevering through this incredibly stressful period was becoming spiritually oriented in addition to career-oriented.

* * * * *

It was about noon when I completed a grueling 12 percent grade ascent to Alto de Mostelares. A local entrepreneur had taken advantage of the isolated hilltop location and set up a snack truck for exhausted hikers. I got a banana and *cervesa* (beer) to relax with. Since I was only going 20 km without a pack, I was considering this is a lazy, relaxing day. A beer at lunch was a perfect treat for such a day. I gave the young businessman a donation of 2.5€. It was more than the items were actually worth, but I figured it showed my appreciation for his service to peregrinos.

I took my snack over to a shelter that reminded me of a bus stop. It was made of cement and had a tiled roof that protected resting pilgrims from rain or the beating sun, and I pulled out my service study.

The day 13 lesson pointed out that the Bible contains many examples of how to pray effectively—for example, Jesus's prayers the night before he was crucified in John 17 and those prayers offered by Paul during his ministry and the hardships of his confinement before his martyrdom. We should learn from their prayers, both to enhance our own walk with the Lord and to pray for those we serve.[23]

* * * * *

Repacking my reading materials, I disposed of my garbage in a receptacle provided by the entrepreneur and headed out across the top of the hill. Soon an almost-endless plain of brown farmland stretched out in front of me after a gradual descent. The Camino could be seen for miles weaving its way through the rolling fields. The brown, sun-burned remains of summer crops reminded me how this wide-open, exposed part of the Camino would likely be unbearable on a nine-ty-plus-degree summer day. I thanked the Lord that today was in the low seventies with a light breeze. I was quite enjoying it, comfortably soaking up plenty of vitamin D and working on my tan.

After about an hour and a half, I arrived at Albergue San Nicholas. A very basic rectangular building on the edge of the dirt road, it rested among a small grove of green trees. Virtually an oasis after spending most of the day among the brown fields.

There was a large group of young twentysomethings lounging against the front of the albergue. They were laughing and engaging in loud, enthusiastic conversation in Spanish. I immediately started reconsidering my intention to stay for the night. I counted ten of them. Since there were only twelve beds, they would make up the vast majority of the clientele that night. The loud, youthful energy they were displaying would soon get on my nerves, and since they

---

[23] Fryar, p. 28–29.

were all speaking in Spanish, I would have no idea what was going on. The situation was not appealing at all.

A sign on the front door indicated the albergue would open at 1500. It was only about 1400. I would have to endure the situation for at least an hour to retrieve my pack before moving on.

As soon as I sat down to wait, flies started buzzing around my head ceaselessly. Very irritating. Worse, my insect repellent was in my pack, which, of course, was locked inside the building. Stress, irritation, and frustration welled up inside of me. No, I would not stay here tonight . . . and this would be the last time I shipped my pack!

The hospitaleros arrived at about 1450 and started unloading groceries for the evening meal. Several of the young people offered to give them a hand, and the front door was opened. I attempted to enter and was cautioned to wait my turn. I could not tell exactly what was being said because the hosts did not seem to speak English. Fruitlessly, I tried to explain that I just wanted to look inside and retrieve my pack. They did not understand, and I got the impression that they were trying to tell me that the others had arrived first or had reservations and I needed to wait for them to sign in before I could. I understood this Camino protocol, but cutting ahead in line was not my intent. I pointed to my pack and repeated "*Mochila*" a couple times. Finally I just walked in and grabbed it.

The inside definitely looked medieval. To the left at the end of the rectangular hall was a small chapel. In front of me was a long dining table, and to the right were bunk beds. The entire building was just one long room with a very high ceiling. It was decorated in medieval style with candles mounted on the walls for light. It definitely had the atmosphere I was expecting, and it would have been the great experience to stay here. But it just wasn't going to work out. I tried to explain to the host that I was going to town, and they did their best to try to convince me to stay. The language barrier really made this conversation difficult. Finally I gave up and walked out, heading toward the village of Itero de la Vega on the other side of the river.

The first building I approached at the edge of town was an albergue. There was a large courtyard with several peregrinos relaxing at tables, enjoying drinks and staring at their electronic devices. At the far end of the courtyard was a restaurant and bar. Rooms lined the right side of the courtyard like a motel. I entered the restaurant area and approached the host at the bar.

"Uno cama, por favor. Necesito cama inferior," I said, bending over and moving my hand back and forth about knee level.

I knew this was pretty poor Spanish, but we were successfully communicating. He understood I was asking for one bottom bunk.

"There is only one single bed available, but it is more expensive, 10€." To my relief, the host spoke fairly good English.

"Can I see it?"

"Si, si, no problemo."

I followed him about two-thirds the way down the row of rooms, and he opened a door. Inside there were five single beds with a bathroom off to the right. Four beds were lined up perpendicular to the left wall. All were taken. One bed remained parallel to the right wall beyond a set of lockers. I smiled.

"I'll take it!"

Dropping my pack next to the bed, I pulled out my pilgrim's credential and followed the host back to the restaurant to do the paperwork.

Since I had eaten very little since I left the albergue this morning and the restaurant here was not serving food until dinnertime, I grabbed my guidebook and iPad and limped into town in search of somewhere that was already serving food. I found a nice small restaurant, ordered a hamburger, fries, and some wine and settled in to do mission planning.

The trail ahead was, for the most part, flat, gaining only about fifty meters in elevation over the next 30 km. The weather forecast was calling for cool temperatures, cloudy skies, and the potential for some light rain. I decided to take advantage of these favorable conditions and attempt 28.8 km. Once through Frómista at the start of stage 16, the primary route ran along the side of a paved road. There was a scenic option that followed a river. It was a bit longer but definitely preferable. This said, once committed, I would need to go 11 km before coming to an albergue. If I felt up to it, it would be worth it. I could always change my mind just before embarking on the green detour.

Pleased with the plan, I pulled out my iPad and read through chapter 16 in *Seeking Allah, Finding Jesus*. The main theme of these chapters was Nabeel's experiences carrying out his role of ambassador for Islam to a predominantly Christian high school. Through discussions with classmates, differences between the beliefs of Christianity and Islam were highlighted. It was intriguing to read about their misunderstandings about the Christian faith, as well as some of the particulars about what they believe. The major issue he pointed out that made Christianity heretical in the eyes of Muslims was the belief in "three gods": the Father, Son, and Holy Spirit. Muslims do not understand the one-God-in-three-persons theology. They believe that Christians who believe in the Trinity cannot go to heaven because to do so requires a belief in only one God.[24] I must remember this and the other points if I ever have the privilege of talking to any of Mark's Muslim immigrant friends about Christianity.

After completing the chapters, I returned to the albergue and saw Al sitting at a table in the courtyard. He and his wife, Tara, were the Canadians from the pilgrims' dinner the previous night. I asked Al if I could join him.

"Of course," he replied, reaching out his hand toward a chair.

"Looks like we both opted for a short day," I observed.

"Tara's fighting some pretty bad shin splints. It's been going on for several days, and we're not sure what we should do. I hate to say it, but we may have to stop."

"Take it from me, it may be better to just take some time off and let her heal, and then take it slow for a while. Two years ago we cut out a major part of the Camino because my feet hurt. Look where that got me, back on the Camino doing it again."

Tara overheard this statement as she joined us. "Something to think about!"

---

[24] Qureshi, chapter 16.

"Hello," I greeted her. "I don't know about you, but being a military veteran, I have a type A personality and just could not accept the fact that I did not complete the mission. It bugged me for two years. I couldn't even convince myself to just do the part we skipped. No, I had to do the entire thing to successfully complete the mission. You've already knocked out 340 km. I'm guessing you don't want to do them again!"

A contemplative look emerged on Tara's face.

"So you are in the military," Al stated. "Thank you for your service."

"Thanks, I appreciate that. I'm retired, but it was a great career and way of life."

"It is hard for me to imagine all you've done," Al continued. "Where did you serve?"

"I was stationed at bases all over the US and around the world over almost thirty years in uniform. Combat-wise, I did two tours in Afghanistan, one in Iraq, and my most recent deployment was to Djibouti in the Horn of Africa."

Looking at the braces on my hands, he asked, "What happened to your hands?"

"Combat typing," I launched into my standard response. "That's how officers fight wars nowadays. We type e-mails, reports, and other documents on a computer, go to meetings, and make PowerPoint briefings."

The couple laughed heartily. "We civilians really don't have good grasp about what you do," Tara stated.

"You got that right! I get plenty of people thanking me for my service all the time, but it is apparent few really understand. But it's not their fault, I blame the media. All they ever report on are things that go *boom*." I launched into an explanation of the PRT mission and my role.

"Some reporters came to our base for a few days," I started zeroing in on my point. "We were getting ready to do a mission outside the wire to meet with the provincial governor and check on a couple of projects. I invited them to come along, but they refused. They wanted to go out with the kinetic unit in hopes of getting into a firefight so they could cover something exciting. Mundane meetings and construction projects, not a chance. If one hundred missions went outside the wire on a given day and one gets hit, that's the one covered on the evening news. There is never any mention of the ninety-nine peaceful convoys and all the good that they accomplished."

"So as a female, did you have any problems in the military?" Tara asked.

Interesting question, since I had been reflecting on my problems with Jones earlier.

"Yeah, I had to deal with some real jerks now and again. But I'm pretty sure there are jerks in civilian world. No matter what you do or where you do it, there will be people you don't get along with, who have different values and ways of doing things."

We discussed various other subjects for a while before Al and Tara excused themselves to attend the peregrino dinner. I headed back to the room to turn in early.

# CHAPTER 19

## Itero de la Vega to Villalcázar de Sirga, 28.8 Kilometers
## 13 Sep 2015
## D+15

When my alarm went off at 0700, the room was completely dark, and not a sound could be detected. I grabbed my cell phone and activated the light function, shielding it with a cupped hand so only enough light escaped to help me find my toothbrush and other hygiene items. I then made my way across the dark room to the bathroom. After completing my tasks, I returned to my bed to start packing up.

After fumbling around in the dark for a few minutes of trying to be as quiet as possible, Tara spoke up.

"You can turn the light on. Everyone else is gone."

I found the light switch, and sure enough, the light revealed that it was just Al, Tara, and myself left in the room.

"Incredible," I exclaimed. "How did they all get out of here without a sound? Those guys have a system down pat!"

After leisurely preparing my feet and packing my bag for the day, I got breakfast at the albergue's restaurant and was on the trail, with my pack on my back, by 0800. The weather forecast showed a 50 percent chance of rain starting at about 1500 hours. If I was going to be able to make almost 29 km before then, I needed to move out quickly.

\* \* \* \* \*

My thoughts returned to yesterday's reflections. The problems I had with Lt Col Jones, less-than-satisfactory results from the IG, and the extreme personal stress that sent my life into a tailspin was very similar to what I later experienced in Afghanistan and Iraq.

With twenty-twenty hindsight, I can see the big picture. Jones *and my boss in Iraq* were ultimately forced out the DoD, and I retired at a higher rank than Jones, thus my retirement income is significantly higher. I smiled. I guess in the end, there was some justice!

Although this realization was somewhat satisfying, it was egocentric. A more constructive perspective was that these extremely difficult times were vital episodes in my long journey to a closer relationship with God. Romans 8:28 says, "And we know that all things work together for good to those who love God, to those who are called according to His purpose."

In difficult and stressful times, it is extremely hard to detect this promise at work in your circumstance. At least it is for me. When religious friends tried to comfort me with this passage, in my frustration I perceived it as an empty Christian platitude, or "catchall phrase" used to explain away the painful and unexplainable. Their intent was to comfort me and give me hope that some good would come of my suffering. Of course, they always followed up with other "standard Christian responses," such as, "We cannot always understand God's purposes" or "God's timing is not our timing." Job's struggles are used as an example. "Who are we to question what God does?" I often wonder if I am the only Christian in the world that does not find this type of counsel comforting when their life is falling apart and they have no ability to stop it and God does not seem to answer their cries for help. Or is my attitude a telltale sign of a lack of faith?

I do not believe that God caused these hardships to happen, but I guess He can use difficult situations to shape us and draw us closer to Him. I believe that there are times when He sets in motion tough times for us because some of us just don't listen unless we are hit upside the head with a two-by-four. Maybe this is what happened with me, or maybe He just used the situations that unfolded to divert my eyes toward Him.

Up until my turmoil with Jones, my spiritual journey had been a roller coaster. There were many times when I felt very close to God and other times when He didn't seem to be a real part of my life.

I was raised in a strong Catholic home. We went to mass every Sunday and always attended Confraternity of Christian Doctrine (CCD) classes. My older sister and I were the first girls in our parish to serve as altar girls. We were fortunate to have a priest who was open to nonconventional ideas. As a teenager, I was confirmed into the church and took on the confirmation name of Joan, after Joan of Arc. I admired the strength of her faith and her warrior ethos. She was the prime example of how a woman could be strong in faith and deed. She seemed like the perfect role model for young woman bound for a military academy.

One day in the late '70s or early '80s, I was in our basement at home in Anchorage listening to a radio program that was discussing how, in the speaker's opinion, the Bible's prophecies that pointed to the end of the world were playing out in society. According to him, all the signs were there. Armageddon and the rapture were just around the corner. His warning and plea was that everyone would accept Jesus as their Lord and Savior before the end came, lest they be condemned to hell for eternity. There was little time remaining for people to make their decision.

The prospect scared me. Although the church had always been a major part of my life, what if I had never said the right prayer to actually be saved prior to this day? To be on the safe side, I repeated the radio preacher's prayer of salvation. I have often wondered if this was my personal day of salvation, my spiritual rebirthday? Or did I not have a solid-enough understanding about Jesus's sacrifice and what it meant for individuals to "accept the gift of salvation" based on faith alone? At that time, did I have enough belief and faith for my prayer to be effective, for salvation to "stick"?

During my freshman year at the academy, I was a regular at Catholic mass, even routinely attending weekday morning services. I found the services helped me handle the stress of fourth-class year. In fact, one of the most vivid memories I hold of that year is the sight of a large number of cadets bundled up in black parkas with black hoods covering their heads streaming like monks across the terrazzo and up the ramp to the beautiful academy chapel whose spires were reflecting the dawn's light on a cold winter morning against the beautiful backdrop of the snow-covered Rampart Range.

As the workload of my academic and military studies became overwhelming, I found myself going to fewer and fewer weekday masses. There just wasn't time to do everything. I needed every minute of sleep I could squeeze in. The other phenomenon that I experienced was going to mass too often resulted in a perception that I was just going through the motions. Catholic mass is ritual-oriented. You say the same prayers and kneel and stand at the same times, mass after mass. The only difference is the priest's homily, the announcements, and the specific songs sung. By going so often, I slipped into a bit of a rut. Mass lost its spiritual meaning and impact, and therefore everything else in my overwhelming schedule soon took priority. Out of the habit, I seldom went to mass during my upper-class years.

However, I accepted the invitation to visit an evangelical church off-base a few times my two-degree year. This was my first exposure to contemporary nondenominational Christian services that included praise and worship music, much less ritual (basically the services consisted of praise songs set to modern music performed by a praise team [band], the preacher's message, and communion once a month), and definitely less formal in regards to dress and interaction between the congregation and the preacher. I enjoyed the services and felt a new spiritual invigoration when I was able to attend, but my visits were few and far between due to my academic struggles. Since my friend graduated the year before me, I did not go at all senior year.

At some point during my academy years, I attended a Billy Graham revival event while visiting my sister in Spokane, Washington. An invitation was given at the end of a moving presentation about the plan of salvation. All humans have sinned. It has been our nature since Adam and Eve sinned for the first time in the Garden of Eden. Our ability to sin is a by-product of God's desire to have genuine fellowship with his people, and that's why he gave us "free will." This free will allows us to choose a relationship with God, but it also means we can choose to sin and reject God. Since God is holy and just, He cannot allow sin to go unpunished and He cannot fellowship with those stained by sin. The "wages" of sin is death. There is no level of sacrifice that a human can undertake to adequately pay for their sins. Only the sacrifice of Jesus's horrific crucifixion on the cross can atone for the sins of mankind. As God, Jesus had no sin and, therefore, was the only possible perfect sacrifice. He took all our sins, past and future, on Himself and paid for them with His life after undergoing unimaginable pain. Only by believing that Jesus is the Son of God Who died as payment for our sins and by personally accepting His gift can we be saved.

My soul was moved by the presentation. I believed I understood, and I sincerely wanted to accept the gift and establish a new relationship with God. I went forward to the stage, knelt down, and once again prayed the prayer of salvation. However, the emotion of that night soon wore off as I returned to my hectic academy life. Once again, it didn't seem to "stick."

My six-on-and-three-off schedule in Malmstrom's missile field was not conducive to attending services, and I don't remember ever going to church while stationed in Montana. Comiso was also spiritually dry, as was the beginning of my tour at Hahn.

While at Hahn, my off-duty days often consisted of day trips around Germany, and I really got into Volksmarching, ten- and twenty-kilometer hikes sponsored by villages all over Germany. On

Berg Eltz, Germany.

other days, I enjoyed drives along the banks of the Mosel river and visiting castles. I seldom had Sundays off and was enjoying seeing Germany when I did. I had no motivation to attend a church.

Things changed when I was reassigned to Delta Flight. My flight sergeant, Eric, was a devoted Baptist who attended an Independent Baptist church in the small town outside the base's main gate. The pastor's missionary calling was to minister to the US military stationed overseas. Eric was my right-hand man, so we often talked about what was going on, and he could see how it was tearing me up. He was also distressed by the negative impact the discrimination against me was having on the flight in general. He repeatedly invited me to join him and his family at their church. I resisted for several months before I agreed to go with them. I found out later that he had routinely asked church members pray for me during my time of professional and emotional struggles and resistance to his invitations. Everyone there knew who I was before I ever stepped through the door.

After a particularly stressful day, Eric told me that the church was having several days of revival meetings that week. Since we were working mids part of the week and then had three days off, attendance was possible.

Before agreeing to go, I had to ask the most important question: "How long is a service?"

He bluntly replied with a statement that I will never forget: "If you are there for the right reason, it doesn't matter how long it lasts."

Point taken.

I attended several revival meetings that week. I do not remember the sermons, but the plan of salvation was given every night, along with discussions about living a Christian life in a fallen world. At the end of each service, there was an invitation. This is when the preacher tells everyone to close their eyes and pray. He then asks anybody in the congregation who wanted to come forward and pray to receive Christ and salvation to do so. With every eye in the congregation closed, you could do it with some level of privacy.

Each time there was an invitation, my stomach seemed to tie in knots, and my heart felt compelled to go forward. But my pride and ego kept me in my seat. I felt that going forward would be embarrassing.

After the revival week, I started going to the weekly services when my work schedule allowed. One day Eric invited me his house for dinner with his family. After dinner his daughter disappeared, and his wife, Connie, and he got serious.

"So what do you think about the message at church?"

"I am enjoying the songs and the sermons. Sure gives me a lot to think about. The people are great."

"How about salvation? Are you ready to accept Christ?"

"I think I've already done that." I described the two times I had asked Christ to save me—in my basement as a teenager and later at the Billy Graham revival.

"Did either of those times change your life? Are you doing anything to develop your faith and grow in your relationship with God?" Connie asked.

"Not really, I don't know if I was really saved at these times. I don't know if it 'took.'"

"Only you and God really know that. It's probably something you should pray about and see what God shows you through his Holy Spirit," Eric explained.

"God may know, but I certainly am not sure."

During the half-hour drive home that evening, I was deep in thought. Once again I prayed for salvation and told God that I accepted His gift. Then a couple weeks later, on Easter morning, I finally heeded the tug on my heart and went forward to the altar during the invitation. I explained to the preacher's wife how I had prayed in the car that night, and we prayed again together. After the invitation, we announced my decision to the congregation. Everyone was excited and clapped. Several people came to me afterward and told me that they had been praying for months for me and that they were so glad that I had finally committed my life to Christ.

From then on, I was at the church whenever the doors were open and I was not on duty. I also joined a weekly Bible study that was held at the house of a chief master sergeant.

I became very close to the members of the congregation and started wearing dresses to church events. This was a major change in my life. I had not worn a dress since I was a very young girl. I hated them! However, the Independent Fundamental Baptists believe that women should only wear dresses. I never did buy into this entirely, but eventually I felt it would be appropriate to at least do so while at church.

After a while, I gave up drinking alcohol. Because of the stress and emotional turmoil, I had been steadily increasing my intake of German wine. I loved the taste and often bought it directly from a winery along the Mosel River a few miles from my house. But when I drank an entire bottle in one night after a particularly stressful day, I realized that I was drinking too much. My church taught that Christians should not drink alcohol at all. When I questioned them about Jesus turning water into wine at the wedding and other references to wine at dinner events, they explained that in those days, wine was not the same as we think of it today. It was not fermented, so it was actually more like grape juice. I never was convinced of this since I found Bible passages mentioning being "drunk with wine," but since it was obvious that I was drinking too much, I decided to give it up.

Although my spiritual journey has not been completely smooth since then, I have consistently pursued a relationship with Christ and joined churches and Bible studies wherever stationed. Far from perfect, it seems to have "stuck" this time.

* * * * *

The morning had been cold and windy. A mist hung in the air, and there was an occasional light drizzle. By the time I stopped for lunch just after noon, the temperature had only reached fifty-five degrees. I was still wearing my coat and gloves.

I accessed the restaurant's Wi-Fi and checked the weather again. It was no longer showing rain for the afternoon, at least not for this village. Still, I figured it would be wise to cover my pack with the rain shield for the final leg just in case. It couldn't hurt.

My right foot was feeling better today, so I was confident that I could make the 28 km. It was interesting that as the swollen area started to feel better, the chronic foot problems started to take center stage again.

It was as if my toes were saying, "You are not going to get out of this that easy!"

The pain kept reminding me to limit my stride length and not go too fast.

Encouraged by the rainless forecast, I opted to take the longer scenic green route on an earthen trail through farm fields and along a tree-lined river. It was just a kilometer further. Definitely much more relaxing. Amazingly, I only saw a couple other pilgrims who chose the natural route. The solitude walking through the trees next to a river was extremely peaceful, at least for a while.

Lies, lies, and more lies! I don't know who loads the weather information for my app, but they sure got it wrong this day. About 1415 it started raining and had soon worked its way up to a downpour. For the next forty-five minutes, I regretted not bringing rain pants. My pants were soon soaking wet, and the water flowed from them into the top of my waterproof shoes. Apparently, shoes are only waterproof up to the hole where my foot was inserted.

When I reached the intersection with the country road that would take me back to the main route and my destination for the night, I passed a church where a couple of soaking pilgrims were waiting out the storm under the covered entryway. I was tempted to join them, but it was only 1.7 more kilometers to the village. Who knows how long the rain would last, and I couldn't get any wetter than I already was. So I decided to press on. Once signed into an albergue, I could get a shower and put on dry clothing. Hopefully, they would have a washer and dryer.

I felt bad as I walked across the restaurant to the bar to check in, dripping and sloshing in my shoes the entire way. The hostess did not seem at all concerned; apparently she was used to guests arriving this way. I proceeded to give her my arthritis sob story with renewed vigor since my hands and feet hurt so bad from being wet and cold. She took mercy on me, showed me to a room, and removed the "reserved" sign off a lower bunk.

"You may sleep here," she said.

"Gracias, you are so kind!"

I hung my wet clothes on bed rails and over a chair to dry because they did not have a dryer. Taking the orthotics and metal plates out of my shoes and opening up the laces, I did the best I could to facilitate drying. I found some newspaper and wadded up a few pages to stuff into the shoes. This would absorb some of the moisture. I then headed for the restaurant to plan tomorrow.

I recognized a lady enjoying a glass of wine. Purchasing my own, I asked to join her. Her name was Eunice, and we had run into each other numerous times over the last few days.

"It's good to see you," she said. "Marty is here too. She'll be back in a few minutes."

Marty soon joined us, followed by Joy, whom I had met at dinner two nights before. All from Canada, the three had been hiking a lot together.

Marty was not a happy camper. She was still in her wet clothing. She had shipped her pack today and had yet to find it. We convinced her to ask the hospitalero for assistance. Marty related where she had stayed the night before, and the hospitalero called to inquire about the pack. Sure enough, it was there. The person on the other end of the phone explained that the company had not picked it up because the destination and payment envelope had not been attached.

Marty was baffled. "I checked and double-checked it. I am positive everything was correct and it was attached securely."

Surprised, we surmised someone must have taken the envelope. The hospitalero called a taxi, and it cost Marty 35€ round-trip to go back and get it. We waited until she returned to order dinner.

By then, two other ladies from Canada that I had first met on the third night joined us. We found it interesting that everyone was from Canada except me. The rest of the group decided that I could be an honorary Canadian since I lived only about fifty miles south of the border. Close enough, they said.

The attacks of 9/11 was the primary topic of conversation as we enjoyed our pilgrims' dinner together. Once again I related the stories about what had gone on at Luke in the aftermath of that fateful day. Everyone else explained what they had been doing and how they felt when they heard the news. Marty had been hiking in the mountains that day and had no idea what was going on until she returned to the trailhead in late afternoon.

They were also interested to know why I wore braces on my hands.

"Combat typing," I dove into my standard speech. "It does a real number on a person's joints!" I concluded.

# CHAPTER 20

## Villalcázar de Sirga to Calzadilla de la Cueza, 23 Kilometers
## 14 Sep 2015
## D+16

The beautiful sunny day started by sharing breakfast with Eunice and Marty. Ordering freshly made "tortilla con chorizo, no pan" was the second sign of a good day! This was the first time I had been able to order a sausage omelet without a loaf of bread. During the second half of the 2013 hike, this had become a staple for me.

After getting a "puppy fix," petting an energetic black Lab that greeted us as we stepped onto the street, two of my Canadian friends and I followed the yellow arrows through town. It turned out that the dog was hiking the Camino with his owner. We saw him a couple more times during the day's first stretch. I stopped to pet him each time.

The path was a wide dirt trail along the side of the busy road I had successfully avoided yesterday. I must've pushed too hard yesterday. The forward section of my right foot screamed in pain with each step. I was also developing a blister on my right heel. It was quite a struggle to keep up with Eunice and Marty, but I managed for five clicks until we got to the end of stage 16, Carrión de Condes.

While enjoying a coffee break, I informed my companions I was going to need to slow down and could not keep up with them.

"See you along The Way," I said, slinging my pack.

With a joyous "Bein Camino," they headed out at their normal quick pace.

The map in the guidebook showed the rest of today's trail was an earthen path, well away from the road. There was a mobile café a little more than halfway, but that was about it for the next 17 km. I stopped at a small grocery store before leaving town to purchase an apple and a large Swiss chocolate bar to take along as snacks.

My pace was slower than it had been for quite some time. Regardless of how my foot felt, I would not be able to stop early since there were no facilities until the end of this stretch. It was far too early to stop, so I really had no choice but to give it a go. I just needed to take my time and not push my foot too hard, as I had obviously done yesterday.

\* \* \* \* \*

My reflections turned to my next assignment at Little Rock Air Force Base near Jacksonville, Arkansas. I was stationed there from September 1992 until November 1994.

I was assigned as the readiness officer at the prestigious 314th Ground Combat Readiness Evaluation Squadron (GCRES), better known as Volant Scorpion. Combat support teams came to our schoolhouse to prepare for potential deployments. The program was unique in that it conducted integrated, multifunctional training with numerous career fields. Besides SPs, our training included field medics, combat camera, explosive ordnance disposal (EOD), civil engineering (CE), communications, prime ribs (food services), and Tactical Airlift Control Element (TALCE) teams. Our integrated training allowed the various career fields to learn about each other's mission and how they could best work together to establish and operate remote, austere airfields where C-130s could deliver personnel, equipment, and supplies to Army combat units near the front lines.

It was an honor to be assigned as a member of the cadre in this "selectively manned" unit. I held the distinction of being the first female officer ever assigned to Volant Scorpion. There had been a couple of enlisted females assigned, but none in a leadership position.

As the readiness officer, I was in charge of supply and logistics support for the training courses and our own unit mobility deployment tasking. I also managed the unit budget, facility upgrades, and equipment acquisitions. Finally my flight was responsible for the care and maintenance of ninety vehicles. Since I did not have a direct role in the instruction or evaluation of the student teams, I was often available to perform duties as OPFOR. I had really enjoyed doing this at Comiso and was excited to have the chance to do it again.

Capt. Meck (back right) and other GCRES OPFOR team members.

Besides the classes that we conducted in the back woods of Little Rock AFB, unit personnel were tasked with observer/controller (O/C) duties at Army-run Joint Readiness Training Center (JRTC) exercises. During each ten-day exercise, Army units consisting of thousands of soldiers, all sorts of heavy equipment, and even tanks and helicopters descended on a huge training area to practice all aspects of war and contingency operations. The Air Force contributed a multifunctional contingent that operated the dirt runway in the "box" so we could practice supporting Army maneuvers (the "box" was the active exercise maneuver area). The exercise normally started with Air Force Security Police and TALCE personnel working with an Army team to occupy and secure the dirt runway. C-130s would then bring in additional forces who would move out to execute the rest of the mission. It was excellent integrated joint (meaning, more than one military service) training that help me develop fundamental skills that paid huge dividends during joint humanitarian and combat deployments later in my career.

When I first arrived at GCRES, the commander sent me out as a "player" to one of these rotations as a training opportunity. I was assigned as the Air Force's liaison officer (LNO) to the Army Brigade's Tactical Operations Center (TOC), their highest level control center in the box. Not very concerned about taking care of the troops, the Army had no plan for my workspace or sleeping quarters. So my first job was to coordinate work space at a table along the side of the large TOC tent. I had a small tent but ended up sleeping underneath a vehicle trailer for the first few nights. I don't remember why exactly, but it might have been just a matter of being tired and not having the time or motivation to set up the tent.

This was my first real opportunity to work closely with the Army and I often felt like I was beating my head against the wall trying to get things done. This is where I first learned that *joint* is spelled A-R-M-Y. In other words, in joint operations when the Army was the lead (and often even when they were not the lead), you were expected to do things the Army way, and they were not open to alternative suggestions. A phenomenon that I would struggle with many times during joint deployments and assignments throughout my career.

Six months later I returned to JRTC as an O/C for another rotation. This time the weather was very cold. About halfway through the exercise, it rained ice one night. A thick, heavy layer of ice covered all the camouflage netting and tents, and many started collapsing from the weight. Everyone performing outside duties during the exercise's standard "blackout" conditions became extremely wet and cold. With ice everywhere, all movements, whether by the vehicle or by foot, were dangerous. Myself and the senior AF O/C became concerned about the safety of the players. Much to the frustration of the Army, we made the call to implement a safety PauseEx (pause exercise) so that the players could concentrate on dealing with the collapsing camouflage netting and tents, while bringing their freezing personnel into heated areas to warm up. We did not want somebody to get hurt or killed fending off OPFOR attacks in these conditions. The Army tried to tell us we were not authorized to do this, but we held our ground. I am sure they thought the AF was "weak," but we decided that erring on the side of safety was the right thing to do. Even with this precaution, by morning the SP players had managed to burn down one of their sector CPs when something went wrong with the potbelly stove they were using to heat the tent. Fortunately, we just had to deal with a few smoke inhalation cases and plenty of costly equipment damage, but no one was seriously injured.

During the summer of 1993, the officer in charge (OIC) of the Readiness Evaluation Flight PCSed to a new assignment, and I moved up into that position. I was now in charge of the operational instruction and exercise evaluations for our schoolhouse. Additionally, I was the second-in-command of the unit.

By this time, in the AF's spirit of "constant improvement," the name of the Major Command we were assigned to changed from Mobility Airlift Command (MAC) to Air Mobility Command (AMC), obviously a monumental step forward in the history of the Air Force. Because of this change, all "Volant" programs had to change their name to "Phoenix" programs, and we became Phoenix ACE. However, internally the cadre maintained their loyalty to the Volant Scorpion name. Once a Scorpion, always a Scorpion!

One of my proudest moments in this position was on a day when I was manning an M-60 machine gun bunker at the end of the tactical movement course. One of the teams to go through the course that day was a Navy unit led by an overly egotistical, male chauvinistic lieutenant (the Navy rank equivalent to an AF captain). Not even realizing who it was because of his camouflage, I engaged him with the M-60 as he made his way toward the bunker. His MILES gear quickly emitted the piercing, steady squeal that indicated he had been killed. My staff later informed me that he was enraged when he found out that a woman had killed him! Chalk it up as a victory for all of womankind!

Contemplating the list of Murphy's Laws of Combat we often referred to offered some comic relief as I trudged along the lonely, desolate trail:

1. Keep it simple, stupid.
2. If it's stupid and it works, it ain't stupid.
3. Incoming fire has the right-of-way.
4. If the enemy is in range—so are you.
5. Don't look conspicuous, it draws fire.
6. There is always a way.
7. The easy way is always mined.
8. In war, all the important things are simple, and all the simple things are very hard.
9. Try to look unimportant; they may be low on ammo.

10. Professionals are predictable; it's the amateurs that are dangerous.
11. The enemy invariably attacks on two occasions:
    —When you're ready for them
    —When you're not ready for them
12. Fortify your front well enough, and you'll get your rear shot up!
13. Teamwork is essential; it gives them someone else to shoot at.
14. If you can't remember, the Claymore is pointed at you.
15. No combat-ready unit ever "passed" inspection.
16. No inspection-ready unit ever "passed" combat.
17. The enemy diversion you have been ignoring will be the main attack.
18. A "sucking chest wound" is nature's way of telling you to slow down.
19. If your attack is going well, it's an ambush.
20. All your five-second grenades will have three-second fuses.
21. Never draw fire; it irritates everyone around you.
22. When you have secured an area, don't forget to tell the enemy.
23. All warfare is based on deception, with the major problem being to fool the enemy and not yourself.
24. Anything you do can get you shot, including doing nothing.
25. Make it tough enough for the enemy to get in, and you won't be able to get out.
26. Never share a foxhole with anyone braver than yourself.
27. If you're short of everything but the enemy, you're in a combat zone.
28. No battle plan survives contact with the enemy.
29. Each side is convinced they are about to lose—they are both right.
30. Comm will fail as soon as you need it.
31. All your weapons are made by the lowest bidder.

Have a nice day!

Author anonymous

In 1994, my flight and I were tasked with planning for and deploying as the SP HQ unit and the core of the HQ for the various other functional area player units for a JRTC rotation. I was the primary leader during the preparation phases. We developed the operations order (OPORD) for the 369-person, 16-AFSC Combat Support Group (Provisional). I led the planning for a multifunctional Leadership Planning Conference (LPC) and then orchestrated the Intermediate Staging Base (ISB) activities at our compound where the diverse player units came together for final preparatory activities before we boarded the C-130s to travel to the box which had moved to Louisiana.

It was an extremely cold and wet February in 1994. So miserable—in fact, our commander started referring to the ridge where we set up operations as "Piss on Ridge." We spent quite a bit of time trying to walk through knee-deep mud and extracting vehicles that had sunk into it.

Because of the significant unit accomplishments, we were honored as the Outstanding Security Police Squadron (Small Unit) for AMC for both 1993 and 1994. We were also awarded the Air Force Organizational Excellence Award for 1994.

I loved being a part of this unit and its mission, but as I had experienced a few times before, being a trailblazer for military women was not without its frustrations and disappointments. During the summer of 1993, GCRES was tasked to provide a SP HQ element to deploy to Mogadishu, Somalia, in support of Operation RESTORE HOPE. As the second-in-command of GCRES, and based on the official tasking requiring a captain as the team leader, I should have commanded the deploying team. Instead, our new commander requested and received approval to send our operations superintendent, a senior master sergeant (SMSgt), as the team leader. Even though senior-enlisted personnel have extensive experience, it is not normal to deploy them to fill an officer's position. Even more suspect in this circumstance was that his wife had just given birth to two tiny premature babies. He was needed at home, and I was enthusiastic about deploying. Regardless, the commander sent the senior and never gave me an acceptable explanation. He simply stated that he felt the senior was more qualified to lead the team. I cannot imagine this happening to a male officer.

* * * * *

What a long, boring 10.1 km stretch to the picnic area where the mobile café was supposed to be! Traversing an old Roman road that was still usable after two thousand years provided an interesting diversion from the boring, flat landscape.

Regrettably, the mobile café had already closed for the season. The guidebook warned it was only open in the summer but did not designate the dates of closure. I figured there were still enough pilgrims walking that it would still be open, but it was not. Fortunately, there was a potable water spicket available to refill my small water bottle. I removed my pack and sat at a picnic table to eat my apple and read the service study for day 14.

The author demonstrated that prayers recorded in the Bible could be used effectively by believers today. By inserting the person's name or changing a pronoun, you can personalize a biblical prayer to be a praise or request for yourself or another person. Colossians 1:9–12 and Philippians 1:3–11 were slightly modified as examples. I used the example to pray for my Afghan friend who converted to Christianity:

> Lord Christ, I ask that you fill [Mark] with the knowledge of your will in all spiritual wisdom and understanding. Teach [him] to walk in a manner worthy of you, Lord, fully pleasing to you, bearing fruit in every good work and increasing in the knowledge of God. May [he] be strengthened with all power, according to your glorious might, for all endurance and patience with joy, giving thanks to the Father, who has qualified us to share in the inheritance of the saints in light.[25]

---

[25] Fryar, p. 30.

As I was finishing up, Pat and Peggy arrived and joined me at the picnic table. We spent a few minutes talking and sharing my chocolate bar before I embarked on the final leg of the day's trek. They settled in for a leisurely lunch.

I thought the next 7.2 km would never end! The wide, flat gravel trail through the brown remnants of crop fields stretched straight ahead as far as I could see with few signs of civilization.

There was a strong, cold-head wind making my progress chilly, slow, and labored. Once again I was convinced the weight of my pack kept me from being blown away!

It wasn't long before I started to run low on water and decided to ration it. I decided to wait at least thirty minutes between swallows in hopes of stretching the small bottle of water until I arrived at the next village. I should have paid closer attention to the written description of the day's route in the guidebook. It clearly described the need for pilgrims to bring plenty of food and water along due to the lack the supplies over a great distance. I wanted to kick myself. I was allowing complacency to hinder effective mission planning. I should have filled my CamelBak with water!

\* \* \* \* \*

To pass the time, my mind reflected on the development of my spiritual walk while in Arkansas.

My first priority upon arrival was to find a house to rent within a reasonable commute to the base. Still on a spiritual high from my experiences at Hahn, the second priority was to find a new church home. Since Grace was an Independent Baptist church, I sought out the same denomination in Jacksonville. A simple look in the phone book showed one conveniently positioned between my new rental house and the base. I started attending the next Sunday morning.

It turned out to be a good-sized church with many wonderful ministries and support programs. I was especially intrigued to discover they had a Bible study group for single adults. Hanging out with married couples was okay, but I often felt like a third wheel, like I was intruding or that they were inviting me over more as a charity as opposed to developing friendships. I jumped at the opportunity to join the singles group.

Things were starting out great at this new assignment. I loved my new unit, its mission, the other cadre, and working in a combat training environment in the backwoods of the base, and I had a good church to grow in my faith.

It was not long before my two worlds, work and church, began to collide. While at work, I wore the battle dress uniform (BDU), with a black cadre hat, and often put camouflage on my face and maneuvered around the woods shooting lasers at students.

At the church, I often felt like a second-class citizen. Being female meant I could not lead anyone except other females. I had to wear a dress because pants were "men's clothes," and I was extremely limited on how I could participate in events. For example, one day the church was holding a potluck. I arrived a little early while setup was still going on. Assessing the situation, I determined that I could help by bringing chairs over to the tables. I had not even got the first one in place before I was told in no uncertain terms that it was "man's work" and I was not to do it.

After the Sunday evening service a couple months later, the singles group planned to go on a hayride and then roast marshmallows and make s'mores by a bonfire in the woods. Before loading up in the van, I decided it would be best to change out of my dress and put on a pair of jeans for the event. Most people had left when I went into the women's bathroom and changed. As I reemerged into the church foyer, the pastor's wife noticed my attire. She didn't say anything, but I will never forget the ugly, disapproving expression on her face.

I murmured, "We're going on a hayride in the woods," and scurried out the front door into the parking lot as quickly as I could.

In my mind it would have been far more inappropriate for a female to sit on a bunch of hay in the back of a trailer and to sit around a bonfire in the woods with a dress on. No one in the singles group seemed to care that I wore pants, but the damage had been done. I never went back to that church.

I found another Independent Baptist church about a half hour away and started attending it. They were much smaller and less formal. I think they were just happy to have a new member even though I was not perfect. But my mind and heart were in spiritual conflict. Everyone at both churches seemed impressed with my occupation and duties on base. What I could not reconcile is, how could it be okay for me to lead men and run around in the woods with camouflage on my face, shooting at people while at work, and then have to wear a dress and not be allowed to move a chair while at church? How could there be two completely different standards of conduct depending on your location? Shouldn't they be consistent across your life's activities?

I was faced with a terrible dilemma. If what the Independent Baptist church was telling me was true, logically, I should resign my commission, find a husband, and be limited to being "barefoot and pregnant in the kitchen." My perception of their teaching was that a woman's role was to be a mother and submissive wife and maybe a Sunday schoolteacher for children. That's it.

But I could not accept this as being God's will for my life. I had prayed extensively for an appointment to the academy, endured and conquered many hardships and struggles while there, and had managed to survive multiple situations where I was discriminated against because of my sex. I honestly believed that I had made it through these events and managed to successfully progress in my career in spite of them because of God's protection and guiding hand on the flow of my life. He had helped me through all these hardships because He had plans for me and my military career. It had not always been easy, but He had helped me endure and persevere.

These two views regarding what my life should be like where incompatible. They could not both be true. So either I had prevailed in life while going against God's will, or this particular denomination of the church was not interpreting the scriptures accurately.

So I left the second church as well. A friend recommended a nondenominational evangelical church about forty-five minutes away. I visited and immediately felt at home. It was remarkably similar to the church I had attended a few times in Colorado Springs with my friend from the class of '86. Everyone dressed casually, and plenty of women wore pants. There was a praise-and-worship band, and the services were far less formal than either the Catholic church or the Independent Baptists. We were even allowed to drink coffee during the service! The praise-and-worship band was extraordinary. They were so good that they had produced a CD, which I purchased and listened to routinely later while assigned to a remote base in southeastern Turkey. Their music was spiritually uplifting and proclaimed the wonderful message of God's grace, love for us, and His purpose for our lives.

The people in the Bible study groups I joined were very supportive of my military career. When I explained the spiritual conflict I had been battling, many told me that they had also been disillusioned and discouraged by fundamental legalism. They actually had a name for it. They explained that legalism had ruined many relationships with Christ. It puts the focus on a bunch of rules and regulations that are not necessarily biblical, instead of focusing on our relationship with our Father in heaven.

"You shall know the truth, and the truth shall set you free" (John 8:32) became my "life verse" for this period. It is not God's will for us to live in bondage to the repressive rules of man. But rather we are free to worship God, to serve Him, and to follow His will for our life. We obey and serve God out of sincere gratitude for what He has done for us, not out of obligation to fulfill someone's interpretation of the "law." True faith was all about belief and relationship!

New life was breathed into my spiritual walk, and I started to grow again. I developed close relationships with many people in the church, and to this day, I financially contribute to one of their ministries that provides support to two struggling churches in Russia.

\* \* \* \* \*

Down to one remaining swallow of water, I began to wonder if I would ever reach the village of Calzadilla de la Cueza. In the distance I saw a small hill. Maybe the village would be visible from the top! It had to be. How much further could it possibly be? Despair flowed over me as I crested the top only to behold another long, straight stretch of dirt road.

There was another incline about a kilometer away. Maybe this would be it. As the ongoing desolate trail became visible from the top of this second hill, a small amount of guarded hope filled my heart. In the distance, I could see a tower rising above the brown fields. Could this be the village water tower? A sign of civilization?

As I closed in on the tower, I was once again overcome with sheer disappointment. It was just a farm tower with a stack of hay next to it. But wait, the world dipped down out of sight just past the tower. Did I dare to hope yet again?

After another laborious ten minutes and now completely out of water, I finally saw rooftops! Once I started down the hill, two albergues could be seen not even one hundred meters ahead. Praise the Lord! I was finally there.

Just before the albergues, there was a small village park with a water fountain. Almost desperate with thirst, I filled my water bottle and drank it completely down. Filling it again, I proceeded to the municipal albergue on the left side of the road. To my delight, they had a laundry service—wash and dry for six euros.

After dropping off my laundry, I found a restaurant serving bar food at this early hour. I ordered a pizza and wine and then conducted mission planning for tomorrow. According to my weather app, it would be raining starting late tomorrow morning and continuing throughout the rest of the day. I decided I would only go about 10 km and then treat myself to a hotel or casa rural, taking a semi-day off. My feet could use the break, and I certainly did not want to get soaking wet again.

Speaking of the weather, I marveled at how it had changed over the last two and a half weeks. The first few days the temperatures had reached the midnineties. Today it barely reached sixty. I had begun to worry about cold pernio sores developing on my feet due to the cold nights and mornings. They could be very painful to walk on. I was having enough problems with my feet! I needed to take special care to keep them warm.

As I finished my glass of wine, a couple of pilgrims I had not previously met joined me. As we discussed our treks so far, one of them pointed out that we were now halfway through the Camino. Looking at my distance log, I saw that she was correct. We were three clicks past the halfway point!

Back at the albergue courtyard, I read a few more chapters of *Seeking Allah, Finding Jesus*. Chapters 17 and 18 continued to discuss the author's Islamic education and his struggle with the cultural conflict at school and with his American friends.

The theme of chapter 19 hit a lot closer to home for me personally. He describes how the terrorist attacks of 9/11/2001 sent his spiritual life into a tailspin, as it did mine.

As the facts unfolded and it became clear the perpetrators were, in fact, Muslim and they had carried out the attacks in the name of Islam, Nabeel was confused and very disturbed. The Islam he had been taught and loved was a religion of peace. The inconsistency was overwhelming, and he became determined to learn the truth about his faith. His initial research indicated Islam could be a religion of peace or terror, depending on how a particular denomination interpreted the Koran and supporting books. Denominations in Western countries tended to teach that Muhammad only used violence in a defensive context and that jihad was a peaceful, internal struggle against one's fleshly desires. In the East, Muslims are taught to use violence against those who do not believe in Islam and that jihad is a physical struggle against the religion's enemies. Eastern denominations of Islam believe that "Islam will dominate the world."

He points out that, as he contends is common in most belief systems, Muslims believe what they are taught and do not critically investigate the history behind their beliefs. Complementing this tendency, social Islamic norms teach that you do not challenge authority, especially not of religious leaders. You do not question their teachings.

The repeated images of the attacks of 9/11 on TV led him to commit himself to critically investigate his religion with the intent of finding the truth. It was this investigation that eventually led him to convert to Christianity.[26]

The attacks caused me to question my Christian faith for different reasons. My logical mind was amazed the perpetrators had such a strong faith in what they were taught that they were willing to fly planes into buildings, killing themselves and thousands of strangers because they believed that god wanted them to do it. They planned and trained for this event for years. Throughout that time, their faith remained firm, and they truly believed they were carrying out the will of Allah.

My faith was not that strong. I could never tell if God was leading me in a particular direction or if it was my own personal desires motivating me to take my life in a particular direction. God never spoke to me through the flames of a burning bush. There were numerous passages in the Bible that did not make sense to me or seemed to contradict other parts of the Bible. All this combined to confuse me and left me with doubts about the reliability of the Bible. Was it really the inspired Word of God, or was it the interpretations of what man thought God was telling them to write? Did I believe in the Christian Gospel because that was how I was raised and taught? Had I been indoctrinated and brainwashed into believing Christianity as the 9/11 attackers had been brainwashed to believe Islam? Was my faith more a factor of where I was born and the religion of my family, or had I been taught the universal truth by my caring parents, friends, and community? How was I to truly know?

Doubts flooded my spiritual life as my career was increasingly focused on and shaped by the war on terrorism. I entered an extended period of spiritual warfare that had yet to be completely resolved.

---

[26] Qureshi, chapters 17–19.

# CHAPTER 21

## Calzadilla de la Cueza to Moratinos, 12.7 Kilometers
### 15 Sep 2015
### D+17

I awoke just before 0630 to the muffled sounds of peregrinos quietly trying to get ready in the dark. The first order of business was to get an intel update on the weather. Rain was still expected starting around 1000. Obviously, this would be a short day. But . . . not such a bad thing. My feet could definitely use a break. It had been my intention from the start to take periodic days off so as not to burn myself out or cause injury that would require me to stop. Apparently, God was forcing the issue with the rain.

I may fall behind the friends that I spent a lot of time with over the last few days, but no worries. They may take a day off in the near future, or they may even do the same thing I am doing in order to avoid the rain.

* * * * *

I expected to stay in GCRES for at least three years. However, we were informed about halfway through my second year that AMC had decided to move the entire unit to McGuire Air Force Base in New Jersey. The intent was to consolidate our unit with other mobility training units under the umbrella of the new Air Mobility Warfare Center. The move would enhance our training capacity because McGuire was next to the Army's Fort Dix, which had extensive field training areas and a wide variety of weapons firing ranges that we would be able to schedule for our classes.

If I moved with the unit, it would be considered a PCS and would reset the clock. I would not be eligible to move again for three years. Together, that would be five years at GCRES. Not good for career progression. Officers needed to change positions every two to three years in order to develop into the well-rounded officer that was needed at higher ranks. Five years at a specialized unit would be career suicide, so I decided to request an overseas assignment.

The director of security police for AMC thought I would be an excellent match for the chief security police (CSP) position at Pirinclik Air Station (AS) in southeast Turkey. My stomach churned, but I hid my revulsion as best I could. I had once told a friend that there were three places that I did not ever want to be stationed: Turkey (third world, Muslim country), England (six-month quarantine for dogs), and the Pentagon (political puzzle palace). Now one of the most respected leaders in my career field was telling me that he would really like me to take a position in Turkey. How could I say no?

On the plus side, a CSP position was a major step up. The USAF contingent at this small, remote base had less than three hundred airmen and US contractors assigned to it. Everyone was assigned to the 722nd Air Base Squadron (ABS) with the various functional areas being assigned to subordinate flights. The 722nd was a geographically separated unit (GSU) assigned under the command of the 39th Wing at Incirlik Air Base near Adana. I would not be an actual "commander," but I would be the "top cop" on the base.

Approaching Pirinclik Air Station
Dec 1994

It was a one-year remote assignment, so even if it turned out to be as awful a place as I envisioned, the tour would be over before I knew it.

"I can do a year standing on my head," I jokingly told a friend just before I left.

Pirinclik was a small radar and communication site near the city of Diyarbakir about

271

thirty miles from both the Iraqi and Syrian borders. It was also strategically close to the southern borders of the old Soviet Union. The massive radar screens gathered intel from both the Middle East and the Soviet space launch facilities in Kapustin Yar and also provided space surveillance and missile warning.[27] Historically, the base was famous for detecting the launch of *Sputnik* from the Soviet Union in 1957.

I was stationed there from November 1994 until December 1995. During this period, the base had the added responsibility of supporting a helicopter unit that was billeted on the base and traveled to a nearby Turkish Air Base to fly missions into northern Iraq in support of Operation PROVIDE COMFORT (OPC). Not long before my arrival, the unit had lost two Blackhawk helicopters in northern Iraq. Pirinclik was the staging base for recovery operations.

My flight of 51 SP airman was the largest military functional area on base. Because the Kurdistan Workers' Party (PKK) was waging a war against the Turkish government in the area, we were also one of the more important. Our close coordination and combined (*combined* means "involving military personnel from more than one country") security operations with the small Turkish element on the base was vital to protecting both Turkish and US nationals.

There was plenty of terrorist activity in the area around the base. So much so that other Americans stationed in western Turkey were not allowed to go east of Gaziantep. Pirinclik was about hundred miles east of there. Whenever anyone needed to leave the base, we had to be in a convoy of at least two vehicles. This way, if one vehicle was incapacitated, everyone could pile into the other and escape the kill zone. We also were required to have two satellite phones with us at all times, one in each vehicle. This technology was brand-new at the time, and the phones were huge. I estimate one phone weighed over ten pounds. We were not allowed to wear uniforms off-base, had to be back to base before dark, and were often restricted to base completely due to heightened local threats.

---

[27] "Pirinçlik Air Base," Wikipedia, February 21, 2015, https://en.wikipedia.org/wiki/Pirin%C3%A7lik_Air_Base.

Less than a month after I arrived, our base commander and the only other officer that outranked me went to the main US base in Turkey, Incirlik, for meetings. This left me in charge of the base for a couple of days. The first night our Security Control Center received threats against the base over the base radio's security frequency. The Turkish-accented broadcaster warned that they were going to attack our base and rape all of our women. Great! Just what I needed! I was brand-new in-country and left in command of a base for the first time ever, and now, on my first evening in charge, we received an attack threat.

I directed that the threat information be upchanneled to the CP at Incirlik, implemented THREATCON Delta (our highest threat level that indicated an imminent local threat), and fortified the perimeter. Simultaneously, I worked through our interpreters to coordinate support from the local paramilitary police forces that secured the area around the base. It turned out to be a false alarm, and the local police identified and arrested the joker. Still, it was a heart-pounding initiation to the war on terror.

Another day, several bombs exploded along the route normally taken by the base morale bus used by off-duty personnel to go downtown for short shopping trips and dining. This incident highlighted the fact that this practice made us vulnerable and the lone, armed Turkish soldier that rode in the front of the bus was basically useless, providing little more than a psychological sense of security.

On another occasion, a two-van convoy en route to Incirlik came under fire, and one of the vehicles was damaged enough that it could not be driven further. Per SOP, everyone crowded into the other van and sped out of the area. They were unable to identify where the shots had come from, and we were never able to determine if our vans were actually the target or if they were just in the wrong place at the wrong time. There was some speculation that the shots could have been errant bullets from a wedding celebration.

In another incident, I was central in the orchestration of the investigative response and host nation coordination when an American contractor was stabbed while patronizing an off-limits establishment downtown. Our actions to extract the wounded contractor and coordinate his medical evacuation to Incirlik ensured his survival. It was kind of frustrating. What part of "off-limits" did he not understand? This particular one was a brothel, and he paid a high price for his lack of self-control. In my opinion, he should have been required to reimburse the US government for the price of his rescue!

On less exciting days, I worked diligently with my staff to improve security procedures and infrastructure to protect the base. I thrived in this high-threat environment and ended up loving the assignment that I had earlier vowed to avoid. I was awarded Company Grade Officer of the Year for the 722 ABS for both 1994 and 1995, and for the 39th Support Group (the group our squadron reported to at Incirlik) for 1995.

Suffice it to say, things were looking up for my career.

\* \* \* \* \*

One kilometer into the day's hike, I diverted to the scenic option. The path veered off to the left across a river and then followed the river which paralleled the road, but a considerable distance away. The river flowed through a beautiful wooded area which produced an amazing feeling of tranquility.

The scenic path rejoined the primary at the end of stage 17 in Terradillos de los Templarios. My initial intent was to stop here for the night, but it was just before 0930, and forecast now showed the storm would not hit for another one to two hours. I decided to press on to the next village 3.2 clicks away.

\* \* \* \* \*

As great for my career as Pirinclik was, there were some frustrations—primarily with how the Turks treated the United States. In my humble opinion, they had an inferiority complex. It was as if they were always trying to prove that they had power over us. Obviously it was their country, but they used our desire to respect their sovereignty to establish and demonstrate their dominion over us in very frustrating ways.

My first encounter with this mind-set was when I had to fill out paperwork on each of my electronic devices that came in my personal item shipment. This was because any electronic devices that were brought into country became the property of the Turkish government after they had been in-country for ninety days. Our government negotiated an exception for individual personal property.

US government electronics of any type, such as computers and even airplanes, became the property of the Turkish government after being in-country for ninety days. Because of this, the 39th Wing at Incirlik had to rotate their planes with new ones every eighty-nine days. What an incredible waste of US taxpayer money. When Pirinclik closed, all computers and other electronic equipment on base became the property of the Turkish government.

In another example of their domineering mind-set, Congress voted to reduce the amount of money that the United States gave Turkey in foreign aid. In retaliation, the Turks decided the US military was not allowed to have a post office at Incirlik. As the central air hub that supported all US bases throughout Turkey, the post office was vital to troop morale. The base commander's response was to change the name of the building to a "paper redistribution center." Similarly, the Turkish government informed the Incirlik commander that they were not allowed to have a swimming pool on base.

In response, he redesignated it as an "aboveground water storage tank."

What a ridiculous game!

\* \* \* \* \*

By the time I reached Moratinos, it had started to lightly sprinkle. I headed for a small café at the entrance to town in hopes of connecting to Wi-Fi and checking on the weather forecast. As it turned out, there was a hotel upstairs. I ordered my café con leche and inquired about a room.

"I know it is still early, but I was wondering if you had any rooms available for tonight? I am willing to wait down here until it is ready to be occupied."

"Yes, yes, of course, we have rooms available. I have a private room for 30€. It will be ready in one hour."

Since I would be inside most of the day, a private room sounded good.

"I'll take it!" I smiled and added an OJ, croissant, and honey to my coffee order. I then settled into a table to conduct my daily service study.

Today's message discussed how, even in Old Testament times, the hustle and bustle of daily activities made it difficult to carve out time for prayer. The psalmists frequently discussed praying in the middle of the night and getting up early in the morning to focus on prayer before the day's tasks overwhelmed them. We can also be creative and make time to pray while we are executing our daily routine. We can pray, listen to Christian music, and reflect while driving or working out at the gym. When we hear negative news on the radio or TV, we can pray about it. We can even take a few minutes of our lunch period at work for prayer and study.[28]

I could not help but chuckle; obviously peregrinos had plenty of time to reflect and pray during their daily trek!

Contemplating the study, I gazed out the window and down the road leading into town. Numerous small groups and individual pilgrims trudged by, rain hoods up and heads down trying to protect their faces as they labored against the wind and pouring rain, water flowing from their rain gear and pack covers. A few entered the restaurant, creating a long puddle from the door to the counter. A little pride welled up inside as I observed the suffering souls. By paying attention to the weather reports and planning accordingly, I had been able to avoid the miserable predicament that these pilgrims found themselves in.

To my surprise, many headed back out into the rain after a short respite. Were they dedicated and gung ho, or did they lack wisdom?

The forecast for tomorrow morning didn't look much better than this afternoon: 80–100 percent chance of rain through 0900,

---

[28] Fryar, p. 32–33.

60 percent at ten, 50 percent at eleven. I guess I would be forced to sleep in and lounge around until it stops raining. I could then make my way nine clicks to Shagún in the afternoon.

Besides avoiding the rain, a down day allowed some healing for my foot. Considering my ongoing daily battle with significant pain, I remembered a particular scene in the movie *An Officer and a Gentleman*, where the drill sergeant was trying to break the lead character and get him to self-eliminate from the course. Dripping wet in the pouring rain, the trainee was in tears from pain imposed by intense physical stress and mental anguish, but the taunting added an element of anger and determination. He kept repeating "I won't quit, I won't quit." Gritting his teeth, he redoubled his efforts. His determination inspired me not to let the pain beat me.

Just before noon, the hospitalero told me that my room was ready and took me upstairs. It was a very basic but had a nice bed, pillows, sheets, blankets, towels, and a couple of nightstands. The bathroom was off the hallway by the stairs, to be shared with three other rooms on the floor. I was very pleased. This was going to be a real treat.

Settling into my room, I spent some time enjoying the privacy and read chapters 20 through 23 of *Seeking Allah, Finding Jesus*. Nabeel picks up a few weeks after the attacks of 9/11. His new friendship with a strong Christian (David) led to many deep discussions between the two regarding the reliability of the Bible and Koran and why each believed as they did. David challenged Nabeel to be as critical regarding the Koran as he was in challenging the reliability of the Bible. However, there was a deep resistance to conceding to David's arguments—to do so would mean Nabeel would have to consider that his parents and teachers were wrong. Such a thing is unheard of in the Muslim culture.[29]

My thoughts returned to my reflections from a couple of days ago about how 9/11 had exasperated the doubts I tried so hard to suppress. There are so many different translations of the Bible. In the

---

[29] Qureshi, chapters 20–23.

centuries after the death of Christ, men had determined which letters and scrolls to include in the Bible and which ones they believed were not inspired and therefore left out. Various translators over the centuries also came up with different interpretations of the meaning of passages they were translating. How could we be sure which translation was most accurate?

An even more important question I had been struggling with was, How could I be sure that I had faith in the truth? How could I be sure that I did not believe what I believed just because that is what I was raised to believe? The terrorists who flew those planes into buildings believed in Islam because that is how they were raised. They were willing to give their lives and kill thousands of others because they were indoctrinated to believe that they were doing God's will. How could I be sure that my faith was not a result of indoctrination?

The other aspect of faith that I had struggled with was how God could allow such evil to prevail in this world. I understood the concept that this is a fallen world and that people have the free choice to sin. God does not want us to obey Him and have a relationship with Him because we are programmed to do so like robots, but rather, He wants us to choose to have a relationship and to serve Him. But still, the destruction I saw on 9/11 and as a result of numerous terrorist attacks around the world before and since were unfathomable. Why doesn't God step in and stop the massacres?

I wondered the same thing about natural disasters that claim countless lives. Hurricanes, tornadoes, tsunamis, earthquakes, and other tragedies are not because of the sins of man, but cause massive indiscriminate death, destruction, and despair.

Contemplating all this over the past decade and a half had caused serious spiritual struggles for me. Lots of counseling and study was slowly helping me to work through this, but I definitely still had more of the journey to travel ahead.

Maybe the story of Nabeel's journey would help me with mine.

* * * * *

My thirteen months at Pirinclik were not only rewarding career-wise but also socially and spiritually, not to mention some extremely meaningful travel experiences.

Similar to Comiso, it was an unaccompanied assignment. A handful of officers got together most nights to play cards and have barbecues. I was introduced to the card game Phase 10, and it became almost like an obsession too many of us.

I was very active in the base chapel community. I was part of the parish council, attended (and even led a couple of) Bible studies, helped with monthly chaplain-sponsored ice cream socials, and even joined the choir. I wasn't much of a singer, but it was a small base, so they took anyone who showed an interest. Besides, the Bible states "make a joyful noise unto the Lord" (Ps. 100:1). It does not say that it has to be pleasing to human ears. Actually, we weren't too bad as a group.

I became friends with the chaplain, and he was a normal participant in our evening social events. When he rotated out at the end of his tour, I eagerly welcomed his replacement, showed him around, and invited him to join our activities.

I must have been doing something right because about ten years later, an officer who had been a lieutenant in the operations flight and visited the chapel a couple of times tracked me down via the Air Force global address Listing (GAL). She made the effort after all those years to let me know that my words, accompanied by my daily conduct, had laid the foundation for her eventual acceptance of Christ as her personal Savior. She wanted to thank me for the seeds that I had planted. I was stunned. To this day, I do not remember any details of our interactions that might have had this impact.

Turkey is in the cradle of civilization. In fact, the local population believed that the Garden of Eden was in a wasteland just outside of Diyarbakir's ancient city walls. Just south of us was a dilapidated well that was said to be "Jacob's well." The Turks were not too interested in preserving historical sites, so airmen from our chapel occasionally went down and cleaned up the site. There were even rumors that Noah's Ark had been discovered high up on a mountain in eastern Turkey.

Taking advantage of the historical significance of this country, the base morale welfare and recreation (MWR) office and the chapel organized several tourist expeditions. I was able to go on two of them.

The first was to Cappadocia. According to Acts 2, people from this area were present in Jerusalem on the Day of Pentecost when the Holy Spirit came to dwell in the souls of believers. Ancient inhabitants of Cappadocia dug their cities into volcanic rock spires that rose out of the sparse land. Today tourists can see the windows, doors, and staircases from a distance and join guided tours to explore the rooms carved into the rocks. But the city went far deeper than this—five stories underground, in fact. Our tour guide told us that the Christians who had lived there centuries ago frequently had to retreat into the underground city for years to avoid annihilation from Muslim invaders who were trying to conquer and dominate the area. There was an entrance passage that could be sealed with a giant rock in a way that hid its purpose. I was fascinated by the tour.

The second trip I went on was organized by my first chaplain friend. We toured the seven churches of Asia Minor from the book of Revelations (Revelation 1–3), which were all in what is now western Turkey. At the ruins of each church, our chaplain read the verses from the Bible that referred to the church where we were standing. It was

Seven Churches tour group at Pergamon, May 1995

a very moving experience to be at these biblical locations—to read the passages while sitting there and praying. Amazing! Except for Ephesus, few people visit these run-down sites.

Ephesus is a major tourist attraction that is a common stop on Mediterranean cruises. As such, I was able to visit a second time when my parents joined me for a vacation during the summer of 1995.

Because of the dangers posed by the PKK, I told my parents I did not want them visiting Turkey. Instead, we met in Israel for the religious tour of a lifetime and then went to Athens for a few days before boarding the Mediterranean cruise, which took us to many Greek islands, including Patmos, where John lived in a cave while he penned the book of Revelations. We also spent one day on a shore excursion to Ephesus, their only incursion into Turkey.

At first we marveled at the ruins of ancient temples and religious sites throughout Israel and Athens. However, as we neared the end of our Mediterranean cruise, we became weary of visiting broken-down old buildings.

# CHAPTER 22

## Moratinos to Calzadilla de Los Hermanillos, 23.5 Kilometers
## 16 Sep 2015
## D+18

I slept an extra half hour due to the forecast and headed down the hall for personal hygiene at 0700. Closing my room door behind me, I was surprised to find it locked when I returned a few minutes later. Of course, my keys were sitting safely on the nightstand next to my bed.

I must've been quite a sight—with my towel and hygiene kit, in the shorts and T-shirt that I slept in, and of course, bare feet—when I went down to the café to inquire about an extra key. Well prepared for this contingency, the hospitalero broke away to get a key from the back room. The café was packed. I felt guilty about interrupting the busy host, not to mention a bit embarrassed about having everyone hear that I had locked myself out of my room.

Forty-five minutes later, I checked the forecast while enjoying an American-style breakfast of scrambled eggs, bacon, toast, OJ, and of course, coffee. The rain would stop by 1000 instead of noon. The rest of the day looked very nice.

My feet were feeling pretty good, and I'd had a good rest, so I was excited for the opportunity to go farther than planned. I decided to go at least 15 km to Calzada del Coto. Once there, I could assess the situation, and if it was early enough and I was feeling up to it, I had the option of continuing on another 8.4 km to Calazadilla De Los Hermanillos.

By the time I finished breakfast around 0830, the rain had pretty much stopped. There was just a light sprinkle in the air. I decided to take my chances and head out. I protected my pack with its rain cover and wore my raincoat just in case. The rain turned out to be a nonissue, but the wind was as strong if not stronger than the day prior. Besides relying on the weight of my pack to hold me down, I frequently had to dig my poles into the ground for extra resistance to prevent myself from being blown across the field like a tumbleweed.

\* \* \* \* \*

After a rare Christmas with family, I reported to Whiteman AFB in Missouri in January 1996 to assume the position of operations flight commander with the 509th Security Police Squadron. I would not be the "top cop," but it was a very large squadron, so I would have over three hundred people working under my leadership, including several lieutenants who were our shift commanders. This was the first time I directly supervised junior officers. It was my honor to have the role of shaping the foundations of their professional careers.

The wing was in the process of standing up its new mission as the only base operating the new B-2 "Spirit" stealth bomber. With the new mission came significant additions and upgrades to security equipment and systems and an endless string of higher headquarters inspections to certify the base as operationally capable of executing its new mission, to include certifying the effectiveness of the new security systems and procedures that were being instituted. During the two and a half years I was assigned to the position, there were eight higher headquarters inspections conducted by our Numbered Air Force (NAF), MAJCOM, Headquarters Air Force (HAF), and the DoD. In each case, it was critical that the wing excel. Failure was not an option. This meant two and a half straight years of extremely long days, plenty of work on weekends, and an incredible amount of stress that really wore me down. When the MAJCOM, HAF, and DoD inspectors arrived for "the inspection to end all inspections," I had already shipped my household goods and was staying at the visiting officers' quarters (VOQ) in preparation for my PCS to England a few days after the inspection.

Failure during these inspections could have dire consequences. Serious mistakes, even if they did not result in all-out "failure," could have a detrimental effect on an individual's career and that of their squadron leadership. If a young troop had a case of "stupid on station," it could cost his commander his career. We had a close call with one such incident.

On the first day of the inspection, a young entry controller (EC) at the weapons storage area (WSA) failed to notice an error on the inspectors' entry authority list (EAL) that should have prevented a couple of them from being granted access. The young man was nervous, and the inspectors were displaying an attitude of impatience and superiority that was putting a lot of pressure on him. He choked. He caught the mistake after the inspectors were inside and deployed a patrol to detain the team and investigate their status and the reason for the error. He was trying to do the best he could to mitigate the impact of the lapse. Of course, their detention alerted the inspectors that a mistake had been made. After the details were determined, the inspectors' initial reaction was to recommend failing our squadron since the EC did not catch the problem before allowing them to enter.

Back at the squadron office building, my senior staff and I looked further into the problem. We determined that the inspectors had made a mistake when typing up and submitting their EAL. It was not an intentional mistake to test the unit but an administrative mistake they did not catch. We approached them with this fact and discussed how they were as much at fault as the EC. Although I did not say it in as many words, I implied that as senior DoD inspecting officials, they should be held to an extremely high standard and they should have known better. Their mistake was therefore worse than that of the young EC, who realized his mistake within minutes of making it and did everything he could at that point to mitigate the situation. The EC had taken responsibility, brought the problem to light for everyone to see, initiated the appropriate security response to ensure there was no threat to the resources, and then stood tall, waiting for the consequences. This is exactly the type of integrity we expect of airmen. People are not perfect. When you make a mistake, you need to own up to it, take corrective action, and let the chips fall where they may.

At first the inspectors resisted our line of logic, but the following morning they informed us that instead of considering it an automatic failure, they would reevaluate our entry control procedures. They fixed the EAL, and there were no further discrepancies during entry processing for the remainder of the inspection. The incident did not make it into the final report.

Besides accepting the fact that their mistake had caused the incident in the first place, they likely implemented a mind-set that an inspector had explained to me during a previous inspection. He described his evaluation philosophy as, "Once is an anomaly. Twice is a trend. Three times is policy." Since all other entry processing had been textbook, they chocked the first one up as an anomaly. Our careers had been saved.

In conjunction with constantly preparing for the next inspection, bringing on a new mission required a complete review and update of current procedures and the creation of new SOPs for the upgraded priority A and new priority B restricted areas. We established SOPs for new sensor systems in both areas and ensured that the operators were highly knowledgeable and capable of operating them. We developed and exercised contingency procedures to protect our new resources during potential attacks, increased Threat Conditions, and when generating our resources to support national defense requirements around the world.

Because of the worldwide reach of the B-2, we had numerous US DoD and foreign military contingents visit the base. I had the privilege of providing security briefings to the Director, Security Programs, Office of the Assistant Secretary of Defense; the British Air Vice Marshal; and the Russian Commander-in-Chief (CINC) of Long-Range Aviation. Little did I know at the time, but these briefings laid the foundation for similar high-level briefings all the way through my final deployment to Djibouti, Africa. In the end, I was very comfortable providing briefings to anybody, regardless of their level of responsibility.

Other portions of our law enforcement and security mission also excelled. The Investigations section achieved an astounding 79 percent solve rate, and we increased the military working dog (MWD) evaluation pass rate by 69 percent. We also proved our mantle during a training deployment to JRTC (for my fourth time!).

A leader is often credited with the accomplishments of the personnel under their supervision. Hence, leaders must always remember that they cannot be successful without supporting, caring for, and motivating their troops. Keeping this in perspective, I racked up a long string of personal achievement awards, none of which I could have earned without my innovative and motivated operations staff. The awards included being selected as one of two Air Force nominees and one of three federal finalists for the Julie Y. Cross Memorial Award for Women in Federal Law Enforcement for 1996, the 509th Bomb Wing's Company Grade Officer (CGO) of the Year for 1996, and the wing's Lance P. Sijan Leadership Award winner for 1997.

Together with the exceptional performance reports from my very supportive squadron, group, and wing chain-of-command at both Pirinclik and Whiteman, I came out on the promotion list for major.

I was a workaholic in a workaholic's paradise, and in many ways, I thrived. But there were also costs associated with dedicating oneself to work for over twelve hours on most weekdays and four to eight hours on Saturdays and Sundays over a period of two and a half years.

\* \* \* \* \*

Crossing into the province of León, I entered Sahagún a little after 1100 and found a wonderful bar and café with an intriguing old European atmosphere. As I entered and started for the bar to place my order, a familiar voice rang out.

"Tracey, it is good to see you!"

Sitting just inside the door was Pat and Peg.

"Wow, I really didn't expect to run into you. I figured you'd be long gone by now."

"We decided to take the day off. They told us we could keep our beds at the albergue, so we slept in and are just now having a slow leisurely breakfast," Peg explained.

"We aren't interested in walking another day in bad weather," Pat added.

After ordering a café con leché, I joined them at their table.

"I bet you got soaked yesterday if you came this far," I said as I took my pack off and stowed my rain gear.

The sun was starting to come out, and I was pretty sure I was out of rain danger for the day.

"It was miserable," Pat growled. "Our clothes aren't dry yet, and our shoes are soaked."

"I stopped in a small village just as the rain started yesterday and decided to stay the night in a pension there. Had my own room with sheets and towels. Paradise! I actually got quite a kick out of watching people walk by fighting the rain and wind."

"Great plan, we'll have to consider doing that next time!" Peg said, obviously disappointed that they had not thought of it.

After a few more minutes of light conversation, I took the last sip of my coffee and bid them "Bien Camino" as I prepared to head out into the now partly sunny early afternoon.

"Bien Camino," they replied in unison.

I navigated through the city streets and headed across the Rio Cea toward Calzada del Coto.

* * * * *

Although on paper my career was progressing quite nicely, the stress of the position and continual inspections resulted in the first surfacing of my struggles with excessive stress. Just prior to the final inspection, my commander ordered a mental health evaluation because I was having trouble controlling my temper when people around me did or said stupid stuff. The result was that I was "fit for duty," but it was recommended that I attend a stress-management course as soon as I arrived at my new assignment at Royal Air Force (RAF) Mildenhall, England. As the doctor put it in his letter to my commander, "Sometimes we put too many expectations on people. In such situations, it is natural for someone to get overly stressed."

Managing stress would be a continual struggle throughout the remainder of my career as my level of responsibility continued to increase and the burdens of over a decade of war dominated the latter portion of my career. Ultimately, it was a major factor in my decision to retire in 2012.

After we passed the final intense inspection, the unit held a farewell dinner for me. The concluding comment of my commander's presentation testified to how overwhelming and all-encompassing my duties had been during this tour. After describing what a wonderful job I had done, he ordered me to "get a life!"

He would not be the last boss to say it. This was one order I never really obeyed.

* * * * *

The weather was still partly sunny, and I was feeling decent as I entered Calzada del Coto, so I decided to press on via the green route that followed the ruins of the ancient Roman road, aptly named Via Romana.

The trail was a fairly wide dirt road that cut relatively straight through desolate fields with occasional trees along the edges. Periodically, you could see the remains of the old Roman road off to the side of the dirt track.

During this entire stretch, I saw only one other pilgrim. At first the young man was ahead of me, but he stopped on a bridge over some railroad tracks to put his rain gear away. I greeted him with a friendly "Bien Camino" as I moved past. Soon after, I found myself becoming a little worried about the situation. There was nothing threatening about him, but as I looked around and saw no one or any structure as far as the eye could see, I could not help but think about how great a place this would be if somebody wanted to attack a lone woman. If such a thing were to happen, I could scream at the top of my lungs, but nobody would hear. Yes, I was a military veteran, but I was not a front-line fighter! That's what I had troops for! I was what we often referred to as a "back-office weenie." This was the first time on the Camino, either this time or two years ago, when the hair on the back of my neck stood up on alert. Every few minutes, I looked back to assess the situation.

Such thoughts would not normally have occurred to me because crime along the Camino was not at all common. A couple hundred thousand people walk the Camino every year with few issues. However, just a couple of days ago, we saw a newscast about an American girl who had disappeared on the Camino in April. Spanish authorities had finally found her body and arrested the man who had attacked, raped, and killed her. Apparently, he had been masquerading as a pilgrim to gain her trust. Many peregrinos were talking about it, and the women were a bit nervous.

"Hundreds of thousands of people walk the Camino every year. One has been killed in who knows how many years. When you think of it in that perspective, the odds are strongly in our favor," I had offered as encouragement to others during one such conversation.

But now that I was alone in the middle of nowhere on an alternate, less traveled route with a lone man following me, my mind was obsessing on the worst-case scenario. My nervousness ratcheted up a few extra notches as the road entered a wooded area a couple miles before the village. I stepped up my pace significantly, ignoring my two aching feet.

I sighed with relief upon emerging from the forest at the outskirts of town. He passed me when I stopped to fill my water bottle at a fountain. I gave him a faint smile. He tried the first hostel at the edge of the village and was coming out as I caught up.

"They are full," he stated with a strong German accent as we greeted each other and together headed across the street and down another block to the municipal albergue.

His manner was very kind, and I started to feel guilty about my previous nervousness.

The albergue was very basic. There were two short hallways connecting several cubicles with two bunk beds each. In the common area, pilgrims sat around two long wood tables on benches that could easily have been from the middle ages. The hospitalero was feeding a small woodburning stove that provided the only heat for the hostel. Al and Tara were there checking e-mail.

"How are your shin splints?" I asked Tara, happy to see that she had not allowed the pain to defeat her and they had decided to press on.

"Much better," she smiled. "I think it's going to be okay!"

"We expected you to be well ahead of us by now," Al said.

"I only did 12 km yesterday. I stopped before the rain started," I explained. "Last time my shoes got soaked and they took several days to dry out. They stank to high heaven until I was able to wash them in the machine back home. I wanted to avoid this at all costs, so I enjoyed a nice break at a pension in Moratinos."

"Smart," Tara smiled. "We walked 27 km in that miserable rain and wind! Not the most enjoyable day we've had."

After showering, I went looking for food since I had had nothing since breakfast except a cup of coffee. The village was practically deserted, but after weaving my way through the empty streets for about twenty minutes, I eventually found a nice outdoor patio bar that had only been open for two days. The only food they had was small tapas that they served with your drink order. I had two hours to kill before dinner, so I ordered a wine anyway.

As I relaxed, I took out my service study book and read lesson 16. To put it in law enforcement terms, it warned the reader to put out a BOLO (be on the lookout) for various sins that plague many who serve others. Depending on their perceptions of their effectiveness, self-righteousness, and a judgmental attitude toward those they serve, impatience can overtake the servant. One irritated comment, or even a raised eyebrow, can ruin days or months of relationship-building. But take heart, if you recognize when these sins sneak into your life, repent and ask God for forgiveness, healing, and an attitude adjustment; He is faithful to restore and encourage you.[30]

---

[30] Fryar, p. 34–35

The portion of the message about the stray comment or raised eyebrow reminded me of the saying I had reflected on many times since my academy years: one "awe shit" wipes out a thousand "attaboy's." It can sure apply to countless areas of one's life!

It occurred to me that this study topic also applied to my experiences at Whiteman. Maybe my endurance and self-control would have been better if I had had some spiritual balance in my life. My grueling work schedule gave me little time to be involved in a church community. Besides not having much free time, when I was off I was tired and just wanted to rest.

I made it a point to join and regularly attend the Officers' Christian Fellowship (OCF) group on base. We met in another officer's home most Tuesday nights. Since I lived about a half hour from the base, I would work until it was time to go and not get home until around 2200. This made for a tough start to the next morning. I checked out several churches near the small town where I lived but wasn't able to find one I was comfortable with. So I attended the base chapel with some of my friends from OCF. I tried furthering my singing "career" by joining the praise and worship team that led the music during the contemporary service. The leader of the team was a B2 pilot who attended OCF. He once told me I was decent at harmony, and he admired my commitment. I think that translated to "You aren't so good, but when we sing together, it is not a problem, and I am happy to have someone on the team I can count on to show up." It was an honor to get to know him. Most pilots I had met during my career had huge egos and could be rather juvenile in their conduct. This pilot was a humble yet confident servant of God.

Attending OCF and singing on the praise team kept me somewhat connected to my spiritual walk, but this only accounted for a few hours a week. The rest of the time, I was totally immersed in my military duties. I would not call this assignment a spiritual void, but there was little growth.

I ordered a coffee instead of a second drink and was enjoying it when a couple came in and sat next to me at the bar.

"Aren't you the one who locked yourself out of your room this morning?" the man asked.

"That was me." I smiled sheepishly. Great, now I had a reputation.

"Don't worry," the lady said, "there are worse things a pilgrim could be known for!"

"I guess you're right." I chuckled as I finished my coffee and got up to leave. "I need to go find something to eat. I'm famished. Bien Camino! Enjoy your evening."

I hobbled out of the patio café. Once I had stopped for the day and taken my hiking shoes off, both feet had begun to get progressively more painful. I now walked with a two-legged limp.

I went in search of the village market the bartender told me about. It was very difficult to find, and my feet had almost convinced me to give up when I finally saw it. It was a tiny "hole-in-the-wall" establishment, and I think half of the albergue guests were crammed inside. I found a small package of mixed nuts that would tide me over until dinner.

I was once again amazed about how few people I saw in the village besides peregrinos. It seemed almost abandoned. In fact, I actually saw more dogs than people, and there weren't many of them. The handful of people I saw were at the bar and the market, and most of them looked like pilgrims. Even so, many of the buildings were modern and well-kept. It was weird.

Our albergue did not have a dinner available, so I headed across the street to the hostel at the entrance to town. The young German man had the same idea, and we walked over together. We both felt that this was the best option in town because it was only one hundred meters away. No use walking to the other side of the village!

Since we arrived together, the hostess seated us at a four-person table.

"Feel free to have other people join us if they don't have anyone to eat with," I told her in hopes of meeting additional new people.

I'm not sure that she understood me because she did not sit anybody else with us. This gave the young German man and me time to talk extensively. His name was Roman, so it was fitting that he had taken the "Romana" detour.

"What brings you to the Camino?" I asked the standard introductory question.

"I just finished my bachelor's degree and am taking a semester off before starting work on my master's," he explained in broken English, but it was clear enough that I had little trouble understanding him.

"The Camino is a good way to spend my time of rest. I don't know when I will have this much time off again once I start working after graduation," he concluded.

He was not the first from whom I had heard such an explanation. Two sisters I met the first week were in a similar situation. One had just graduated from college, the other from high school. Both were taking a break before starting their next chapter.

"Did you notice how deserted this town seems to be?" I asked, thinking about my earlier search for food.

"Yes," he replied. "I have seen this many times along The Way. I did not expect it to be this way."

"I have been told that it is because people are moving to the big cities to find jobs, or at least they are commuting there so they don't spend much time in their village," I related the explanation I had been told.

"Could be, I really don't know. There are definitely more jobs in the city."

We continued our small talk throughout dinner. By the end I was convinced that the guy that had caused me such discomfort on the trail this afternoon was actually a fine young man with great potential. I guess there is a lesson to be learned here about letting your imagination get the better of you.

As I was walking out of the dining room, an American couple sitting at a table I passed greeted me. They obviously recognized me. I found them slightly familiar but could not place them.

"We met you on the first night in Roncesvalles," the gentleman explained.

"Oh yes," my confused look changed to familiarity. "It is good to see you again! How is your Camino going?"

"We have had our struggles, but we are making it, even if slowly," his wife replied. "Jim has artificial knees, so this has slowed us down a bit."

"Really? It is amazing that you are doing this at all! I am impressed by your determination."

"It is not so unique," Jim replied a little embarrassed. "We have traveled a lot with a man who has artificial hips. His condition seems to be a bit more challenging than mine."

"I guess I need to quit complaining about my sore feet!"

Finding someone who is defeating more serious challenges than yours can really help motivate you to achieve victory over your ailments.

Once back in the cubicle at the albergue, I read chapters 24 and 25 in *Seeking Allah, Finding Jesus*. In chapter 24, David asked Nabeel if he really wanted to know if Christianity's doctrines were actually true. Hesitantly, Nabeel said yes and no. He really wanted to know the truth and follow the true path, but it would cost him his family. His parents would lose a son and all the respect they had in the Muslim community. He was not sure he could live with that. David's response was to ask who should win, God or the family?[31]

This discussion enlightened me to the difficulties Muslims have even considering the possibility that other religious doctrines could be true. Over the years, I had seen similar sentiments in Christians who were exposed to other denominational doctrines. Most were very resistant to other views and tended to cling tightly to those they were raised to believe.

I went to sleep contemplating the significance of the book's discussion. As I had struggled intellectually with doubts during my spiritual walk over the years, I read several books about the historical reliability of the Bible as compared to other literary works handed down through the ages: *Evidence That Demands a Verdict*, *The Case for Faith*, and *The Case for Christ*.

---

[31] Qureshi, chapter 24.

Apparently, I am not the only one with doubts. My pastors have all known about the books and recommended them to help me work through the doubts. I got the impression that it was one of their counseling SOPs on their "Confronting Doubts Checklist." *Seeking* should be added to the list!

One of the books said that it is normal for Christians to occasionally have doubts and that Satan will use our propensity to doubt what we do not clearly understand as a weapon to prevent us from developing our faith and serving God with earnest. The reality of that theory was apparent throughout my spiritual walk.

# CHAPTER 23

## Calzadilla de Los Hermanillos to Reliegos, 17.3 Kilometers
## 17 Sep 2015
## D+19

It was a very chilly forty-five degrees Fahrenheit when I headed back to the albergue at the town entrance for breakfast. I ordered a tortilla con chorizo, consisting of a sausage and egg omelet inside a half loaf of bread. A large breakfast was actually beneficial today. I planned to continue along the green route. The guidebook showed no villages all the way into Reliego where I planned to stay tonight. Not even a mobile café. To prepare for this, I took the top layer of bread off, cut it in half, spread jam on it, and wrapped it in a napkin to have for lunch.

Roman soon joined me, and we had another nice discussion. Once again, I was struck by his kindness, intelligence, and obvious potential. A large group of women occupied the big round table in the corner of the dining room. They were energetic and laughing loudly.

"I bet they are tour a group," I commented to Roman. "There are so many of them, and the lobby is filled with regular luggage tagged for shipment."

"Yes, I think so," Roman replied.

"We met a group like that when I was here in 2013. They have a completely different experience than the rest of us. The tour company plans every place they will stay, even when and where they eat. They meet very few peregrinos outside their group, and of course, they don't carry their stuff with them in a pack. I don't think I would like it. No flexibility to take an easy day or care for injuries. You do what the tour company says and when they say it, and they charge you a lot of money that goes into their pockets. That is not what the Camino is about."

"I agree," Roman said as he took a sip of coffee. "It is not a true Camino experience. I think this place was full last night because they had reservations."

"Most likely," I nodded. "Oh well, the municipal albergue was not all that bad. I thought it actually had a lot of character."

"Yes, it was fine. The hospitalero was very nice, and he kept the place warm with the fire."

"Well, I think I will head out," I said as I got up and started putting my pack on.

"Bien Camino."

"See you along The Way." I smiled.

It was still extremely cold as I stepped into the street at 0815. I would obviously be wearing my coat, gloves, and pant legs for some time today! The weather forecast suggested that this could be the new normal. I probably needed to consider purchasing something to keep my ears warm in the mornings.

\* \* \* \* \*

I arrived at RAF Mildenhall in June 1998. The base primarily operated an Air Refueling Wing. I was assigned to a tenet unit on the base, Headquarters Third Air Force (3AF). Third Air Force was responsible for seventeen USAF facilities throughout the British Isles and on the mainland north of the Alps. We were also responsible for supporting contingency operations in sub-Saharan Africa. The head-quarters unit itself was tasked with being prepared to deploy as the core leadership contingent for any Air Force–led JTF that European Command (EUCOM) might stand up to deal with wartime or humanitarian contingencies within our area of responsibility (AOR). If the Air Force was not the lead service, our personnel would still fill slots in each of the functional directorates (the "J Staff") and provide the core leadership for the subordinate Air Force organization that would direct the air arm of the JTF's overall operation. During nor-mal day-to-day operations at home station, I was the chief, security forces. When deployed to a JTF, my role would be provost marshal—an Army term used in joint operations.

While I was at Whiteman, the Air Force had changed the name of our career field from security police to security forces. At the academy, there was a saying that "West Point had two hundred years of tradition unhampered by progress. USAFA had forty years of progress unhampered by tradition."

Apparently this was true in the "real Air Force" as well. Initially, the career field was called air police, or AP. Later, it was changed to security police to clarify that we were responsible for both resource security and law enforcement. The most recent change was to emphasize our wartime Air Base defense mission. Personally, I think we kept changing our name to keep our enemies, to include terrorists, guessing. By changing our name, they would have trouble keeping up with who we were.

I was the top cop again. Although it sounds impressive, it really wasn't. There were four enlisted personnel on my staff. Our role for overseeing the subordinate 3AF bases was limited. USAFE provided guidance and direction for day-to-day operations of USAF units in Europe. The bulk of our role was managing over five hundred rotational deployment taskings on an ongoing basis. While I was at 3AF, these rotational taskings supported US operations in both Bosnia and Southwest Asia (SWA).

We also determined what subordinate units would get tasked to support new taskings that developed in response to world events. This was called "sourcing." For instance, when the US embassies were bombed in Kenya and Tanzania, we were directed to source two thirteen-man SF squads to deploy and augment security during the US response and investigation.

Finally we determined security requirements and tasked units to provide Force Protection personnel to secure short-term theater events, such as the annual Farnborough International Air Show.

Pop-up contingency taskings seemed to always present themselves late Friday afternoon. It became such a routine that one Friday around 1600, we received a call from the SF chief at Ramstein Air Base in Germany. He seemed very concerned and wanted to know if we were okay. Mike, my superintendent and right-hand man, answered the phone and was soon laughing hysterically. When I inquired as to what was so funny, he said the chief was worried that we must be sick since we had not called yet that afternoon to task him to send troops somewhere over the weekend. It had been his unit we had tasked to send the two squads to Africa after the embassy attacks.

\* \* \* \* \*

After about a half hour of not seeing anyone, I momentarily caught sight of someone on the horizon. Thirty minutes later I recognized him as Roman coming up behind me.

"You are the first I have seen so far," he said as he came alongside me. "I think all those peregrinos we saw in the village are fakers. They must be taking taxis. I saw none of them yesterday, nor today."

We both laughed and once again wished each other "Bien Camino" as Roman moved on ahead. A few minutes later, a biking pilgrim passed me. Then I was alone again.

\* \* \* \* \*

In early 1999, Serbian President Slobodan Milosevic escalated his ethnic-cleansing campaign against Kosovar Albanians by sending forty thousand troops into Kosovo. This set in motion a massive refugee crisis and prompted NATO to respond with an intense air campaign against Serbia and its forces in Kosovo.[32]

We stood up a contingency response cell (CRC) to provide guidance and support for US units tasked to contribute to the campaign dubbed Operation ALLIED FORCE (OAF). My office was responsible for determining what security enhancements needed to be implemented at 3AF bases in general and sourcing SF personnel to deploy to augment security at Southern European bases that were launching missions against the Serbians. Since European bases were

---

[32] Gregory Ball, "Operation Allied Force," Air Force Historical Support Division. http://www.afhso.af.mil/topics/factsheets/factsheet.asp?id=18652

increasing security, we had to reach back to the Air Force Security Forces Center (AFSFC) in San Antonio, Texas, to arrange for stateside SF personnel to fill the gaps. In all, we coordinated the deployment of 170 personnel to enhance security at eight bases launching combat sorties.

As the air war intensified, so did the flow of refugees from Kosovo into Albania. The international community identified the need to establish refugee camps in Albania, and NATO took the lead. EUCOM tasked USAFE, who tasked 3AF, to lead Joint Task Force SHINING HOPE (JTF-SH) with the mission to coordinate military and civilian international governmental and nongovernmental organization's contributions to the humanitarian effort.

\* \* \* \* \*

I arrived at the rest stop, which I judged to be a little more than one-third of the way around 1000 hours. Removing my pack, I leaned it and my poles against a picnic table in a clearing about fifty feet from the trail. According to today's map, this would be the best place to have lunch, albeit too early. I removed my right glove to enter some notes into my phone. The cold ignited the arthritis in my fingers. I could not wait to put the gloves back on. Pain can be a wonderful motivator for brevity!

The large tour group we had seen at breakfast walked by. They were still loudly chatting and laughing. I wondered if they would ever find peace on the Camino? Not if they continued to stick together so closely! I was relieved that they passed by my small sanctuary.

It wasn't long before I was bundled up in my snivel gear once again and heading down the Camino, hoping the exercise would we restore my body heat. I collapsed my poles and attached them securely to my pack so I could stick my gloved hands in my pockets. The pain lessened as they warmed.

\* \* \* \* \*

We had a heads-up that we might be deployed on Thursday. Early Saturday morning I got a phone call instructing me to report to the CRC ASAP (technically stands for "as soon as possible," but really means "immediately"). Once everybody had arrived, we received a deployment mission briefing and were told to get our affairs in order and report to the airfield in three hours to board a C-130 and fly to Germany where the JTF-SH HQ would stand up. I would be the provost marshal, and my cell would be responsible for Force Protection for military units in Albania and for securing the refugee camps which the JTF was building. I contacted Mike and another member of our staff, and we determined the more junior NCO would join me. Mike would stay to manage our support to ALLIED FORCE but would be on standby in case we needed him to deploy after we arrived and got our situational awareness (SA).

On my way off base, I stopped at the base post office and provided them a forwarding address. Once back home, I contacted my landlord and let him know I would be out of town for an undetermined amount of time. He agreed to keep an eye on the house and yard while I was gone. I loaded all the clothes I would need into the washing machine and got it going. I then pulled out my mobility bags and checked to make sure I had everything I needed. Once the washing machine cycle was done, I took the wet clothes out and stuffed them into a large garbage bag that I put into one of my large green Air Force issue mobility bags. No time to dry them.

A few hours later, we found ourselves at Ramstien Air Base in Germany. A military transport bus picked us up and took us to a small satellite base, Einsedlerhof, where USAFE held its Noncommissioned Officer Academy courses. The scheduled course had been canceled because of Operation ALLIED FORCE, so we moved into the student dormitories. After taking a few minutes to deposit our gear in our assigned rooms, we got back on the bus and headed for a warehouse where contingency Command and Control exercises were frequently held. This was where we would set up our headquarters operation because it already had the office cubicles, furniture, security, computers, and communication networks we would need.

After setting up our offices, we returned to the dormitory about 2100. Only then was I able to put my wet clothes into the dryer.

Countless times after this, I heard troops whining about only having a couple of weeks or even a month's notice before a contingency deployment. Each time I would chuckle a little, roll my eyes, and then relate my experience of rushing home from the briefing, washing my uniforms, putting them into a plastic bag wet, flying to the deployment location, and then drying them. That usually stopped the whining.

\* \* \* \* \*

After being back on the trail for about a half hour, I passed the large group of women. They were having a picnic lunch at another rest area. My guidebook only showed one rest area, but apparently there were two. I wondered which was the one depicted in the book?

About thirty minutes later, I could hear them coming up behind me. Boy, did they talk a lot and very loudly! The hair stood up on the back of my neck, my stomach churned, and I could feel frustration and anxiety invading my mind. Breathing deeply, I stepped off to the side of the trail so that they would quickly catch up and pass by. I could not help but notice how small their packs were. Most were about half the size of the daypacks we used on our day hikes back home. No wonder they were going so fast and had the energy to chatter so much!

\* \* \* \* \*

We set up our headquarters operation in Germany because a major part of our mission would be to coordinate logistical support—i.e., airlift to get equipment, supplies, and personnel into Albania. We had exceptional phone and computer connectivity that we would need to coordinate with various US and international military headquarters and civilian organizations from around the world that would be contributing to the humanitarian operations in Albania. Satellite bandwidth availability from a contingency base in Albania would be limited, and it needed to be dedicated to the forces conducting the tactical mission on the ground, not HQ staff functions. Finally, from our central location in Germany, our commander would be able to meet face-to-face with influential leaders from contributing entities in European countries.

To ensure effective Command and Control, the general established a JTF HQ forward element at our logistics hub at the international airport in Tirana, Albania. Staff members whose jobs revolved around day-to-day operations in-country and coordination with the Albanian government deployed to the forward HQ, while those that could best do their international coordination and orchestration from the rear stayed in Germany. Some, like the commander and his deputy, rotated back and forth.

The provost marshal (PM) cell stayed in Germany but maintained close contact with our forward security elements in-country via secure (classified) satellite phone and Internet. The AFSFC deployed SF troops to provide security for the AF compound on one side of the runway and for the cargo aircraft that brought in personnel, equipment, and humanitarian supplies. Army military police (MP) secured the Army sector on the other side of the runway where their helicopters staged to transport personnel and supplies to remote villages and the refugee camps we were building in collaboration with international aid organizations. A Marine Expeditionary Unit (MEU) came ashore and was charged with providing security for the refugee camps. My PM cell oversaw all of this US security and FP activity.

Several weeks into the operation, I had the opportunity to go to Albania to evaluate firsthand the FP and security operations at the Tirana airport. I also planned to travel out to evaluate the security at the refugee camps. I was able to secure authorization to fill an empty seat on a VIP-support leer jet that was heading down range from Ramstien. This was my first experience on such a plane. Every other military flight I had ever taken was on cargo aircraft, and we sat in webbed jump seats along the edge of the plane's fuselage. None too comfortable. The other special aspect of this flight was that the pilot turned out to be a classmate of mine from my squadron at USAFA. I had not seen him since graduation day. We had the opportunity during the flight to get caught up.

The observations that stuck with me the most during my time on the ground was the stark difference between the AF and Army camps. I made arrangements with the AF SF flight commander to stay with his unit on the our side of the runway. After getting settled, the flight commander and I visited his sector security CP and then conducted post visits at the ECP and the perimeter-security positions.

While we made our rounds, we stopped for lunch at the DFAC (made up of several tents connected together) and at the small base exchange (BX, similar to a small convenience store) in another tent. Both were impressive and were serving the needs of AF personnel well. CE had brought in a lot of dirt and built the ground up, so it was dry and relatively flat. They had also made plywood floors for each of the tents that were used for office space and lodging. Every tent had a heating and air-conditioning unit attached that were powered by a large generator. In the middle of the compound, a volleyball court had been erected and a group of off-duty airmen were playing in shorts and T-shirts. For a newly established contingency base made up primarily of tents, it actually it was not too bad.

After lunch, we drove around the end of the runway to the Army camp to meet with the MP commander and see their operation. The differences were striking. The ground had not been built up, and the entire camp was in deep mud. They had taken wooden pallets and laid them out end-to-end to make walking paths. The tents did not have floors in them, nor did they have AC. Instead, the sides of the tents were rolled up to provide airflow and cool off the insides. All the soldiers we saw moving around were weighted down with full combat gear to include helmets, ballistic vests, ammo, med kits, gas masks, and M-16 rifles slung over their shoulders. Even soldiers who were obviously going to the showers wore their combat gear. What a miserable dump!

"Soldiers often walk an hour around the end of the runway to buy snacks and personal items at our BX and to eat at the DFAC," the flight commander explained after I commented on the dismal conditions at the Army camp.

"Crazy," I replied.

Once we met up with the Army's MP commander, I asked him why everybody was in combat gear since the base was in Albania, hundreds of miles away from the fighting.

"You never know when the enemy may attack us," he explained. "For instance, they could launch a helicopter attack."

I raised my eyebrow. "The enemy is hundreds of miles away over a mountain range. I don't think they have that capability. Besides, I don't see why they would be interested in attacking this humanitarian effort. They've got their hands full in Kosovo right now."

I left my comments at that. No need to be too critical. It had been my impression for some time that the Army took pride in being miserable.

We turned our discussion to how to better coordinate security between the two US compounds, the international airport security personnel, and all the other international camps that circled the runway. We all agreed that there needed to be one overarching security control center and commander. Currently, everyone was securing their sectors as they felt appropriate. There was no integration or coordination. This was unacceptable. One of the first things you learned at ABGD school was the need for well-integrated and coordinated security operations. This was my major takeaway from the visit that I needed to discuss with the EUCOM FP staff. The two US commanders agreed to start local discussions to this end with the rest of the units on the airfield. EUCOM would be able to help the effort through communication with their counterparts on the NATO staff.

When I got back to the AF sector CP, I was informed that my office in Germany had called. The general wanted me back in Germany ASAP. There was a meeting regarding an emerging aspect of the operation that needed to be discussed, and the general wanted my input. I called Mike to find out what was going on.

"You know as much as I do about all this, can't you attend the meeting?"

"The general made it clear he wanted you to represent, PM, not me."

Frustrated, I asked the security controller to find out when the next flight to Germany was and to see if he could get me on it. Within a couple hours, I was on my way back to Germany. The meeting turned out to be fairly basic and could definitely have been handled by my senior NCO. I was never able to break away again to see the refugee camps. Very disappointing!

Our workdays in Germany were long and very busy. We spent a lot of time on e-mail and phone conversations, monitoring progress and security events in-country, determining manning and equipment requirements, coordinating formal requests, and orchestrating the deployment of these resources to the locations in Albania where they were needed. Staff meetings took up far too much of my time. This is how military leaders fight wars nowadays: by reading and sending e-mails, creating and briefing PowerPoint slides, and attending meetings.

Eventually we had four personnel on staff. Three us worked twelve to fifteen hours on what could be called a dayshift, and we had one working mids. During contingency operations, a six-and-one, twelve-hour shift schedule was common. Normally, that meant six days on, one day off. We worked a different type of six and one;

six weeks on, one day off. Since the operation lasted approximately ninety days, what that really meant was each of us got one day off about halfway through the deployment. By the time I took my day, I was completely exhausted and could hardly think straight. Several slots on a Rhine River cruise were contracted by the JTF, and I signed up for the tour. I really loved the German countryside, especially around the rivers with their small villages, vineyards, and castles on hills overlooking the strategic waterways. We had fun and managed to get some relaxation in. A late morning departure meant I even got to sleep in, which I desperately needed. I returned to work the next day rested, with clean clothes, and eager to get back in to the thick of things.

Day-to-day the staff work at the headquarters of the JTF was fairly routine. However, there were a few memorable events and issues that have stuck with me over the years.

A major issue for the PM staff was acquiring the equipment necessary to adequately care for the MWDs we were using to detect explosives at the ECPs at the various operating locations and to assist the Albanians in screening people using the commercial operations at the airport. The major issue was the heat once we entered the summer months. In order for the dogs to be effective in their detection tasks, they needed air-conditioned shelters to rest in between shifts. The issue actually became the JTF's top priority for several days as my staff labored tirelessly to acquire portable air-conditioned dog kennels and arrange airlift to Tirana.

Another surprising requirement teetered on becoming a major international incident. Obviously, bringing in shippable bathroom and shower compartmentalized units was vital to maintaining proper sanitation and a healthy environment at the refugee camps. The JTF acquired units for use at the airfield and the refugee camps. Once they arrived at the refugee camps, a major uproar ensued. The refugees refused to use the Western-style toilets. They were used to squatting over Eastern-style holes in the floor. I had used these Eastern-style toilets while off-base in Turkey. There were footpads on either side of a hole. A person needed to squat down and do their best to aim for the hole. At least in my experience, misses were the norm. A bucket of water sat nearby for use in cleaning up the floor area and flushing the waste. Personally, I found the system repugnant.

For a couple of weeks, this was a major topic of discussion during our daily meetings with the senior JTF staff. Our logistics directorate (J4) turned to international aid organizations to assist in orchestrating the delivery and installation of Eastern-style restrooms. It boggled my mind, and the minds of many others, that refugees for whom we were spending millions to provide shelter, food, security, and other supplies to would be so insistent and inflexible that they demanded we spend an excessive amount of extra time, money, and precious logistical resources to get them the type of toilets they wanted. I felt blessed that I was merely an observer at staff meetings and not a part of dealing with this debacle.

On another day, I was attending the daily staff meeting and offered a status update on some topic when asked. I don't remember what that topic was or what I said about it. Who knows, maybe it had something to do with delays in the delivery of the air-conditioned MWD kennels. What I do remember was the general's response—not the words that he said, but the tone. He gave me a strong tongue-lashing, chewed me up one side and down the other. I was shocked and obviously became determined to fix whatever the problem was, somehow, someway. At the end of the meeting, the general always went around the table, asking everyone if they had anything else to contribute. When he got to me, I hesitated, still a bit in shock.

He smiled the biggest smile I ever saw on his face.

"Kind of hard to talk when you have no lips," he said, playing on a common military saying indicating that he had 'ripped my lips off."

The entire senior staff got a good laugh at my expense. I admit it, I even managed a light smile.

"No, sir, nothing further."

About two months into the three-month operation, I was surprised and a bit disappointed when they brought in a lieutenant colonel to assume the position of provost marshal and I had to step down to deputy. My type A, perfectionist self felt betrayed and concerned. Had I done something wrong? Was I not performing up to standard? The general assured me that neither of these were the case. He just felt that FP and security were extremely vital functions of the operation. As was standard in my field, failure was not an option. Most of my staff "peers" (the leaders of the other functional areas) were colonels with just a couple of lieutenant colonels. I was a newly pinned on major.

I could definitely see his point; this reality had made my job a bit more difficult. Some of the colonels were easy to work with. Others had huge egos and were opposed to being persuaded to change their mind by a young female major. This was not a huge issue with the colonels from the 3AF staff. However, by this point the staff had expanded from the core JTF we had deployed with. Several of the key leaders were now from either the Army or Marines; hence the word *joint* in Joint Task Force. They seemed to have more of a problem working with a female in a security and FP leadership role than the AF colonels did. And it wasn't just the crusty old colonels that seemed to have a problem with my sex. I had to dress down a Marine lieutenant quite strongly one day for treating me with blatant disrespect when I tried to coordinate something with him. My ego was bruised when they brought in a senior-ranking man, but looking back, I think the general made the right call. We had a mission to accomplish and did not have time for this kind of crap.

Even though—like the majority of military officers—I had always been a conservative Republican, I was excited when President Clinton visited our headquarters during the last couple of weeks of the operation to thank us for all that we had done and to get our opinions on how things had gone and how similar operations could be done better in the future.

This line of questions was standard after military operations. We always looked back on what happened to determine what worked and what didn't to derive lessons learned that could be recorded and shared to benefit future operations. We called this an after-action review (AAR). The idea was constant improvement based on realistic critiques of outcomes and impact.

The biggest question was, "So what?"

Did we achieve the objectives of the mission? What actual, lasting impact did we have on the people we were trying to help? After determining the effectiveness of our operation, we would then ask how could we have done it better.

Anyway, after receiving a briefing from the general officers assigned to the JTF, President Clinton visited the office cubicles. When he arrived at the PM cell, I had no idea what he might ask. At the time, I was the ranking person in the cubicle, so he directed his question at me.

"How do you think your operation has gone so far?"

Behind the president, I could see my home station supervisor and the general tense up. They both knew that there had been a few hurdles that we had struggled with that I was not happy about. I think they thought I was going launch into internal AF SF issues.

"As with all operations, there were many things that went well and other areas where we could improve," I said as diplomatically as I could. "We are already in the process of discussing lessons learned and improvement options with EUCOM and Headquarters Air Force Security Forces."

I perceived a deep sigh of relief from my superiors as the president shook the hands of my staff and asked us much safer questions about where we were stationed and where we called home. He then thanked us for what we had done and moved on to the next cubicle.

* * * * *

It was just before 1300 when I entered the village of Reliegos and found Al and Tara studying their guidebook on a street corner. I greeted them, and we set off together to evaluate lodging options. We found a very nice, new albergue tucked away on a remote side street on the northwest side of the village. On the ground floor they had a very nice restaurant and bar with outdoor seating. Above there were a couple floors with six-person bunk rooms. For only 7€ we felt it was a nice treat. We were the first three to be assigned to our room on the second floor, so we had our pick of beds. As per SOP, I made up my bottom bunk and headed for the shower.

Once settled in the bar with a drink, I proceeded with my mission planning. By the end of tomorrow, I would be approaching León, the largest city yet. As we were jumping forward in 2013, we stopped there for two nights to explore the city. We stayed in the middle of old town—which, of course, was filled with people, noise, and activity. I planned to avoid it this time.

Via the green route, there was a village a little over eighteen clicks out that the guidebook described as "the last chance to take a rest in the relative quiet before we hit the city traffic."[33] That piqued my interest, and at first I decided this would be my COA.

Just to be thorough, I looked into the following day's options. There was a green route starting at the far side of León. If I wanted to take it, the lodging options were very limited. If I executed COA 1, it would be over 29 km to the first lodging opportunity. Alternatively, I could follow the main route along a busy highway. There were closer lodging options this way, but following the road was not appealing. Back to the drawing board.

I noticed that there was lodging on the outskirts entering León. The Albergue Santo Tomás de Canterbury was 5.6 km from the village I was considering in COA 1. From there I could quickly pass through León the following morning, and it would only be 23.7 clicks to the lodging along the green route. Much more reasonable. I decided to go with COA 2 tomorrow.

I checked the weather forecast next. It had been only fifty-four degrees when we arrived at the albergue this afternoon. It was not going to get much better. From now through at least next Sat, the lows were forecasted to range from thirty-nine to forty-five. Highs would range from sixty-three to seventy-two. I found it surprising how much colder it is this time. We did not have to deal with cold until well into October last time.

At least there would be no rain for the next couple of days!

Next, it was time for my daily Bible study on serving others. Day 17 cautioned God's servants not to allow their contributions to lead to

---

[33] Brierley, p. 178.

pride or arrogance, let alone a feeling that you are entitled to receive something from God in payment for your service. When God works through you, the credit for the results go to Him. You are a vessel with the honor of being used by Him to achieve His purpose. That is your reward. Serving Him is a privilege. God does not owe us. He has already given us the greatest gift of all, the death of His Son on the cross in payment for our sins so that we can live with Him in heaven for eternity. We can never do enough for Him to earn what He has already given us.[34]

I would have to be on alert for this issue. I could easily see how my ego and desire for self-achievement could lead to pride.

Focusing my thoughts on spiritual things reminded me of a major blessing during SHINING HOPE. The Air Force chaplain that I had befriended when I first arrived at Pirinclik was assigned to the JTF as our headquarters chaplain. I was very thankful for the opportunity to reconnect with him and attend midday Bible studies that he held for the staff. We enjoyed reminiscing about getting hooked on the card game Phase 10 during our evening group get-togethers, the monthly ice cream socials, and of course, the Seven Churches tour. Once again I was reminded how great the assignment that I did not want had turned out to be!

When peregrinos stop walking in the early afternoon, we sure have a long time to kill before dinner. I decided to pull out my iPad and read some more of *Seeking Allah, Finding Jesus*. Nabeel was now really getting into the specifics of his internal conflict as he seriously considered arguments for Christianity and struggled to find trustworthy counter arguments from his family and Islamic books and scholars. He was deep into a very long yet intriguing journey. I was captivated and continued reading for five chapters.

The concern of betraying his family and faith was emerging as the greatest obstacle in his hesitancy to accept Christianity as the truth. But another issue started to emerge that made him question all that he thought he knew. Whether it was from studying books or observing Muslim scholars debate with Christians, Muslim experts

---

[34] Fryar, p. 36–37.

continually denied and ignored evidence against their Islamic beliefs. Often they did not even try to argue logically against the Christian conclusions, just basically stated the Muslim perspective and denied of validity of the Christian perspective. Nabeel's conclusion about a specific Muslim scholar's presentation was, "His skepticism of the data was unwarranted, and he applied nowhere near the same level of skepticism to his own position. This inconsistency had to be the result of his bias, one that I could see even as a Muslim who wanted to agree with him."

As Nabeel looked at each piece of doctrine that he was confused about and applied a logical and systematic evaluation of historical and biblical evidence, he consistently saw flaws in the Muslim perspective and discovered that the Christian perspective was the best explanation based on the totality of evidence.[35]

An interesting point Nabeel brought out that helped me with my ongoing spiritual struggle was that there were seldom any perfect theories. If one examined something from various perspectives, one could always find arguments for and against any of the perspectives. It all depended on your interpretation and where you put your emphasis.

So many times specific verses in the Bible did not make sense to me in relation to other verses or in relation to personal observations of the world around me. For instance, there are verses that indicate that if God will take care of the birds and flowers, why wouldn't He take care of humans? But when I look around the world, I see so much suffering and people dying due to disease, tragic weather events, hunger, accidents, and because of evil that is allowed control people in the world.

Another set of passages that I stumble over discuss how if you have the faith of a mustard seed, you can move mountains. My understanding was that a lack of faith was often the reason for unanswered prayers. Yet I have seen very faithful people pray fervently for somebody to be cured of a fatal injury or crippling disease and various other things that would make extremely positive impacts on

---

[35] Qureshi, chapters 26–30.

people's lives. Yet these prays often do not result in a positive answer. This is explained by the standard Christian response that God knows what is best from the big-picture perspective. He has a plan, and He knows how things will turn out, so we should trust Him. Who are we to question His decisions? In that case, why should we bother to pray? If He knows what is best and will do what is best for people in general and for His kingdom, why should we get involved by praying for our desires? What is the purpose of those prayers if God is going to do what He knows is best, anyway?

This type of analysis has always caused me to struggle with believing in the divine authorship of the Bible. Maybe it is Satan casting doubt in my mind, but it makes me focus on the fact that men wrote the chapters of the Bible; other men decided which documents to include in the Bible; and of course, others translated it into various languages. All these steps opened the door for inaccuracies. For me, this was a reasonable possible explanation for the inconsistencies and passages I could not understand in relation to my limited observations.

I remember going around and around with a pastor about these types of arguments. After a while he laid out the bottom line. Sooner or later, I was going to have to just decide to believe or not to believe. Nabeel's journey helped me with this by emphasizing that the key was to find the explanation that aligned best with *all* the evidence and go with it.

Expanding my reflection to my memories of SHINING HOPE from earlier in the day, I remembered something that I had thought about numerous times during the refugee operation. Terrorist attacks against the West had been occurring for multiple decades at this point, not to mention repeated periods of violence throughout history. In the case of Kosovo, it was interesting to note that it was the Christians who were persecuting Muslims. The refugees that were fleeing into Albania, and whom the Western coalition was working hard to support and defend, were Muslims. Could it be that our assistance and support of Muslims in need would change the general negative perceptions of the West held by the Islamic world? My logical Western mind said yes, this should be the outcome.

As time went on, I looked for evidence that Western actions during ALLIED FORCE and SHINING HOPE were leading to reduced tension between the Muslim and Western worlds. As far as I could tell, there was no broad recognition in the Islamic world that a Western coalition was spending an excessive amount of funding and time,

Tent stands ready to receive and stage UN humanitarian supplies at the Tirana International Airport.

not to mention risking Western lives helping Muslims, both by helping the refugees and fighting against the government that was persecuting them in Kosovo. The hatred of the West continued unabated in Islamic countries, and terrorist attacks continued.

To my Western mind, this made no sense. Could they not see that we were helping Muslims who were being treated viciously? That we were standing up for human rights and justice regardless of religion? Why wouldn't this soften their hearts and open their minds to the prospect that maybe we could live together in peace? This same hope for proving peaceful coexistence was possible clouded my evaluation of our efforts in Afghanistan when I was assigned to the PRT almost a decade later. Once again I believed the West was spending a lot of its treasure to help an Islamic country and that these efforts would soften their hearts and decrease their hatred. Again, I was disappointed and now realize that I was naive to hold on to this hope for so long. I now understand much better that no matter what the West does, the Islamic world will hate us unless the entire world converts to Islam and submits to Sharia Law. In their minds, nothing else matters.

Just before I went to bed, I received a couple texts from Mike back at the American Legion. The Washington Department Service Officers in Seattle continued to give him a hard time about coming back to the office and helping veterans with their claims. One of the people that Mike had butted heads with was gone, but the other was still there, and he was saying that under no circumstances was Mike to be allowed to resume his duties as a service officer. Our district commander was supporting Mike and trying to fight on his behalf, but it did not sound like much progress was being made. This was a major travesty! Mike was the best service officer in the state, maybe the country and the legion officials were preventing him from serving veterans because he had rubbed them the wrong way somehow. Just the year prior, the Stanwood–Camano community had voted him Man of the Year for his work as a SO.

Once again, I became very frustrated as I read the communications. I decided I needed to pray about the situation and contemplate if it is time to resign. One thing was for sure: I had had about all I could take of the Seattle office. The key people in the Department Service Division were the worst leaders I had ever seen. The problems did not stop there. The more I found out about American Legion officials in general, the more I suspected that they were far more interested in protecting their empire than fighting for what is best and fiscally realistic for veterans. The national leadership seemed to fall on their swords over every proposed change. They were not open to new ideas. For example, the organization's structure assumed women were spouses and high school programs for girls were run by the Auxiliary (which was comprised of only women since "obviously" there are no male military spouses). The Post (the part of the organization that are only vets) focuses its community support activities and programs for boys. Leadership positions at all levels rotated between members of the inner click, basically a "good ole boy" system.

I slept poorly all night, thinking about all this. The whole thing had been causing me an excessive amount of stress for some time. While working at the Legion and dealing with these issues, I often experienced the emotional and physical symptoms that I had struggled with prior to leaving the service due to being physically and mentally beaten to a pulp. Working at the Legion meant continuing the downward spiral. Maybe I needed to resign and find less stressful and more spiritual ways to contribute to the world and make a difference in my community?

# CHAPTER 24

## Reliegos to Puente Castro, 22.5 Kilometers
## 18 Sep 2015
## D+20

"I plan to stay just this side of León tonight and pass straight through it tomorrow," I informed Al and Tara while prepping my feet for the day's trek. "We spent two days there seeing the sights in 13. I have no need to put up with the crowds again."

"Walking in the city and fighting the traffic is not something we are looking forward to either," Al replied. "We decided to go 6 km today to Mansilla and then take a bus into the center of León. We'll tour the highlights and then may take another bus tonight to a village on the other side. We'll stay there."

"We are not such hard-core pilgrims that we are opposed to using a bus to skip walking the streets of such a large industrial city," Tara explained.

"It is your Camino! You can do it any way you want to," I said, remembering how many pilgrims were on the bus that Ria and I had taken to skip stage 11. "I, on the other hand, took a bus, taxi, and train last time. I am determined to walk every inch this time!"

Examining the outside of my tender right heel, I surmised that it was calloused and red but was not yet a blister—i.e., the textbook definition of a "hot spot." I covered the area with Compeed and applied medical tape around the edges as a preventive measure. I then took another cross-lace out of my left shoe to give my foot more room. Hopefully, that would relieve the growing pain there.

"That will put you at least a day ahead of me. I may not see you again!"

"Who knows, anything could happen," Tara said as she and Al slung their packs onto their backs, grabbed their poles, and bid me "Bien Camino." They were much faster at getting ready than I was.

When I finally got downstairs, I saw that the bar was closed up tight. I decided to try a private albergue I had noticed yesterday and see if they were serving breakfast. Passing the village fountain on the way, I filled my water bottle and added my vitamin powder mix.

After leisurely enjoying a coffee and croissant with honey, I bundled up with every piece of snivel gear I had and set out about 0830. Maybe I was starting to acclimate because the thirty-nine degrees didn't feel quite as bad today as it had a few days ago. Even my ears did somewhat better today.

* * * * *

In mid-February torrential rains caused severe flooding in five southern African countries: Mozambique, South Africa, Botswana, Zimbabwe, and Zambia. 3AF was tasked to lead JTF ATLAS RESPONSE in support of (ISO) the DoS, the UN and responding international aid organizations. Our mission was to assist in the coordination and synchronization of relief efforts, provide air transport for humanitarian relief supplies and personnel, and to provide aerial assessment of the status of roads to determine when we could transition to ground operations in each area.[36] Numerous other countries contributed to the humanitarian operation to include Britain, Germany, Malawi, Mozambique, Portugal, Spain, and of course, South Africa.[37] I even saw an Iranian cargo plane on the tarmac in Biera, Mozambique.

My staff formed the provost marshal cell again. We were among the first to deploy to Air Force Base Hoedspriut, South Africa. Our initial mission was to determine requirements and coordinate the

---

[36] "Atlas Response / Silent Promise," GlobalSecurity.org, May 7, 2011, https://www.globalsecurity.org/military/ops/silent_promise.htm

[37] "Atlas Response / Silent Promise," GlobalSecurity.org, May 7, 2011, https://www.globalsecurity.org/military/ops/silent_promise.htm

deployment of USAF Security Forces personnel to integrate with the South African Air Force in order to enhance security for their airfield as it transitioned to a busy logistical hub. Humanitarian relief supplies and personnel flowed into the airfield from numerous contributing countries and international aid organizations. Our C-130 aircraft and helicopters then transported the supplies and personnel to the areas cut off by floodwaters.

This time we had a bit more notice before deployment, much to our frustration. When 3AF was initially given the deployment tasking, one of our primary tasks was supposed to be search-and-rescue. We spent a good week planning as best we could from England while watching news broadcasts depicting people on rooftops and in trees in need of rescue. One particular story captivated my attention. A woman delivered a baby while clinging to a tree a few feet above the floodwaters. While this was going on, we sat in our offices and front rooms next to our packed mobility bags helplessly watching it on TV. Meanwhile, our rescue helicopters and cargo aircraft sat idly by on the RAF runway. All this while diplomats spent days trying to resolve several apparently contentious questions about where we would operate from and how. We finally received permission to deploy to South Africa, but by then the need for lifesaving rescues had subsided. Now the main issue was getting food, water, and other humanitarian supplies to the people who were cut off by floodwaters.

Complicating our contingency planning prior to and immediately after deployment was a timing conflict with Operation BRILLIANT LION. Since returning from Operation SHINING HOPE in late summer 1999, the 3AF staff had been planning a humanitarian relief and MEDFLAG (medical) FTX with the country of Cameroon in Central Africa. The exercise was scheduled for early March, within a week of our deployment to South Africa. Third Air Force was supposed to be the JTF HQ, and my office would make up the PM cell. We tasked several USAFE SF units to provide security for the exercise. Now, the staff and some of the support forces were being diverted to the "real-world" emergency, but the exercise would continue. In the midst of deploying to ATLAS RESPONSE, my staff and I were busy developing a new leadership plan for BRILLIANT

LOIN and adjusting SF taskings to cover both operations while continuing to support the ongoing contingencies in Bosnia, Kosovo, and Southwest Asia.

The other major issue I had to deal with at the start was convincing the State Department and the South African government to allow our security personnel to carry weapons while performing security duties at the airfield. This issue was a constant headache whenever US aircraft deployed with security anywhere in Africa. The host governments were not inclined to allow US personnel to be armed while on the ground in their country; this included security personnel assigned to secure the aircraft. The problem was our regulations required armed US security because, in general, African security was less effective, poorly equipped, and generally did not meet our standards. This was more important than usual because of all the other countries (some not so friendly to us) and countless aid organizations involved. There would be way too many "unknowns" wandering around the airfield.

I drafted a compromise proposal that allowed US security personnel to be armed with pistols while on security duty. The weapons would be securely stored in an armory between an individual's shifts. Normally we would carry M16s "long guns" for these duties, but M9 pistols were less aggressive, and therefore less offensive. Additionally, US forces would work closely with armed South African military security in recognition of the country's sovereignty and ownership of the airfield they were allowing us to use. After USAFE SF and EUCOM Force Protection staff approved my proposal, I worked closely with the commander of the Hoedspriut security unit, the defense attaché, and regional security offices at the US embassy to get it coordinated and approved by the South African government.

Soon after we were successful at this endeavor, it was decided that we would stand up a smaller logistical support base at the Beira Airport in Mozambique. Once again we had to obtain an international firearms agreement. Although our enemy was Mother Nature, security was vital because we were operating in poor countries in the middle of a devastating humanitarian crisis. The humanitarian supplies on the airfield were very tempting.

The majority of PM staff work in-country was done at our office at the JTF HQ at Hoedspruit. It is funny how staff work is pretty much the same regardless of if you are in an office at our historic headquarters building in England, a cubicle in a warehouse in Germany, or at a host country base in South Africa. The job entails making phone calls, processing e-mails, writing SITREPs, and attending staff meetings—all with the goal of orchestrating joint and combined (multinational) operations to achieve mission objectives.

Soon after we stood up our small logistical base in Beira, I seized the opportunity to go visit and check on the security situation, integration, and coordination with the many multinational organizations who were also supporting the relief efforts from the airport. The operation there was much more austere. Security Command and Control

High-Speed Security Control Center at Beira, Mozambique.

operated from a few chairs and a radio at a folding table in a large room with representatives from every organization you could think of. A bit of a madhouse if you ask me, but the close quarters made it easy to coordinate with your counterparts across the room.

While in this room, I had the pleasure of running into the deployed US military chaplain supporting the troops there. He was a fellow academy graduate who was currently stationed at Mildenhall. I often attended services he led and was a part of his weekly Bible study group. We had become friends, but I was unaware that he had deployed because I was already downrange when he got his tasking. It was great to see a familiar face.

The local chief, security forces (CSF) took me on post visits around the airfield and a drive around the exterior perimeter of the base. I was stunned by how poor the country was. Along the sides of the roads, we could see whole communities composed of shanties obviously constructed from discarded wood pallets and other garbage. These structures could hardly provide shelter from the elements, let alone be considered reasonable housing.

The SF captain I was with explained that Mozambique was the poorest country in Africa. Across the border, where I was working, was Africa's richest country, South Africa. I found it amazing how these two extremes could border each other. Similar to Mexico and the United States, people from Mozambique routinely attempted to illegally enter the wealthier South Africa. However, South Africa had a very effective border security system. Covering two million hectares along the South African side of the border was Kruger National Park. It was a large wildlife refuge patrolled by lions, elephants, wildebeests, leopards, cheetahs, and other large, dangerous animals. Many would-be illegal immigrants become prey while attempting to cross the park.

We were not there long enough to get a day off. The operation only lasted about thirty days. I did, however, take a couple of partial days. For the first one, we left the lodging area about 0300 to rendezvous with a local safari guide who had us out in Kruger Park before six to observe the wildlife engage in their early-morning activities before the African heat drove them to rest in hidden shaded areas.

I was amazed at all the wildlife that we saw—pretty much everything that you would imagine seeing on an African safari: impala, zebra, hyenas, lions, baboons, packs of wild dogs, giraffes, elephants, and water buffalo. The only animal we were looking for, but never caught a glimpse of, was a rhinoceros. We were fortunate enough to observe a couple of cheetahs take down an impala for breakfast. Kind of violent, but a firsthand view of how the food chain works in the wild.

We were back in the office and hard at work by 1200 hours.

A couple weeks later, I was able to leave work a little early in the late afternoon to enjoy another MWR trip and experience a night Safari and African dinner. This time we watched the animals at dusk and then continued to look for them with spotlights after dark. The most amazing thing about this trip was approaching a lion and lioness lounging on the side of the road. Our open-topped safari jeep stopped just a few feet from the lion, and the guide shone the spotlight right on him. It didn't faze him a bit. The guide explained that they were used to seeing the shape of the jeeps and did not see them as a threat. The jeeps were also too big to attack. However, they warned us that simply putting parts of our body outside the edges of the jeep or completely getting out would prompt a far different and extremely violent response.

I could not believe that I took a picture of a lion lying comfortably on the side of the road not three feet from me!

\* \* \* \* \*

I stopped for a coffee break about 1130. After a day and a half in the middle of nowhere, I was thoroughly enjoying the frequent villages.

I was not, however, enjoying the trail. The first leg was along a quiet green path, but after Mansilla de las Mulas, the Camino was merely a dirt trail beside a very busy road; frequently we were on the road's shoulder. The traffic noise was a constant irritant. The vehicles zoomed by as if we were not there. How I longed for the green path on the far side of León. But that was more than a day away. Until then, I had to endure the city and "zona industrial."

I was determined to somehow persevere and get through this! I must remember to smile and greet everybody I encountered in the city. That would help calm my nerves. This coping mechanism did not work so well with speeding traffic!

\* \* \* \* \*

The e-mail from Mike regarding his struggles with the Seattle office reinvaded my thoughts. My obsessive-compulsive tendencies took over, and my mind churned the details of the whole situation over and over again for the rest of the day's trek.

Between sometimes-overwhelming number of clients, phone calls, walk-ins, system abuse, bad client attitudes and frustrations resulting in them lashing out at us, the bureaucratic frustrations working with the VA and dealing with the stress generated by the major leadership deficiencies up the chain of command, I could feel my body and mind continuing to spiral downward. I kept returning to the thought "I am retired now. I am supposed to be relaxing and healing my physical and mental ailments. Instead, I have put myself into a position which in some ways is more mentally taxing then my military duties were." Although my AL duties helped individual veterans, the negative pressures beat the positive impacts into sub-mission. As a result, I felt I was getting worse, not better, and I wasn't even getting paid for putting up with the crap!

At this point I was about 98 percent convinced that the right thing for me to do for my mental and physical well-being was to resign. I just didn't need the frustrations and stress! I had been on the verge of literally working myself to death before I retired. Besides mental struggles, I could feel my body falling apart and always knew that I'd pushed too hard when I got pains and tightness in my chest. I had been experiencing this same feeling more and more recently. I had also been recently diagnosed with prehypertension and prediabetes. All of this could be easily attributed to too much stress in my life. A majority of that stress came from my duties at the Legion.

\* \* \* \* \*

Finally, back on a green route somewhat offset from the busy road that the Camino still followed, I was able to enjoy a couple kilometers of relative peace. About two-thirds of the way through this relaxing section, I stopped at a small out-of-the-way café a couple blocks off trail in the village of Arcahueja—where the guidebook suggested we RON if our objective was to avoid staying in busy and noisy León. The book was right; the small village was a quiet, peaceful oasis before the coming storm.

I treated myself to a healthy rotisserie chicken and salad. This was the first time that I had found rotisserie chicken and could get a meal with a lot of protein and no bread for lunch. While enjoying the secluded rest, I took advantage of the relative peace to read day 18 of my service study.

In today's study, followers of Christ are cautioned to remember that their work planting the seeds of God's message is a service to both God and the people receiving the message. However, the responsibility for the results is God's and, of course, whether or not the person receiving the message is willing to accept it. God's servants should not feel discouraged if the seeds they plant do not produce the fruit they hope for. That is between God and the person being served. God's servants must keep this in perspective, persevere in their dedicated service, and rejoice that God is allowing them to be a part of process. The two major scriptural references used today were 1 Corinthians 3.7 and Luke 8:4–15.[38]

As I started out on the final leg of the day's trek, I contemplated relating this to my ongoing turmoil about the American Legion. Is this telling me to just suck it up and continue doing the best job I can in spite of the circumstances?

Although any service to God's people is looked favorably on by God, my American Legion duties were not directly related to this message in that I was not evangelizing the Gospel message of salvation. The principal might apply, but not the technical details. Besides, I don't think that God would want me to work myself to death. What good would I be to Him if I was not mentally or physically capable of serving with a joyful demeanor? Trying to do the job while extremely stressed out could easily lead to mistakes that could cost a veteran a lot of money and continued stress.

No, I think God wants joyful and effective servants!

My other volunteer position as an admissions liaison officer for USAFA was an incredibly positive experience, not only for myself, but for the young students who dreamed of excelling as officers, being a part of something bigger than themselves, and dedicating

---

[38] Fryar, p. 38–39.

themselves to excellence. This also was not a missionary endeavor, but setting up high school students to achieve their dreams and be the best that they could be is something that I think God supports. Military service brings a lot of people to a saving relationship with God.

After all, as the saying goes, "There are no atheists in foxholes!"

Obviously, it is inappropriate for me to push applicants toward a relationship with God. Still, my soul gets great satisfaction knowing that I am helping them launch an incredible career and life of service to their country.

The other great aspects of this volunteer position are that I have complete control of how much work I accept and the flexibility to drive my schedule as long as deadlines are met. To this point, how much time I have been able to dedicate to this service has been limited because my Legion duties have demanded two full days a week. By resigning from the Legion, I could more aggressively reach out to my assigned schools IOT do a better job educating career counselors and students on the opportunities the academy and the Air Force offer.

Having more time to focus on this service position would be a win-win situation for both me and potential applicants, not to mention the academy and the country as a whole.

Of course, there was no question that I would continue serving at Camano Chapel and people throughout our community who needed assistance as a volunteer at His Pantry. Although busy days—especially near the holidays—could be stressful, for the most part it was a very positive experience, and I enjoyed working with not only the clients but the other volunteers. Many were now friends, and from this service I had developed a strong connection to the chapel, ministry staff, and fellow members of the congregation. It was the means by which I had become more closely connected to a church family than I had ever been in my entire life. I believe the chapel and the community received benefit from my service, but I also received a lot from that service. The closer I became to the chapel community, the closer I felt to God, the more I was able to address the causes of my spiritual struggles, and slowly but surely my faith and relationship with God was strengthening.

The day's last kilometer entered the outskirts of León. Industrial buildings and small businesses lined the streets. By the time I got to the Albergue Santo Tomás de Canterbury, I was among standard city streets. However, we were still far enough away from old town and the tourist areas that the population and traffic on the streets was relatively light. Not ideal, but it would do.

The albergue was a very nice, new facility, obviously built specifically for peregrinos. They even had a bicycle storage room for those riding the Camino. A very nice, relaxing lounge area hosted a book exchange library, microwave, and of course, a cof-

Comical way-marker
on the outskirts of León
with yellow arrows.

fee machine and a vending machine that sold beer in addition to water and sodas. They had a laundry service, so I took advantage of it and had them wash and dry my clothing. Across the street and down a block, I found a place where I could get a drink and a light early meal.

While relaxing there, I completed my mission planning for the following day. The first ten and a half clicks would be through León's downtown, old town, and industrial areas. I expected masses of people, but would concentrate on passing through as quickly as possible. After a small community on the far end of the León metropolitan area called La Virgen Del Camino, a green trail veered south of the major road, N-120, we had been following. After a couple of kilometers along a country road, the Camino took off across open fields for another 10 km to Villar de Mazarife. That would be my next mission objective.

Returning to the albergue, I settled in to a comfortable chair in the lounge and read chapters 31 to 34 in my *Seeking* e-book. These chapters dug deeply into significant reasoning that supported believing in the foundational tenets of Christianity and continued to demonstrate the fallacies of the Islamic faith when studied critically and realistically.

After returning to my bunk, I drifted off to sleep in deep contemplation about the fresh perspectives presented in the book. My logical mind definitely appreciated the scientific thought process that was laid out.

# CHAPTER 25

## Puente Castro to Villar de Mazarife, 24.3 Kilometers
## 19 Sep 2015
## D+21

After enjoying a small coffee from the machine in the lounge, I set out for the lion's den at 0755, enduring a brisk forty-one-degree morning. It was just under two clicks to get to old town León. I planned to reminisce about this short stretch of familiar territory over breakfast at one of the many cafés near the cathedral. I also looked forward to the opportunity to find something to keep my ears warm and a resupply of travel-size antiperspirant.

\* \* \* \* \*

"I think I've moved into an oven," I thought as I got out of my air-conditioned car in the parking lot of the temporary lodging facility at Luke AFB on a blistering 110 degrees afternoon in Glendale on the west side of Phoenix, Arizona.

It was the middle of July 2000, and I had just arrived from cold, rainy England to take command of the 56th Security Forces Squadron. This time I would officially be "on orders" as the squadron commander. Being on orders meant that I had more autonomy to run my unit. I also had nonjudicial punishment authority for discipline matters. Previously, I could issue letters of counseling, admonishment, or reprimand, but now I could punish wayward troops under Article 15 of the Uniform Code of Military Justice (UCMJ) and refer the most serious infections and crimes to the legal office for court-martial proceedings. Additionally, I had a higher level of authority regarding squadron policy and procedures, budgeting, infrastructure and equipment enhancements, work schedules, and all day-to-day unit operations. I was responsible for all security, law enforcement, and Force Protection for the base. My wing polo shirt had my new nickname "Sheriff" embroidered on it. My boss was the 56th Mission Support Group commander. He also oversaw Civil Engineering, Services, Communications, and the Mission Support Squadrons.

Originally known as Luke Field, the base was named after 2Lt Frank Luke Jr., known as the "Arizona Balloon Buster" for shooting down eighteen enemy planes and balloons during World War I. The base started training AT-6 advanced fighter pilots in the summer of 1941. During World War II, Luke was the Army Air Corps' largest fighter training base and became known as a Home of the Fighter Pilot.[39] Today the 56th Fighter Wing's mission was to the train new pilots to fly the F-16 Fighting Falcon. We fell under the Air Education and Training Command (AETC).

Besides turning the base into a fortress after 9/11, there were a couple of significant events that occurred during my time at Luke that will forever affect who I am.

Late one afternoon, the LED called me while I was working on e-mail in my office.

"Senior Airman Smith [not his actual name] was hit by a car while riding his motorcycle off-base. The Glendale Police are requesting somebody from the squadron come to the accident site and identify the body. They also want to know if we want to assist with notifying his wife."

I sat stunned for a few seconds. SrA Smith was one of our young LE patrolmen. He had just worked a day shift and would have been on his way home. The Glendale Police probably recognized the SF badge on his uniform. Since we worked so closely together in the aftermath of 9/11, they knew who we were and how to get ahold of us.

"I'll come get the information from you. Let them know that I will be there as soon as possible," I managed to respond in a fairly

39 "Luke Air Force Base," Wikipedia.com, September 1, 2016, https://en.wikipedia.org/wiki/Luke_Air_Force_Base.

steady voice even though my stomach was churning and my hands were shaking.

I took another minute or so to regain my composure and then went down the hall to the desk. The desk sergeant gave me the location of the accident. Fighting to hide my shakes, I wrote down SrA Smith's home address and returned to my office to call my boss. It was standard protocol to upchannel information about serious incidents involving group personnel. The colonel suggested that his deputy accompany me to the accident site. He was a lieutenant colonel who had been through this sort of thing before. I gratefully accepted the offer. About ten minutes later, the deputy picked me up, and we headed off-base. In the meantime, the colonel made arrangements for the on-call chaplain to meet us at the accident site and join us when we went to the couple's apartment to notify his wife.

When we arrived, I sat in the car for a minute or so, taking in the scene. I was still preparing myself mentally for the difficult task ahead. When our airman was killed in the accident at the training area on Sicily, I was spared the pain of visiting the accident site. The flight commander had gone instead. Now I was the commander, and with that prestigious job title came responsibilities such as this.

The accident had happened on a wide thoroughfare. There were three lanes of traffic going in each direction and a center turn lane separating them. I could see two vehicles in the middle pointing in different directions and a mangled motorcycle lying on its side. Among all this was a body covered in a blanket. That would be my airman.

An NCO from my unit approached me as I got out of the car. It was SrA Smith's supervisor.

"Thank you for coming, ma'am," he said with a quick salute. "I went ahead and identified the body for the police."

"Thank you," I said, feeling both relief and a little guilt that I would not have to see the body. "Did they tell you what happened?"

"It appears that Smith was accelerating after stopping at that red light. That van was attempting a left turn but did not get entirely into the turn lane. The other car ran into the back side of the van that was still in the traffic flow lane. They must have been going fairly fast, because the impact pushed the van across the turn lane and into Smith, hitting him head-on. It all happened so fast there was nothing he could do. It was Smith's body versus the van."

I took a deep breath and closed my eyes for moment, trying to process what I had heard. My NCO then introduced me to the patrolman in charge of the investigation who repeated the same story.

"From the evidence we have so far, Airman Smith did nothing wrong. He was just at the wrong place, at the wrong time. There was nothing he could have done, and human bodies don't fare well when they hit a vehicle with that much momentum."

"I understand. We have a chaplain on the way. We'll take care of notifying his wife," I assured him.

About a half hour later, the four of us arrived at the couple's apartment and knocked on the door. When his young wife opened the door and saw us standing there, the chaplain in dress blues, she knew that something had happened to her husband.

She started to cry, "Where is my husband? What has happened to him?"

I swallowed hard, took a deep breath, and recited the death notification statement.

"It is with a heavy heart that I regret to inform you that [*John*] was killed in a traffic accident on his way home."

I was actually relieved to have the script because I don't know if I could have spoken professionally otherwise.

She started crying hysterically. My NCO and the chaplain started comforting her. My heart was breaking. I could not imagine a harder thing to be a part of. We stayed for close to an hour, telling her as much as we knew about the accident and how the unit would help her deal with the coming days.

"I will assign one of my officers to help you with all of the paperwork and arrangements. If it is okay with you, our unit would like to have a formal military memorial service for him."

The next day she stopped by the squadron to tell me that she had just been to the doctor and found out that she was pregnant with the couple's second child. Again, my heart was breaking as I hugged her. I had no idea what to say.

A couple of months later, my group commander decided to capitalize on the fact that I was now experienced in death notifications and called on me once again. An airman at another base had been killed in another motorcycle accident. He was single, so the death notification needed to be made to his parents. They lived in Phoenix, so the responsibility fell to Luke AFB. I put on my dress blue uniform and rendezvoused with the chaplain. We discussed the situation and then set off in his vehicle for the parents' house. This time I did not even get out the standard statement before the mother started screaming hysterically. Military families are fully aware what it means when officers in their service dress uniform knock on their door.

After that night, I decided that I would keep my experience in this area a secret at future bases. I didn't want any more bosses assigning me this task just "because I knew what I was doing."

\* \* \* \* \*

It only took about fifty minutes to arrive at the square in front of the enormous and ornate León Cathedral. It was still very cold, and I was bundled up in every piece of snivel gear I had. I timed my pass through León well. The streets were practically empty, only a few city employees cleaning up debris from the previous day's

León Cathedral

activities. I'm not sure why I had not remembered this, but it was consistent with what we had previously seen in big cities. The Spaniards love to stay up late at night and therefore did not get moving until late morning. The downside to this was that none of the stores were open, so I was unable to shop for ear covers or replacements for items I was running low on. I didn't even find an open café until I reached the cathedral square.

I took advantage of the peaceful morning and beautiful view of the cathedral by enjoying a coffee and croissant while completing day 19 of the service study.

Similar to yesterday's, readers were cautioned not to let our service lead to a sense of pride or entitlement or, on the negative side, discouragement. Referencing 2 Corinthians 9:8 and 10:12, we are also cautioned not to compare ourselves to the service of other Christians. God has a different role for each of us, and we must be content to serve as He asks us to.[40]

This is definitely a lesson I must learn. As a type A perfectionist and workaholic with obsessive-compulsive tendencies, I am constantly striving to excel. I must admit, I find pride when my efforts achieve positive results and I am recognized for these achievements. Of course, recognition is very important in the military where it is vital that you prove yourself in order to be promoted and assigned greater responsibilities; moving up is a must in our "up-or-out" system. Awards attest to your past success, set you apart from your peers, and indicate your future potential.

My two years at Luke continued the successful trends of my career and resulted in several awards that set me on course for promotion to lieutenant colonel. I was selected from our 22,000-plus career field to receive the AF Col Billy Jack Carter Award for the calendar year 2000. This award is given to the security force member who was deemed to have made the greatest contribution to securing Air Force resources and protecting personnel that year. I received this award based on my accomplishments in planning security for Operation BRILLIANT LION in Cameroon, serving as provost marshal for JTF ATLAS RESPONSE, and several other things we had done in 3AF during my last six months there. My initial successes at Luke—such as, dealing with a shooting incident just outside the base, drastically improving our enlisted upgrade training program, providing lessons-learned information based on my 3AF deployment experiences to the AF Research Lab to help with the development of guidance for Humanitarian Relief Operations, having our

---

[40] Fryar, p. 40–41.

Force Protection program cited as "Outstanding" by the Joint Staff Integrated Vulnerability Assessment team, and numerous error-free mobility inspections and exercises—rounded out my award-nomination package.

My unit continued to excel by building on the improvements started the previous year, increasing security after 9/11 and deploying multiple teams to the new combat zone. I was personally recognized as the 56th Mission Support Group's Field Grade Officer of the Year, and my unit was selected as AETC's Outstanding Active-Duty Medium Security Forces Unit for the year 2001. Both awards were exceptional feathers in my cap.

Now that I am retired, I needed to guard against continuing the mind-set of pride and awards. I am realizing more and more that my new identity should be to serve God and his people here on earth. I must learn to be humble and accept whatever role God will ask me to have, no matter how menial I may see it to be. I must be content to do God's will and humbly give Him all credit. I must not seek recognition for myself. I should only discuss what I do to serve when my purpose is merely to let people know that I am available and willing to fill a need. Likely easier thought than done!

At 0910, I headed out across the cathedral square and embarked on the last major section I had not walked in 2013.

\* \* \* \* \*

Another significant event that occurred while in command was the crash of an F-16 near Gila Bend, Arizona, on 23 July 2001.

Prior to my arrival in the summer of 2000, the base had experienced a string of crashes. The F-16 had gained a reputation for crashing and was therefore commonly referred to as a "lawn dart." The base had gotten a handle on the situation and had gone thirteen months without a crash. Fortunately, the pilot safely ejected and was rescued by a search-and-rescue helicopter. He was quickly released from the hospital after being thoroughly checked out.

The aircraft did not fare so well. Debris was scattered across an isolated desert area. The base fire department (FD) and a contingent of my security troops were the first ground personnel to arrive. The FD put out the associated fires while my troops established security of the crash site and set up entry control procedures. The crash area was large, but its isolation helped minimize the security manpower required.

Similar to the response to 9/11, my role initially was to represent security at the Wing Battle Staff to assist with coordination of the emergency response and coordinate with local law enforcement. While I did this, my senior staff recalled off-duty unit members and organized follow-up personnel and equipment to set up twenty-four-hour security at the site. We had to secure the site for the duration of the crash investigation, which lasted close to ten days. Since it took almost three hours to get there, a bivouac had to be established on-scene. Personnel were required to stay out there for several days before being relieved by another crew. It was extremely hot, so air-conditioned tents and electric generators to operate lights, equipment, and the AC were vital. Each time we relieved a crew, we sent out water, food, fuel, and other supplies to get them through the next few days.

The night shift tries to sleep in the partial shade from camy-netting at an F-16 crash site in the Arizona desert.

I took a day off from my tedious office duties to visit the troops on-site. I was amazed, as usual, at how well they were faring in the miserable, austere conditions. Leave it to the gung ho cops to make the best of every situation! Nobody was whining. They were actually happy to have been selected to do their part. I delivered some junk food I had purchased at the commissary as a way to show my appreciation for their sacrifice. They could not have been happier! In conditions like this, the littlest things can make a huge difference.

The NCOIC showed me around the crash site. It was incredible how small most of the pieces were and how large an area they were dispersed over. The violence of the impact was very apparent. Thank the Lord for ejection seats!

* * * * *

I stopped at a small park on the outskirts of León to top off my water bottle before leaving the built-up area and reentering the rolling hills of rural farmland. I was excited to see an old friend.

"Tom, how's it going?" I greeted my friend from Philadelphia.

"Good to see that you are still going strong," he smiled in greeting.

We decided to walk together for a while. With our common military background, our conversation quickly headed in that direction. Somehow the discussion progressed to my thoughts about the plight of the local nationals who had worked for coalition forces in Afghanistan and Iraq and my personal experiences with one of them.

* * * * *

Not long before the end of my PRT tour, an event occurred that was on one hand exciting and on another, alarming. Of course, I had no idea at the time how this event would affect my life for most of the next decade.

After myself and the incoming XO met with a village Shura as part of the right seat–left seat changeover training, I decided to visit the personnel manning the security perimeter around the village. I walked from one uparmored HMMWV to the next, stopping at each one to talk to the crew for a few minutes. While walking away from one of these posts toward the next, I heard somebody call out "Colonel" with a strong Afghan accent. I turned around to see one of our new local national interpreters coming toward me.

"I have been looking for a chance to talk to you," he said as he got within about ten feet of me.

"What can I do for you?" I asked smiling in greeting.

"I was very happy about what you said and did at the school a couple weeks ago." He was referring to the official opening of a school the PRT had funded, contracted, and monitored the construction of in Charkh District. Myself and the provincial governor, along with many other local dignitaries, had given formal speeches before officially cutting the ribbon across the entryway and officially handing the building over to the Afghan government.

"You said that the school supplies and gifts you presented came from your parents' church in the United States. I was very happy when I heard this! That was when I knew that you were a Christian."

My parents' church had collected money, clothing, and school supplies as a service ministry. My mom had taken the donated money to a local Walmart to purchase additional items for Afghan children. When she told the Walmart employees what she was doing, they gave her an incredible discount so she could buy a lot more items with the available funds. The church itself donated about $2,000 to cover the shipping costs. I used the ribbon-cutting ceremony as a venue to present the items to the children that would be attending the school. I explained to the several hundred people in attendance that the items had been donated by my parents' church as a sign of friendship and support from America. He had obviously keyed in on the word *church*.

"Yes, I am a Christian," I said a bit nervously.

Proselytizing was strictly prohibited by General Order 1 (GO1). It was vitally important to avoid any activity that could possibly be misperceived as violating GO1. He had brought up the subject, but I still had to be very careful.

"I am also a Christian," he explained with a broad smile on his face. "I have been looking for a chance to talk to you. I became a Christian when I was a refugee in England when the Taliban ruled my country. Now I want to be baptized. Can you help me?"

I was stunned. Did this Afghan actually just say what I thought he said? This was a Muslim country. Converting to Christianity meant a death sentence for a Muslim. If I was accused of participating in a conversion, my career would be over; I'd probably be court-martialed. This was not a good conversation to be having. My stomach started churning, and the hair on the back of my neck stood up. I needed to be very careful with my reply. However, a convert was looking for help from another Christian. I had to do something.

"I am not sure. I will ask the base chaplain what can be done."

"Thank you," he replied enthusiastically. "When I knew you were a Christian, I knew you would help me!"

I returned a slight smile and told him I would get back with him soon. He then returned to the security team he was supporting, and I continued on to visit the next post.

That evening I went to the base chaplain and asked what I should do, explaining my concerns about GO1. It would be really bad if the commander was accused of evangelizing. He told me the best thing to do was to bring him to the chapel, and he would take it from there.

The next day I went to the small building right outside the base gate where the interpreters lived—off-base, but within the protective range of our perimeter security forces. I was nervous about what the other interpreters would think, but I asked for the young man, anyway. I was directed to a room around the back side of the building, knocked on the door, and called out his name.

"Come with me, and I will show you where the chapel is," I said very softly when he came to the door.

I wanted to make sure that none of the other interpreters heard what I said. If they knew that he wanted to visit the chapel, his life would be at risk. It was suspicious enough that the commander had come to the interpreter hut to get a specific "terp." Normally, the only one I talked to was their leader who was assigned as my personal interpreter and acted as the manager for the rest of the team. I had never gone to the hut even to look for him. I always sent for him, and he would report to my office or the conference room when we needed to discuss an upcoming mission or other issues. Merely being at their house would pique the curiosity of both Afghans and any Americans who noticed. Walking across the FOB together was another suspicious activity. Once at the chapel, we quickly entered and closed the door behind us. I introduced him to the chaplain and then immediately left them to talk alone. I was determined that I would take no further part in what would happen next. I was out of it, or so I thought.

Mark (the Christian name he took while working in Kabul) continued to work as an interpreter with the PRT after I left. Later he transferred to another position supporting the US military at a base in Kabul. In all, he worked for the United States for about five years. During this period, he put his life on the line on a daily basis as an interpreter and cultural adviser. It would be impossible to determine the number of convoys he completed (all subject to attack) and how many meetings he interpreted for where anyone in the audience could have been the enemy and could have attacked at any moment. Throughout, he served with bravery, distinction, and determination to assist the coalition achieve its goal of peace and stability for Afghanistan.

In his off-duty hours, he attended Bible studies and services at the chapel at each base. Eventually, his religious affiliation was discovered by the other interpreters and Afghan employees. They harassed him a lot and called him "kafer," which basically meant he was a traitor to Islam. However, because he resided on a US base, he had some semblance of a shield from physical harm.

While at the Kabul base, he applied to immigrate to the United States through the Afghan Special Immigration Visa (SIV) program. Similar to its counterpart in Iraq, this program was designed to provide US immigration visas and permanent residency to local nationals who had worked for the United States for more than a year. They risked severe injury or death by Afghans who were a part of, or sympathized with, the Taliban or Al Qaeda. The US government felt it only right that their immigration applications should carry a significant priority.

A US service member and an Afghan American (an Afghan who had immigrated to the United States, spent five years as a legal permanent resident, and then had been granted citizenship and a security clearance) counterintelligence employee conducted the required interview as part of the SIV application process. During the interview, Mark was asked his religion, and he proudly stated he was a Christian. The Muslim interviewer took great offense to this admission and immediately started belittling and insulting him and yelling at him that he should be ashamed. He called him a kafer. The interviewer was very emotional in his verbal attacks, and the report he submitted for the SIV process was negative. Additionally, somehow a note was added to his official file that he had tested positive for tuberculosis (TB) even though he had never had a test that indicated a positive result. Combined, the report and TB positive note stopped all hope Mark had to immigrate to the United States. It also cost him his job at the base.

He went back to live with his family and got married. He was seriously injured during a couple assassination attempts motivated by his previous employment with the United States. His nephew was kidnapped and killed for the same reason.

It wasn't long before his wife found his Bible and informed his brothers that he was a Christian. She left him; his brothers beat him and threatened to kill him. He fled to another part of Afghanistan. His brothers informed their Imans at the mosques, and word went out to his home community that he had converted to Christianity. He did not dare to return. He assumed that the police would have been informed and that they would arrest him if they found him. At that time, Christians were being routinely executed for violating the Muslim blasphemy law.

At some point during all this, he received what was commonly known as a "Night Letter" from the Taliban. He sent me a translation of their message to him:

> This is the final decision of Taliban organization's scholars; that you [his name] son of [his father's name] resident of [hometown] . . . that you have been working for long time with Americans, Jewish and Christians as interpreter in Paktya and Logar provinces and you spying for them a lot and you handed over lots of innocent young Talibans to these Jews and Christians. Also, you invited lots of people to the religion of

Christianity. So the solid and authoritative scholars of Taliban's organization declared this decision; if you (his name) do not stop supporting
them you will be beheaded by the brave soldiers
of Taliban. "Inshallah."

It was in the midst of this hopeless situation that he contacted
me in 2012 through Facebook and asked for my assistance in getting his immigration application approved. I had read several articles
about how many Iraqis who had worked for Britain and the United
States in Iraq before the coalition pulled out had been killed once
they were no longer protected by the foreign military forces. This
was becoming a problem in Afghanistan as we started drawing down
our forces there. Based on this knowledge, combined with my understanding of the threat he was under for converting to Christianity,
my heart went out to him, and I made it my mission to help him.

I wrote letters to the State Department's SIV office and to my
senators and representative in Congress. I explained how the faulty
and biased information in his record had stopped his application and
how much danger he was in. I then asked for their assistance in getting to him a new, unbiased interview and a medical test to confirm
that he did not have TB.

Apparently, my request worked its way to the right office and
was granted. He was given a new interview and medical exam. Finally
he was approved for immigration and arrived in the United States
near the end of 2013. I then went to work trying to help him get
settled.

We soon discovered that World Relief had been contracted by
the State Department to help immigrants and refugees get settled.
He contacted them, and they arranged for him to move into an
apartment complex with other immigrants from Afghanistan, Iraq,
Pakistan, Somalia, and various other Islamic countries. He then went
through their eight-month integration program. To help make ends
meet during this process, World Relief paid the rent for the apartment that he shared with several Muslim immigrants. The immigrants also received food stamps and medical care from the state's

social services program. They all attended classes on American culture and English as a Second Language. During the final month, World Relief helped the immigrants get jobs with the goal of them becoming self-sustaining.

* * * * *

"Personally, I think that they could have done a better job teaching the immigrants the basics of functioning in our society," I commented to Tom as I was nearing the end of my story. "I was talking to Mark on the phone one day, and he told me that he had been trying to mail a letter. I don't remember if he was trying to pay a bill or send something to the immigration office regarding his pending Green Card, but he said he had put it in the outgoing mailbox several times, and it kept showing up back in his mailbox. After contemplating his dilemma for a few moments, I asked him if he had put a stamp on the envelope. The phone went silent for a while, and then he asked, 'What is a stamp?' I could not believe they had not taught him such a basic thing."

As we laughed together about how the most basic things we grew up with can be completely foreign to an immigrant, we started passing through the outskirts of Villar de Mazarife. On the right side of the Camino was an albergue with a large number of pilgrims lounging in the grassy front yard.

I recognized Joy as she called out, "Tracey, Tom, good to see you! Come join us here. It's very nice."

"We were hoping to get a room at Tio Pepe in the center of town. We are not interested in fifty people in one room," Tom explained.

"Both of the other places are already full. They have smaller rooms here. You could see if any of those beds are still available," Joy replied.

"It's great to know that the others are full! Thank you! No use walking all the way there just to have to return." My feet were happy to be spared the extra effort and pain. They were really hurting this afternoon.

Tom and I were each able to get a bed in four-person rooms with dinner and a breakfast buffet included for 23€. Joy was correct;

it was a very nice place, and it was not long before we were cleaned up and outside on the front lawn lounging with the others while enjoying an afternoon glass of wine.

"I signed up for a massage," I told Joy.

A lady I had not met before sat down next to us as Joy and I were talking about the massage.

"I just got done with one. He is wonderful. Have him work on whatever is hurting. He'll work out the kinks."

"My feet are killing me today, but having him work on them would be way too painful."

"That is exactly why you should have him work on them! By the time he's done, they should feel much better," she encouraged me.

"Hhmm. I'll think about it."

A half hour later, I went in for my massage and decided to bite the bullet. I had him spend the majority the time working on my feet with about a third on my somewhat less painful back. Throughout, I just kept reminding myself of the saying on a T-shirt I had bought while at the academy: "No Pain, No Gain."

If the level of pain meant anything, my "gain" should be immense!

An hour later, I was back in my room. My feet still hurt. Maybe the relief would take awhile. I decided to give them a rest and sat on my bed with my feet propped up. I fired up my iPad to read a couple chapters in the *Seeking* book.

Nabeel, David, and their Buddhist friend continued the discussion about how God loves us as a Father, and that is why He willingly paid for our sins Himself, allowing Him to forgive us so we could live with Him in heaven for eternity. Nabeel gained some understanding of this concept by comparing it to his father's love for him. He told his friends that he assessed the historical evidence about Christianity as having an 80 percent chance of being accurate, but the case for Islam was 100 percent.

Nabeel explained his reasoning, and the others started asking intellectually critical questions regarding his arguments based on other passages from the Islamic holy books that they had found in preparation for the session. By the end of chapter 36, Nabeel realized that his evaluation of Islamic beliefs was not based on critical investigation. He had intensely investigated Christianity, but his mind-set had been that Islam is true, period. He agreed to study Muhammad in-depth while focusing on the question "How do we know?" for each point. The group would then continue the discussion at their next meeting.[41]

At 1900, we gathered at long tables in the dining room for the communal dinner. I sat next to Tom. Joy was a couple of seats away at the end of the table. Sitting across from me was the young German girl that I had met in Roncesvalles the first evening. This was the first time we had run into each other since then, and we enjoyed telling each other the highlights of our pilgrimages.

She was sitting next to a very interesting couple from Germany. I was astounded to hear that the husband had started his Camino at the front door of their home in Hamburg, as the pilgrims of old would have done. He had been walking since April. His wife was not as committed to being authentic as he was. She joined him in France about 770 km before St. Jean.

---

[41] Qureshi, chapters 35–36.

# CHAPTER 26

### Villar de Mazarife to Santibanez de Valdeiglesia, 19.5 Kilometers
### 20 Sep 2015
### D+22

I hit the trail solo at 0805. I encouraged Tom to go on ahead because my feet slowed us down yesterday and I could detect no positive impact of the massage. It was going to be another painful day. To limit my day to around 20 km, I expected to stop about two-thirds of the way through stage 22. Tom was intent on finishing the stage by going all the way to Astorga. Per SOP, I had no intention of staying in a town that large. Hence, another good reason to stop at my day's objective— Santibanez, if I even made it that far. There were three closer options starting around the ten-click point if my feet wanted to stop earlier.

\* \* \* \* \*

My command at Luke went well enough that I was rewarded with another command, this time overseas. On 29 May 2002, I had the first of several nerve-racking experiences of flying into the Tegucigalpa airport in Honduras. I had been warned by the major I was replacing about the unique landing at the country's capital nestled among a mountain range. The runway was situated such that an approaching plane had to fly very low over the mountains, turning sharply to squeeze between two at a low-enough altitude to enable a landing on the nearby international runway.

His warning might have actually made it worse for me. Maybe it would've been better to have been in an ignorant bliss. Instead, knowing what we were in for, I anxiously watched out the window as the large commercial passenger plane rolled to the left for a sharp turn while continuing to lose altitude. We were so close to the ground that I could swear the wing was about to hit the side of the mountain. Obviously, the pilots had flown this route before and managed to get us safely onto the ground. Once the brakes engaged, a round of applause broke out throughout the plane. Apparently, I was not the only nervous passenger onboard!

My relief was short-lived. The major and another unit member were waiting for me outside the customs area. They explained that we had about sixty miles to get to Soto Cano Air Base near the city of Comayagua. Because we would be traveling on third world roads, it would take us close to two hours. I had always thought the driving in Sicily was hair-raising. Sicilian drivers were quite tame in comparison to Hondurans!

They race along roads barely wide enough for two cars, passing one another with absolutely no regard for oncoming traffic. This harrowing conduct did not seem to faze our enlisted driver (my new supply sergeant, S4) in the least bit—not even when it happened going around a blind mountain curve. The passing vehicle took his half in the middle, the vehicle being passed simply moved to the right shoulder as my driver calmly moved to left. Somehow we managed to get three vehicles abreast speeding down a road that was barely wide enough for two. After this happened a couple of times and I saw my life flash before my eyes, I decided it would be best if I refrained from looking out the front window. Instead, I kept my eyes fixed on the outgoing commander and tried to focus on our discussion about the unit I was about to take command of—that was, if we arrived alive.

Soto Cano Air Base, affectionately referred to as "SCAB," was established temporarily in 1983 on the Honduran military base that supported their Air Force Academy. It was still considered "temporary" nineteen years later. This designation was a major problem because the "powers that be" were not willing to put a significant amount of funding toward upgrading the living and working conditions at a temporary base. Hence, we lived and worked in small, very basic plywood buildings known as hooches. As a unit commander, I was fortunate to be assigned an entire hooch to live in. Senior NCOs and junior offices lived in half hooches, while the junior enlisted lived in a quarter of a hooch. Work and morale buildings where larger but of similar construction. All of the structures had very poor insulation, so heating and air-conditioning costs were sky-high, as was maintenance. The base had been fighting for a brick-and-mortar buildings

JSF Commander's Hooch

for some time, but funding was never approved since the base was temporary.

There were Air Force and Army units assigned to the base who worked together under an umbrella organization called Joint Task Force–Bravo, or JTF-B. We had many mission taskings. Day-to-day we were a US presence in Central America. We operated a C-5 capable airfield that was used as a staging base and logistical hub for HUMROs in Central and South America. We filled the same role during exercises including MEDOPs and civil engineering construction operations in remote areas throughout Central America. As part of these exercises, medical teams practiced deploying from the United States to provide medical care in remote villages, which normally had no access to care. Similarly, the civil engineering (CE) teams completed small construction projects such as bridges and wells. Besides giving US teams the experience of deploying with their mission equipment and personnel, establishing and conducting operations at remote forward locations, these operations built goodwill with our Southern neighbors and presented opportunities for our troops to work closely with their counterparts in the host nation.

My unit was the Joint Security Forces, or JSF. About half of the unit consisted of SF airmen on one-year remote tours. The other half rotated between Army military police (MP) and Marine security units on six-month deployments from their home stations. Our mission was primarily to secure JTF-B's section of the base and US resources on the airfield and coordinate all security activities with host base security personnel. We also provided a couple personnel to work with Honduran security forces at the base's main gate. Occasionally, we were tasked to provide security personnel for off-base medical and CE missions.

\* \* \* \* \*

I stopped in Villavante for a twenty-minute coffee break about 1030. The first 6 km today had been along an isolated country road. The trail then veered off along an earthen track, passing rows of cornfields. The terrain was basically flat, with only a couple slight hills.

As anticipated, both feet were really painful, possibly one of the worst days yet. Added to the toe and ball pain, I was obviously getting a blister on my left big toe. That made three blisters on the left foot. The old one on the right foot was almost healed but still ached somewhat when I put weight on the foot. The ball of my right foot was feeling a bit better, and I was almost able to walk normal on it after loosening my shoestrings a bit more. This was a true blessing because now the ball of my left foot screamed in pain. I suspected blisters were forming because of my recent two-legged limp. My neck and shoulders were also giving me a hard time. They were stiff and constantly ached. My head was pounding accordingly, emanating from my tense upper-body muscles. Frequently, as I moved one way or another, stabbing pain exploded in my neck for the few seconds. Each time it seemed like eternity.

I concluded my massage had been a complete waste of money. Plenty of pain, no gain. I don't think I will seek out any further massages until I get home and no longer have to walk long distances with a pack every day. Until then, perseverance and endurance would have to prevail.

As I rested and enjoyed my café con leche, I sent a text to Mom to brag about passing the three-hundred-mile mark yesterday. I gloated that I had now walked further than she had in 2013. Since Ria and I had taken the bus and a taxi during stage 11, she had hiked 24 km, or about fifteen miles, further than we had. Her total was 300.8 miles. As of last night, I reached the 305-mile point. Mom quickly replied that she was heading over to make up the lost ground.

"I will not allow you to exceed my record!" She ended the text with the winking emoji.

* * * * *

Upon taking command of the JSF, I set about reviewing local policies and procedures and did an assessment to identify vulnerabilities and determine what sort of equipment upgrades were needed. I guess the "temporary" designation of the base also impeded normal procedures over the decades. I found both policy guidance and physical security equipment lacking and implemented corrective action plans.

We also dispatched Force Protection (FP) assessment teams to locations frequented by JTF-B personnel during exercises and morale activities off-base throughout our AOR.

Identifying what should have been obvious to any security leader, I found each service had their own SOPs that they were well versed in. We found it necessary to merge the best practices into specific local procedures to ensure unity of effort and consistency throughout our joint force.

From a physical security perspective, we lit a fire under contractors to compel them to complete a long-pending project to install an enhanced base security alarm and closed-circuit television system throughout the US portion of the base and around the base perimeter. We also initiated new projects to enhance the emergency notification system and install phones in all the Honduran perimeter guard towers so they could sound the alarm in the event that they identified a security threat approaching the base. Looking to the future, we developed project proposals and budget requests for future projects to rectify other identified security deficiencies.

My troops were honored to have the opportunity to provide security support for numerous off-base missions. Our FP teams enabled over eight thousand patients to be treated in several Central American countries during numerous MEDOPs. We also provided port security for cargo staging yards and ships receiving US-provided civil assistance equipment destined for Civil Engineering "New Horizons" missions in Belize and Panama.

Tragically, I had to leverage my aircraft crash response experience in December 2002 to help organize the initial response to the site where one of the Army Aviation Regiment's UH-60 helicopters crashed into a mountainside, taking the lives of all five soldiers onboard. Once again I found myself participating in a memorial ceremony for unit members. This time with a "fallen comrade" ceremony where we lined the route and saluted as their flag-draped coffins were driven to the flight line and loaded onto a US cargo aircraft.

My time at SCAB entailed long hours most days of the week, but was not without some relaxation time. I normally took Saturday mornings off and rode my bike around the perimeter of the base, then swam laps in the base pool, followed by about an hour of sunbathing.

After baking in the sun for a while one sunny Saturday, I noticed that the sun had moved to the point where I was no longer lined up effectively. I needed to adjust my vector. Straddling the lounge chair, I planted my feet firmly on the ground on either side. I shifted my weight to my feet and raised my body slightly in order to rotate clockwise a few degrees. There was a loud crack, and pain shot through my foot and up my calf. One of my toes was bent underneath my foot. An X-ray soon confirmed my suspicion. I had actually broken my toe sunbathing! The taunting soon began in earnest.

This was one assignment that my parents did not come to visit. However, my sister from Alaska flew down over her Christmas vacation from teaching school. We visited ancient Mayan ruins at Copan and went kayaking, white-water rafting, and hiking in the rain forest. Although I would not drive in-country when there was another option, I was not in favor of my sister driving. She did not object when I insisted on driving our rented SUV. I had decided to rent the SUV instead of a car because its larger size would fare better if we were to get into an accident. We managed to make it through about a week of touring without any incidents directly affecting us. However, one afternoon we drove by the scene of a pedestrian traffic death, obviously soon after it had occurred. It was an unsettling sight.

To my great relief, we finally reached the portion of our trip were we turned in the rental vehicle and took a boat out to Roatan

Island. There we stayed in a rustic Caribbean beach resort village and spent five days getting certified in scuba diving. Roatan boasts some of the best coral reefs in the world, and we had the privilege of diving among them for several days. Simply astounding colors in a wide variety of plants. Another treat was an evening at a rustic outdoor pavilion constructed from local foliage watching a movie on a large TV screen in the middle of the jungle—complete with popcorn, of course.

We were really depressed when an extremely strong storm passed near the island the morning we were scheduled to leave. The seas were rough, so all ship transport activity was canceled, and we were forced to stay in paradise for an extra night. Experiencing the storm was just another part of a grand adventure.

Commanding the JSF was another very successful assignment for me. My unit's Antiterrorism/Force Protection (AT/FP) program was praised by the Inspector General as the "Best in US Southern Command," and my unit was selected as Air Combat Command's Outstanding Small SF Unit for fiscal year 2003. This was my second command, and both units had been recognized as the best in their MAJCOM within their size category. Not a bad accomplishment.

Just before I rotated back to the states, the JFT-B commander presided over my promotion ceremony to lieutenant colonel.

\* \* \* \* \*

I limped into Santibanez about 1330 and made a beeline for the first albergue I saw. My feet hurt so bad I could go no further.

A rustic "Albergue" sign hung above a set of ancient wooden doors. The doorway opened into a relaxing, tile courtyard where pilgrims lounged enjoying drinks in the sunny afternoon. Laundry hung on racks and railings. On the left side of the courtyard was another doorway that led into the bar. I secured a lower bunk and reserved a seat for the pilgrims' dinner.

As the hospitalero showed me around the private facility, it was apparent that the ancient-looking doorway was just for looks. It was actually a very new facility. The hostel rooms were upstairs along the walkway overlooking the courtyard. I was guided into the second room at the far end of the walkway. There were four sets of bunk beds, split between the right and left side of the room, and a single bed along the back wall—already claimed,  of course. In the front of the room near the doorway was a table with four chairs. I had not seen tables and chairs in a sleeping room yet.

Conducting mission planning and getting caught up on my notes at the table in relative solitude was a special treat. Tomorrow I would be passing through Astorga. It was only 11.5 km away, so I should be able to make it through and on to another village fairly easily. There were lodging options 3, 5, and 9 km on the other side. I would let my feet decide which one I would stop at.

Day 20 of my service study was based on James 5:16, which states, "Confess your sins to one another and pray for one another, that you may be healed." The author pointed out that if we confess and repent, we can be blessed with the peace that comes with being forgiven, but sometimes we have trouble with this because we seem to commit the same sin over again. In these situations, it may be helpful to find a Christian friend that you can trust and talk about it with them. Pray together about the issue. Confiding in a trusted Christian can add the accountability you need to break the cycle of recurring sin.[42]

I have plenty of recurring issues and problems that seem impossible to just put behind me and never repeat. Some could be blamed on physical and mental exhaustion and overwhelming stress. Then again, maybe I use stress and exhaustion as an excuse for what is really sin. The Bible says that we should not be anxious but to trust God.

---

[42] Fryar, p. 42–43.

Does the fact that I have an anxiety disorder and other stress-related mental and physical struggles mean that I don't trust God with my life? If so, is that really sin? Isn't it a human reality to be able to take only so much? Isn't this the way God made us? Can faith really overcome the effects of stressors such as working 24/7/365 in a high-pressure job and in dangerous combat zones? Could faith eliminate the anxiety that naturally comes from mental abuse and mistreatment that threatens your career and your entire way of life? The psychologist at Camp Victory in Baghdad said that I was having "a normal reaction to an abnormal situation." Is this being human, or is it sin?

Either way, confiding in someone that I was struggling with something was not in my nature. It was one thing to talk to God about it in private prayer, but to talk to another Christian would mean admitting that I have a problem and need help. A type A, perfectionist senior officer does not struggle with problems. They certainly don't need help.

Obviously, today's lesson taught a concept that I really need to contemplate and pray about in order to figure out how to apply it. I guess a certain amount of courage would be needed to implement the concept. Do I have that type of courage?

My contemplative struggle was mercifully interrupted by a gentleman who appeared to be in his midsixties.

"Hello," he greeted quietly since there was somebody sleeping in a bunk on the other side of the room. "Do you have carpal tunnel?" he asked, pointing at the braces on my hands.

Smiling, I gave my standard explanation about arthritis.

"Aren't you a little young to have arthritis?"

"Combat typing," I explained. "I'm retired military. That's how officers fight wars nowadays. We spend all day on the computer doing SITREPs, PowerPoint slides, reports, e-mails. Real PowerPoint Rangers!"

"I'm also retired military, Air Force Reserves." His face brightened with the familiar look of comradeship that veterans share. "What service were you in, and how long did you serve?"

"I was Air Force, about twenty-nine and a half years. I retired in November 2012."

"I just retired about six months ago," he explained. "What are you doing now, besides walking the Camino?"

I gave him my "professional volunteer" speech. When I got to the academy ALO reference, he smiled and lifted an eyebrow. "That was my job in the Reserves for the past twenty years. I just retired from it in May."

"That's incredible," I exclaimed. "Who would've thought I would run into another ALO out here?"

The person sleeping across the room stirred, and we both realized we were likely disturbing him.

"Let's go downstairs to the courtyard," I suggested. "We can get a drink and exchange war stories."

He glanced over at the sleeping pilgrim and nodded in agreement.

We were soon basking in the afternoon sun, enjoying a drink.

"I think they are abusing my volunteerism, I have responsibility for forty-five schools," I joked. "Actually, I really enjoy it, even though the only compensation I get is a whooping fourteen cent per mile tax deduction. HOOAH!" I said sarcastically.

"I only had about twenty schools. Where we live in Wisconsin is pretty rural, so there aren't that many schools," he explained. "Beside the tax break, I got credit toward my reserve retirement, so that was nice."

"I guess the sense of self-satisfaction I get from helping these kids get set up for an incredible career in the Air Force is reward enough," I continued. "Seeing the pride and excitement on their faces when I present their appointment certificate at Senior Awards Night gives me an awesome feeling inside. I feel like I am still contributing to the world around me and the Air Force, that I am earning my retirement and disability checks each month. Working with them also gives me hope for the next generation. So often you see teenagers nowadays who seem to be lazy and really have no clue about the world around them or how to be successful in life. Most have been indoctrinated with the destructive political correctness and entitlement philosophy that is destroying our country. They don't even seem concerned about setting themselves up for the future, let alone being part of something bigger than themselves. The kids I work with are intelligent and dedicated to their studies and community service. They are motivated to serve. Maybe there is still hope for America's future."

By this time, his wife and other peregrinos had joined us and the conversation expanded to more inclusive topics about Camino experiences and plans for tomorrow's hike. Surprisingly, Tom pulled up a chair about a half hour later.

"I didn't expect to see you here," I said in greeting. "I thought you were going to Astorga."

"That was the plan, but 30 km was too much," he explained. "I was tired, and this place looked nice. I am not really in a hurry. At the rate I am going, I'll get to Santiago several days before I'm scheduled to meet my wife. Someone told me about doing half days once in a while instead taking full days off," he continued, referring to an earlier conversation we had had. "I decided to try the tactic."

I laughed.

We all continued socializing until we moved into the dining room for the communal dinner at 1900.

After dinner I retired to my bunk and read chapters 37 through 39 of the *Seeking* book before going to sleep.

All three chapters discussed what Nabeel discovered while preparing to defend the historicity of Muhammad. He found that most of the accounts of Muhammad's life were revisions of revisions. Other concerns included a Hadith clearly instructing Muslims to fight, kill, and take the property of anyone who would not convert to Islam (as opposed to the peaceful message he had learned growing up); various Holy Islamic texts strongly contradicting each other on basic foundations of the faith; and countless examples of acts committed by Muhammad that were contrary to the tenets of the faith. The myriad of conflicting information led him to doubt the trustworthiness of the books used to describe and defend the Islamic faith.[43]

---

[43] Qureshi, chapters 37–39.

As I put my iPad away and settled into bed, I recalled several books that discussed the reliability of how the Bible had been handed down through the centuries and the historicity of the evidence regarding the foundations of Christianity. Some of these books had been written by secular scholars and atheists who had set out to disprove Christianity but in the end were themselves convinced that the evidence proved Christianity beyond a doubt. They had converted to Christianity and were now leading apologetics of the faith. Reading about Nabeel's investigation was helping me gain confidence in the Bible and Christian faith.

(Note—if readers would like to explore the critical evidence for Christianity for themselves, the following books may be useful: *The Case for Faith* and *The Case for Christ* by Lee Strobel, *Evidence That Demands a Verdict* by Josh McDowell.)

# CHAPTER 27

## Santibanez de Valdeiglesia to Santa Catalina de Somoza, 21 Kilometers
## 21 Sep 2015
## D+23

I embarked on the earthen green trail toward Astorga just after 0800. My right foot continued its trend of feeling better. The left foot was trending the other way. It was now swollen and hurt as bad as the right one had a week ago. I guess I should consider it a blessing that my feet are taking turns.

I hoped to go twenty-one clicks to Santa Catalina de Somoza, but I was keeping my options open. Villages would be frequent today, so I could make a decision as I approached each. One thing was for sure: I would be moving very slowly.

\* \* \* \* \*

After leaving Soto Cono the last week of June 2003, I was assigned to the Air Force Security Forces Center (AFSFC) at Lackland Air Force Base for four years. Lackland is the Air Force's basic training base and the home of the Security Forces Academy.

With this being the home base for the career field, I guess it was logical to put the AFSFC there. The "Center" (as we called it) was actually a geographically separated Field Operating Agency (FOA) reporting directly to the Security Forces Directorate at HAF in the Pentagon. By law, there can only be so many military personnel assigned to the Pentagon. The SF career field was only allocated a handful of slots. Minuscule compared to other career fields. The small staff didn't cut it for a 35,000-person career field with such diverse and important missions. Hence, we had a much larger "below-the-line" headquarters staff at Lackland.

As the antiterrorism (AT) branch chief, I supervised a civilian contractor and one SF officer. Together, we were responsible for the development and updating (constant improvement) of AF AT policy and program implementation worldwide. AT is the defensive part of combating terrorism, so this guidance included procedures, infrastructure, and equipment requirements to defend our bases and personnel from a wide range of potential types of attack. As we were working on this, we were also reaching out to the Joint Staff (JS) at the Pentagon and our counterparts in the other services to contribute to DoD-wide guidance and integrate our policies with the rest of the military community.

Our contractor was the computer software developer who created the AF's Vulnerability Assessment Management Program (VAMP), which we used to track AT and FP vulnerabilities and deficiencies identified at Air Force bases and to prioritize funding for projects to fix them. The JS liked our program so much they developed one of their own. We tried to convince them to just adopt ours, but they insisted on developing their own similar program.

This launched a long, complicated, frustrating process of continually having to modify our program so that it could communicate and integrate data sharing with the JS system. Every time they made even the slightest change to a code line, our contractor spent anywhere from hours to weeks trying to determine why we lost cyber contact and how to fix it. We resisted dumping our system and converting to what was known as the Core VAMP (CVAMP) because our program contained capabilities that were not in the CVAMP, and thus we believed ours met the AF requirements far better than CVAMP. Additionally, since we controlled the software, we could program new capabilities as requested by AF users without having to coordinate with all the other services and the JS. Our office could make the requested changes in hours. Coordination with other stakeholders would be prolonged (months) and very complicated as everyone tried to protect their own system so that it would meet their vision. After about a year of struggling to maintain interoperability, we finally surrendered and adopted the CVAMP. We lost a lot of cherished capability, but in the end resistance was futile.

Another major area my branch was responsible for was disseminating terrorism awareness information to our subordinate commands and units. Three days a week, we scoured public news publications for articles about terrorism. We would consolidate these articles into an electronic periodical that we would send to all of our units (intelligence officers put out a similar, yet more focused and in-depth intelligence-based product on the classified side).

Although this sounds easy, it was not long before we realized it was, in a way, the toughest part of our job. Spending countless hours reading and analyzing terrorism information became very emotionally draining. The vast amount of information made my head spin, and it was hard to resist developing a sense of hopelessness concerning the worldwide situation that seemed to be spinning out of control. It was very apparent that there were no easy solutions, no quick fixes, and everything we tried based on a Western mind-set failed. Understanding the enemy's mind-set was very difficult. I found it almost impossible to fathom their perspective. If the leaders throughout the Western world were having similar struggles, that would explain why it has been so hard for coalition leaders to develop an effective strategy to defeat and eliminate radical Islamic terrorism. After a few months of myself and the major on my staff taking turns consolidating the articles and publishing the periodical, we each started to dread the task and sought ways to get the other one to do it. We were tempted to just stop the program, but we continually received positive feedback from our readers who encouraged us to continue.

Occasionally, I was asked to lead a vulnerability assessment team (VA) when one of the normal team leaders was on leave or not available for a trip. Our mission was conduct multifunctional AT/FP program assessments at bases worldwide. In addition to security, we looked at civil engineering, infrastructure, communications, first responders, and Command and Control (C2). We assessed how effectively these areas worked together to protect the base. In a way, it was an inspection. However, we tried to emphasize that we were really there to help them improve their programs and to identify physical vulnerabilities, which would require major project funding to resolve. Unlike a normal inspection where a "write-up" could be detrimental to the commander's career, a write-up from a VA actually helped the unit. They would take the vulnerabilities noted and enter them into the VAMP so that they could compete for money from the AF and DoD budgets to fix the problems.

I was honored to be given such responsibilities at a time when combating terrorism was the major focus for our country and the world as a whole. From a staff and program oversight perspective, I was the point person for the AF's AT program. I wrote Air Force AT policy and was the AF's voice for the development of joint DoD policy. It was great to be so immersed in world events, to be a part of such important work.

This said, this continual deluge of intense, horrific terrorism information and daily focus on improving our capability to defend personnel and resources from terrorist attack intensified the spiritual doubts and questions I had been struggling with since 9/11.

\* \* \* \* \*

Just before 1030, I reached Cruceiro de Santo Torilio at the summit of a hill. The climb to the day's second summit was also fairly gradual, but looking down from the top, I could tell the descent was going to be steep. At the high point was a large stone cross overlooking the sprawling city of Astorga in the distance.

View of Astorga from Cruceiro de Santo Toribio.

I decided that this would be a great place to take a break and complete the day's service study. I found a comfortable place to sit and opened the booklet to day 21. The bottom line of today's message was that even when things don't go as we expect them to, we should continue to pray and remember that God is in control. Events in this world will not always work out in the way that "we" think they should, nor will the outcomes always be positive. Bad things happen in a fallen world. We should not let this get us down. We should trust God and remember that in the end, God wins and His kingdom will prevail. During the bad times, we should reflect on Romans 8:28:

> We know that for those who love God all things work together for good, for those who are called according to his purpose.

Isaiah 55: 10–11 is another verse that we should consider when depressed by events around us:

> For as the rain comes down, and the snow from heaven, and do not return there, but water the earth, and make it bring forth and bud, that it may give seed to the sower and bread to the eater, so shall My word be that goes forth from My mouth; it shall not return to Me void, but it shall accomplish what I please, and it shall prosper in the thing for which I sent it.[44]

In thought about this, I headed down the steep path toward Astorga.

These were humbling passages to consider. In other words, similar to the message in the book of Job: Who are we, mere humans, to question God's ways? We must trust that in the end, all things work out for the best from the perspective of God's ultimate kingdom. I have heard this message many times during my Christian walk, but I find it is much easier to say than to actually trust in it when the world around me is falling apart. Sometimes it feels like this is just a Christian platitude used to explain the unexplainable (easy copout).

---

[44] Fryar, p. 44–45.

Is this the devil putting doubt in my mind? Maybe someday I will be able to just accept it and quit trying to understand it through my limited human reasoning.

The dirt road down the steep hill was very rocky, and I found it difficult to find relatively flat places to put my feet. I preceded extremely slowly, picking every foot fall with care. Since this required me to continually look down, my neck and left shoulder soon became very painful. This led to a splitting headache. But all of this was nothing compared to the exploding pain I was experiencing in my left foot whenever I hit a rock wrong. I was not a happy camper!

As I approached a small village at the bottom of the hill, the path turned to flat pavement. No longer worried about rocks, my pace picked up somewhat. However, I was still routinely passed by other pilgrims. There was certainly plenty to humble me today.

I greeted Tom as I arrived at a café in the middle of the small village. He and a large number of other peregrinos were there eating and checking e-mail. The Wi-Fi at the albergue last night had not been working, so everyone was getting caught up on communications with home. After doing the same, I set out into the busy outskirts of Astorga.

Per SOP, I controlled my tendency toward increased anxiety when among crowds and traffic by focusing on smiling and greeting people that I passed.

I had been told not to miss the Museum of Chocolate, but I didn't notice any signs directing me to it. Most likely because I was so focused on getting through the city as quickly as possible. Just as well, if I had gone, I probably would have bought a lot of chocolate, which I really did not need!

For me, the best part of passing through Astorga was that I was now embarking on stage 23! After this, only ten more stages!

* * * * *

As I left the craziness of the city behind me, my mind returned to reflecting on my time in San Antonio.

One of the major blessings of my assignment there was the opportunity to attend Oak Hills Church where Max Lucado, a popular Christian author, was the senior pastor. I found his books to be very refreshing and down-to-earth. He had a definite gift from God to present the Word in a way that was refreshingly easy to understand. There were many times that I would read a section and want to hit my hand against my head and say, "Wow, I could've had a V8" referencing the old TV advertisements. To put it another way—"Duh, now why didn't I think of it that way before?"

Besides the enlightening Sunday sermons, another advantage of this church was a large adult group for singles over thirty. Smaller churches are lucky to have a singles group at all, and if they do, it is normally focused on college-age singles. This gave me the opportunity to make friends with single believers in my age group. Even so, I found that my life experiences still set me apart from most of them.

I was astonished to discover that many in our group had never been outside the greater San Antonio area, not even venturing as far as Dallas! I hosted an event at my house one day and was surprised by their fascination with my pictures, furniture, and decor procured during my travels around the world. They found it hard to believe that somebody had been to so many places. From my perspective, I found it hard to comprehend that so few of them had done any traveling at all. How could anybody live out their life in such a small "world," limited to their birth community?

There was one member of this group with whom I hit it off immediately. He was also an Air Force Academy graduate who had taken advantage of a military downsizing program that allowed him to retire after only fifteen years as a major in order to help his dad through a period of terminal illness. We enjoyed each other's company because our lives had so much in common and we understood each other's mind-set and vocabulary. We could talk in military acronyms and actually understand each other, while everyone else looked at us in total confusion.

As an example of how God works in mysterious ways, it was through this group that I established the dialogue with a Pakistani immigrant who had converted to Christianity from Islam. Because my job centered around studying and dealing with the threat of terrorism, my spiritual struggles had taken a turn for the worse, along with my growing mental exhaustion and increased sense of fertility and concern for the future for the western and American way of life. I was perplexed by not only the Islamic assaults on the West but also our growing problem of political correctness that prevented us from dealing with the situation effectively. These were all issues that he understood well and we could talk about in-depth.

\* \* \* \* \*

About a click before the village of Somoza, I passed a clearing where a couple of police cars and what appeared to be a TV news crew were parked. A few policemen were gathered together talking at the far end of the clearing next to a small wooded area. A TV cameraman was off to the left filming them. Interesting. I wondered what was going on as I passed.

The first albergue, El Caminante, had a nice write-up in the guidebook. Sixteen beds split between two rooms. The front of the building was constructed of the typical rock wall in the intriguing old European-style. A statue dressed in an outfit that I figured was common a couple of hundred years ago  guarded the entryway. A Camino shell hung around his neck, and another was attached to the front of his hat. His left arm was raised and pointing inward, obviously inviting weary pilgrims to enter.

Attracted by the decor, I decided to inquire about a room. I was able to secure a bottom bunk for only 5€, another four paid for a load of wash. Several clotheslines were strung along the left side of the secluded back patio where my clean but wet clothing soon joined those of other tenants. The lines were placed perfectly to take advantage of the afternoon sun.

Soon settled in and enjoying a glass of wine in the bar, I purchased a large Swiss chocolate bar to make up for missing the chocolate museum. Chocolate and wine, not a bad combination.

Studying the options for tomorrow, I noticed the closest village to my goal of 20 km was a tiny place called Manjarin. To my dismay, the book described it as a very basic facility with an outside toilet. A well provided the water. A solar panel was able to create "some" hot water. The place was heated by an open fire. Instead of discussing beds, the book said thirty-five mattresses were available. It sounded like an adventurous option, but I was not interested.

The problem was that the next potential RON opportunity was another 6.8 km. I feared this was too far for my feet. Stopping earlier meant only about a 16.5 km day. Also not appealing.

I decided to wing it and make my decision as the day progressed.

"Flexibility is the key to Air Power" was quickly becoming the best description of my Camino.

Dorthy, the wife of the ALO I had met the night prior, asked if she could join me.

"Sure!" I offered her a seat. "Good to see you again."

"I love the atmosphere of this place," she smiled, looking around the rustic bar.

"Did you pass the police and the TV crew just before town?"

"Yes! I asked about that when I was talking to a local awhile ago," she explained. "Apparently they are looking for the hands of the girl that was killed back in April. They found her body in the woods behind that clearing. The body was dismembered, and they have yet to find the hands."

Pictures of the suspect being apprehended had been on the news a few days earlier.

"Such a tragedy," I said. "There is such little crime on the Camino, something like this is the last thing you would expect. I wonder how it has been affecting the number of people walking the Camino?"

"The lady I talked to said that the locals are very upset about the whole thing. They are convinced that the police knew who did it within two weeks of the murder because two other girls reported they had also been attacked and fought him off with their hiking sticks. They gave a good description of the guy. That testimony and DNA evidence quickly led to the suspect. However, for some reason, the police had stopped pursuing the case. Recently the victim's brother objected to the lack of action and made enough noise in the international media that they started working on it again. Finally, last week they arrested the guy. Today they are looking for more evidence. The people in this village are furious that the guy that attacked three pilgrims, killing one of them, has been totally free since April. Obviously, they are concerned for the safety of the pilgrims that they rely on for their livelihood."

"Incredible. You would think that everybody in this area would have the same concerns and that catching the murderer would have been the top priority," I said, shaking my head. "It certainly has shook up a lot of the women pilgrims that I have met along the way. Everyone is talking about it."

After a few more minutes of small talk, her husband, Jim, arrived, and they dismissed themselves to go for a walk around town.

I turned my attention to reading a couple chapters in the *Seeking Allah* book. Chapters 40 and 41 started Nabeel's examination of the Muslims' belief that the Quran was inspired by God. Critically scrutinizing the actual words of the Quran and the evidence cited by the scholars in support of these assertions, his studies revealed a pattern: "the protocol always called for redefining the clear statements of the Quran to say something they did not, and then glossing over the "strain" (difficulties/inaccuracies). Nabeel found that to defend his Muslim beliefs, he had to be "willing to redefine certain terms and emphasize certain points in favor of my position."[45]

As I struggled with my Christian faith after 9/11, somewhat similar concerns had plagued me. Was the Bible really the unaltered, inspired Word of God? After all these centuries, the Bible had been translated many times. Councils of men had studied various ancient writings and together decided what was inspired by God and what

---

[45] Qureshi, chapters 40–41.

was not. There are so many English translations today that say things in slightly different ways. The Catholic Bible has several books that Protestants do not believe are inspired. People constantly interpret the meaning of passages based on the version that they believe is the closest to accurate and how they are taught to understand the meaning of the original words. There are over a hundred Christian denominations who each insist they maintain the "true" interpretation of various sections of the Bible and all the other denominations are leading believers astray.

Have not those Christians who have accepted Christ as their personal Savior been indwelled by the Holy Spirit, Whose mission it is to guide and teach the believer and reveal God's truth to them? How could so many believers who are "on fire" for Christ and sincerely seeking God's truth through prayer and listening to the Holy Spirit come to so many different conclusions?

Could it be that Christians, like Muslims, believe the way they do because they have been indoctrinated?

I believe that God knew that I was struggling with this and put someone in my life to help guide me through my struggles, the singles' pastor at Oak Hills Church. As a convert from Islam, he was able to help me pray and talk through my concerns. We met one-on-one at a common area in the church lobby once a week for many months to discuss my spiritual dilemmas. The root of my struggles was the fear that I may be deceived, as I believed the hijackers of 9/11 had been deceived. They believed what they believed because they were raised to believe it. They believed what they were taught so deeply that they were willing to train for months to fly planes into buildings and kill thousands of people because they had convinced themselves and each other that this was what God was calling them to do. One thing was for sure: my faith was not as strong as theirs apparently was.

Our discussions included many points supporting the accuracy of the history of Christianity based on secular records and the dedication that early servants put into ensuring the accurate copying of Bible scriptures to preserve the original words in the original languages. In general, these arguments were very familiar from sermons and books. But there was another level of understanding and clarity when he described his conversion process and the reasons that he had decided Christianity was truth. I don't think anyone else could have addressed my specific internal intellectual struggle as well as this Pakistani immigrant turned Christian pastor.

I joined Jim, Dorothy, and a young man from South Korea at the pilgrim dinner. After the normal pleasantries, our discussion turned to economic issues that America was struggling with. We three Americans were very concerned about our national debt nearing $19 trillion and rising by tens of billions every day.

"It is almost impossible to comprehend what this really means," I said, shaking my head in confusion. "The amount is just unbelievable!"

"Yet the current political candidates continue to propose major new social aid programs which will cost billions more every year," Jim agreed in dismay.

"Well, that's how they buy votes," Dorothy bluntly said what we were all thinking.

"Here's my political platform," I offered. "No new social aid programs, we have enough already. Focus all efforts on deleting regulations and other impediments to economic development so businesses can be created and grow, thus hiring more employees. This will result in more people earning enough money to pay taxes while decreasing the number of people getting entitlements such as welfare, food stamps, and Medicaid. Simple. Tax revenue goes up, spending on entitlements goes down."

"Those would have to be decent-paying jobs because, as it is, people have to take a pay cut to accept a reasonable job," Jim pointed out. "Besides that, why work if the government will pay you to do nothing?"

I agreed. "Our government has created a welfare state and locked people into a downward spiraling cycle of dependency! This is passed from generation to generation. When my mom was working as a teacher's assistant, she often heard kids comment that they could not wait to turn eighteen so they could get their own welfare check. They were not looking forward to getting a job and starting a career so they could support themselves. They intended to do as their parents had done and live off government assistance. Our tax dollars could be much better spent on programs that would break this cycle of dependency!"

"Yes," Jim agreed. "Our national and community leaders, not to mention parents, should be emphasizing the importance of working hard so that you can achieve self-sufficiency for yourself and your family, to contribute positively to society instead of taking from it. If this was taught to children in poor communities from a young age, they would be motivated to succeed. It used to be shameful to take handouts!"

"Not only are we ruining our own country, but we are exporting dependency to countries like Afghanistan!"

I launched into my standard soapbox speech about the irrigation canal example and how we were creating a government-run health-care system there that was completely incapable of sustaining itself and providing care to the people.

"The government cannot provide adequately educated doctors and nurses, clinics, equipment, medications, ambulances and gas, operations and maintenance funding (not to mention people knowledgeable enough to carry out the required tasks), or even pay health-care workers without massive contributions from the international community.

"We had an Afghan American on our PRT who was convinced that the greatest enemy to Afghanistan was not the Taliban or Al Qaeda but corruption. The more money we sink into the situation, the worse the corruption gets! Not only that, but there are indications that a lot of the money that is flowing from the international community into Afghanistan ends up in the hands of the bad guys. We found out after-the-fact that the majority of the money that we paid a contractor to clear snow from roads leading to remote villages so supplies and assistance could get in actually ended up in Taliban hands. If they did any clearing at all, it was a narrow one-lane section of the road. We were beating our heads against the wall trying to get the contractor to do the job we hired him for while people starved in the remote villages, only to find out later of his close ties to the Taliban and how he was funneling our money to them. Crazy!"

Throughout this discussion, the South Korean intently listened. I wondered what he was thinking about the dismal US situation we were discussing. So many people around the world look up to America for inspiration. I bet he was not inspired today!

# CHAPTER 28

## Santa Catalina de Somoza to Foncebadon, 16.5 Kilometers
## 22 Sep 2015
## D+24

While discussing plans over breakfast, it was apparent that I was not the only one who was not intrigued by the albergue at Manjarin. Most pilgrims had resigned themselves to a short day of 16 km to Foncebadon, an isolated mountain hamlet. Although this description gave a rustic impression, there were five lodging options with beds and restaurants. Definitely more inviting then Manjarin.

It was forty-eight degrees with a significant breeze when I hit the trail at 0730. I don't know what I was thinking, but I had my pants configured as shorts. Regretting my attire decision, I stopped at a bench on the side of The Way, found the legs of my pants, and zipped them on. Combined with my jacket and gloves, and the exertion of walking, I was able to warm up fairly quickly.

\* \* \* \* \*

After a year at the AFSFC, I had had about all I could take of the Terrorism Periodical. As a way to reduce the stress, I started looking for a deployment opportunity. A friend at the Air Force Personnel Center (AFPC) put me in contact with the man who sourced support group commander and deputy positions in the Central Command AOR. The next rotation was already filled, but he was looking for volunteers to deploy in early 2005.

"The support group commander positions are filled by colonels," he told me. "But I am looking for a lieutenant colonel to be the deputy for the 455th Expeditionary Mission Support Group (455 EMSG) at Bagram."

Naturally, I had been following the flow of the Global War on Terrorism (GWOT) and was generally familiar with Bagram Airfield, normally referred to as BAF. It was the largest US base in Afghanistan. Our Current Operations section at the AFSFC was charged with sourcing cops for 120-day rotations to provide airfield security.

"I am definitely interested," I replied, excited about the opportunity. "I will run it by my commander and let you know what he says."

I had been wanting to deploy and do my part for the war on terrorism ever since the attacks of 9/11. My request had been turned down at Luke when I was told that I was needed there, that I needed to stay and command my squadron. No one deployed from Soto Cano except to short-term contingency operations within the Central American AO. Now I was a staff officer. Maybe this time my request would be granted!

The commander wondered about my sanity but agreed to allow me to apply for the position after I explained to him that my country had been at war for three years and I had never been in a position to do my part. I explained to him that I had been denied the opportunity to deploy to the Gulf War because my squadron refused to send women. Ten years later, things had changed and women were routinely deployed to the combat zones, but I had always been "too important" to the home station mission.

"What's the reporting date?" he asked, obviously a little concerned about a couple of major events that were scheduled in the next couple of months.

"Early January," I said. "It's only 120-day rotation, so I'd be back in early May."

"That shouldn't be much of a problem. Tell him you have my support."

The unit received the official tasking order about a week later. It was not until I had a copy in my hand that the gravity of what I had done sank in. I was on my way to the combat zone, to a base that was frequently the target of rocket attacks.

My stomach started to churn as I wondered if I had made a mistake. The next time I got the ninety-day notification that I needed to change my password for computer access, I used the first letter of each word in the sentence "Lord protect me as I go off to fight the terrorists in Afghanistan." Since I had to think through this sentence each time I needed to type my password, I said this prayer countless times every day for the next several months until it was time for me to board the plane and head across the pond the war zone.

\* \* \* \* \*

It took me just over an hour to get to the next village. It was very small, appeared almost abandoned, and many of the buildings needed some serious tender loving care. However, I was intrigued by the name of one establishment: the Cowboy Bar. Being an American, I felt obliged to stop in and look around. Although not very American, the interior had a very inviting rustic decor. To my surprise, no other peregrino had stopped. After a couple of minutes, a hostess emerged and happily served me a café con leche. I was soon back on the trail.

\* \* \* \* \*

Ken, the other USAFA grad in the singles group, picked me up at 0-dark-30 (pronounced oh-dark-thirty; meaning "in the middle of the night") and took me to the airport to catch the commercial flight to Baltimore International Airport. From there I would catch a military-chartered flight for the trip into theater. I was smartly dressed in my desert camouflage uniform (DCU) with sand-colored suede boots. As we loaded four military A-bags stuffed with my uniforms and required deployment gear, to include a M-9 pistol securely locked in a government-issued carrying case, my stomach started to churn.

This was it. I was finally on my way to the combat zone to do my part as a military officer. I had been training and waiting my entire career for this opportunity. On the other hand, I was very nervous. I was heading to where there was a no-kidding war going on. As the primary US base in Afghanistan, I knew BAF would likely be attacked while I was there, if not by a ground attack, at least by indirect rocket fire; maybe both. Obviously, it was possible that I would not be coming back. It was also possible that even if I made it back, I could be wounded and disabled for life. Then again, this was not a normal war. We were fighting terrorists and insurgents— not a large, well-organized or well-trained conventional army. There were no large-scale battles where thousands died in a single day. The survival rate for individuals during deployments was incredibly high, especially for those not going "outside the wire."

My job would be on base. The mission of the EMSG was to secure and manage the operations of the airfield. As the deputy commander, I would assist the commander in providing oversight and guidance to numerous subordinate squadrons including Security Forces, Communications, Civil Engineering, Logistics, Airfield Operations, Military Personnel, and Services, which included lodging and Morale, Welfare, and Recreation. Our scope of responsibility was limited to the Air Force operations on and around the runway and within the AF camp, Camp Cunningham. We were not responsible for the actual base perimeter or any of the other thousands of forces on the base, which included not only camps operated by units from the other US military services but also from our international coalition partners. The US Army was the executive agent with the responsibility of operating and securing the base and synchronizing the activities of the vast array of units operating out of BAF. There would be little reason for me to leave the secure perimeter of the base. Hence, the main thing I had to worry about were the rocket attacks. Those could come with little to no warning and they could be deadly.

Ken and I prayed together at the curb of the airport's departure area. I then set off alone, with my overloaded luggage cart and weapons case, to the check-in counter.

About twenty-four hours later, I found myself watching intently out the window as we flew across Iraq. It was the middle of the night, and I was amazed at how little light could be seen on the ground.

The use of electricity was not widespread outside major cities such as Baghdad. Many of the points of light that I did see appeared to be large flames. I wondered if these were the oil fires I had been hearing so much about.

A couple hours later, we landed at Manas AB in Kyrgyzstan. The United States was leasing the base as a major staging area for personnel flowing into and out of theater. Chartered commercial airliners brought the troops this far and then picked up those rotating back to the States and returned home. The inbound troops were assigned space in a tent to await theater airlift to their assigned base in Afghanistan.

As a deputy group commander, I had priority for seating on a flight into country. I was not sure if this should be considered a blessing.

Within twelve hours I boarded a C-130 heading to Bagram, and it really hit home that we were heading into a war zone. We were required to wear our combat helmets, heavy protective vests, and blast-resistant goggles throughout the flight. We were packed in like sardines, sitting in web-backed jump seats along both sides of the fuselage with two back-to-back middle rows facing the outer rows. There was very little space between the rows. For over three hours we sat shoulder to shoulder with the person on either side of us, and with our legs interlocking with those of the people facing us from the middle row. You simply could not move. There was a toilet seat at the rear of the aircraft with a curtain that could be pulled around it for privacy. However, to get to it, you would have to walk over everyone's legs. For all practical purposes, you were stuck where you sat.

We approached Bagram about midnight. The loadmaster warned us that the flight was about to get very interesting. We were going to execute a combat landing.

I had been warned about this. Because of the threat of the enemy shooting a surface-to-air missile (SAM) at inbound aircraft on final approach, we remained at an altitude above the range of the missiles until we were over the airfield. We then quickly descended in a steep corkscrew path before straightening out and leveling off just in time to touchdown. I was surprised that I did not throw up!

My commander's aide met me at the passenger terminal with a truck to help me get my stuff to my assigned B-Hut in Camp Cunningham. B-Huts were small plywood buildings divided into eight small rooms only big enough for a bed and a closet to hang our clothes and store some of our gear in. The rest of the gear had to be stored under the bed. A blanket was hung across the opening to the center hall. Bathrooms and showers were in separate facilities strategically positioned around the camp. As basic as these facilities were, at least I had my own private eight-by-ten-foot space with a bed and mattress.

We put my bags in my room and headed to the Alaska shelter that served as the headquarters offices for the 455 EMSG to meet my new boss. She was a colonel from the Wyoming Air National Guard who had only recently arrived herself. After about thirty minutes of introductory discussion, she informed to me that we needed to get going so we could stand in a fallen comrade ceremony.

"A what?" I asked, not liking the sound of it.

"The Army lost a couple of guys," she explained. "They're being flown out on the plane you arrived on."

We walked out Camp Cunningham's gate and lined up shoulder to shoulder with other airmen and service members from units across the base. The road in front of our camp lead to the airfield. Service members lined both sides from the airfield to the intersection on the far side of our camp. The human lines then turned left and extended down the base's main road named Disney after a soldier who had been killed in action (KIA) in the early days of the war. We all quietly stood at parade rest until two HMMWVs turned the corner and slowly drove down the road between our lines. As the first HMMWV approached each person's position, they would come to attention, saluting until the second one had passed them by. The back hatches were open, exposing the flag-draped coffins.

I swallowed hard as they passed by me. Welcome to Afghanistan, I thought. This is no kidding the real thing!

One of the first things I was briefed on as I got a tour of the base the next morning was the dangers posed by land mines that the

Russians had buried before abandoning the base when the Mujahedin pushed them out in the '80s. All new arrivals were strictly warned to stay on the sidewalks, roadways, and other paved or graveled areas or risk stepping on a land mine. The known minefields were marked with red triangular signs with the word "MINES" stenciled on them. However, the pesky mines had a habit of moving when the ground was saturated with water. Therefore, they were sometimes found in places that had previously been cleared. Later during my deployment, this phenomenon turned deadly for a couple of soldiers when their HMMWV ran over a mine that had "migrated" into a dirt road off-base.

A civilian company had been contracted to clear the base of mines, but it was a long, slow process, and there were still numerous fields around base. The one I found the hardest to comprehend was a field next the tent complex used as the US's primary trauma hospital in-country. A narrow road had been cleared and paved through the field to facilitate safe transport of patients from the MEDEVAC helicopter pad on the other side of the minefield to the hospital. I had to take a picture of a truck and ambulance backed up to the edge of the parking lot against a field with "MINES" warning signs prominently displayed.

"MINES" sign    Paved route through minefield from MEDEVAC helo pad.

I asked the executive officer who was giving me the tour why that field had not been cleared.

"EOD would have to blow the mines in place, but they can't do that so close to the hospital tents," he explained. "We can't evacuate the hospital long enough."

One day a C-130 blew a tire while landing and slid off the runway into a minefield in the grassy area between the runway and the taxiway. Miraculously, the plane did not set off any of the mines before coming to a rest in the middle of the field. This put both the aircrew and emergency responders in a rather precarious situation. Somehow they had to get the crew off the plane and to safety. It was also necessary to pull the plane out of the field. Utilizing the path taken by the skidding aircraft, EOD painstakingly searched for mines and mapped out a safe route. The crew was extracted after a couple of hours. It took a couple more days to get the plane out.

We were not just concerned about explosive ordinance in the ground. As expected, several times during my deployment, insurgents fired rockets at the base. These were called indirect fire attacks. An example of direct fire would be shooting a gun pointed directly at the intended target. Indirect fire is propelled from a distance in an arcing trajectory. Fortunately for coalition forces, the insurgents did not have effective aiming technology. Their attacks were far from "precision."

During my first experience, several rockets impacted around the base, but fortunately did not hit any populated areas. It was hard to determine how many rockets had actually been shot at the base because some impacted minefields and set off some of the mines as secondary explosions. I guess that was one way to clear the minefields; maybe we should have been appreciative for the assistance!

Base security and intelligence personnel used radar systems to determine the point of origin (POO), but the insurgents were gone before the response teams could get there. The evidence that was left behind was indicative of the low-tech enemy we were fighting. Apparently, they had merely rested the rockets against the side of a ditch, pointed them in the general direction of the mega base, and hoped for the best.

Even so, the odds were not exactly in our favor. We had to be lucky 100 percent of the time; they only had to be lucky once. If they kept lobbing rockets at us, sooner or later they would hit something and people would die. A month later, they got much closer to being "lucky."

The warning sirens went off at 0-dark-30. Because of my security forces background, the group commander had tasked me with being responsible for Command and Control of Camp Cunningham's response to such incidents. I donned my Interceptor Body Armor (IBA) and helmet, strapped my M9 around my leg, and pulled on my boots. While most people were hustling to the nearest bunker, I took off across the compound toward BDOC.

About halfway there, I stumbled and took a hard fall. Besides scraped-up knees and elbows, the twenty-plus-pound IBA and attached equipment did quite a number on my back and neck. I would have to worry about that later. I scrambled back to my feet and resumed my sprint.

By this time the inbound rockets had impacted, and the base had started its response. Each unit was tasked with sweeping their camp and assigned areas for injured personnel, damage, and unexploded ordinance. Our SOP required personnel to remain in the bunkers or wherever they had taken shelter while security teams conducted the sweeps. We did not want mass confusion with everyone running in various directions, let alone chancing someone detonating an unexploded mortar. Since the base operated in blackout mode, it was pitch-black. The standard little red-and-green pin lights we used at night could not detect the potential hazards.

Our sweeps of the AF areas came up negative, but we soon learned of impacts in two other camps. Bagram's Joint Defense Operations Center (JDOC) requested assistance from our explosive ordnance disposal (EOD) unit to respond to the points of impact (POI). The base EOD team was responding to the POO.

God must have been watching out for us that day. Two rockets had impacted in populated areas, but miraculously there were no casualties.

One hit the empty bed of a semitruck and exploded, creating a hole in the bed and a lot of broken glass and shrapnel damage in the truck itself and nearby connexes and buildings. The miracle was that the driver of the truck had gotten out of the cab a few minutes before the attack and had gone inside an office building to fill out some paperwork. He was not injured.

An even greater miracle was that a rocket hit a B-Hut where eight people were sleeping. It smashed through the roof and cut a gash down the plywood on the front wall. When it hit the air-conditioning system, somehow the ignitor was disengaged from the explosives, and the device buried itself, unexploded, under the wooden stairs.

Minor damage, no casualties! God is good!

After everything settled down and life returned to normal, I walked over to the hospital compound and asked to see my doctor. He was a reservist who had been activated and deployed as the anesthesiologist. In his civilian life, he was a chiropractor. Although the connection didn't make sense to me, I felt blessed that there was somebody there that could help me when my neck and back got all out of whack, which happened every time I put my IBA and helmet on. Because of the fall, this time it was far worse than usual. I had to wait until he wasn't in surgery performing his primary duties; obviously my pain was secondary to saving the lives of the wounded US, Afghan, and coalition service members and locals.

My duties typically entailed mundane office work, meetings, e-mail, checking the status of projects, and occasional visits with troops in our various work centers. Except for the fact that you worked in a tent, slept in a plywood shelter with no bathrooms, and constantly put up with loud aircraft engines at all hours of the day and night, not to mention the occasional rocket attack, the job was very similar to any base-level job anywhere in the Air Force. Eager to experience more, I joined a few off-base missions.

Our EOD team, part of the CE squadron, had acquired a large stockpile of captured enemy munitions, rockets, mines, and other unexploded ordinance. Once the storage area reached a specific net

Controlled blast

explosive weight, the ordinance needed to be destroyed. It was loaded onto trucks and taken a short distance off-base to a safe area called "the range" and arranged per checklist in a hole in the ground. C4 was then used to destroy the entire batch in one large explosion. Several of us from the EMSG staff joined them one frigid winter day. I was amazed at how long it took to set it all up. Once it was ready to go, we all pulled back to a safe distance and took cover. Someone pushed a button, and it was all over in about two seconds. Somehow I managed to time a picture just right to capture the explosion.

On another occasion, I was asked to join a team whose mission was to detect and investigate indicators of a potential enemy activity in the area around the base. They had received information about a potential munitions cache buried in a farmer's field outside a nearby village. Our cops often provided security for them on off-base missions. Hence, I had an inside track for an invite. I jumped at the opportunity.

I was fascinated by my first close-up view of Afghan society. The roads were muddy and deeply rutted, so we drove very slowly and were constantly jostled around inside the vehicle. Between that and the weight of the IBA and helmet, my back was once again in a pretty bad state by the time we got back.

The Afghan buildings and fences were made of mud. Typical large family compounds with high walls surrounding them looked like mud fortresses. The local nationals (LN) were dressed in typical Afghan robes. The women wore burkas or at least had scarfs covering their head.

Contrary to what you would expect after listening to the news that portrayed the United States as being hated as an occupying force, the Afghans were excited to see our vehicles drive by. The children ran to the side of the road, waving at us. When we stopped at the objective and the mission team went into the house to discuss the cache with the farmer, myself and the SF personnel provided security for the area. Within seconds, the villagers started gathering around, doing their best to communicate with us. They were happy that we were there, and the men and boys asked repeatedly to have their pictures taken with us. I did not understand this since there was no way for us to give them a copy of the photos. The women quickly moved out of sight, but occasionally you could see a curious little girl watching us from the protection of a mud wall or behind a tree.

The farmer showed the team where the suspected munitions were buried. The intent was to bring the munitions back to base for examination, but a quick evaluation determined that they were not stable. The security team worked with local police officers who had joined us to move the villagers back to a safe distance, and then the munitions were blown in place.

My third off-base mission was to participate in what we called the Adopt-a-Village program. Units from all over base participated in this program. Service members contacted family, friends, churches, and schools that they were associated with back home and requested toys, clothing, and hygiene items. Boxes of donated items arrived through the postal system almost daily. The Bagram Provincial Reconstruction Team (PRT) orchestrated the program by selecting villages and coordinating the missions. Volunteers were selected from the sponsoring unit, in our case the 455th Air Expeditionary Wing (AEW), to hand out the items to the villagers. I was privileged to be selected for one of these missions.

Once again I was amazed at how the Afghans lived in very primitive conditions with none of the basic luxuries that Americans take for granted—like running water, electricity, paved roads, well-stocked stores, solid building construction, etc. I likened their living conditions to what it must have been like in Jesus's time.

As on the earlier mission, the children ran to the side of the road to wave as our long convoy passed through villages on the way to our objective. Once we stopped, a large crowd quickly gathered. We suspected that they came from several villages in the area. There were far too many for the small village we were in.

It was an incredible feeling to be there handing out toys, clothing, and other items to the children. They were all so excited. The adults either stood with the children or nearby watching with smiles on their faces. The crowd was so excited that it was difficult to control the distribution in an organized manner and keep track of who had already received items. To ensure that everyone got something before seconds were handed out, we marked the children's hands with red pens to indicate that they had received something. But this was not a foolproof procedure. In one case, we observed an older boy steal a stuffed animal from a younger boy and run away. The younger boy was very upset. Fortunately, a member of our team saw it, and we gave the child a new toy.

I know where many of America's Beanie Babies went. By this time the fad was dying out, and people were wondering what to do with their collections. Thousands of them ended up bringing smiles to Afghan children's faces.

About a week into May 2005, I boarded a C-5 to start my journey home. I found myself facing four flag-draped coffins. Just as my first official "duty" upon arrival was to stand in a fallen comrade ceremony, such a ceremony was also my last. I do not recall the circumstances of their deaths or their names. I did not know them personally. But I will never forget the gut-wrenching feeling of staring at the caskets throughout the flight back to Manas.

The sight caused me to reflect on an earlier incident where fifteen service members and three civilian DoD contractors had been killed when their helicopter crashed near Ghazni. Of course, the Taliban claimed credit for shooting it down, but the word put out at staff meetings was that the cause was actually weather-related. The following Sunday at chapel services, the pastor related that one of the fallen had been a regular attender at the same service I normally attended. I thought I had remembered seeing her joyfully clapping and praising the Lord during the worship songs the previous Sunday. Knowing that she had been at the same service I was three days prior to her death really made me think about the realities of war. One day you're going about your business as normal, and then in a blink of an eye something happens and you are gone. The marathon fallen comrade ceremony that followed the crash was particularly hard to stand in. For the entire time the eighteen HMMWVs carrying the flag-draped coffins slowly drove by, one could not help but contemplate how fleeting young life could be in a war zone.

On the trip home, I struggled with mixed feelings. I was happy that I had finally had the opportunity to complete a deployment in support of the war on terrorism. Our country had been at war for almost four years since the attacks on 9/11. Hundreds of thousands had deployed. I had finally been one of them. On the other hand, it was only for a little over four months, and I had been primarily stuck on a major US base with thousands of others. Granted, running the airfield was critical to US and coalition operations. Personnel and supplies flowed in and out of country on the cargo planes. Smaller tactical fixed wing and rotary wing aircraft then carried the personnel and supplies to Forward Operating Bases throughout the country. Other aircraft provided Close Air Support (CAS) for ground troops. None of that would be possible without the AF operating the airfield.

I had been a part of that, but for some reason, I did not feel like I had completely done my part. My fair share. Every day when I went to the chow hall, I observed dirty soldiers who had obviously just returned from off-base missions. I was certain they were making a difference while taking great risks. I also thought a lot about the Bagram PRT whose mission I had been exposed to through the

Adopt-a-Village program. They convoyed outside the wire almost every day, meeting with locals, coordinating construction projects, and delivering humanitarian aid. All these people were out there making an incredible difference, while I sat safely behind a computer in a tent in the middle of a huge base.

Still, it was time to go home. I would have to be content with the small contribution that I was able to make.

\* \* \* \* \*

It was not far past the tiny, practically vacant, village that housed the Cowboy Bar that the trail started its long, mostly gradual ascent to the highest point on the Camino. I ran into Tom in Rabanal del Camino, and we decided to walk together for a while. The Way became fairly steep as we approached the mountain hamlet of Foncebadon. The trail became much thinner, uneven, and incredibly rocky. It now reminded me of the trails I hiked back home in the North Cascades with our Wednesday hiking group. The difference was, I did not do them with painful, swollen feet, nor was I wearing a twenty-pound pack. Even though there was a cold, moderate wind, I started sweating as we chugged up the incline. Twice I decided to take my coat and gloves off because I was so hot. I regretted it both times, and within minutes I was stopping to put them back on. Between the painful feet and the weather, I decided that going another 11 km past Foncebadon to Acebo was out of the question.

"Somebody I met along The Way taught me that hiking half days was a good way to take some downtime," Tom once again reminded me of our earlier conversation. "I'm ready to call it a day!"

Five albergues stair-stepped up the steep main road. We selected the middle one. After signing in and getting our credentials stamped, we were led past a small dining area and out the back door into a courtyard. Several lodging rooms circled the courtyard, and community toilettes and shower rooms were in the far back left corner. The altitude made the strong wind frigid. We were the first pilgrims to be assigned to our room with three sets of bunk beds. We chose the set to the left of the door. Tom was kind enough to take the upper bunk.

As I headed across the courtyard, chilled to the bone in my shower shoes, I had to chuckle. This reminded me of both of my deployments in Afghanistan. January and February at Bagram were cold, and snow often covered the ground. It was worse at FOB Gardez, where our base was at 7,650 feet; that is about a mile and a half above sea level. Take that, Denver! It was even higher than the academy, whose "altitude of 7,250 feet above sea level—far, far above that of West Point or Annapolis" was required knowledge that doolies were frequently ordered to recite when upperclassmen asked them for an "altimeter check."

Anyway, trudging through snow while shivering in the cold winter air to get to the bathroom and showers was standard during both deployments. A few years later, when we were both stationed at the Pentagon, my senior enlisted adviser (SEA) from Gardez and I reminisced about these treks.

Air Traffic Control Tower in Camp Cunningham

"Do you know how you can tell if a veteran was deployed to the mountains in Afghanistan?" he asked me over lunch in the Pentagon's food court.

"Tell me," I encouraged him to continue.

"When they get up to go to the bathroom in the middle of the night, they always put on their coat and boots."

This "habit" would come in handy tonight!

Once we were cleaned up and our beds were made, we headed out in search of food.

We found a tiny market and bar on the ground floor of the next albergue downhill from ours. I could not imagine a more cramped place. There was a small table off to the side that could seat six in very close quarters. There was little walking space between the table and the counter, so everyone wanting to purchase something crowded the table. After getting a hot café con leche and a sandwich, I took the seat at the far end of the table to isolate myself from the crowd as much as possible.

Tom introduced me to three ladies who were already sitting. He had met them the night before. They were friends from Arkansas who had started their Camino only two days earlier in Leon. Their fresh excitement and nonstop talking, not to mention their lack of major pain, was a dead giveaway that they were new to the trail.

Both my feet were throbbing. My back and head ached. I was tired, and the cold made my arthritic hands hurt something awful. Then there was the wall-to-wall people in the tiny cramped space—topped off with these jubilant ladies spouting their liberal perspectives on various issues that my conservative viewpoint thought were just downright crazy. Normally, I can take such discussions in stride, but all in all, my anxiety level shot up and my attitude plummeted!

I lasted about twenty minutes and then had to escape back to my bunk.

Blissfully alone in the bunk room, I lay down, took some deep breaths, and enjoyed the solitude for a little while. Feeling much calmer, I pulled out my service study booklet and opened to day 22, hoping that this would lead to an attitude adjustment.

Today's theme was that God's love for us does not change based on the success or failure of our service. The key is to keep serving, motivated by our love for God and knowledge of His ceaseless love. This said, we are warned not to let His enduring love tempt us not to work for Him. If we decide not to serve because He will love us, anyway, we don't understand our relationship with Him and we may want to consider whether or not we actually have a relationship with Him. We don't serve Him to earn His love. We serve Him "because" He loves us and we love Him.[46]

---

[46] Fryar, p. 46–47.

Contemplating this uplifting message, I drifted off to sleep.

About forty-five minutes later, a couple came in and started settling into the bunks on the other side of the small room. They were Spanish speakers and spoke loudly and nonstop. By this time, Tom had returned and was in the bunk above me. The fact that we were both obviously trying to sleep had absolutely no impact on the conduct of our new roommates.

After thirty minutes or so, they settled down and appeared to doze off. The blissful silence did not last long. Another Spanish-speaking couple came in, and it was quite apparent that they were good friends with the first couple. Now there were four people talking loudly with each other.

I waited ten minutes, hoping that they would notice we were trying to sleep and stop talking. They did not. I could not stand it any longer, so I grabbed my iPad and left seeking peace.

I went back down the hill to the first albergue. The guidebook said that it had a popular bar and restaurant. It was a very nice and apparently an upscale place with rooms upstairs! We should have stayed there. Too late now, but I decided I could at least hang out for a while!

I ordered a glass of wine, logged into Wi-Fi, and engaged in an extensive text exchange with Mom. After I was done whining about all my physical pains and our rude roommates, Mom suggested I consider stopping once I got to Ponferrada, my goal for the following day. This was the city that we had taken the train to after touring León last time. She pointed out that once I reached that city, I would have completed all the portions that we had skipped.

"You don't need to go the rest of the way," she wrote, offering me an escape. "You could also skip forward from there to Sarria and just do the last 100k so you can get your certificate."

"No! I didn't come all the way back over here and walk this far to quit now," I replied. "I don't think I could live with myself if I didn't finish it again. I am sure my attitude will be better if I can make the 27.4 clicks to Ponferrada tomorrow." Arrival there would represent a gratifying milestone. "I'll get a single room in a hotel there. That should do wonders for my attitude problem! I just need a break from the albergue scene."

"Okay. Just remember you have options. We won't think any less of you if you skip forward a bit." She signed off to get a start on her day on the other side of the world.

It was now early evening, and I decided to get some dinner. Since I had eaten a sandwich in midafternoon, I was not very hungry. I definitely did not need a full menu peregrino. I ordered a bowl of soup and started reading chapter 42 of the *Seeking* book.

In this chapter, Nabeel dug deep into the history of the Quran. It is a foundational belief of Muslims that the Quran has been perfectly preserved over the centuries. Similar to his studies of the other tenants of his faith, this premise did not stand up to scrutiny. The supporting holy books of the hadith, Sahih Bukhari, Sahih Muslim, and Sunan ibn Majah all recorded the initial struggles to determine the contents of the Quran to include different versions of versus relayed orally by Muhammad himself. The four people Muhammad designated as his best teachers remembered oral versus from the prophet differently. It was even recorded in the holy books that some material had gone missing over the years following Muhammad's death. Once again Nabeel had found that the most trustworthy Islamic sources related a different story than what he had been taught from the pulpits of the mosques.[47]

As I shivered against the howling cold wind while climbing the hill back to my albergue, I contemplated how similarly important the authenticity of the Quran is to the Islamic faith as the Bible is to the Christian faith. If the religious and secular evidence does not support the reliability of the scriptures, it is hard to justify putting one's faith in them. I mentally reviewed some of the points made in the various books I'd read that laid out very strong evidence for the reliability of the Bible.

---

[47] Qureshi, chapter 42.

I decided I needed to warm up again before heading to bed, so I went to the small check-in area where I had seen a pellet stove earlier in the day. I found a roaring fire in the stove, and the small room was very toasty. Tom was there with the same intention, so we talked for a few minutes about our plans for tomorrow. We decided we should get an early start in anticipation of a much longer hike than we did today.

We then spent a couple minutes complaining about our roommates.

"They could've started their Camino in León and just haven't learned pilgrim etiquette yet," Tom suggested, giving them the benefit of the doubt.

"Maybe we should educate them!" I replied.

# CHAPTER 29

## Foncebadon to Molinaseca, 19.3 Kilometers
## 23 Sep 2015
## D+25

Our rude roommates set the alarm for 0530. When it went off, they turned on the light and started talking very loudly. This was just not the right protocol for the Camino! Tom and I tried to go back to sleep after they left, but it had been too long. After about thirty restless minutes, I got up and headed across the courtyard for personal hygiene. By the time I got back, Tom was done packing up his gear and was ready to head out. I guess he couldn't get back to sleep either.

We decided to return to the small café where we had lunch yesterday in search of breakfast. Tom recognized one of the ladies sitting at the lone table enjoying a hot breakfast with a couple of friends.

"Jacque, I'm so glad we ran into you," he greeted her. "This is the other retired Air Force officer I told you about," he said, pointing his hand in my direction. "Colonel Tracey Meck." Then pointing at her and looking at me, he said, "This is Jacque."

"Wow, how long have you been retired?" I smiled, a little surprised at the revelation.

"Officially, 1 September," she explained, obviously intrigued that we had finally met. "I have been told by several people that there was another retired Air Force officer on the trail. I was hoping that we would run into each other."

"One September," I replied, focused on the first part of her statement. "And you're already this far into the Camino?"

"I've been on terminal leave. My last duty day was back in July. I retired out of Korea and had to get settled in California before heading over here. I actually started the Camino on my official retirement date."

Terminal leave is very common among military personnel. Active-duty personnel get thirty days of paid leave per year. If it is not used, it remains on the books and carries forward as long as you don't exceed the accrued leave limit. Most people plan it so they have at least two months leave on the books when they want to retire. They take their remaining leave after their final duty day.

"You're making pretty good time," I observed after doing the math and realizing that she had started three days after me.

She explained that she retired as a lieutenant colonel and had been a maintenance officer. She then mentioned that she thought I looked familiar, so I listed all of the places where I had been stationed to see if we had had any in common. We finally determined she was at the Pentagon at the same time I was prior to her final assignment in Korea. We discussed the issues and projects we worked there to see if we might have attended any of the same meetings. There did not seem to be any overlap to explain how we might have met in the world's largest office building. Finally we discovered that we had both attended a military women's symposium at the National Women's Memorial just outside Arlington National Cemetery.

"That must be it," I said. "I stood up during one of the discussions and talked about how important it was to balance rest and relaxation with being a type A workaholic. I failed to do that, leading to a long struggle with physical and mental exhaustion. I cautioned everyone to make the time to rest because you are no good to the mission or your people if you're so exhausted that you can't do your job."

"Yes, I remember that!" she exclaimed, happy that we had finally figured it out.

"Well, now that that's settled, I think I would like to get going." Tom, who had been politely listening to our discussion while he ate his breakfast, broke in. "I would like to be at the cross for sunrise."

The cross that Tom was talking about was called La Cruz de Ferro, one of the most famous monuments on the Camino. It is a small, nondescript iron cross on top of a tall pole that extends out of a mound of dirt and rocks. It is customary to bring a rock from home or some other place of special significance and carry it to this point. Then, in contemplation of the significance of where the rock came from and why they are walking the Camino, each pilgrim ceremoniously deposits the rock on the growing pile around the base of the pole.

Until Tom said this, I had not realized that we were approaching the monument. I guess my mission planning last night had been lacking.

"It's only 2 km away," Tom explained. "I hear it is a very moving experience to be there at sunrise."

Caught off guard, I did not have the opportunity to think it through. My mind was focused on how hard it would be to walk on the steep, rocky, rutted trail in the dark. My feet and back hurt just thinking about it.

"It would be best if I waited until the sun comes up," I said.

"Sunrise at the cross would be awesome." Jacque smiled. "I'll go with you!"

The other two ladies at the table were also intrigued by the idea. The four of them slung their packs onto their backs, grabbed their poles, and headed out into the cold darkness. I ordered another café con leche and enjoyed about thirty minutes of solitude before venturing out into what could now be called the "dawn's early light."

Within minutes I discovered that my wait was not necessary. Just after the last building in the small hamlet, the trial leveled out significantly and became a wide, smooth dirt walkway. I wondered if the steep, rough trail into the hamlet was actually a marketing scheme to discourage pilgrims enough to convince them to RON there? Either way, not a big deal. Except for the rude roommates and the cold, there was a lot of great things about the rustic hamlet. And of course, I had met a new friend this morning.

* * * * *

About six months after returning from my first deployment to Afghanistan, I received a mass e-mail seeking applicants for six PRT commander jobs. AFPC had sent the e-mail to every lieutenant colonel in the AF. My exposure to the Bagram PRT had left me intrigued with the mission. Still feeling that I had not done enough to contribute and feeling a little guilty that I had spent the entire deployment relatively safe on a huge base, I saw this as an opportunity to rectify those issues.

I headed straight for my commander's office and explained my desire to apply for one of the positions. Once again, he agreed to support my application for deployment. The PRT positions were not SF taskings, and I would be gone for fifteen months—about three months of training and then a full twelve months in-country. I would have to be "released" from my career field for the duration of the deployment. The commander said that he would contact our general, the director of Air Force Security Forces, at the Pentagon and explain my request to him.

To my great surprise, by the end of the day, I had received permission from the general to apply. I submitted my application to the personnel center's action officer before I went home that night. I was later told that about eighty lieutenant colonels applied. Six of us were chosen by the Pentagon.

US Army Civil Affairs (CA) units had created the PRT concept. PRT Gardez (named after the capital of Paktia Province because the FOB was located just outside of town), the one I was assigned to, had been the first to stand up in February 2003. Initially they were responsible for reconstruction and development in five provinces. Over time, new PRTs stood up and took over some of the provinces originally assigned to Gardez. Others, run by the United States and other nations that were members of the coalition, were initiated in other parts of the country. By 2006, most of the thirty-four provinces had a PRT assigned. The handful that did not have their own normally shared one with a neighboring province, as was the case for my PRT. When we arrived, the United States was operating twelve PRTs. PRT Gardez was down to just Paktia and Logar Provinces, immediately south of Kabul.

The DoD wanted to free up the Army CA units to institute the PRT concept in Iraq, so they tasked the AF and the Navy to deploy teams to replace the Army units in Afghanistan. Each service took six. Since PRT's were a new concept and CA was an Army mission, anyway, there was no career field in either the Air Force or Navy that mirrored the requirements to command these teams. So . . . we all came from different career fields and backgrounds. This would be new to all of us, almost entirely outside our comfort zones and professional skill sets. Upon reflection, we decided that security forces actually had the most relevant skills. PRTs conducted convoys, secured contingency bases and operations, fired weapons, were trained to engage the enemy in self-defense, and coordinated with host nation officials. These were skills I had practiced and implemented frequently as an SF officer. As far as the rest of the PRT mission elements and skill sets, I was equal with the other commanders. We were starting from scratch.

The twelve commanders reported to Fort Bragg, North Carolina, in early February 2006. About three weeks later, personnel tasked to fill several key positions on each PRT joined us: CA, information operations, intelligence, the first sergeant, ops officer (S3), and logistics officer (S4). A week or so after that, the rest of the AF and Navy team members arrived, and we trained mostly together until it was time to deploy in mid-April. The Army National Guard platoons that would be our security force (SECFOR) arrived around the same time as the main Air Force and Navy contingents, but trained separately most days.

For many reasons, this training left a lot to be desired. Since the PRTs were a new concept, there was no established history of an organizational structure, SOPs, successes, or failures around which to form a training program. The schoolhouse at Fort Bragg was given the mission to conduct the training for over one thousand new PRT members about two weeks before the commanders arrived to start training. The instructors had no experience with the PRT mission. Prior to this course, their mission had been to train combat battalions to deploy for direct combat. Except for the areas of security, base operations, convoys, and response to enemy activity, they seemed to be as clueless as the students. They did their best to pull together whatever useful information they could from the current Army PRT units in theater and the civil affairs schoolhouse also located on Bragg. The individual instructors were not CA troops, and those that had combat deployments under their belts had served in Iraq, not Afghanistan. Contrary to common assumption, the contingency operation and the social and threat environments were quite different. Tactics, Techniques, and Procedures (TTPs) that worked well for combat ops in Iraq would not necessarily be effective for the PRT mission in Afghanistan. But our instructors did not understand that. The result, in essence, was the blind leading the blind; and more often than not, the instructors just read whatever was on the slide. If we asked a question to dig deeper, they had no idea and reread the slide in response.

A prime example of the training disconnect was that every meeting we had scheduled with host nation role-players during practical field exercises almost immediately transitioned to a response to hostile action. Either the convoy was attacked and we never arrived, or the meeting place was attacked within minutes of us sitting down to talk to the village elders. We never actually got to exercise using translators or conducting meetings about projects and security issues with local officials, yet this would be the foundation of our mission in-country. Instead, we battled off ambushes by the Taliban and Al Qaeda and practiced our combat lifesavers skills on simulated dead and injured. All necessary skills, but we never practiced our actual mission!

* * * * *

Before I knew it, I had arrived at the cross. Tom and crew had already moved on. As I took my rock from my pack, I could not help but feel a little relieved that the pack would be lighter from here out. I bet it weighed half a pound!

I brought the small rock from my yard and wrote my name and hometown on it with a marker prior to departing for the airport. Now,

using my pen, I added "23 Sep 15." I then climbed to the top of the rock mound and found a place to prop the rock up so that the writing could be read. I took a picture of it while contemplating my appreciation for God having helped me make it this far in spite of the pain I had endured so far.

I then headed toward the high point of the entire Camino.

Everyone was passing by me yet again. It was bothering me less at this point. I was getting pretty used to it. What I still wasn't used to was when they came up and hovered behind me. As usual, anxiety kicked in each time it happened. For some reason, people found the need to get right on your tail.

\* \* \* \* \*

The AF element of PRT Gardez at Ft Bragg, NC, in March 2006.

Each PRT was a joint team composed of service members from at least two military services. Either the AF or the Navy commanded the PRT and provided a variety of functional skills to include intelligence, communications, a physician's assistant (PA) and several medics, information operations (IO), personnel administration, supply, food services, vehicle maintenance, civil engineering, and a police training and advising team (PTAT). The Army provided the SECFOR, seven CA officers and NCOs, and three individuals that the Army felt really needed to be from the Army in order for the PRTs to effectively work in a combat zone under the Tactical Control (TACON) of an Army brigade: the first sergeant, the operations officer (S3), and the logistics officer (S4).

Regarding these three positions, there apparently was a lack of communication internal to the Army concerning their importance. At least in the case of PRT Gardez, the Army manned these "vital" positions with personnel at least one level in rank below the stated requirement and with no experience in the job they were sent to do. This proved to be a major problem in all three functional areas, including significantly contributing to the accountability procedural issues identified during the investigation into the missing set of NVGs.

Although I initially suspected the Army was trying to destroy us, I came to realize I saw conspiracies where there were none. The positions were filled through the individual augmentation (IA) process, meaning that an Army unit was tasked to provide one person for the position. Although fairly standard in the AF, these types of taskings were unusual in the Army. They normally tasked entire units to deploy together for a specific mission; the unit determined the exact makeup of their team based on the mission they were assigned. Anticipating the potential for their own unit taskings, it was likely the home station commanders kept their best people and instead selected new troops or those that they saw as expendable for one reason or another to fill the IA taskings.

\* \* \* \* \*

A couple of clicks past La Cruz de Ferro was the austere albergue with the thirty-five mattresses and solar panels providing limited electricity. It really had a lot of character and looked like it would have been a lot of fun for a young, adventurous peregrino. However, considering how cold it had been the night before and how the wind had cut through my clothing and chilled me to the bone, I was extremely relieved that I had not attempted to stay there.

By 1035 I reached the highest point on the Camino. The route itself did not go to the Alto Altar Mayor but rather passed by it at twenty meters less elevation. I took the optional side trip up to a prominent cairn (a trail marker constructed of stacked rocks) where the elevation was 1,535 meters, or 5,036 feet. To my surprise, everyone else was opting to remain on the primary trail, so I found myself alone at the peak.

After spending a few minutes soaking in the exceptional views of the endless rolling hills and farmland, I found a comfortable rock to sit on and read day 23 of my study on the Christian service. Today's message urged us not to judge someone else's service, even failures, nor judge them for not living up to "our" expectations of what "we" think they should be doing for God. What they do and how they serve is between them and God. We do not know what else is going on in their lives or how God wants to use them, let alone why. Our judgmental attitudes toward other members of ministry teams can undermine the mission and destroy the team. The author refers us to Romans 14:4 and 15:5–6 to illustrate God's perspective on this principle.[48]

How many times has my perfectionist character been guilty of this, both in my professional life and what limited service I have been able to do in God's community? Now that I am retired and seeking to increase my service to my Savior, I will need stay alert for signs that I am being tempted to violate this principle.

A young man arrived as I sat gazing out over the Spanish landscape from my perch at the Camino's high point. He was an American from Georgia who had started in León. He was a mere four stages into his Camino.

Terrible at selfies, I seized the opportunity to ask him to take a picture of me at the cairn as proof that I had been there. I, of course,

---

[48] Fryar, p. 48–49.

returned the favor. Bidding him a hearty "Buen Camino," I headed down the hill, leaving him to rest and reflect in solitude as I had had the privilege to do.

The path quickly became steep, rocky, and uneven. Steep down-hill trails were always much harder for me than going uphill. The rocks and deep ruts made it almost unbearable. It had been a long time since my left ankle had caused me problems, but this terrible trail made it scream! I could not help but wonder why the steepest ascents and descents had the worst trail conditions. I slowed down to my slowest pace yet.

It was becoming apparent that I would not make it to Ponferrada today.

\* \* \* \* \*

The PRT's mission included three primary focus areas: governance, security, and reconstruction and development (better described as infrastructure development). In addition to duties on base within their functional areas, many of the AF and Navy PRT personnel had advisory responsibilities at the provincial and district levels. For instance, not only did our doc and enlisted medics operate a clinic on the FOB to take care of the medical needs of PRT personnel, they were also advisers to the provincial directors of public health and their subordinates at the district government level. This included facility and resource assessments and occasional advising directly with doctors at the clinics we visited. Our civil engineering officer and NCO were primarily focused on project proposal development, contract solicitation and selection, and monitoring construction progress via quality assurance/quality control (QA/QC) evaluations at project sites throughout our AOR.

After getting a good look the Afghan society, I would argue that *reconstruction* was not the appropriate word, but rather, *construction*. In my assessment, it is realistic to compare the infrastructure outside of major cities to how it would have been for people living in the time of Christ.

We were briefed that back in the 1960s, major Afghan cities were surprisingly more modern and Western-leaning. But outside these major metropolises, the population had always lived in fairly primitive conditions. After close to forty years of extremely violent turmoil, fighting first the Russian occupation, then Taliban oppression, and finally struggling alongside the international coalition to push the Taliban out of power and resist extremists like Al Qaeda had decimated their cities and sent their rural areas even further into the ancient past. Vast areas that had lush forests and farmland were now barren, brown, lifeless wastelands.

There was poor or no basic infrastructure. No running water or electricity. Buildings were constructed from a mixture of mud and straw. The agricultural support systems, such as major irrigation canals, were decimated. The majority of the people were illiterate.

Government officials were normally uneducated, inexperienced, and corrupt. Members of the Afghan National Army (ANA) and Police (ANP) were also illiterate, and their leaders were inexperienced. The midlevel officers and NCOs had only slightly more knowledge and experience than the raw recruits.

The objective of our reconstruction mission was to work with village elders, district leaders, and provincial government officials to improve the infrastructure by constructing roads, schools, clinics, government buildings, irrigation systems, electrical production and distribution systems, and other infrastructure to provide government services to the people and improve the livelihoods of the population.

A representative from the United States Agency for International Development (USAID) was assigned to each PRT. In theory, this person was the "lead" for reconstruction and development efforts. Reality was a little more complicated. The USAID rep had access to USAID project funding. His projects did not need to be coordinated with the military. I had access to military funding for reconstruction projects. Military projects did not have to be coordinated with USAID. However, I commanded the team, and USAID was a member of the team. My military chain of command made it clear that I was definitely responsible for the safety and security of the US government civilians on the team, but beyond this, the extent of my authority was a bit cloudy. Turf wars could be a problem at various levels.

Fortunately, on PRT Gardez, we got along very well and were able to work together mostly in one accord. We felt it was important to have a united effort between all the US government agencies and the Afghan officials that we worked with. To be successful, this was vital. I saw myself and our USG civilians as a leadership team. I was the tiebreaker and final decision authority, but the vast majority of the time the decisions were made together.

Afghan graduates from a USAID power generator operation and maintenance course in Gardez. A USAID project installed the generator and distribution system to give power to the provincial capital.

The USAID rep was supposed to be a "development expert," and therefore we were to lean on him for this part of the mission. Shams, our rep, was an Afghan American banker from Colorado. He had fought against the Russians with the US-supported Mujahideen and later immigrated and became a US citizen. He was well respected by the Afghans we worked with and obviously knew the culture and language. This made him a very valuable member of our team. In fact, it was he who educated me on an important point that few others, especially in the US media even today, understood. The correct term for a citizen of Afghanistan is *Afghan*, not the more commonly used term *Afghani*. *Afghani* is the term used to describe their currency. So referring to them as Afghani was like calling an American a "Dollar."

Shams was as new to the development world as myself and the rest of our team. USAID hired him specifically for this mission. One thing was for sure: his heart was in it! He was on a mission to use what he had learned in America to help his native country pull themselves out of the dismal pit they found themselves in after four decades of bloody, horrific conflict.

A couple of months after my team's arrival, we were thrilled to have a representative from the United States Department of Agriculture (USDA) join our team. Both provinces were historically agricultural, so we were one of the first four US PRTs to receive a USDA representative when the agency joined the Afghan development effort. We saw the rejuvenation of this industry as the key to improving the Afghan economic condition.

Opium (poppies) was currently a major crop because it did not take much water to grow and obviously sold for a lot of money. To counter the allure of this crop, we needed to improve the irrigation systems to enable what we called "alternative livelihood" crops. Our USDA rep was definitely motivated toward the mission, but once again his background and expertise did not really sync with what was needed. His experience was with the veterinarian portion of the agency. Fortunately, like the rest of us working outside our comfort zones, he was open-minded, eager to learn and do what was expected of him. When he rotated out, his replacement had a background in forestry. Again, not exactly what we needed.

The folks in DC seemed to be randomly assigning volunteers to slots irrespective of what expertise was required in the area of operations. They did not seem to understand that individual members of USDA were not experts in every area that fell under the department's umbrella. We got a USAID rep to do development. We got a Ag rep to do Ag stuff. That seemed to be the level of thought that had gone into the personnel assignment decisions.

Anyway, back to the projects themselves. The PRT did not actually do any of the construction projects. Rather, we contracted out to international and local companies with the stipulation that at least 80 percent of the employees working on a project had to be Afghan—the majority of whom needed to be from the local area.

The projects were not just about constructing infrastructure; we were also focused on building the "capacity" of the people in the community. The projects provided job skill training, experience, and income for the local men. It was the "give-them-a-fish vs. teach-them-to-fish" theory in action. The vision was that one day they would be able to do all this on their own without the assistance of coalition forces or international businessmen. By building skills and providing incomes sufficient to care for a family, we believed that the work would produce hope for a better future for their families and this would decrease their motivation join or support terrorist organizations.

Our "governance" mission was to work with provincial officials to improve their "governance capacity" and together establish a Provincial Development Plan (PDP) by working closely with village Shuras and district officials to determine local infrastructure needs and priorities. Our greatest challenge was that this concept was rather foreign to their culture.

In support of local United Nations Assistance Mission–Afghanistan (UNAMA) representatives, we helped facilitate monthly Provincial Development Council (PDC) meetings. But instead of focusing on identifying and prioritizing requirements, we spent months explaining the difference between a goal and an objective, and why it was important to have a five-year plan to address the endless array of "requirements" in an organized, methodical fashion. We seemed to be starting from scratch trying to educate them on how to develop both short-term and long-term goals and objectives and then use those to build development plans that would achieve them. Based on their culture, their inclination was to push for the project associated with the most recent person that visited their office asking for something. Each time a representative from a village or district brought a new proposal to the governor, his priorities changed. Suddenly this became the most important project he was requesting funding for.

Similar to the other US government agency personnel discussed above, each PRT had a US Department of State (DoS) representative assigned whose primary responsibility was governance capacity building. This person was supposed to be our governance expert. The State rep that was in place when we arrived was outstanding. She knew what she was doing and had formed close working relationships with our two governors and other key provincial officials. Sadly, the old adage is true: "All good things must come to an end." Three months after our arrival, she rotated home. The DoS was having difficulty finding volunteers to fill these front-line field positions. It was six months before we received a replacement. When we finally got a new rep, he had no experience in governance capacity building and not a lot of motivation to figure it out.

Unbeknownst to us military folk, "governance capacity building" is not an actual mission of the State Department. We were told that by virtue of working for State, they were governance experts and we should look to them to lead these efforts. It turns out that State Department employees work in embassies around the world, coordinating US interests with local officials and issuing cables about the status of their host nation from their cubicles. They do not teach local government officials how to govern.

All this meant that for nine months, I had to assume the role of the lead for governance and as the primary contact and adviser to the two governors. Of course, I didn't have any qualifications for this role either. I was a cop. What did I know about governing a state (our equivalent to their province)? Fortunately, the governors I worked with were intelligent and had spent time living outside of Afghanistan. One had even worked for the United Nations. They spoke English fairly well. Together, I think we did a fairly good job figuring it out.

Our final mission pillar was security. When PRT Gardez initially stood up, this was a very important part of the mission. Training and advising the local ANA and ANP units concerning tactical operations was the intent of the PTAT. However, over the years, much more robust security training programs were implemented. In fact, Gardez was home to the regional ANP Training Academy. There was also a new ANA base with a significant US training and advisory unit about five miles from our FOB. Therefore, the role of the PTAT was now in question. I had to put my foot down numerous times to prevent them from being sucked into the SECFOR and assigned base security duties. Instead, they frequently went to the ANP Academy to assist the US-based company that had been contracted by the DoS to run the facility and train the recruits. We also had them go out to police stations and checkpoints to conduct assessments to determine what support and equipment we could provide them.

Taking the initiative, our team developed a couple of training courses to provide "continuing training" for ANP troops who were already on the job. Finally, when we conducted combined missions with Afghan government officials, the ANP had a significant role in providing security for the event. During these activities, the PTAT visited the ANP posts and provided advice and assistance to ensure adequate and integrated security was being provided.

\* \* \* \* \*

After descending over five hundred meters, the steep trail finally mellowed slightly as I approached the small village of Acebo. This had been my mission objective yesterday. Since it was now just after noon, I realized how aggressive that goal had been.

I found a café and stopped for lunch to take a break from my trail struggles. I checked the guidebook elevation map for stage 24 and saw that the next three clicks would be slightly less steep, but after the next village, the map was marked with a caution symbol (!) indicating that it would get nasty yet again. Fortunately, it did not appear that it would stay bad for as long as what I had just endured—maybe a kilometer, two at the most. The Camino would then transition to a mild descent into a good-sized village of about eight hundred people.

I decided this would be my objective for today's mission.

\* \* \* \* \*

My PRT was in-country for one year. There was never any real downtime, at least not for the leadership. Besides my midtour leave, I got three days off the entire year, and they were not what I would call "relaxing."

While attending a regional governors meeting at our Brigade HQ in Salerno, I came down with a bad case of food poisoning. I had eaten local food countless times during my tour. Whether it was provided by our interpreters for base barbecues, dinners at the governors' compounds, or celebratory lunches during ribbon-cutting ceremonies at completed project sites—I had never had a problem.

Our brigade commander decided to honor the governors by bringing them to a US base and feeding them a catered normal Afghan meal. You would think it would have been nice to let them sample typical American cuisine. Anyway, about halfway through the meal I started feeling nauseous, my stomach felt like it was doing flip turns. I became light headed and rotated between chills and sweats. I knew exactly what was wrong. I stopped eating the meat; I am not sure if it was chicken or goat. But the damage had been done.

Because I had quit eating, I was still hungry, so I went to the Green Bean Coffee Shop after the official event ended and purchased a strawberry smoothie. A couple hours later, the smoothie and everything I had eaten at dinner started coming up. Before long I developed diarrhea and awful stomach cramps. All night long, everything that I consumed came out one end or the other, even the water I tried to drink in order to stay hydrated. By morning I was exhausted and so dizzy I could hardly walk. When it was time to head for the LZ to catch a helicopter home, one of the other commanders noticed my condition and talked me into getting checked out at the hospital tent. The doctor said I could not get on the helicopter until I had at least three bladders of IV solution. Somehow we managed to do that just in time for me to get on the helicopter with strict orders to see our doc immediately upon landing at Gardez. Doc filled me with another IV and sent me to my room with a few days' supply of Imodium. For the next three days, the only time I left my room was for the frequent treks across the compound to the restroom.

Not exactly the ideal three-day weekend. I would rather have been working!

Anyway, during our busy year, we normally had at least one, and frequently more, off-base missions each day except Fridays. On one particularly busy day, we conducted six different convoy operations.

Friday was the Islamic holy day, and Afghans did not work. Most of the PRT used Fridays to clean and repair equipment and conduct training within their functional area. We called it our training and maintenance day. The leadership team spent these days reviewing our strategic and tactical situation, updating our rolling schedule for the next four weeks and conducting detailed planning for the next week's specific missions.

In all, PRT Gardez conducted approximately 450 off-base missions during the year in support of the Afghan National Development Strategy (ANDS) and focusing on strengthening the legitimacy of the Government of Afghanistan (GoA) in the eyes of the population. We conducted countless meetings at the provincial, district, and village levels and worked on over 150 projects involving a total of $17 million from DoD and USAID development funding. Our projects included schools, medical clinics, wells, bridges, orphanages, government buildings, agriculture, water management, and electrical systems. We also funded governance, security, and vocational training programs.

Crowds gather for the ribbon cutting ceremony for a PRT-built school.

Additionally, we assisted with surveys, coordination, and QA/QCs for nationally directed and funded projects that were ongoing or being started in our AO, including road construction, district center complexes, district police headquarters, a large hospital, and police communication systems.

We also conducted several MEDOPs. Although the medical care given would only have a short-term impact, the strategic objective of these operations was to win public support for the GoA and the coalition. After a couple MEDOPs where US medical personnel did everything, our doc insisted that we could have a longer-term impact if we included Afghan medical personnel in the operations. This provided the local doctors training and experience and built the population's confidence in their own medical system and personnel.

Sometimes villages were selected because there was a lot of support for the bad guys in the area and we were trying to separate them from the insurgents and win their support for our side.

Other villages were selected as a reward. For instance, one of our convoys was heading up the main rough dirt road out of Gardez toward districts closer to the Pakistani border. As they approached a small village, an elder came into the road and waved for them to stop. Through the mission commander's interpreter, the elder explained that someone had put a suspicious item in the road ahead. He suspected it was an IED. The convoy stopped, established a secure perimeter, and requested an EOD team be dispatched to investigate the item. It did not turn out to be an explosive device, but we still appreciated his warning and his concern for the team's safety. A couple of weeks later, we returned to the village and conducted a MEDOP as a way to say thank you. The villagers were ecstatic. For years, US convoys had driven through their village, but no one had ever stopped to meet with them, let alone do anything for them.

As our understanding of the local situation evolved, all our missions started taking on the characteristic of including Afghan officials. Whenever possible, we put them in the front, especially when interacting with local villagers. The intent of all our work was to build economic capacity, solid governance, and public confidence so the people would have hope for a better future. If they could see the end of the dark tunnel of conflict and could start trusting that there was hope for their society, they would eventually be able to envision a secure community where they could raise and support their families in peace. This would make them less likely to support the Taliban and Al Qaeda insurgents. We believed that this was the key to long-term stability and security.

This sounded great and rather simplistic. In reality, it was very complex. There were always many layers of contributing factors behind every motivation and action in the community. Everything we did had second, third, and even fourth orders of effect. It was never "if this, then that," never simple cause and effect; nothing was ever black and white.

Over the year, we learned a lot of lessons but also redeployed with many dilemmas still unresolved. One thing was for sure: our experiences provided a treasured trove of war stories.

\* \* \* \* \*

Relieved to be done with the worst trail conditions so far, I collapsed into the bed in my private room in El Palacio Hotel in the outskirts of Molinaseca. I propped my feet up on a couple of pillows in hopes that the swelling and pain would decrease. I was now just 7 km short of Ponferrada where Mom, Ria, and I had started trekking again in 2013.

Reflecting back on the last portion of our previous hike, I could not think of a section as tough as the trail I was on today. I was confident that I was through the worst of it!

In chapter 43 of *Seeking*, David courageously pointed out that the Quran and the supporting holy books allowed—in fact, *encouraged*—Muslim men to rape captured women that they had enslaved. David cited three verses from the Quran in his argument (4:24, 23:6, and 70:30) which allow men to have sex with "those whose their right hands possess." Nabeel was familiar with this phrase but was appalled by David's interpretation and the implications concerning the character of Muhammad and Muslims in general. This was not the loving, kindhearted freer of the oppressed that Nabeel had learned about in the mosques he attended. He set out to prove David wrong by studying the evidence in the holy books. What he found in the Hadiths (Sahih Muslim, Sunan Abu Daud, and Sahih Bukhari) supported David's accusations. Even Islamic religious commentaries supported David. Nabeel was disgusted. This is what finally broke his faith in Islam.[49]

I could not help but wonder how many Muslims ever questioned what they were taught enough to notice these types of conflicting interpretations. As explained earlier in the book, the culture

---

[49] Qureshi, chapter 43.

demands that Muslims accept what they are taught by their religious leaders without question. Everything about their life, upbringing, culture, and education impeded such discovery and critical analysis of the evidence in their own holy books.

After snoozing for a half hour or so, I went to the bar for a drink and ran into numerous friends. Jacque, the Air Force retiree I met at breakfast, told me how moved she had been, watching Tom at the cross. He used the opportunity of being where people leave their burdens at the base of the cross to pay tribute to friends he had lost in Vietnam. No wonder it was so important for him to be there at sunrise. I regretted not joining them!

# CHAPTER 30

## Molinaseca to Valtuille de Arriba, 26.3 Kilometers
## 24 Sep 2015
## D+26

Strolling lazily into the restaurant at 0800, I enjoyed a wonderful breakfast buffet. Jacque and Lora appeared just as I was finishing up, so I ordered another cup coffee and stayed to talk for another twenty minutes or so while they ate. Together we embarked on stage 25 toward Ponferrada around 0900.

It was 6.2 km to the old city castle. I was looking forward to touring it. We were there on a Sunday in 2013, and it was closed. Intrigued by the ancient walls, we had to settle for walking around the outside. Timing should be just about right today.

\* \* \* \* \*

Besides my perception that our development efforts in Afghanistan were "strategically" creating a culture of dependency and a welfare state, there were numerous other "tactical" dilemmas that we juggled during mission planning. The most puzzling was, Should we use our projects as a reward for villages who produced stability and supported the Afghan government and coalition forces, or as an incentive for people in unstable and hostile areas to stop supporting Al Qaeda and the Taliban and instead work toward stability and peace by changing their allegiance to the GoA?

When the provincial governor and I visited villages, we explained to the Shuras that "with peace and stability comes reconstruction." We emphasized the importance of security if we were going to invest and convince contractors to construct facilities, roads, irrigation systems, hydroelectric systems, and other requested infrastructure. Many schools had been built only to be bombed and burned to the ground within days or weeks of completion, sometimes even before completion. On more than one occasion, road construction crews had been attacked and many workers killed. Convoys of humanitarian aid had been hijacked, the aid stolen, and the truck drivers killed. We explained that this was a waste of precious resources and lives.

Even though we preached this at our Shura meetings, we did a lot of projects in unstable areas in the hopes of building goodwill. The clinic in Zurmat where we did the ribbon-cutting ceremony during my right seat–left seat ride with my predecessor and got into the security wall discussion was a prime example of this. In fact, if memory serves, I think about two-thirds of our projects were in unstable areas. This reality was not lost on the Afghans. Many times in the my first few months, leaders of stable areas expressed their frustration with the obvious trend after we gave the standard spiel.

The residents of one village in the most secure district in Logar, Muhammad Agha, took their observation of the discrepancy a step further. They orchestrated an "ambush" on an Afghan "Jingle" truck transporting food from farms to a market along the main road heading toward Kabul. No one was killed or even injured, but the truck and the load were destroyed. During the incident investigation, the very competent Logar provincial police chief discovered that the attack had been staged in order to prove to us that they "had insurgent problems" so that we would consider their village for a project.

We decided to change our approach in deciding what new projects to work on. From then on, our methodology was rewarding stable areas with major projects such as schools, clinics, and hydroelectric systems. Unstable areas got small, relatively cheap projects such as wells or government facility refurbishment such as a paint job.

Cancellation of pending projects in unstable areas was a stick we could use to "punish" villages that supported and harbored terrorists. We did this in response to the major attack on our convoy in Chamkani District near the Pakistan border while I was on leave. After the devastating ambush, the Paktia governor invited the district commissioner and major Shura leaders to the governor's compound in Gardez to discuss the attack. During the meeting, I made the announcement that I had been forced to cancel a school project just a few miles from the site of the attack because it was just too dangerous to go through with it. A few days later, the governor made the same announcement during the PDC meeting. He further announced that we were taking the money that had been approved for that school and using it to build one in Sayid Karam District instead. This was by far the most secure district in Paktia and had, therefore, received very little attention, let alone projects.

Finally we were making good on our claim that "security brings reconstruction."

\* \* \* \* \*

We arrived at the entrance to the castle at 1045, only to discover it opened at 1100.

"I am going to stay here tonight and spend the day looking around town," Lora told Jacque and me. "I think I will go find a place to stay and then come back to tour the castle this afternoon."

"Okay, Buen Camino," we replied as she turned and headed toward the center of old town.

We decided to wait in a café. As we approached the door, Tom called out to us, and we waited for him to catch up before going in.

We discussed our mission objectives for the day over coffee. Tom was also planning to spend the day seeing the sights of Ponferrada.

"This is where we started back up two years ago. We arrived by train midday, so we had quite a bit of time to look around. I don't need to do it again," I explained. "However, we were here on a Sunday and the castle was closed. I'll spend about forty-five minutes looking around inside, and then I'll head on down the trail."

"Think I'm going to try to get all the way to Villafranca today," Jacque explained.

I opened my phone's calculator app and added up the distance based on the waypoints in the guidebook: 23.1 km.

"Wow, that's a long way since it's already eleven. Added to the 6 km we've already done, that's way too far for me!"

"I'm pretty sure I can do it as long as I don't stay at the castle very long. I'll get in and out in ten to fifteen minutes."

"I've waited two years to tour this castle. I'll take my time. There is a village about 4.3 km before Villafranca with a casa rural. The book doesn't show how many beds. I think I will call and make a reservation just in case."

The lady who answered the phone said there was plenty of room but asked if I could be there before five because she needed to go to an appointment. I told her I should be able to make it by then. Just under 18 km in about five hours. No problem . . . Right! I was going to have to hustle. Maybe I should limit my time in the castle to thirty or forty minutes.

"I better take off and find a place to stay," Tom announced as he gulped his last sip of coffee and geared up.

Jacque and I bought our tickets together and found a place to stow our packs in a small courtyard to the left just after the entrance. Wishing each other "Buen Camino," we parted ways so Jacque could make a quick visit of it.

Enjoying the walk on top of the castle walls, I found the views of the small city and the surrounding green hills typical of Europe. The mix of ancient structures, modern European construction, and the surrounding tranquil landscapes had always been something that I can only describe as "cool." I guess I could use the word *awesome*, but that has become so overused and misused in the lingo of today's young people that I avoid using it whenever possible.

I made my way up the steep enclosed spiral staircases leading to the fighting platforms of each guard tower. I marveled at the slits through the thick walls. They were about six inches wide from the inside and then narrowed to about two inches on the outside. Being an AF defender, I was very familiar with this type of design.

It was common in modern cement DFPs that surrounded the perimeters of several bases I was stationed at in Europe. The angle allowed the sentry to observe a wider area than a straight slit and to shoot an arrow or firearm anywhere within the same "field of fire." The small exterior opening provided significant protection from incoming fire for the sentry on the inside.

I was also intrigued by the large open courtyard and refurbished living, working, and socializing rooms that enabled tourists to imagine what life in the castle must have been like.

After about forty-five minutes of wandering, I retrieved my pack, departed the castle across the drawbridge, found a yellow arrow, and started out toward my day's objective at a brisk pace.

\* \* \* \* \*

A major dilemma that plagued not only the PRT but also the kinetic forces and the coalition in general was how much of the information provided by local nationals could be trusted. This included not only information obtained through formal intelligence efforts but what we were told during numerous meetings with both government officials and regular citizens.

During our PRT commanders orientation briefings in Kabul, we were briefed on a strikingly tragic incident where coalition kinetic forces acted on intelligence received that they believed was reliable and the implications of which would be devastating enough that immediate action was required to save lives, specifically Hamid Karzai on his Inauguration Day. Besides the president-elect, the lives of attending senior government representatives from coalition nations—to include the US vice president and secretary of defense—were at risk.

The coalition received information from an Afghan warning that a good-sized group of terrorists were on foot heading for Kabul through a specific mountain pass. The Afghan said they were suicide bombers intent on attacking the inauguration, targeting Karzai and the senior coalition diplomats attending.

Coalition aerial surveillance located the group where the intelligence indicated they would be. There was not enough time to effectively vet the information. The stakes were extreme. To prevent a catastrophic and horrific attack on a critical event in the stabilization of Afghanistan, the group was taken out by an aerial strike.

The tragedy was that the group turned out to be an official provincial delegation who were traveling to attend the inauguration to show their province's support for the new president. Among those killed was the son of the province's governor. Investigation into the incident revealed that the Afghan who initially provided the information was a member of a family that had been feuding with the governor's family for an incredibly long time. He gave the coalition false information in hopes that the coalition would do the family's dirty work for them. Tragically, the coalition did just that.

Another motive for lying to coalition forces and Afghan government officials was to conceal their affiliation with, or at least support of, the Taliban or Al Qaeda. A prime example of this was during an initiative implemented by myself and Governor Hakim Taniwal of Paktia Province. Based partially on orders from brigade headquarters, the governor and I met with Shuras from villages and districts that were hotbeds for insurgent activity with the objective of convincing them to cut off their support to the Taliban and join with the government to build a safe and secure province. For security purposes and to demonstrate the authority of the governor, the Shuras were asked to come to the governor's office complex for the meetings. One of these meetings will forever plague me.

We were meeting the Shura from Gerda Serai, one of our most unstable areas along a key "Line of Communication" (LoC) (road) connecting Gardez with Khost Province through the K-G Pass. I was sitting next to the governor, but he was doing the talking. An interpreter was quietly translating the conversation for me. After the traditional greetings, the governor began by pointing out that their area had experienced more than its fair share of violence from Taliban activity. Government police and army forces were frequently attacked, and buildings constructed by the government and coalition were bombed or burned. He encouraged them to quit supporting the Taliban who were operating in their area—rather, to fight against them and push them out. Several members of the Shura insisted that the good people of Gerda Serai did not support the Taliban. They were being oppressed and intimidated by them. The poor villagers had no way to defend themselves, so they did not resist in order to ensure the safety of their families and livelihoods. The line of reasoning that the people were actually victims went on for quite some time. Finally Governor Taniwal had had enough. He sat up very straight and glared at the Shura members.

"You know as well as I do, that is not true. Your tribe is fully supporting the Taliban. Now, quit lying about it, and let's talk seriously."

I could not believe my ears. I knew what the governor said was true. Yet I could not believe that he so blatantly confronted them with the knowledge. We were both quite sure that not only did the tribe support the Taliban, but it was very likely that more than one of the Shura members in attendance were Taliban; we just didn't know precisely which ones. I do not remember how the remainder of the meeting went, but I did not come away with a good feeling that we had made any progress.

Gov Hakim Taniwal speaks at a PRT project ribbon cutting ceremony before his assassination.

The next day I went to BAF. The evening before I was scheduled to return a couple of days later, I was called into the office of my Air Force boss (ADCON) who informed me that Governor Taniwal had been killed by a suicide bomber. Apparently, a man had been hanging out all day in the traffic circle outside the governor's office compound. The security force did not consider this odd. With the dismal state of unemployment, it was quite common to see men just hanging around somewhere all day. At the end of the day, the governor, his security chief, and his nephew (who was his assistant) departed the gate on their way to the governor's house. The man approached the soft-shelled vehicle, leaned into it, and blew himself up, killing everybody inside.

My XO, information ops (IO), and doc assembled a convoy and sped to the hospital where the victims had been taken. The IO took some photos for the report and showed them to me when I got back. I wish he had not done that because I will never be able to forget the picture of the dead governor, nor of the suicide bomber's severed head.

Instead of returning to Gardez, my Army boss, the brigade commander, sent a helicopter to Bagram to pick me up and take me to his base of operations at Selarno in Khost Province. The governor's funeral would be held nearby in the capital of Khost because that was where his family was from. The intent was for me to attend the funeral as a representative of the United States and coalition. After several hours of planning, it was determined that this was not the best idea after all. The security presence that would be required for me to attend would be so great that it was felt it would not be appropriate at a public event in honor of a beloved leader who had been the governor of Khost prior to moving to Gardez the previous year. Instead, the colonel arranged a helicopter to take me home.

Upon my arrival at FOB Gardez, I was hit with another shocking announcement. A suicide bomber had attacked the DV section at the funeral, and six influential Afghan officials were killed, many others wounded. It immediately occurred to me that if I had been present, I would have been seated in that section.

I strongly believe that the people responsible for these two attacks had been present at our meeting with the Greda Serai Shura. I cannot help but feel at least partially responsible for the nine deaths. Although I did not tell him to say what he did, I was the one that suggested to him that we conduct the meetings with the Shuras.

Another possible example of deceit revolved around the September incident when the high-value target (HVT) was killed during a combined US and Afghan raid near the Pakistan border, setting off an extensive round of tit-for-tat violence, to include the ambush on my team's convoy in November. A couple of days after the raid, the district commissioner came to FOB Gardez to lodge a complaint against the forces involved. He told me that the individual killed was innocent and had been killed in front of his family members, including children. He insisted there was no Taliban in the village. Skeptical, I reported his allegations to Brigade and suggested they initiate an investigation to determine the actual facts.

At the time of the district commissioner's visit to the FOB, I was completely unaware of the raid, let alone any intelligence regarding the HVT. I felt it was my duty to upchannel the commissioner's version of events and let the brigade figure out the details based on intelligence and kinetic data that I was not privy to. If it actually was a war crime, it was essential that I report it. If it wasn't a war crime, I was sure that no negative action would be taken against US personnel as a result of the investigation. Still the mere fact that I reported the information I received and an investigation was conducted made me persona non grata at the outpost. I even got the impression that the brigade commander held the report against me.

To this day, I have no idea if the information I received from the district commissioner was true or deceitful. My inclination is to believe that the target of the raid was in fact an HVT that was taken off the battlefield, thus potentially saving many lives. I suspected as much at the time, but having received information regarding a potential war crime and having absolutely no knowledge of the incident outside of what the district commissioner reported, I still believe it was my duty to upchannel it for proper investigation at a level where there was access to all the relevant data. Yet another negative experience with the Army!

A nonviolent example of deceit on the part of Afghans was when they attempted to convince me to fund the construction of the security wall around the USAID-built clinic in Zurmat during the ribbon-cutting ceremony when I first arrived. Then there was the attack in Logar that was staged in hopes of getting a project funded.

Of course, these are a handful of examples of Afghan deceit and underhandedness. Definitely not all our interactions with local nationals (LNs) met this description. The villager who waved our convoy down to warn them of the potential IED is a great example of positive and honest support from the Afghan public.

Another example of positive communication involved a mission that we were planning in conjunction with UNAMA to visit the remote village of Shai Kot. The village was located in a rugged, mountainous hotbed for insurgents. Numerous historic battles had been fought in this area over the millennia. Most recently was the infamous Operation Anaconda in

"Road" to Shai Kot

2002. Our hope was that the "innocent" civilians that lived in the village supported the Taliban because they were intimidated by them; it was a matter of survival. The Afghan National Security Forces (ANSF, consisting of the ANP and ANA) never went to the area, so the villagers had no hope of protection if they were to oppose the insurgents. Our plan was to motivate them to support the Afghan government by determining their needs and initiating a few small projects—such as water wells and, yes, even irrigation canals. ANSF personnel were to accompany us to encourage confidence in the villagers that if stability increased, ANSF would be able to operate in the area and protect them. Of course, our "long-term" message was that with stability would come major projects.

It was decided that I, as the PRT commander, should not attend this meeting. First of all, the governor was not going, and it would not be proper for someone at my level to conduct a major meeting with a local Shura without him being there as the Afghan government lead. Additionally, it was considered an honor to have the PRT commander visit and offer projects. Obviously, the situation was not stable enough to bestow that honor. This was just the foundational first meeting to open up communications with a hostile community.

The day before the mission was scheduled, we got a call from UNAMA who had been communicating with the village elders to arrange the visit. The elders had notified them that the Taliban had arrived at the village and were making the rounds, extorting money

Shai Kot boy smiles after receiving a gift from PRT members.

from the villagers. The elders could not guarantee the safety of our team. The warning was in accordance with the ethics of Pashtunwali; if the elders invited you to their village, they guaranteed your safety and went to battle against anyone who tried to attack you. The elders would contact UNAMA once the Taliban left and it was safe to travel to the village. We put the mission on hold and conducted it about two weeks later after getting the green light from the elders.

There were many examples of positive, honest communication, and just as many examples of deceit. One thing was for sure: it was blatantly obvious to me that I had to take everything the LNs told me with a grain of salt. I should never assume that anything they said was true without having it checked out in detail. This is a vital lesson that should be learned by the world's media and those that acquire their knowledge of international events from the sound bites the media puts out.

It was normal for Afghans to feel a much greater sense of loyalty to their tribe and family than to their country. This tribal loyalty, combined with their government's incompetence due to a lack of education and their cultural tendencies toward corruption, made one of our three mission pillars very difficult to work toward—that being to encourage the people to trust and support their government.

The more interactions I had with government officials, the more I realized the level of incompetence and corruption. Shams, our Afghan-American USAID rep, told me and other US military leadership multiple times that the greatest threat and impediment to a stable Afghanistan was neither the Taliban nor even the thriving illegal poppy industry. The biggest threat was corruption. Corruption permeated every aspect of the government, thus enabling the Taliban, Al Qaeda, and illegal drug industries to exist and have such a great impact on the culture and society as a whole. In many parts of the country, government officials not only tolerated the insurgents and illegal drug production but were major players in those sectors.

The provincial chief of police (CoP) of Paktia was a prime example. The man holding that position when I arrived had been extorting money from the population for years. He also skimmed money from the paychecks of his men. Money for their paychecks was transported from Kabul to the provincial capitals and then out to the district capitals. The policemen would line up to personally receive their pay. Officials involved in each part of this process skimmed some of the money until the actual policeman received less than 50 percent of what he was owed. The CoP had many other moneymaking schemes. After six months of investigation and documentation by the PRT, US intelligence personnel and the maneuver unit in the area, the United States was finally able to convince President Karzai to fire him. However, none of the money was recovered for the government or for the people who had been robbed. Instead, the ex-CoP built an enormous fancy mansion to live out the rest of his days in luxury.

Still, we were ecstatic that he was out of the picture. We needed a CoP that could be trusted and that the people could have faith in. However, the person that the national government replaced him with made the first guy look like an angel. It was not long before we dubbed him the "King of Corruption."

Again, we built a package of evidence and lobbied to have him removed from office and arrested for his extensive corruption and crimes. After several months of evidence being elevated to the president and minister of the interior (MoI, who was responsible for the ANP), the second CoP was called to Kabul for a meeting with the minister. We were sure that this was it—that he would not be coming back.

Two days later, he was back at work as if nothing had happened. He had had a large truckload of firewood delivered to the minister as a bribe to keep his job. We kept forwarding evidence of corruption and other illegal activity, and he kept bribing his way out of trouble. He was still in place when I rotated out.

The new governor who replaced Governor Taniwal worked closely with us and tried to get this second CoP removed through his official Afghan government channels. I really felt sorry for Governor Rahmat. He was competent and honest. He quickly exhausted all his savings trying to keep the provincial government running while national officials withheld (pocketed) funds that were supposed to cover his salary and pay for gas for the police cars, electricity for government facilities and other standard expenses. When Governor Rahmat complained, the MoI boss told him that he "had to give something to receive something." In other words, he was expected to give the minister a sizable portion of the provincial budget as a payment (a bribe) to receive the rest. The governor refused for several months, using his personal funds for as long as they lasted. I was later told that he himself was removed from his position several months after my departure due to allegations of corruption. He was not corrupt when he got there. If the allegations were true, it was the system that forced him into corruption because he had no other choice.

The more I dealt with these issues, the harder it was for me in good conscience to try "to connect the Afghan people to their government." It didn't take long for Governor Rahmat to become just as disillusioned as I was becoming. About two months after assuming his position, his frustration prompted him to confide in me that, in his assessment, 80 percent of "his staff" was either corrupt or incompetent.

As bad as the quality of his staff was, the bigger problem was, he had absolutely no say in their assignments or, ultimately, their actions. Although they were expected to work "with" him, they did not work "for" him. Instead, the government structure was set up so that the functional directors in the provinces (director of health, director of agriculture, CoP, etc.) reported directly to the national minister for that functional area. Working with the governor and following his guidance was merely a courtesy that was not necessarily maintained with any reliability.

"How can I be expected to govern a province honestly and effectively under these conditions?" he sighed in utter exasperation.

I could find no words to encourage him, nor did any amount of reporting about the situation to my chain of command have any impact whatsoever. We both felt like we were beating our heads against the wall.

Even though activists around the world have accused the United States of being occupiers, our influence over the politics and culture were extremely limited. Afghanistan was a sovereign country.

\* \* \* \* \*

I quick-walked as fast as my aching foot allowed. I didn't even stop for coffee, let alone lunch. However, I was hungry by the time I passed through Cacabelos, about five clicks before my objective. I took a couple of minutes to buy an ice cream bar to eat while I walked.

After wandering around the windy village streets of Valtuille de Arriba for about ten minutes, I finally found the casa rural at about 1640, twenty minutes before the hostess was due to leave. Fortunately, this gave us enough time for her to show me around the facility. I was the only one there, and she said she was not expecting anyone else. This made sense. I had not seen another peregrino since the trail split into two options about a kilometer and a half before the isolated village.

Before leaving, the hospitalero showed me her stash of pasta and sauce for me to make my dinner. She also provided vegetables she had procured from her neighbor's garden and showed me where her basil plant was in her front yard. She encouraged me to take what I needed to add flavor to the pasta and salad. She then showed me how to use the typically small European washer and dryer. Lastly I was presented a bottle of wine, which I would have to myself since there were no other guests.

The evening was very relaxing in the rustic, old-style European house. The outer walls and fireplace were made of rocks cemented together. The wood beams that supported the planks of the second floor reminded me of my log home in Washington. There were even full logs used as major support beams for the structure—again, just like home. It was as if this place was constructed just for me.

While enjoying dinner, I completed day 24 of my study on Christian service. Today's lesson continued the discussion about people frequently making mistakes while serving. As an example, Peter denied he knew Jesus three times the night he was arrested. Even so, Jesus forgave him after his resurrection, and Peter resumed serving with renewed enthusiasm and determination until he himself was martyred. The study also referenced several verses that described how Paul and Barnabas had a falling out and went their separate ways. Paul still considered Barnabas a close friend and brother in Christ whom he valued throughout the rest of his ministry (Acts 13:5–13, Acts 15:36–39, Col. 4:10–11, and 2 Tim. 4:11).[50]

As I contemplated this, I pondered that Jesus had once said that Peter was the rock on which his church would be built (Matt. 16:17–19). He said this before Peter betrayed him. Jesus is all-knowing and therefore knew what Peter was going to do. Yet He said it, anyway, and when it happened, He did not give up on Peter! Similarly, we should not give up on other Christians just because they make a few mistakes.

Taking the concept a step further, I realized that I should apply the concept to my judgment of my perfectionist, type A self. I should not beat myself up endlessly because I am not the perfect servant of my Savior. I cannot let the devil convince me to condemn myself for my imperfections to the point where it interferes with the effectiveness of my service to Christ.

There is no such thing as a "one-mistake Christianity"! God's children are not kicked out of the family just because they make a mistake.

---

[50] Fryar, p. 50–51.

# CHAPTER 31

## Valtuille de Arriba to La Portela de Valcarce, 19.6 Kilometers
## 25 Sep 2015
## D+27

The hospitalero said she did not plan to get up until about nine, so I could just leave payment for my room on the kitchen table. After she went up to her private section of the house, I discovered I was going to need to break a 50€ bill to pay her. This gave me the opportunity to sleep in. I timed it fairly well and finished doing the dishes and foot maintenance about 0910.

I knocked on her door. No response. I tried a couple more times, and she finally leaned out a window on the second floor.

"I am sorry to wake you, but all I have is a fifty. Do you have change?"

"I think so," she replied. "Let me get dressed, and I will be down in a few minutes."

That handled, I set out for Villafranca del Bierzo about 0930.

\* \* \* \* \*

How little the American public knows about what's really going on in Afghanistan can be extremely frustrating. Of course, it's not the public's fault. Since only 1 percent of Americans are serving in the military at any given time, and less than 7 percent have ever served, the vast majority have no firsthand information about the front lines. They only know what the media tells them, and that is tainted by the worldview of the media outlet and what they think will "sell."

Based on watching the media coverage about what I was involved with, it is my assessment that the media only gets about 30

428

percent of what they report correct. They are constantly giving their opinions and arguing over skewed superficial talking points as if they were discussing gospel facts. Yet they have absolutely no depth of understanding; they know none of the details involved. They never ask "How do I know that this is actually true?" Nor do they ask "Why is this the way it is?" Obviously, what the American people think they know about a situation or incident is therefore incorrect and even more superficial than the media.

For example, when I heard a media team arrived at FOB Gardez, I tracked them down, introduced myself as the PRT commander, and invited them to come on a couple missions with us.

"Tomorrow we are meeting with the governor, representatives from UNAMA, and Afghan officials that make up the Provincial Development Council. You can come see how we are working with international organizations and the Afghan government to map out plans to develop the province's infrastructure and economy. You're also welcome to come with us the next day. We are doing a medical operation out in a remote village."

"Thank you," the lead reporter replied. "But we will have to pass. We are going out with the maneuver unit on their mission tomorrow."

"Perhaps you could join us the next day then," I offered, trying to keep the door open.

"We'll see," she replied and then headed toward the maneuver element's TOC.

I never saw her again even though she was on base for several days. The situation was clear. They wanted to see something go *boom* and to be there to cover it—to get action video, to be filmed in a helmet and protective vest reporting while a battle raged around them. This is the sort of coverage that sells news reports and makes reporters famous. As far as they were concerned, the American public did not want to see video of Afghans planning for their future or of American service members providing medical care in remote villages. It just wasn't exciting. It also did not fit their preferred message that the wars in Afghanistan and Iraq were all about occupation, improvised explosive devices, air strikes, and overall destruction, not to mention the deaths of innocent civilians.

My assessment of the situation was validated several years later when I was assisting the State Department train people from nine federal agencies who were preparing to deploy to Afghanistan to assist in the reconstruction and development mission. I was pleasantly surprised that a reporter was interested in the field training and planned to spend a week writing a story about our program. I took the opportunity to have lunch with her one day and told her my Gardez media story.

"I believe it," she said. "My boss sent me to Afghanistan a couple of years ago to embed with a PRT and write their story. I spent over a week going on missions with them. It was an incredible experience. I was amazed how dedicated they were to the mission and how much good they were doing. I thought I had an exceptional piece, but when I got back, the editor refused to publish it. Not exciting enough, I guess."

"Those in charge of the media must assume that the American public is only interested in things that go *boom*, but in reality, I think they are interested in all the good things that American service members and civilians are doing over there," I theorized. "I did several presentations and a radio interview about the PRT mission when I was home for my midtour leave from Afghanistan. At the end of each presentation, several people came up to me to express their surprise about what they had heard. They wondered why they never heard about the reconstruction and development mission. My reply was always 'Because the media refuses to report on it.'"

\* \* \* \* \*

After about 4.5 clicks, I entered Villafranca and stopped for my morning break. As was the case during the first twelve stages, memories from 2013 flooded my mind as I walked through the familiar town. Descending down a steep street on the far end of town, I recognized the albergue where we had stayed. It was a three-story skinny section in the middle of a block-long building divided into separate businesses, all sharing walls like the row of town houses where I rented in Burke, Virginia, when I was stationed at the Pentagon. The entry floor was a café/bar where you checked in. A staircase at the back led up to the rooms on the second and third floors.

After taking a shower in 2013, I had gone down to the bar to enjoy a drink while I waited for Mom and Ria to shower and get settled. After forty-five minutes, Mom came down and wondered if I wanted to walk around town.

"Sure, will Ria be joining us?" I asked.

"I haven't seen her. I thought she was down here with you," Mom replied with some surprise.

"Nope, she hasn't come down yet."

"Interesting, I'll go back up and look around again." A few minutes later, she returned with a puzzled look on her face. "She's not up there!"

I started to get a little worried. Ria wasn't real good at navigating strange city streets and had been counting on me to guide Team Camino through towns. What if she had gone out for a walk and got lost?

"We better go look for her."

"I'll go with you," she said before going back up to get her jacket.

A few minutes later, she came back down with an embarrassed smile. Shaking her head, she said, "I found her. She's curled up sleeping on the back of her top bunk."

We tried to wake her for dinner, but she said she wasn't hungry and went right back to sleep. The following days were similar. She seemed to have sufficient energy during the day and maintained a commendable pace but had no energy for much activity once we settled in for the evening.

While the three of us enjoyed breakfast the next morning, a couple, most likely in their sixties, kept glancing in our direction. Finally the gentleman introduced himself and his wife. They were pilgrims from Germany. They both spoke English extremely well. As the days passed, we ran into them over and over again, and they became part of our Camino family.

On the far side of town, I selected the same green route we took in 2013. It headed up a hillside to a trail that generally paralleled the primary route next to a road far below, but was far enough away that you could not see or hear it most of the time. It was earthen track and farm roads through chestnut orchards until it reconnected with the primary after 10.4 clicks. I would then have to join the dangerous route along the busy, loud, high-speed N-VI, but at least I would miss a substantial section of it and could spend the time walking through the woods and quiet orchards. There was only one small village about 8 km into this section, and it was at least a kilometer off of the trail.

As I climbed the hill, I noticed that the trees seemed to be infected with disease, and there had apparently been a fire since I was here last. The hillside was really in bad shape. Once I got home and had access to my photos from the first trip, it would be interesting to compare them to the ones I was taking today.

Pesky tiny black bugs swarmed ceaselessly around my head. They didn't land, let alone bite, but the swarming was relentless. I pulled out my bug repellent for the first time, applied it to my face and neck, and sprayed it in my hair. It had no effect on the obnoxious flying bugs.

The only pilgrims I saw were two bikers with strong Italian accents who rode up behind me and stopped to talk. They seemed very excited to see me and said I was "the winner" in broken English. They apparently were quite impressed that I had tackled the challenge of this route. I countered by telling them that it was far more impressive that they had ridden their bikes up the steep hill. That would have been grueling, far more difficult than walking up it!

After taking a couple of group selfies with our various phone cameras, the bikers

Bikers tackling the challenge

pushed ahead with a wave and a friendly "Buen Camino," and I returned to my reflections.

* * * * *

Sitting in on operational briefings and intelligence updates, I became more and more frustrated when I saw media reports about civilian deaths.

The first problem was how the media portrayed civilian deaths as terrible travesties that should never have been allowed to happen if only we had competent military leaders. Throughout history, civilian deaths have been a normal, inevitable part of war. Even though most Western countries no longer purposefully target them, there have always been civilian deaths. The term "collateral damage" is normally used to describe damage to the civilian infrastructure and unintended civilian deaths. Many non-Western countries and insurgents actually target civilians as a way to pressure the enemy government.

The Taliban and Al Qaeda definitely fall into this category. In fact, although the media never specifically points it out, civilians are their primary target. As soft targets, their gruesome deaths instill horror in the minds of the public. Government forces seem to be a secondary option, likely because they are expected to be targeted in war and therefore not perceived by the public as such a horrific travesty.

The acceptance of civilian deaths during war diminished in Western societies after the use of precision weapons became common based on GPS technology, a relatively recent development. The pendulum has swung so far in the other direction that now even one unintended civilian death caused by an errant US bomb causes furious outrage from both first world countries and the developing world.

Interesting that those outraged people don't seem to care that the Taliban, Al Qaeda, and other terrorist and insurgent organizations actually target civilians, not to mention using them as shields to protect themselves and their munitions, thus preventing themselves and legitimate military targets from being attacked. The international community and media is mostly silent about these atrocities.

Anyway, when there is an accidental civilian casualty resulting from legitimate coalition action targeting insurgents or defending themselves from enemy attack, the media covers the local "outrage" constantly for days on end, fueling the "outrage." It also fuels condemnation from "peace organizations" around the world. Local nationals never riot when the Taliban and Al Qaeda kill civilians, and of course, the media never points out that when civilians are killed by the United States and most of our coalition partners, it is the result a terrible accident.

We never targeted civilians in Afghanistan or Iraq. In fact, following the Rules of Engagement (ROE) routinely prevents us from taking decisive hostile action if there is more than the slightest chance that civilians could get caught in the crossfire. Many American service members have died because of adhering to these ROE.

The Taliban and Al Qaeda, on the other hand, know our ROE and take advantage of it by purposely using their family members, innocent civilians, and prisoners as human shields to protect their hideouts and command centers. They also use hospitals, mosques, and schools to store their munitions and as command centers for planning and resting. They know that we are not allowed to target such facilities. If mentioned by the media, it is a passing comment that is seldom repeated and is easily missed by the vast majority of the unknowing public.

The more familiar I got with the kinetic side of operations, the more I wondered about another aspect of media reporting on civilian deaths. What exactly is the definition of a "civilian"? Who decides if a particular person killed during an attack was a civilian or an enemy combatant? Terrorists and insurgents never admit who they really are, certainly not to the media. Family members and members of an individual's tribe constantly deny their loved ones' ties to the insurgency. Anyone who understands the culture will know that family members of a dead insurgent are not likely to admit that he engaged in terrorist activities. One major reason that they don't want to confess their loved ones' wrongdoing is that the coalition pays families of accidental civilian casualties large sums of money in restitution for their loss.

I saw one media report where they interviewed a man from a nearby village after a US air strike. He was quite insistent that everyone killed were innocent civilians and that there were no Taliban in the area; rather, it was a poor, peaceful community. Just because the person interviewed was an LN does not mean he had any idea what he was talking about or, if he did, that he was telling the truth. Yet the media and international community took his words as gospel.

Media reports of local outrage over civilian deaths came so quickly after an incident that there was obviously no time to investigate and determine who was who. This was especially true when those that died were women or children under the age of eighteen. To the media, women and children are obviously innocent victims. Yet there have been many examples of women hiding munitions under their burkas, and both women and children have been used as suicide attackers.

A little bit more complicated situation is when these women and children are related to and living with terrorists. If the women are supporting their husbands or brothers, feeding them, tending to their wounds, and giving them moral support—are they really "innocent civilians," or are they aiding and abetting the terrorists? They may even be coconspirators. If a sixteen- or seventeen-year-old "child" helps his father perpetrate attacks, is this really an innocent child or a terrorist in training?

Is it really coalition strikes against high-value targets (HVT) and terrorist camps that is endangering "innocent" women and children? Is this the great evil? Or would it be more prudent to blame the supposedly loving terrorist husband and father who is purposefully using his family as human shields to protect himself, bomb-making materials, and munitions and trainees from attack?

I think it would be interesting for someone to investigate how many truly innocent people (both Westerners and Muslims) have been killed because the coalition Rules of Engagement (ROE) compel us to refrain from attacking a HVT because the terrorist's family is with him.

Bottom line—what exactly is a civilian, and who determines who the "innocent civilians" are on the battlefield? In a guerrilla insurgency, one should not jump to conclusions like the media and numerous international "humanitarian" organizations always seem to do.

After observing battlefield dynamics over the course of four combat deployments, one thing I am convinced about is, you should never take a media report at face value. They seldom look below the surface at the underlying details or root causes. They just rush to get a story on the news in a way that will have the greatest possible emotional impact on viewers. Nor should you believe everything international human rights groups say, especially when they have an agenda they are trying to convince you of.

Even if you are naive enough to believe that people tell the truth all the time, don't forget that the "fog of war" is a basic principle of war. Seldom is anything in a combat zone what it appears to be at first glance.

\* \* \* \* \*

A little over three clicks into the green route, I took a short rest at a vista to admire the rolling hills that surrounded me and drink some water. I was concerned to notice my water bottle was already half gone. I dug out the guidebook to see if there was a fountain along the trial. Obviously, I had become complacent in my mission planning. Not only was this stretch sparse in regards to villages, but there were no fountains marked along the entire route. Not good! The guidebook was not clear, but even getting to the small village with the bar that was well off The Way was likely a good 5 km ahead of my current position.

If only I had paid closer attention, I could have filled up my CamelBak to get me through this long stretch. Too late now. Even with strict rationing, I was out of water well before I saw a sign pointing toward the bar. The village was advertised as 1.5 km away, but this was closer than the village where I would connect with the primary trail, so I turned right and headed down the side trip.

By the time I got to the village, my mouth was extremely dry. To my dismay, the café/bar was closed for the season. Apparently, too few pilgrims stopped by this time of year to justify keeping it open. I was not a happy camper.

I went in search of a village fountain. After about a block, I saw a local and showed him my empty water bottle and asked, "Donde esté agua?"

He did not speak English but indicated there was something up the street. I headed off in the direction he pointed. Soon I was exiting the far side of the village. I had not seen a fountain. I started to panic. I would have to go back into the center of the village and try again.

As usual, the village appeared almost deserted. A bread truck was making its way through town, and people started coming out to procure their daily bread. After buying a loaf, a farmer headed toward his barn. I got his attention and showed him my empty bottle.

"Necessito agua por favor?" I pleaded.

He waved me into the barn and pointed out a water spigot on the back wall. I smiled and thanked him profusely. I filled the bottle and drank it completely dry. Refilling it, I thanked the nice man again and headed back toward the Camino. Near the edge of the village, a woman came out of her house with a pitcher of lemon water and offered it to me. I politely declined and showed her my full bottle of water. Thanking her, I proceeded out of town, wondering if this could have been the wife of the first man I had talked to who had pointed me toward the fountain.

\* \* \* \* \*

Some events stand out in a person's memory much clearer than others. As you would probably suspect, mundane activities such as planning missions, writing reports and other administrative tasks, meeting with governors, attending weekly security meetings with key Afghan officials, checking on the progress of construction projects, and even ribbon-cutting ceremonies became routine, and I don't remember many specifics. However, some activities could be categorized as "significant emotional events," thus burning an image in my mind that cannot be removed. These contribute to what we affectionately call "war stories."

One such story is actually a couple events that were rather serious while they were occurring but I now find humorous when related together—that is, humorous in a military sort of way.

The person with ADCON over all AF personnel assigned to PRTs was the commander of the 755th Expeditionary Mission Support Group (755 EMSG). The person in this position was my official supervisor while in-country. Day-to-day, I took orders from the TACON chain of command, the Army brigade commander in charge of Regional Command-East (RC-E). But Colonel Mike wrote or endorsed all Air Force performance reports, had final say for disciplinary actions, and ensured that his personnel were being used in a manner consistent with the job description the AF agreed to when they signed up to fill the joint position. To adequately fulfill his responsibilities, Colonel Mike occasionally traveled to the PRT FOBs to touch base with his troops.

His first visit to FOB Gardez was in June 2006. During our evening staff meeting the night he arrived with the chief master sergeant (CMSgt) who served as his SEA, I asked him if he wanted to get the "full PRT experience" by accompanying our convoy to conduct a QA/QC at a school construction project. He jumped at the chance! Of course, the chief wasn't going to let the colonel have all the fun, so he decided he needed to go along. We added a vehicle to the convoy for them and assigned two soldiers from our SECFOR and my SEA to accompany our group leadership. I stayed back to do my favorite pastime: combat typing.

In midafternoon, I was returning to my office from grabbing something from my room when our operations officer ran up to me, obviously worked up about something.

"Ma'am, the convoy hit an IED!" he exclaimed.

"Crap," I mumbled as I took off running toward the Joint Operations Center (JOC) with the Lt hot on my heels.

The JOC was a buzz of activity. As soon as we entered, the JOC captain briefed us that the convoy was on the way back from the QA/QC at the school when the second vehicle hit an IED. The uparmored HMMWV had sustained significant damage, and there were some injuries, but nothing too serious. The team secured the area, and our medic was treating the injured. A medi-vac helicopter was en route from Bagram, and the maneuver unit was generating a convoy with EOD, intel, and a recovery vehicle (large armored tow truck) to investigate the scene and bring everybody home.

"The DVs are fine," the captain assured me. "They are helping provide security."

I raised my eyebrows, somewhat intrigued but not really surprised. That was consistent with their personalities.

"Very good. Sounds like you have everything under control. I'm going to go next door and get on a secure line to notify the wing commander," I said, assuming that the JOC had already notified the brigade commander.

The wing commander was the brigadier general in charge of the Air Force Forces (AFFOR) component in Afghanistan. He was also Col. Mike's direct supervisor. This was not a phone call I was going to enjoy.

A major answered the phone. "He is in a meeting and cannot be disturbed," he informed me when I asked if the general was available.

"I think he will want to talk to me right away," I explained. "Colonel Mike was on a convoy that just got hit by an IED."

The major went to get the general.

A bit nervously, I explained the situation as best I knew at the time. I wondered if the general noticed the slight quiver in my voice.

"The colonel and chief were not in the vehicle that was hit. They were right behind it."

"How is everybody?" he asked.

"There are some injuries, but amazingly, nothing life threatening. A medi-vac is on its way from Bagram."

Once he was assured everyone was alive, his manner lightened. "When you send someone off on a trip and tell them to have a blast, you don't expect them to take it literally."

My tension evaporated, and I couldn't help but chuckle. Apparently, he had a good sense of humor.

When everybody returned to base, I got the full brief. The intel troops suspected that the Taliban had observed the convoy go into the project site. There was only one road to the school, so the convoy had to come out the same way it had gone in. They had had enough time to place the IED while the team conducted the inspection of the construction site.

Miraculously, everybody inside the vehicle got away with little more than bumps and bruises. Even the gunner who had been thrown about a hundred feet had only sustained an injured leg and arm; and possibly a concussion, but no broken bones.

The next time Col. Mike and the chief visited was Thanksgiving. As was tradition, myself and the maneuver commander were helping serve the meal to the enlisted personnel and junior officers. Col. Mike and the chief joined us. They were supposed to return to Bagram the following day, but a winter storm grounded all the helicopters. They could not get through the Terra Pass due to low cloud level and blowing snow. We had a supply convoy scheduled to depart that afternoon for Bagram. A bit leery because of what happened the last time I sent them on a convoy, I offered to have the convoy take them. To my surprise, they were not concerned and quickly agreed.

As far as I knew, everything went fine, and the convoy arrived at Bagram the following morning on schedule. It was not until a few days later when the team got back that I found out the colonel and chief had another close call. The road down the far side of the Terra Pass was very windy and somewhat steep. It was cut out of the mountainside, had no shoulder, and had a five-hundred-foot drop-off at the edge. There was no guard rail to stop vehicles from going over the cliff, just some flimsy plastic poles marking the side of the road. Apparently, the HMMWV with the DVs hit a patch of ice and had trouble stopping as it slid sideways toward the edge. The driver managed to get the vehicle stopped with only inches to spare.

Both Col. Mike and the general, by this time a three-star, attended my retirement ceremony at the Pentagon in 2012. I told the story of how I had tried to kill Col Mike twice, but for some reason he still talked to me and even traveled from his retirement home to attend the ceremony. Everyone got a good chuckle about the general's comment about not expecting to be taken literally when he told the colonel to have a blast.

* * * * *

When I reached the bottom of the hill and entered the village, I was distressed to find signs on both fountains warning the water was not guaranteed to be safe. I had gone about four clicks since filling up my bottle, and it was empty once again. I saw a supermarket sign to my left toward the middle of town. It was the wrong direction, but I could buy a bottle of water there. When I arrived, the supermarket was closed. I looked at my watch: 1420. They were closed for the afternoon break / siesta. This was just not my day. The universal conspiracy against me was reemerging!

I had only covered about fifteen clicks so far. Too soon to stop. So, hot and thirsty, I resumed my trek along the side of the busy road. Fortunately, cement Jersey Barriers about a meter tall separated the trail from the traffic most of the way. Still, the loud traffic noise was very aggravating after my long day walking through chestnut orchards in almost complete silence; my parched mouth did not help my mood any.

* * * * *

Sharing a meal at the UNAMA compound.

Our close relationship with the UNAMA office in Gardez resulted in an opportunity for me to participate in a serious incident and help shape a positive resolution.

UNAMA had the "lead" for the PDCs that we participated in, and they had good working relationships with nongovernmental organizations (NGOs) who were doing development projects within our AOR. These NGOs would not communicate or coordinate with the PRT because we were part of the military coalition. Sometimes it was because communicating with us would be a violation of their principles, as they were anti-military. For many others, it was more practical. If they were perceived as collaborating with the military coalition, Afghans associated with the insurgents or who feared for their lives if they opposed the insurgents would not work with them. For the NGOs working in these unstable areas, it was dangerous for there to be any hint of contact between themselves and us. UNAMA was often able to bridge this gap by being a go-between. This was not a foolproof solution, however. Some NGOs refused to even talk to UNAMA. They insisted that they were independent and were not about to coordinate with anybody, sometimes not even Afghan officials.

Hence it was very important to have a good working relationship with UNAMA, and we did. Besides joint missions such as the visit to Shai Kot, collaborating in regards to PDC meetings, and conducting joint meetings with the governors—we often visited each other's compounds to discuss development theory, long-term objectives, and how best to advise the Afghan officials. They would come to the FOB to shop at our mini base exchange (BX) and join us for dinner. In turn, they invited myself and my leadership team to their compound for dinner. We not only had a good working relationship but also developed friendships.

So one day when they called in a bit of panic and asked for help, we swung into high gear.

"Omar is surrounded by Taliban who want to kill him. He can't get away," the leader of the Gardez UNAMA office explained. "He went to his home village in Zurmat District to visit family. The Taliban found out he was there and have surrounded the house. They are ordering him to come out and threatening to kill him and his family because he is working for us."

I went to the JOC and asked them to upchannel the report to RC-E and then contacted the Paktia governor. We agreed to meet at the Provincial Control Center (PCC) at the ANA base about twenty minutes from our FOB. The governor notified the Afghan general in charge of the PCC, and he reached out to representatives from all the local security organizations to send a rep to the command center. By the time we generated a convoy and arrived, there was a full house.

As the ranking US military officer in the room, I assumed the responsibility of facilitating and guiding the meeting. Local security officials familiar with the area in question informed us that it was a hotbed of the insurgency. Any overt attempt by ANSF to rescue Omar would be met with strong and lethal resistance. They could not get anywhere close to the residence. After extensive discussion, we decided to send in several ANP in civilian clothing and in a civilian vehicle.

After several hours of preparation, which to me was aggravatingly long, the team was dispatched from a nearby ANP HQ. After another long wait for them to negotiate the extremely poor road conditions, the ANP HQ informed us our deception had worked. The team was able to get all the way up to the house and somehow extracted Omar under the cover of darkness. They were safely on their way to Gardez.

What an incredible feeling to have been a central part of such a noble mission.

\* \* \* \* \*

My feet were screaming "Enough!" very loudly by the time I approached the next albergue after about four clicks. Altogether I estimated 19.6 km for the day. I had hoped for more, but it was not to be.

I was the first person assigned to my room, but as was typical, another lady had arrived by the time I was done with my shower. She was from Arizona, so we had a good discussion about my time at Luke and the second home I now shared with my parents in Gold Canyon, east of Phoenix.

When we went to the bar for social hour, we ran into Diana. This was the second time I had met up with her today. We had had coffee in Villafranca. She had taken the main route along the busy road and reported no problems finding water.

Sharing a bottle of wine, we visited throughout social hour and then went together to dinner at 1900.

I took the day off from my service study. Looking over the guidebook, I determined mission planning was not necessary. The maximum distance between albergues from here to the middle of stage 27 was 3.4 km. After about midday, I would just take it one village at a time and see how I felt. After all, "Flexibility is the key to airpower."

Before turning in for the night, I read chapters 46 and 47 in the *Seeking* book. Nabeel was done investigating and decided to give up trying to make the decision on his own. Intellectually, he had found extensive evidence for Christianity, but his strong ties to his Islamic upbringing and love for his family made his heart yearn for Islam to be the truth. He prayed countless times over five months that God would reveal to him whether he was the God of the Quran or the God of the Bible. Nabeel promised that if God unmistakably showed him which was the truth, he would believe it no matter the cost.

When God gave him a vision that indicated the Gospel was the truth, he still battled with himself in a way that I was all too familiar with as I struggled with my own doubts over the years. He asked questions that I had asked myself and others many times when trying to sort through my confusion. He wanted to know how he could be certain that the devil was not trying to mislead him so his soul would belong to the devil forever. His decision on this issue would affect the status of his soul for all of eternity. How could he be positive he was interpreting the vision correctly? Similarly, how could he be sure that his subconscious, his own intellect, was not leading him astray?[51]

I have never had anything that I believed was a vision or dream from God. But many times I have prayed for guidance regarding what to believe and what to do in a particular situation. I have asked God many times to reveal to me what His will was for me to do.

"Should I take the deployment orders to Iraq or retire in a few months?" was a prime example of this. At times like this, I wished

---

[51] Qureshi, chapters 46–47.

that God would burn a bush in front of me and speak to me from the flames, tell me in no uncertain terms what to do.

I felt that I should take the assignment. Was that God whispering to my soul? Was it my ego who did not want to revert to lieutenant colonel for retirement? Or was it my intense desire to prove to myself that I had finally conquered the professional and mental hell I had been going through for several years, that I had gotten my act together and could honorably and successfully complete a combat deployment?

This was just one example of the common intellectual dilemma I faced countless times over the years. How could I know when it was God talking to me, or when it was my own personal desires, or when the devil was leading me astray?

Man, I could relate to Nabeel's mental struggle!

# CHAPTER 32

La Portela de Valcarce to Alto do Poio; 23.4 Kilometers
26 Sep 2015
D+28

The restaurant was closed, so I headed out into the dim morning light at 0750. The guidebook showed a café in the village about 2.4 km away. No problem, I often enjoyed exercise before breakfast. I wore my headlight as a safety precaution since the trail was merely the skinny shoulder of the road. There were no Jersey Barriers shielding us from the traffic. Fortunately, the early Saturday morning traffic was light.

It wasn't long before life found me enjoying a tortilla con chorizo (no pan), OJ, and coffee while warming myself up after a chilly start of the day. I studied the guidebook to refresh my memory about today's mission. In about four clicks, I would start a steep climb I distinctly remembered from 2013. Anytime now, I should start seeing signs advertising horses for rent to help pilgrims get up the hill.

\* \* \* \* \*

It is amazing how combat has a habit of changing one's perspective regarding their military profession. When I first met the platoon that was assigned as our security force (SECFOR), they were gung ho young infantrymen eager get into the fight. In fact, they were more than a little upset that they had been assigned as the SECFOR for a PRT. In their minds, they were being relegated to the menial tasks of bus driver and babysitting for civilians and noncombat forces on a diplomatic mission. They had no concept of how the reconstruction and development mission played into the overall war effort. And frankly, they didn't care to learn. What they wanted to do was to hunt down and kill the enemy, to destroy their capability and will to fight.

This was likely the basis for the friction between them and the rest of the PRT from day one. They routinely referred to the rest of us as "the PRT." Although I tried, it proved impossible to convince them that they were part of the PRT. In their minds, they were assigned to protect the PRT; they were not part of it. Their platoon and Army ADCON brigade leadership did not attempt to change their perception. In fact, their words and actions reinforced it, both during training and while in-country.

Although we never really resolved their perception, their attitude toward the mission—and combat in general—evolved as the year progressed.

Possibly due to warrior bravado, they wanted nothing to do with wimpy add-on protection for their IBA, such as the neck and groin protectors. They were not comfortable, and in the case of the groin protectors, frankly they made a warrior look stupid. I ordered the items be worn but eventually discovered they would remove them once outside the gate and away from the sight of my senior staff.

After the IED hit our convoy in June, I did not hear as much trash talk about wanting to be in combat or complaining about being babysitters for diplomats.

During the ambush in November, several members of the SECFOR sustained serious injury, and one had to be medically evacuated to Germany. Afterward, they no longer had any interest in engaging the enemy in combat. The horrors and dangers of war were now strikingly real to them. The glamour of heroic battle as portrayed in Hollywood movies had been revealed as the falsity it was.

The incident also changed their opinion regarding wearing the neck and groin protectors. The soldier that was injured the worst had shrapnel wounds all over his legs. The medic reported he could see the outline of the groin protector in the wound pattern.

"If he hadn't been wearing it, he would not be able to have children," the medic explained, getting to the heart of the matter.

After that, the soldiers were more than happy to wear the protective gear.

The closer we got to going home, the harder it was to motivate them to go on missions. They didn't understand why I would risk their lives just to check on a stupid project or meet with some government official. Why couldn't the governors come to the base for meetings? Why did we have to go to their office? I tried to explain to them that they were the governors of the provinces. Equating their office to the governor of a state in the United States, I tried to impress on them the importance of treating them with respect in their country. They didn't buy it.

The last week was the hardest. It was like pulling teeth to get them out of the gate. Obviously, this is why discipline in the military is so important. After a while, people are not too inclined to continue risking their lives. It is incumbent on military leaders to compel them to carry out their mission despite the risks. Without a disciplined chain of command, this would be impossible.

Reflecting on the evolution of their attitude prompted me to think about how so many in humanitarian organizations, the general American public, and of course, the media believe that military leaders are dangerous. That given the chance, they will resort to violence and war at the first sign of trouble or disagreement with another country. Nothing could be further from the truth. Those that have experienced war are the least likely to recommend war if there is reasonable hope that the situation can be resolved in a peaceful manner without compromising the security and sovereignty of the United States.

This said, military leaders who have fought and sacrificed for their country are not going to recommend rolling over and bowing down to the demands or hostile actions of dictators, terrorists, or countries who want to harm us. They will recommend war if peaceful means have little chance of achieving our national objectives, and if we go to war, they expect that the country will be "all-in." If we're going to risk the lives of military personnel, political leaders need to be willing to take decisive action that will overwhelm the enemy and compel surrender as quickly as possible. Half measures to make political points are a stupid waste of the lives of those who have volunteered to defend their country.

While in the RC-E commander's office after Governor Taniwal's assassination, I was awed to see the photos of each soldier, sailor, airman, and marine who had died in RC-E since he took command. He hung the pictures so he would be reminded every day, and every time he made a decision, how serious the stakes were. He needed to ensure that the mission got accomplished in the most effective way possible, while at the same time not *needlessly* risking the lives of those under his command. The troops didn't mind risking their lives as long as they were not throwing them away in some useless half-hearted action that had little chance of success. If they were going to die, they wanted it to count for something.

\* \* \* \* \*

After a few short kilometers, I stopped for another grandé OJ before starting the steep climb. I would need sugar to get me up the hill. At least that was my excuse.

Because Ria was tired and the standard stage 26 trek was 29 km, we planned to stop early and stay at an albergue in Herrerías. It was still a commendable day's trek, 20.9 km. Ria shipped her pack there. When we arrived, we were not at all impressed with the accommodations. There was talk among other peregrinos that the place had been having a bedbug problem. Even though the hospitalero assured us that the problem had been resolved/eradicated, we were leery. It certainly didn't look clean us. So we decided to grab Ria's pack and proceed about halfway up the steep hill. It was 3.4 clicks to the next albergue in the tiny hamlet of La Faba. In that 3.4 km, we ascended 215 meters in elevation. It was very difficult for the exhausted Ria. Not only were we making a strenuous climb after already walking 21 km, but Ria now was carrying her pack for the first time since day one.

It took us quite awhile to make the ascent, stopping to rest frequently. Our efforts were rewarded with what was likely the albergue with the most character that we stayed in during the trek. It appeared to be relatively new but boosted a rustic mountain atmosphere. Our room had eleven beds and wood plank ceiling supports like my log home back in Washington. The showers were downstairs where the walls and floor were made of rugged rock tile. It had been love at first sight.

\* \* \* \* \*

I still get a good chuckle out of the ending of one of my war stories.

After Gov. Taniwal's death, it took a few weeks for President Karzai to appoint a new governor. We had to encourage the deputy governor to make a public speech and transmit it over the radio to assure the citizens of the province that the government was still in place and functioning. He was nervous about doing this because he feared he might be next. The governor in Logar Province almost completely curtailed his activity outside the capital for the same reason.

I submitted a project request to brigade for two armored SUVs for each of my governors. They were very expensive and would have to be imported, but it would allow the governors and their security teams to confidently travel out to engage the public.

The day after the new governor assumed his position in Paktia, he came to the FOB for a tour and briefing by both myself and the maneuver commander. A major part my briefing was to discuss the list of ongoing and requested projects. Of course, I told him about my request to get him two armored SUVs.

"Please encourage your superiors to get them here before I die," Governor Rahmat said casually. I smiled. The new governor obviously had a sense of humor.

Lt. Col. Meck delivers armored SUVs to Governor Rahmat at FOB Gardez.

Finally the brigade commander was enthusiastic about one of my ideas. Not only did he approve the four vehicles I requested, but he approved two vehicles for each of the ten provinces in RC-E.

I am happy to report that we were able to deliver before Governor Rahmat died!

\* \* \* \* \*

Galicia border sign.

After ascending another 150 meters in 2.5 km, I crossed the border from the province of Castilla Y León into Galatia. To my surprise, Tom arrived just as I was looking for somebody to take my picture next to the welcome sign. We hiked together for the next 2 km into the picturesque rustic mountain village of O'Cebreiro. Many buildings dated back to the ninth and eleventh centuries. At an elevation of over 1,300 meters, I'm sure the thick stone walls where designed to protect villagers from the cold mountain air and biting wind. I think this is my favorite village along The Way. Although timing did not make it reasonable either time, this would be an awesome place to RON, but I would recommend getting here no later than 1400 to have plenty of time to explore the historical chapel and museum.

Tom saw some friends sitting at a table outside a café in the village square and decided to eat lunch with them. All morning I had had been thinking about the restaurant where we ate breakfast two years before with anticipation of having lunch there, so I took my leave and went inside the building across the square. I was treated to an exceptional bowl of garlic soup and a cerveza while I studied the guidebook to determine how much further I wanted to go. After a gradual 8.5 km ascent, there were two albergues at the summit before the trail started a long, sometimes-steep descent. I decided this would be my goal for the day.

Although I looked through the attached gift shop and bought a yellow arrow hat pin, I resisted the temptation to buy any other souvenirs. With another six stages to go, the last thing I wanted was extra weight in my pack.

I stopped to touch base with Tom before leaving town. He hoped to do another 15 km before stopping for the night.

"I'm going to have a look around here a little before heading out," he said.

"I wouldn't mind that myself, but with my feet, I think it best that I get going so I can take it slow. See you along The Way." I smiled and headed down the street. I knew I had been slowing him down when he walked with me the last 2 km. It was best for me to go it alone.

\* \* \* \* \*

In the weeks leading up to our rotation home, a couple more of our major project proposals were approved. A lot of work had gone into preparing and coordinating the proposals. We would not get to see the projects completed, but I was happy that they were at least approved before we left.

The dream of the new Paktia governor was to build an agricultural university in Gardez. Before the Soviets and Taliban decimated the province, it had a thriving agricultural economy. His dream was to rejuvenate it. The university would provide the intellectual foundation for the population. In an interesting twist to the norm, he was able to raise the funding needed for the university buildings themselves.

Governor Rahmat turns the first shovel of dirt at the ground breaking ceremony for the Gardez University, Apr 2007.

All he asked of the PRT was to fund the security wall. It would be quite large because of the size of the campus, but with so much funding coming from the Afghan government and international sources, my superiors had no problem funding the wall. One of my last missions, and one of the first for my replacement, was to participate in the groundbreaking ceremony for the Gardez University.

Additionally, the project that was my pride and joy was also approved. To emphasize our intention to reward good security and local support for the Afghan government with major impact projects, we worked with Afghan provincial and district officials for six months on a project proposal for a hydroelectric plant along a small river in the stable Ahmad Abad District. Numerous site surveys and evaluations were required to determine the best location. A series of meetings were conducted with the Shuras of the affected villages who needed to approve the use of the land and the installation of the infrastructure that would distribute the electricity to the buildings. Extensive coordination was also required with district, province, and national officials from several affected ministries. We then had to get bids from at least three Afghan contractors. Because of the size of the river and the amount of water flow, the plant would only be able to provide electricity for a handful of nearby villages, but it would give electricity to 1,500 families and businesses who had never had it before. I wished we could do more, but this was at least a good start.

As exciting as it was to see these projects get started, I left with some concerns about the overall reconstruction and development mission. The PRT had worked on 120 projects that were funded by the US military and 35 funded by USAID. We had also conducted surveys and coordination for numerous big-ticket projects that were part of multiprovince initiatives, such as district government headquarters and district ANP facilities. Our communications team installed solar-powered police radio antennas and receiving systems in each district.

I felt that our accomplishments for the year were impressive. However, I was leery about the sustainability of what we had accomplished and the ability of the Afghans to continue the progress.

National funding was a major problem.

USAID had funded the installation of a generator in Gardez. It provided electricity for about half the city for three to four hours a day. USAID even funded a training course to train locals to operate and maintain it. What was uncertain was how the government was going to fund fuel for the generator and maintenance parts, and who was going to train eventual replacements for the current employees. We helped them set up a billing system to charge users for the electricity. When we left, the entity with the largest outstanding bill was the provincial government complex.

With the intent to strengthen security, the US State Department delivered a large number of police vehicles. However, the vehicles were used sparingly because the government could not afford the fuel to keep them moving, let alone the maintenance costs.

Similar problems were experienced with the clinics and school buildings that we funded. There was no effective system or national budget to pay the medical staff and teachers. They also lacked funding for medicines, medical equipment, and school supplies such as books. Any funds that did become available for these purposes came from the international community.

Basically, the lack of an effective economy prevented the establishment of a credible tax system that would provide the funds needed to implement and sustain programs that were designed to be government-funded. Speaking of government-funded programs, I suspected that we were dooming them to failure by basically setting up a socialistic government that was responsible for funding way too much.

An example of the major impediments to developing an economic system that could sustain the country was the dangerous security situation. One of the largest copper deposits in the world was in Logar Province. Throughout our year, there were discussions of building and operating a copper mine at PDC meetings. Extensive plans were developed by international organizations and the provincial government, which not only included the mine itself but the construction of a village to support the mine and where the workers would live. The problem was that it would take an extremely large investment by a company willing to build and operate the mine. It was very difficult to find a company willing to take the risk because of the lack of security and the insurgents' SOP of blowing up projects that benefited the community and helped the government enhance its legitimacy. Of course, the government's lack of legitimacy in the eyes of the population was in part due to their inability to provide effective security and fund social support programs. Without an economic base that would be jump-started by such a large mining operation, the government would never have the funds needed for the expected services, to include providing adequate security.

I heard a rumor before I left that a Chinese company was considering it, but I have no idea if anything ever came of it.

One thing I understood clearly by the time we left was that things were very complicated. Every situation had countless factors at its roots. Every possible action we could take had numerous potential third and fourth "orders of effect," many of which were difficult to anticipate. Nothing was black and white. One plus one rarely equaled two. Cause-and-effect relationships where elusive at best.

Bottom line—if there were easy answers, we would not still be there trying to solve the same issues fifteen years later!

\* \* \* \* \*

Normally I can go pretty quick across flat traverses, but today I might as well have been low crawling. It was after 1600 before I dragged myself up the steep last half kilometer to the Alto do Poio summit. The nice albergue was full, so I checked into the hotel across the road. The title "hotel" and cost of twenty euros made me think it would be nicer than the albergue, but it was not. After my shower, I went back across the street for a drink and the early dinner they served at the bar.

I decided my objective for the next day would be a casa rural 24 km away. It was just a half click further than I had gone today, so I figured it was doable. However, anticipating a late arrival, I decided to call and reserve a room. This locked me into going that far since I had to give them my credit card number to hold the room.

After dinner I returned to the hotel and read through day 25 of my service study before turning in early.

The central verse for today's study was Acts 3:6. A poor beggar who could not walk asked Peter and John for spare change. They did not have any, but they gave something better.

> I have no silver and gold, but what I do have I give to you. In the name of Jesus Christ of Nazareth, rise up and walk!

The message emphasized that giving money, food, clothing, etc. to the poor benefits them and helps them get through today and tomorrow. However, a major part of our ministry should be to inform them of Jesus's eternal gift of salvation. In the long run, this is a far better gift. The implication was to be cautious that we don't get so busy helping people with their daily needs that we forget to help them with their eternal needs.[52]

This, of course, is wise teaching: the "teach them to fish, rather than give them fish" theory. I think of this philosophy often when considering our welfare system in the United States. It also applies to short-term mission trips conducted by caring Christian organizations. My church sends teams to Mexico and Haiti a couple times a year. The one I'm most familiar with involves medical and dental teams. Their objectives are very similar to the medical operations that we conducted in Afghanistan. Our PRT doc and I had the same concerns about these operations. What good were we really doing? Treating a wound or giving them a couple weeks' worth the pain medications and vitamins had absolutely no long-term effect on their physical well-being. For the PRT, we justified our MEDOPs because they helped us build goodwill, which contributed to stability. Although not our objective per se, we occasionally were the recipients of some useful intelligence offered by grateful villagers. In order to have a long-term medical impact, our doc started insisting that Afghan doctors join us so that he could mentor them and improve

---

[52] Fryar, p. 52–53.

their medical capabilities. We started this about halfway through, making both of us feel much better about doing the operations.

Stability and intelligence benefits did not apply to short-term Christian mission trips. As I considered today's study, I thought about the religious aspects of the mission trips that I had heard about during post-mission dinner events at the chapel. Our missions pastor often related stories about non-Christian people that came to the churches where the medical operations were happening in order to get treatment. While there, the pastor would explain the gospel to them through Haitian interpreters. Several people who had practiced witchcraft (very common in the area where our teams went) had accepted Jesus as their Savior and converted to Christianity. Many had become strong members of the local churches where they had been saved. Now this was a worthy outcome!

# CHAPTER 33

## Alto do Poio to Pintín, 24.2 Kilometers
## 27 Sep 2015
## D+29

My disappointment with this accommodation continued to grow in the morning. The host knocked on my door at 0720 to ensure I was getting ready. A first—and I would not call it a friendly courtesy wake-up. He was actually rather rude and impatient. Fortunately, I was ready to go when he knocked. I picked up my pack and followed him down the stairs to the bar.

"Do you want coffee?" he asked abruptly.

"Si, por favor," I replied.

Noticing the mother-and-daughter hiking pair I had met briefly at check-in eating toasted bread, I asked the host if I could have some. I had to say it three times before he acknowledged that he had heard me and went to the kitchen in an irritated huff.

After a few minutes, he brought out a large toasted croissant already cut in half. I was impressed. This is the first time that I had a toasted croissant. He gave me some strawberry jam, which I spread on each side. Not bad at all.

I was about halfway done when the two ladies left with a friendly wave and a happy "Buen Camino!" The host started glaring at me from other side of the counter, not even trying to hide his impatience.

Irritated, I stuffed the remaining bread in my mouth and gulped the rest of my coffee.

"Baño?" I said, indicating I needed to use the restroom before leaving.

He was not happy but pointed to a hallway at the back of the room. He continued to stare at me as I put on my pack and prepped my headlamp since he was kicking me out thirty minutes before the sun came up.

"Tres euro," he said with a bit of hostility in his voice.

"I thought it was included in the price of the room," I mumbled, remembering that the mother-daughter team had told me breakfast was included when I was registering the night before.

He ignored me, so I gave him a 5€ note, and he indicated he wanted change instead. I dumped out my money bag to show him I didn't have exact change. Irritated once again, he went to the register and brought back two 1€ pieces. He quickly shook my hand, wished me Buen Camino, and pointed toward the door. He locked the door as soon as I crossed the threshold. It was 0745 and dark. What a jerk.

\* \* \* \* \*

When I left Afghanistan in April 2007, I was exhausted to the deepest part of my being. I had worked sixteen- to eighteen-hour days, seven days a week, for a year. The stress involved in planning off-base missions and sending troops outside the wire every day with the full knowledge that they could be ambushed or hit an IED at any moment can really wear on a responsible commander.

Although discipline and combat scenario training are designed to enable outstanding performance in dangerous and high-pressure situations, I think it is fairly normal to wonder how you will actually respond when faced with sometimes violent or at least high-stakes situations in a combat zone.

I was surprised at how well I was able to handle the daily stressors of our mission. The off-base missions I went on were not as stressful as I thought they would be considering the threat. I actually enjoyed them as a break from the administrative office work and dealing with the Army. It was on these missions when I felt like I was doing something that would make a substantial difference for the Afghans. I often thanked God for the opportunity to be a part of such an honorable mission—one that I was convinced would bring prosperity, security, and hope for a better future to the people of Paktia and Logar provinces. Still, my dedication, enthusiasm, and intense focus on doing as much as possible before leaving was exhausting!

The seemingly constant emotional badgering (friendly fire) from my Army superiors certainly did not help the situation. We had arrived in April, and the problems had started in May when the SECFOR private was caught sleeping while on perimeter security. Then of course, there was the IG complaint about the SECFOR being forced to work for the "noncombat Air Force," the alleged inappropriate photo by a junior officer, the investigation after the ambush near the Pakistan border, and the final straw, the NVG investigation. This all combined to progressively wear me down.

The exhaustion from the daily stresses had significantly diminished my ability to emotionally handle the firestorm from above. Although relieved and very appreciative that the general had stepped in and taken low-level, local action, I was devastated. Negative paperwork was not something I was accustomed to receiving!

Of course, being placed on administrative hold and not allowed to fly home with the rest of my team was a gut-wrenching punishment in itself.

Safely behind closed doors in a borrowed office at the 755 EMSG HQ tent after my infuriating encounter with the Army private who had been ordered to make sure I did not get on the plane with my team, I had a mental breakdown. I started crying uncontrollably. After a while, I was able to pull myself together enough to call the mental health section at the base hospital. I asked for the doctor that I had talked to when I was stressed out about the ambush investigation a few months earlier. He already knew some of the background of what was happening and how I was handling it, so I figured it was safe to talk to him. To my dismay, he had recently rotated back to his home station.

"Can I arrange for you to talk to somebody else?" the clerk who answered the phone asked, obviously noticing my broken emotional condition.

"No. Thank you," I said and hung up. I really didn't want to start over with somebody I didn't know.

This made me even more upset. Not only was my world falling apart around me and the Army was treating me like a criminal, but now I didn't have anybody I could really talk to.

I called the general's office to tell him what the Army had done at the passenger terminal, but he was not available. I was able to talk briefly with his executive officer who was aware of the general situation.

"Can you please tell the Army to just leave me alone?" I managed to blurt out between sobs.

Apparently he was worried about me because about five minutes later, the EMSG exec knocked on the door to check on me.

After the LOC meeting with the general, I was cleared to fly back to Lackland AFB in San Antonio, TX. Even though my career was protected, my struggles with anxiety had just begun.

* * * * *

I found a very inviting café in the second village I came to. It was so relaxing that I decided to do the day's service study while drinking a large glass of OJ.

The theme for day 26 was that when things don't go as planned and unexpected circumstances throw you off, God may be using the circumstances for great things in support of (ISO) His greater purpose. It is so easy for us to get frustrated and even mad at God because our plans are disrupted, sometimes even our plans to serve God. Why would God obstruct our service for Him or important things in our life dealing with our family or jobs? When we feel this way, we must consider that Paul was imprisoned for two years. Obviously, this interfered with planting new churches and conducting discipleship of the leaders of those churches he had already started. Why would God interfere with such important work by allowing Paul to be imprisoned? So he could write several books of the New Testament and spread the Gospel to the prison guards—that's why. We must remember that God is wise and omnipotent. He has a plan that we may not be able to fathom at the time. We must trust in His wisdom and be on the lookout (BOLO—a cop term) for the good He is doing through the circumstances we are going through. The text referenced Paul's words in his letter to the Philippians, chapter 1 verses 12–13: "I want you to know, brothers, that what has happened to me has really served to advance the Gospel, so that it has become known throughout the whole imperial guard and to all the rest that my imprisonment is for Christ."[53]

\* \* \* \* \*

Once back on the Camino, I found myself in a steep, sometimes-dangerous descent. The elevation graph in the guidebook had a danger [!] symbol indicating danger, so I was expecting this development. As I carefully selected the spot for each step, my thoughts drifted to how the concept I had just read about could be applied to the hell I went through at the end of my PRT deployment and the years that followed. It had certainly changed the trajectory of my career.

Under normal SF progression, one would expect to go to a headquarters staff position after their third command, be promoted to colonel, and then become the director of security forces for a MAJCOM, or a Mission Support Group (MSG) commander at the base level. The majority of senior SF officers retire after completing one or both of these assignments since there is only one one-star general officer position in the career field. After retirement, colonels often go on to executive-level civilian jobs with six-figure salaries.

In line with the standard, about halfway through my deployment, I received PCS orders to Headquarters Central Command (CENTCOM) to work in the Joint Security Office (JSO). CENTCOM is a "joint" Combatant Command (COCOM), meaning that members from all US military services worked together on the staff to plan and support joint operations in their assigned region of the world. CENTCOM's AOR extends from Egypt, through the Middle East and the Arabian Peninsula, and into South and Central

---

[53] Fryar, p. 54–55.

Asia. The command provides joint guidance, support, and oversight for operations in and supporting the wars in Afghanistan and Iraq. My two deployments to Afghanistan and my anti-terrorism duties at the AFSFC qualified me to join this critical HQ staff.

CENTCOM AOR

However, my struggles with anxiety interfered with the performance of my duties there. I lost confidence that I could handle the stress of being a MAJCOM SF director or a MSG commander, so I never sought an assignment to those positions. Who knows how the remainder of my career would have gone if I had been mentally up to the normal challenges. I am sure I not would not have ended up in the Pentagon, nor deploying to Iraq or even Djibouti.

It is impossible to know where I would've gone, what I would have done, and how my spiritual journey would have developed if I had followed the normal course. But I am sure I would have missed out on the exceptional experience of the Djibouti deployment, and I might not have retired to my log cabin in the woods, across the street from a lake, on Camino Island. Without living there, I would not have started attending Camano Chapel where I have been honored to serve in many ways, made many close friends, and grown spiritually with the help of pastors and friends helping me adjust to my anxiety struggles and the stress of transitioning from a career military life into the alien civilian world. It is probable that I never would have walked the Camino since I would likely have started an impressive (and very stressful) second career as an executive somewhere in the crazy, dog-eat-dog, step-all-over-people-to-get-to-the-top corporate or federal civilian workforce. I would not have served in any of the secular and Christian volunteer service positions that have kept me so busy since retirement.

Without the unexpected emotional turmoil disrupting my career path, my life definitely would have been different. I must trust God's wisdom that He has me where He wants me, doing what He wants me to do, even if I had to deal with a lot to get here.

\* \* \* \* \*

By the time I entered Triacastela at the end of stage 27, I had descended 660 meters. I was a little over halfway to my objective, so this was a good place to have lunch. I took the opportunity of being in a decent-size city (population 900) to stop at an ATM and withdrew 200€. By my calculations, this would be enough to take me through to Santiago.

As I entered a café, I recognized one of the three women I met from Arkansas and asked if I could join her. She was more than happy to have company.

"Where are your friends?" I asked.

"I needed a break today, so I took a taxi," she explained. "The others are walking from O'Cebreiro. They will join me here later this afternoon."

I could certainly relate!

\* \* \* \* \*

I spent the rest of the day's trek thinking about the difficult two years I spent at CENTCOM.

I was very fortunate that my division chief was a fellow Air Force SF officer and friend, Col. Don. I had originally met him when I was a newly pinned-on first lieutenant attending the Ground Combat Skills Level 4 course prior to my assignment at Comiso AB, Sicily. He had been a captain at that time and was the OIC of the course.

Between me and Col. Don was my branch chief, an Army LTC (the Army way of abbreviating *lieutenant colonel*). He was nice enough, but it seemed odd to be working directly for another lieutenant colonel. He had more time-in-grade than me, and situations such as this were not unheard of in headquarters staff jobs.

The JSO director was above Col. Don. He was an Army colonel. He was never negative or obnoxious around me and actually treated me with a lot of respect. However, I guess I had developed a phobia against Army colonels. Every time I had to talk to him, my stomach would churn, the hair on the back of my neck would stand up, and I would have to fight to control strong feelings of anxiety. It was ridiculous. He had given me no reason to feel like this, but my reactions were a reality I had to deal with.

When I met my new primary care manager (PCM) at the base clinic, I explained my mental struggles. Besides my reaction to the division chief, I felt overwhelmingly exhausted, was easily flustered, had trouble controlling my emotions, and could not sleep without medication. We came to the mutual agreement that I needed to see a mental health professional and was soon meeting with him weekly.

It seemed every doctor and nurse I spoke to over the next couple months, regardless of specialty, asked me if I was suicidal. Maybe they flagged my record. I had soon had about enough of this question. One day when I got back to my office after an appointment, I went into Col. Don's office to let him know I was back.

"If one more person asks me if I'm suicidal, I am going to shoot them," I joked.

"So you're not suicidal, but you are homicidal?" he asked laughing in reply.

Fortunately, Col. Don was someone that I could confide in. Since we had known each other for a while, he knew that this was not normal for me. He knew of my intense dedication to the AF and my duties. He had been the one who predicted that I would find a husband at Comiso. My reply had been that I had married in the AF on May 27, 1987. He also knew my history of earning unit-, wing-, MAJCOM-, and AF-level awards. Because of this, he knew that my condition was not just because I was weak and unable to handle stress. He made it clear that he was there to support me and I could talk to him anytime.

"The pressures of war and the high ops tempo even at stateside bases are getting to a lot of people," he explained. "The cop that had your position before you was a friend of mine. He also came here after a deployment. He lived just a couple blocks from me. His wife called me for help one day, and I rushed over. He had committed suicide. I tried to revive him but was unable to. The ambulance crew had no success either. I don't want the same thing to happen to you. You have nothing to fear from talking to me whenever you need to. Call me at home if you need to after hours."

What a blessing to be working for an individual who was so understanding!

After a few weeks of the situation just getting worse, my psychiatrist and I agreed that I needed to take some time off. I suggested two weeks, and he said that that would be the minimum he would recommend. He thought I should take longer, but I insisted it would be enough.

During the two weeks, I met with him two to three times a week and did nothing work-related. I didn't even do my grocery-shopping at the base commissary. I was starting to feel somewhat better, but two days before I was scheduled to return to work, my anxiety peaked again. I had no desire to face the office. It churned my stomach even thinking about going in. Monday morning, I reported to duty as required and signed in from leave.

My next stop was Col. Don's office. I told him how I was feeling and that I just wasn't ready to come back to work; I needed at least one more week. Because of the unexpected need for an extension, we had to tell the division chief what was going on, definitely not something I wanted to do. Explaining this to an Army colonel was very difficult. What would he think of me and my capabilities? I was sure he would think that he had been stuck with a lemon.

To my surprise, he was understanding and even encouraging. I got my extra week and felt confident that I had not committed career suicide. Although I still struggled with anxiety and some exhaustion symptoms, the following week I was at least able to the resume my duties and start being productive.

Many times throughout my tour at CENTCOM, I became overwhelmed during the duty day. I found it very helpful to go to the gym or take a long bike ride in the middle of the day. During particularly bad moments, I retreated to a secluded spot on the beach a one hundred yards or so from the headquarters building. Sitting there alone, watching and listening to the waves smack against the rocky beach, helped me get the anxiety under control so I could face the stress of returning to the office for the rest of the day.

As the deputy chief of the policies and programs branch, I assigned tasks to branch action officers (AO) and tracked their suspenses and completion. The primary project I was assigned to deal with involved biometric technology. Since JSO had the lead for security and Force Protection, myself and a junior JSO member were the lead for a multifunctional working group consisting of communications, logistics, contracting, and intelligence AOs. Our mission was to determine the required capabilities on the front lines, work through the acquisition and procurement process, and then coordinate shipment and distribution of the devices.

The equipment provided patrols and those controlling entry to coalition installations with the capability to gather biometric data so they could positively identify local national citizens (LNs) who were applying to work for the coalition and enter bases in the CENTCOM AOR. The database was occasionally helpful when investigating the aftermath of terrorist attacks.

It was very interesting work—a pioneering area of the security portfolio that I had no prior experience with. I was honored to be a part of this groundbreaking project, but it also had the drawback of having the active attention of numerous general officers from throughout the headquarters. We were constantly compiling reports and giving briefings regarding our procurement progress, distribution to forward forces, and providing examples and statistics to illustrate successes on the front lines.

With the high visibility came an extremely high level of pressure and, therefore, stress. The hours were long, and the stakes were high because of the variety of insurgent attacks and infiltration attempts in the combat zones. Our efforts had an astounding potential to make a huge difference for troops on the ground. Paradise for a mission-focused workaholic. However, I soon found it overwhelming for my weakened mental and physical state.

I was not the only one who was stressed. The Army colonel we worked with from the forward program staff in Iraq went back to his CHU late one evening and failed to show up for work the following morning. He died in his sleep. I never heard the formal diagnosis of the cause of death, but indications I received was that the stress had gotten the better of him.

I stuck with it for a while, assuming time would heal my issues. However, after a few months, we decided it would be in both mine and the project's best interest if I moved to a less stressful program. Although it was a wise move, it was another major hit to my ego.

My new assignment involved the same project elements, but this time our "product" was the Mine-Resistant, Ambush-Protected (MRAP) vehicles. These vehicles replaced the uparmored HMMWVs we had used in Afghanistan, which were proving to be no match for the ever-evolving capabilities of the enemy's IEDs.

The cycle we were trapped in was a common situation throughout the history of war. One side develops a capability that gives them an edge over their enemy, and then the enemy develops a countermeasure to that capability, and the cycle repeats itself over and over.

In the case of the MRAP, we had much stronger armor all around and a V-shaped undercarriage that channeled the blast affects from a road-level IED out and away from the vehicle.

When I was assigned to the project, they were already well into the distribution process in Iraq. This meant much of the limelight was on the logistics staff, J4, instead of JSO, resulting in less stress on me and the major from our office that worked with me.

The MRAPs proved too large and heavy to operate in Afghanistan. Roads through villages were often very narrow, with buildings hugging both sides. Most bridges were not strong enough to handle the weight. Our working group developed specific requirements (specifications) for a smaller and lighter version that could be deployed and used effectively in Afghanistan, including dimensions, weight limitations, and explosive protection.

Truck belonging to PRT Gardez negotiating the narrow street of an Afghan village.

Although the stress was less with this program, it was definitely still attacking all of us. A couple months after I was assigned to the project, the major who worked with me had a stroke and ended up in the hospital for a week or so and then on light duty for several months. He was in his early forties. Far too young to have such a medical issue.

In the mist of all of this, my doctors warned me that I could be next. With the exhaustion I still felt and the stress of my current duties, they said that the resulting physical impact left me highly vulnerable to a heart attack or stroke if I did not change my lifestyle and priorities significantly.

A trend was becoming quite obvious. With the higher ops tempo, frequent deployments, and constant stressors associated with almost a decade of war—military personnel were literally working themselves to death.

\* \* \* \* \*

The afternoon hike took me up two hundred meters and then back down three hundred to a small village called Pinton where I had called over lunch to make reservations at a casa rural. The path consisted of a mix of dirt trails and walking along the side of small paved country roads through a secluded forest area. I saw virtually no vehicle or peregrino traffic outside of the three villages I passed through. I guess it was just a lazy Sunday in the country.

Upon my arrival, the host started a tab for me to settle up on in the morning. In all, the room, snacks, dinner, drinks, a load of washing and drying, and breakfast came to 60.4€. One of my more expensive evenings, but it was very nice and relaxing.

After my shower, I started reading the *Seeking* book. I was so enthralled by his description of the circumstances surrounding his spiritual surrender, a transformation that had been years in the making, that I could not stop reading. Mesmerized, I read the last six chapters without taking a break.

It was clear from the first paragraph: I was quickly approaching the climax of Nabeel's testimony. Intellectually, he was convinced that Christianity was the truth, but he was still struggling with a deep hope that his entire life was not based on a lie and, more importantly, the pain his conversion would cause his parents. His doubts and confusion led him to wonder if Satan was trying to lead him astray, but which side of his struggle was the false religion?

His Islamic tradition taught that Allah often spoke to Muslims through dreams and visions. He prayed that God would give him dreams that would confirm to him which was the correct path. God answered his prayer and gave him dreams, which he assessed clearly pointed to Christianity being the truth.

Yet he struggled for a couple more months, seeking information from Imams and Muslim texts that could show his interpretations were incorrect. When that did not change his mind, he held off because it made him sick to think of the pain he would cause his parents; it was likely he would be disowned by his family.

God revealed to him through the book of Matthew that sometimes this is the cost of following the truth. Loving your family more than God could cost you your soul for all of eternity. In the grand scheme of things, who is more important—God or your family?

The words of Jesus laid out the bottom line. This was the final piece. He bowed down with his forehead on the ground in the Muslim way of prayer and told God that he believed that Jesus Christ was His Son and that He had come to earth to be sacrificed for the forgiveness of sins for all who believed in Him and accepted His gift of mercy and love. He accepted Jesus as his Lord and Savior.

The scriptures also told him that, as a Christian, he needed to proclaim his belief to God and man. He told his family and got the anticipated reaction. This made him cry out, asking why God would want to cause him and his family so much pain. This time the Holy Spirit spoke to his heart. "This is not about you, it is about God." His perspective changed. He started seeing people outside his apartment as lost souls in need of somebody to explain the Gospel to them. The world around him transformed into a mission field.[54]

How fortunate we are in America that we do not have to go through the turmoil of disavowing everything about our lives—school, family, tradition, daily rituals, and the painful feelings of betrayal to our family and community—when we make a decision to follow Christ. Many of us eventually make radical changes to our lives once we are saved, but seldom are we asked to make such gut-wrenching sacrifices.

---

[54] Qureshi, chapters 48–53.

# CHAPTER 34

Pintín to Mercadoiro, 23.5 Kilometers
28 Sep 2015
D+30

I was surprised to see two other pilgrims eating breakfast at 0745 on the main floor of the casa rural.

"Hola," I greeted them. "Did you stay here last night? Thought I was the only one."

"No," one of the ladies replied with a strong Hispanic accent. "We stayed in Triacastela and have already been walking for four hours. We wanted to watch the super moon eclipse. It was great."

"Wow, I wish I had known that was going on. I would've liked to have seen it. Where are you from?"

"Puerto Rico," she replied. "Are you from America?"

"Sí. Where did you start the Camino?"

"Pamplona," the other lady explained. "This is my second time. Last time I was injured and had to stop there, so my friend and I started where I left off."

I explained my Camino history.

They were soon on their Way. I stayed another ten minutes to finish breakfast and pay my tab.

It wasn't long before I caught up with my new friends. One of them had fallen and hurt her ankle, so they were going rather slow. Could it be because they had gotten up and going at 0-dark-30 and were tired?

We walked together for about twenty minutes. After I revealed I was retired military, we found ourselves discussing a news article I had read on my iPhone earlier that morning. It concerned an injured or sick British soldier who had been told to leave a hospital emergency waiting area in the United Kingdom because the hospital staff was concerned that his uniform might offend somebody.

"I find that completely absurd! A soldier can't seek medical treatment in his own country, the country for which he is risking his life to serve?" I'm sure it was obvious to my new friends that this angered me.

"I'm not surprised," one of them said. "We met a British military man earlier. Someone thanked him for his service, and he was shocked. He said that no one does that in the UK. Pretty sad."

"I'm guessing it's because of the flood immigrants into the UK from the Middle East and the associated political correctness. There was already plenty of Arab immigrants in the country when I was stationed there in the late '90s. I can only imagine what it is like now with the refugee situation going on. What I don't understand is that if these people are immigrating to the UK to escape poor conditions and dangers in their country, why would a British soldier offend them? They chose to go to the UK. If the British culture and people offend them so much, they are free to return home or go to another country with a culture similar to their own. They should not be trying to bring the culture and the problems they are escaping to the country where they are seeking sanctuary. If they want that way of life and are offended by the culture of their host country, they need to go back!"

After my rant, I took a couple of deep breaths and then bid them a hearty "Buen Camino" as I resumed my normal pace and started pulling ahead of them. I was soon in deep contemplation about my professional and emotional turmoil after I returned from my second tour in Afghanistan.

\* \* \* \* \*

During my first year at CENTCOM, I took a total of eleven weeks of leave in several chunks because of my struggles. The fact that I had this much leave on the books was an indicator as to why I was so exhausted and depleted! While I was at work, I spent far too much time at various doctors' offices—including mental health, chiropractor, and conventional back and foot doctors. I was also referred to various specialists to determine causes and potential treatments for my increasingly severe headaches and the problems with thumb joint pain. The arthritis in my other fingers and toes also progressed, requiring two surgeries—one on a finger, the other a toe.

Long-term, chronic symptoms—such as, tingling during exercise, purple coloring, recurring sores when my feet got cold, and circulation issues—started appearing in my feet, which I suspect were results of the cold pernio.

Between all the medical appointments and all the leaves I needed to take because of stress, I seemed to be out of the office more than in. The longer this went on, the more I felt like I was letting my office down. I was not contributing at the level expected of someone of my rank and position. I wasn't pulling my weight, yet I was filling a slot on the manpower document. This really bugged my type A, workaholic ego, hence resulting in an additional level of stress and depression. A never-ending, downward cycle. I was getting paid but did not believe I was really doing my job.

In the middle of all this, my supervisor received notification that he needed to fill out a promotion recommendation form (PRF) for me. The time had come for me to be considered for promotion to colonel in the primary zone, the cycle when my year group had the best chance of being promoted to O-6.

Since I did not believe that I was pulling my weight as a lieutenant colonel, it was my assessment that I did not deserve to be promoted. There were only a certain number of promotion slots available. If I got one and was unable to perform to standard, that meant somebody who was likely in a better position to continue serving adequately would be passed over. In the end, that meant both the AF and the passed over lieutenant colonel would get the short end of the stick. After a few days of tearful prayers, I reluctantly wrote a letter to my chain of command explaining why I felt it would be inappropriate for them to recommend me for promotion. I also requested that the service commitment I incurred when I transferred to MacDill be waived and I be allowed to retire immediately. I explained that this would free up my slot on the manpower document so an able-bodied, hardworking replacement could be assigned who would be far more productive.

I cried the whole time I was writing the letter. The Air Force had been my life since I graduated from high school. Being an officer was my identity. It'd been over twenty years since I graduated from the academy, and I still had no idea what I would want to do if I got out. For most officers, retirement meant they could finally spend quality time with their families. Their spouse and children had been with them throughout their career and would still be there in their post-AF life. They would be that constant that would not change.

I did not have this. Getting out would turn my entire life upside down, and I had no idea what I would do next or even if I could get a job in my current condition. But how could I stay in and burden my unit with my problems? We were still in the middle of two wars, not to mention a worldwide campaign against radical Islamic terrorism. It would be very selfish of me not to step aside and leave the mission to those who were far more capable of being productive.

My hope was that the letter would find its way to the general, he would sign it, and I would be able to fade out with little attention. It was not to be. The deputy J3 that JSO reported to had been the Air Force director of Security Forces before he transferred to his current position. He was the one who had agreed to temporarily release me both times I volunteered for deployment to Afghanistan. He knew me when I was at the peak of my capabilities.

The general called me into his office to inform me he did not agree with my assessment and encouraged me to reconsider. It was his position that my current struggles were temporary, and he was willing to work with me to get through it so I could get back in the game. He knew my work ethic and my previously tireless dedication. He knew all I had accomplished and all the recognition I had received during my career. For the second time in my career, I broke down crying in front of a general officer. I agreed to think about it for a few days and then come back and give him my final decision.

Prior to that meeting, I forwarded a copy of the letter to the current director of Security Forces at the Pentagon. I had first met our new general when I was stationed at Mildenhall. At that time, she was the commander of the SF Group at Ramstein AB in Germany. It was her unit that we often called on Friday afternoons with immediate contingency deployment taskings, such as the two squads we sent to Africa after the embassy bombings. It was her chief that called us one Friday evening to find out if we were okay since he had not received a tasking form us that afternoon. Since then, she had been a mentor to me.

Near the end of the duty day, I received an e-mail from her. She expressed her disappointment in my decision. She said she knew that I had a lot the potential left in me and I just needed some more time to work through the current issues, that it was premature for me to give up my career. Although I had not been diagnosed with PTSD, she felt that that was probably what I actually had and was concerned that if I got out and had to go into the VA health-care system, I would not get the medical support that I needed. What a sad state of affairs when a general officer believes that the VA is so bad it would be better to stay in than to get out and have to count on them for help. She strongly encouraged me to reconsider. Her words were so kind and caring. I could not help myself. I broke down crying once again by the time I got halfway through her e-mail. I printed a copy to keep. Her kindness and encouragement was unimaginable.

What was I to do? The two general officers who knew me best were both encouraging me to stay and to compete for promotion.

The next day I asked the deputy J3 to rip up my letter, and he gave me a strong recommendation on my PRF. I was surprised at the strength of the recommendation written by my AF boss and signed by the Army two-star J3 director. To my shock, the two-star said that I was his number one of the three lieutenant colonels eligible for promotion that year. Apparently, even with all my struggles, I was somehow managing to perform well in the view of my superiors.

\* \* \* \* \*

After a couple of kilometers, I passed an albergue with a popular, intriguing old European-style café and bar where we had stopped one afternoon in 2013. There had been quite a crowd gathered around the bar, guidebooks in hand. We sat next to a couple who explained that the crowd was waiting to get their books autographed by the author, John Brierley. They said he walks the Camino a couple times a year gathering information to update the guide. All three of us were able to get our books signed. Today I was disappointed they were not open for breakfast and I had to pass it by.

Soon thereafter, I entered the outskirts of Sarria, the last place a pilgrim could start their Camino and still earn a Compostela certificate. The pilgrim office at the cathedral in Santiago does not issue certificates unless the pilgrim has walked at least 100 km. This made this location an even more popular starting point than St. Jean.

The last five stages are therefore very crowded. The new people are blatantly obvious—laughing all the time, jabbering away, and taking pictures of everything. After nearly 700 km, the rest of us have said everything that needs to be said and taken so many pictures that we are now only taking them of special milestones or unique buildings or scenery.

What the newbies were wearing also gave them away: tennis shoes, running shorts, and tank tops. Some only have small daypacks and carry their water in plastic bottles in their hands. Another telltale sign is that they walk along without the slightest hint of a limp; some even seem to be skipping. On average, they seemed to be in larger groups than most of the seasoned pilgrims.

As I entered old town Sarria where pilgrims congregate, I saw an excited group of newbies come out of the hotel. Several of them were wearing spandex. Why overweight people wear spandex was a question I had been perplexed about for quite some time.

I shouldn't be negative or critical. The guidebook warns seasoned pilgrims to be tolerant of the newbies, to welcome them to The Way. John Brierley reminds us that not everyone can get six weeks off of work to do the Camino. If this is the best that they could make work, we should not be critical of them. Everyone does the Camino their own way.

For me, the problem is that from here on out, the trail and accommodations would be crowded. RONing in the middle of stages would be even more important from here out. It was my only chance of minimizing the crowds I would have to deal with.

My strategy was working well today. It was 1100 by the time I finished my coffee, refilled my water bottle, and started out on an almost-deserted trail. The crowds were a good three hours ahead of me! This definitely needed to continue to be my SOP!

As I approached a thin, rugged, rudimentary wood bridge on the far side of town at the edge of a forested area, I passed a middle-aged woman with two prosthetic legs. An older man was helping her get a wheelchair across the stream. Amazing. Not many people would attempt even the last hundred kilometers of the Camino with prosthetic legs and a wheelchair. That would definitely take courage, stamina, and determination.

After seeing this, how could I complain about my back and feet?

\* \* \* \* \*

In early summer 2008, I was called to the deputy J3's office.

"The Interagency Action Group is being reorganized and is moving to the J3. I will be dual-hatted in my current position and as the new IAG director. They are the ones who work Afghanistan and Iraq PRT issues for CENTCOM and Phase 0 Stability Operations. They are also the command's lead for Humanitarian Relief Operations. Since you were a PRT commander, I think you would be a perfect deputy chief of their new Development Support Division. I need your boots-on-the-ground experience on the team. Are you interested?"

"Absolutely!"

Although working with the Army had virtually destroyed me, I still believed that the reconstruction and development mission was the foundation for establishing peace and long-term stability in both countries. I considered the HUMROs I had participated in the best experiences of my career. Of course I was interested in the position!

I studied my AAR from my tour at PRT Gardez and got to work developing options to address the problems that myself and other PRT members had identified.

The first item I tackled was to right-size and right-skill the manning document in order to resolve deficiencies and improve the effectiveness of the team. The major problem was that the Army developed the manning document based on what they felt was needed and assigned Army military occupational specialty (MOS) codes to each position. When the teams transitioned to joint units, an attempt had been made to translate each Army MOS into AF and Navy career field identifiers. The problem was that the other services did not necessarily have career fields that clearly matched the Army specialties. The staff did the best they could with neither clear knowledge of all the services specialties nor of the actual needs on the ground. As a result, we ended up with AF and Navy personnel that did not have the skill sets that were actually needed.

For instance, AF public affairs (PA) personnel were put in the information operations (IO) position on AF-led teams. In the AF, PA was in charge of publishing base papers, managing the base's official website, and being the base's liaison to the local papers and TV stations in order to inform the public about happenings regarding the base. Conversely, the objective of the IO function was to develop and execute a well-considered strategic effort in conjunction with provincial governors, directors of information, and other Afghan officials to shape public opinion by crafting information releases. The objective was gaining public support for the Afghan government and coalition and countering the enemy's information operations. The missions may seem similar, but they were as different as night and day. On the AF teams, many of the IO positions were filled by very junior PA officers. Instead of working to shape our message to the Afghan public, they spent most of their time writing articles about PRT projects and personnel for publication in the Bagram Bullet and the ISAF magazine whose audiences were internal coalition forces.

Fortunately, the IO for PRT Gardez was a senior NCO instead of a junior officer. He had worked in Air Force radio and television broadcasting and had had other experiences which had given him an in-depth understanding of the actual IO mission. Instead of working on internal magazine articles, he spent his time working with his counterparts in the Afghan provincial government to establish a network of radio stations and produce radio programs and TV ads with strategic messages for public consumption. For instance, they produced weekly radio shows where the governor would provide local information and answer questions from the public.

One ad campaign was particularly effective in changing the SOP of the enemy. The Taliban were in the habit of burning down schools, clinics, and other infrastructure as soon as construction was completed. After a recently constructed school was blown up and burned down, my IO worked closely with the provincial director of information to create an ad campaign using several media options to include a television ad, radio announcements, and the governor talking about it during his weekly radio address. The message was that denying education to children was contrary to the teachings of the Quran and that the Afghan citizens should not support people who undermined education and, therefore the futures of their children. The public outcry was strong enough that the local Taliban started their own ad campaign to convince the public that they were pro education. They also stopped bombing schools, at least for a while.

Another inappropriate translation of career field codes on the manning document was the radio telephone operators (RTOs). The AFSC assigned was for enlisted communication specialists. What the Army wanted was people to man the radios at the JOC, dispatch and track patrols and response forces, and relay information from higher headquarters to convoys and leadership personnel. They also wanted people who could provide maintenance for typical radios used by the Army. What they got were people who could install, set up, troubleshoot, and fix communication networks—primarily Internet and satellite communications—and telephone maintenance. Although these were very important skills for us to have available, they were not the intent. Some of our assigned communications personnel just happened to have the skills to fix common AF radio equipment, but they were not necessarily familiar with the ones used by the Army. What PRTs really needed was a combination of certified AF Command Post or SF security controllers experienced in Command and Control communications for combat and emergency situations. Separately, they needed Army radio maintenance personnel specifically trained in the radio systems being used by the PRT and, separately, Internet and satellite Information Technology (IT) specialists.

Medical was another place where capabilities were lost in translation. In addition to the physician's assistant, the Army asked for three enlisted medical technicians. In the Army and Navy, enlisted medical personnel are often EMTs and extensively trained in combat medicine (medical corpsmen) so they can embed with units during off-base operations. They are the first line of medical attention when someone is injured in combat. Because the Air Force seldom goes outside the wire, AF medical technicians either perform administrative tasks at the hospitals and clinics or, at the most, take temperatures and blood pressures in preparation for patients to see the doctor. They are not combat medics. Ours received some relevant training during our predeployment course at Fort Bragg, and our doc continued training them once in-country. Eventually they acquired sufficient skills to perform the function that was intended for them.

Similarly, engineers were requested to do project development and management and quality control/quality assurance inspections. What the staffers in their CENTCOM and Joint Staff cubicles stateside failed to understand was that not all engineers are the same and not every engineer knows everything about all types of engineering. Just because somebody was an engineer does not mean that he knows how to build buildings, roads, bridges, electric systems, solar power systems, irrigation systems, and . . . and . . . and . . . Our engineers were also expected to know how to do contracting and finance, which was not within their normal skill set; these are separate career fields.

We had similar problems with our DoS, USAID, and USDA representatives. It seems that their HQ staffers in DC thought all personnel from these departments were interchangeable. State Department personnel are not trained in governance capacity building, but because they were from "State," it was assumed that they were governance experts.

Not every USAID employee knew how to assess requirements, coordinate with local governments, develop and manage projects, and conduct quality-control evaluations during construction (they were not engineers), but it was assumed by the powers to be that the USAID reps they sent to the PRT could cover all these functions for projects funded by the agency.

There are also many different types of employees at USDA. Some specialize in forestry; others, in farming techniques; still others are veterinarians. As with the other participating departments, it was assumed that one USDA representative could cover all these functions.

My objective was to fix these problems and get the right people and the right numbers assigned to the PRTs.

The other major problem I tried to address was the complete loss of continuity and experience when the PRT swapped over as a whole (with the exception of the three civilians) due to the Army's "train as a team" and "deploy as a team" policies.

PRT effectiveness relied on solid relationships with Afghan government partners and in-depth knowledge about resources and social issues in the province, as well as the history behind project selection and development. Major projects could last for two or three years from the time the desired capability was identified. Locations had to be identified and acquired, construction designs developed and approved, coordination conducted with local villagers, contracts developed and awarded, and then of course, construction itself. When the PRTs changed over annually, all the detailed historical knowledge left with the outgoing team. The Afghans understood this and used this dynamic against us—i.e., the Zurmat clinic security wall issue.

It was the initiative to fix this problem that landed me in the two-star general's office trying to convince him to split the team in half within each functional area and rotate only half of the team every six months.

The Army general's reply was that all the maneuver units were also rotating as complete teams and that this was the Army way of doing things. When I asked how it was working out for him, he agreed that it was not. As he put it, "We have had eight one-year wars, not one eight-year war." He signed my proposal and sent it to the Pentagon for further staffing.

Before I PCSed, my proposal had been approved by the four-star tank at the Pentagon and sent to Special Operations Command (SOCOM) to implement. It boggled my mind for several years afterward, as I observed PRT operations during my duties at the Pentagon, that the changes never made any progress at SOCOM. They were never implemented. How could a joint group of four stars approve something and then it not be implemented?

I guess, to be fair, I should put this in perspective. SOCOM was dealing with a lot of higher priorities than this. I wasn't even sure why it had gone to them since CENTCOM was the one that oversaw the PRTs. SOCOM was the ADCON for the Army Civil Affairs personnel assigned to the PRTs, but they did not deal with the PRT as a whole. They did not issue tactical guidance. CENTCOM (my office) should have been tasked with implementation. SOCOM was focused on identifying and hunting down high-value targets. PRT manpower rotation schedules were the least of their worries.

Other major efforts I dealt with during my year assigned to the Development Support Division included enhancing the integration of US government (USG) agencies in regional military planning and working groups, working closely with DoD and the Joint Staff to update civil affairs, Stability Operations, and Counterinsurgency (COIN) guidance and doctrine based on lessons learned from Afghanistan and Iraq, and coordinating with the DoS to identify and source additional State personnel requirements for assignment at the district, provincial, and national levels in theater.

Although I was still dealing with physical and mental struggles, in the end this year proved to be productive and professionally fulfilling. I was uniquely qualified for this position because of my PRT experience and was honored to be able to use what I had learned to really make a difference in the nonkinetic portion of the war against terrorism.

However, I got promoted out of the position.

Since it was a O-5 slot, I had to be reassigned to an O-6 position. The director of Security Forces asked me to come work for her on the Air Staff at the Pentagon in Washington, DC.

I packed up and moved in May 2009. I was now assigned to the last of the three places I had said as a lieutenant that I never wanted to be assigned to: Turkey, England (because of the dog quarantine), and the Pentagon. Was this an example of God's humor, or was He trying to show me that He was in charge?

\* \* \* \* \*

Being offset from the standard stages was paying huge dividends! There were just a handful of late starters sharing the trail with me. This afternoon's walk was actually very pleasant.

About twenty minutes after leaving Sarria, a young Japanese girl passed me, obviously fresh and going fast. When I commented on the fact that she was wearing sandals and they might not be such a good idea, she slowed down long enough to explain that she had started with running shoes. They did not work very well, so she purchased the sandals in Sarria. I wished her luck with them as she hurried ahead. Based on the experiences Samantha had had with her hiking sandals, I doubted the girl would have any more luck with them, but the young idealist was just going to have to learn the lesson on her own. The gear she carried consisted of a large purse slung over her shoulder and a plastic bag with the running shoes. I suppose it is possible that she shipped her gear ahead, but I do not understand why someone so young and fit would need to do that.

I must remember not to be judgmental. The book warned me to keep these thoughts and attitudes in check.

Speaking of the guidebook, after about 3.5 km, I passed the intersection where I had seen its author, John Brierley, in 2013 checking a GPS and making notes for his book update. This was the third time we had seen him that day. The first was at the café where we got the autographs. The second had been as we entered Sarria and had asked to have our picture taken with him. His wife was traveling with

Team Camino with John Brierley in Sarria, Oct 2013.

him. She offered to take the picture, stating, "I am not important. I don't need to be in the picture!" This was fine with us since her offer enabled the three of us to pose with him. By the time we passed him at this intersection, we were familiar enough to him that he recognized us.

Mom and Ria were fifty to one hundred yards ahead of me when I passed him.

"Yep, the youngest is lagging behind again," I joked as he looked at me questioningly.

While I was enjoying lunch at an outside café, the lady with prosthetic legs passed by. This time the older man with her was riding in the wheelchair and she was pushing it. Apparently they were taking turns.

At 1416, I passed the cement one hundred–kilometer marker. Another major milestone achieved!

I arrived at my objective albergue about 1530 and was horrified to see a large group of high school kids, at least thirty of them, loudly chatting, playing loud music, and obnoxiously moving about. The hair on the back of my neck stood up, a chill ran down my spine, and my stomach churned. This was not going to be good. I had already gone 23.5 km. My feet and back hurt. I was tired. I had no desire to go on. I would just have to make the best of it and hope that the kids were in a different building!

As I approached the sign-in desk, I noticed Joy sitting at a table having a drink and reading a book. I enthusiastically greeted her as I passed. It had been over a week since we had seen each other.

After executing my normal settling-in SOP, I joined Joy at her outdoor table. We did not talk much as both of us were engaged in checking e-mail and mission planning. To my great relief and delight, the huge group of high school kids grabbed their packs and left about a half hour later. Apparently, they were off to meet a bus that would take them to a hotel for the evening. Praise the Lord! There was peace in the universe again!

The rest of the evening was relaxing. I had dinner with Joy and a German couple I had seen several times that day.

As often happens, the fact that I am single became a major topic of conversation. I gave them my customary explanation.

"I think I intimidate men," I explained. "How many men want to marry an Air Force officer who is a cop? Both the AF and security are primarily male professions. A senior-ranking female with these credentials could obviously be seen as intimidating by most men. Then there was the issue of me moving every one to three years. What kind of a man with a successful professional career would be willing and able to follow me as I frequently moved around the world? What career could they have that would be that flexible? I think this is why most of the senior female officers I know are single."

We spent the rest of the evening exchanging Camino stories and laughing. An incredible evening.

# CHAPTER 35

## Mercadoiro to Portos, 25 Kilometers
## 29 Sep 2015
## D+31

It was a rough night for sleeping. One of the German ladies in my room snored endlessly. I had taken an over-the-counter sleep aid because I was running low on my prescription; it didn't help much. I carried earplugs but found them so uncomfortable I couldn't sleep with them. It was actually a relief when the alarm went off, signaling the end of my battle.

Arriving at the albergue's restaurant at 0740, I was surprised to find it did not open until 0900. Odd, since pilgrims needed to be out of the rooms by 0800. They were certainly missing out on a lot of business by not being open before their guests departed in the morning.

Disappointed, I put my headlight on and headed out into the cold, dark, foggy morning. It was difficult to see, but I managed not to miss any arrows during the half hour it took the sun to rise.

Joy caught up with me about a kilometer before Portomarín—a nice, moderately sized city of two thousand at the end of stage 29. Together we crossed the bridge over the scenic river Belesar and climbed the long, steep stairway leading to the city's main road with the hope of finding breakfast. I was thankful that we were making this climb early in the day. Last time we climbed it after an exhausting 22 km. It still left us breathless and happy to reach the summit.

The restaurant where Mom, Ria, and I had dinner with the ninety-one-year old from Florida was one of two places open. A large group of energetic and loud high school students crowded the street as they headed off down the trail.

"Sure glad they are leaving now," Joy observed as we entered the restaurant. "They should be well ahead by the time we move out."

Dismayed, I settled for a croissant with honey and coffee because they were not cooking until 1000. They were even out of oranges for fresh zumo! According to the book, there would not be another chance to eat for almost 8 km. Added to the 5.2 we had already done, we would be over halfway through the day's walk before getting a decent meal. Guess I'll be burning some fat this morning!

"I am enjoying the freedom of walking alone," Joy commented as she watched another large group walking down the street outside. "I no longer have to discuss where to stop for breaks with anyone. I'm not waiting for anybody, nor am I slowing anyone else down. I can stop for the night wherever and whenever I need to. It is great to enjoy time with friends in the evenings, but love the freedom during the day!"

"I couldn't agree more!" It was like she was reading my mind.

"Hey, take a look at that," Joy nodded toward yet another group of peregrinos.

I followed her stare to a blind pilgrim with his hand placed on the shoulder of a friend.

"Amazing! Can you imagine how difficult it must for him to walk on the trail sections where all the rough rocks are? I'm having a hard enough time not twisting an ankle."

I decided to have a second cup of coffee and type some notes about what had happened so far today.

"Well, I'm going to head on out," Joy said, adjusting her pack. "I am sure I'll see you again along The Way."

Ten minutes later, as I prepared to depart, yet another, even younger and louder group of kids passed by in front of the restaurant. How many of these school groups could possibly be on the trail at one time? It was late September. Shouldn't they be in the classroom learning to read and write and studying math and history?

I took a deep breath to calm my nerves. I was going to have to adjust to this. There would be crowds the rest of The Way.

\* \* \* \* \*

During my first year at the Pentagon, I was assigned as the deputy chief of the Force Protection and Operations Division at Headquarters Air Force Security Forces. The idea was that I would initially be the deputy and learn the issues and HQ operating procedures. Once the current chief PCSed nine months later, the intent was for me to take over.

Besides the administrative function of assigning taskers to division personnel and tracking progress, I was the primary action officer for developing a new vehicle registration process and coordinating with the other services in an attempt to establish consistency throughout the DoD.

We were still using the pre-9/11 process of registering vehicles and placing registration stickers on the windshield. Before the terrorist attacks, vehicles would merely slow down enough for the guard to get a good look at the sticker and expiration date. If everything appeared in order, they would wave the car through. On 9/11, one of the first security enhancements implemented was requiring 100 percent hands-on identification (ID) checks of everybody coming through the gate. The DoD had no intention of ever allowing the services to return to the process of waving vehicles in based merely on a sticker on the windshield. ID checks was the new normal.

We did not care if the car was registered to be on base. What we wanted to know was whether the individuals "IN" the car were authorized to be on base. As my unit had discovered in the months following 9/11, it was easy for unauthorized people to acquire a vehicle with DoD stickers on it. Although regulations required personnel to remove the stickers before selling their car, my troops found many cars in used car lots with the stickers still attached. Then there was the report about the "Middle Eastern–looking" man trying to buy a truck with the stickers. These two data points reinforced the importance of 100 percent ID checks.

Logically, the question became, Was there a purpose in registering vehicles? Purchasing and maintaining a stock of stickers DoD-wide cost a significant amount of money each year. Additionally, several people were required full-time to register the vehicles of active-duty, retiree, and civilian employees of the base and write day passes for authorized personnel who were driving a rental or a new vehicle that had yet to be registered. Many other enhanced security procedures implemented after 9/11 were manpower intensive and had also become the "new normal." Additionally, SF personnel were in high demand for deployments ISO overseas combat and antiterrorism operations. At any given time, a third of a SF unit might be deployed. Manpower availability and priorities were a major issue.

In the opinion of myself and other key personnel at SF headquarters, the stickers themselves actually increased the threat to personnel. Terrorists could use the stickers to identify vehicles owned by people authorized to enter military bases in order to target them for ambush or place an IED on them. Similar scenarios had happened multiple times to US forces in Europe over the previous decades, and there was no reason to believe it couldn't happen in the United States. The other concern was observing a DoD sticker could result in complacency on the part of the gate guard. In other words, they might not pay as close of attention to the occupants of a vehicle with a sticker as they would to one without one.

Our staff could not think of any real solid reason to continue registering vehicles and using the stickers. It was clear that the manpower and funds could be better utilized for higher security priorities. So we proposed to the other services that we eliminate the requirement DoD-wide.

It was important that we not go it alone for two reasons. First, the vehicle registration requirement came from a DoD directive. That directive would have to be changed, which required all the services to sign off on it. Even if the requirement was deleted, individual services could choose to enhance security by continuing to register vehicles. Since AF personnel frequently entered bases belonging to other services, their continuance of the requirement meant our personnel would have to get a vehicle pass every time they tried to enter a sister service base. This would be very time-consuming and frustrating for personnel living and working in areas where numerous bases were nearby, such as Washington, DC. It was obvious that we all needed to be on the same sheet of music.

To me this was a no-brainer. It was not for the other services. The Navy agreed with our reasoning but refused to implement the new procedures unless the Army was onboard. They did not want to have their personnel hassled and inconvenienced when entering an Army post.

The Army steadfastly disagreed with the proposal. They wanted to periodically check for valid driver's licenses and insurance of those driving on their posts. Registration and renewal requirements provided a recurring opportunity.

To me this was just more proof that the Army did not trust its personnel. None of our statistics showed driving without a license or insurance to be a major problem on bases.

Our disagreement had not been resolved by the time I transferred to work for the Office of the Secretary of Defense (OSD) a year later. Because the Army would not give in, the Navy did not either. The Marines fell under the Department of the Navy, so they followed Navy rules. Frustrated, the AF decided to unilaterally delete the requirement and reallocate the manpower with the approval of the JS, which issued new DoD policy. Sure enough, AF personnel started having trouble getting onto Army and Navy bases. A couple of years after I retired, I heard that the other services had adopted the new AF procedure. Finally!

\* \* \* \* \*

Large group of teenagers

Hungry and ready for a break, I arrived at a café in Gonzar just before noon and ordered a sandwich and OJ. The place was packed. I planned on doing the day's service study over lunch, but there was way too much activity and noise to concentrate. Fighting a surge of anxiety, I wrapped the top layer of bread from my sandwich in a napkin and stuffed it in the outside pocket of my pack to eat later. As I devoured the rest of the sandwich, I unzipped my pant legs and put them and my gloves away. It was finally warm enough to discard the snivel gear for the day. After tightening my shoes and refilling my water bottle, I escaped the chaos back to the relative solitude of the trail. Maybe the next time I stopped I could find a quiet, off trail café to do the service study.

\* \* \* \* \*

Work on several other issues was intermingled between vehicle registration meetings and taskers.

Because SF was responsible for AF confinement facilities, our directorate was tasked to represent the AF on the DoD Detainee Task Force. The TF was charged with identifying and evaluating potential options within DoD facilities to house and try terrorists detained at Guantánamo Bay in Cuba. The effort was in support of President Barak Obama's intent to close the facility and bring the terrorists to the United States for formal legal processing and imprisonment if convicted. Many other law enforcement agencies were evaluating options in civilian communities. Our work was just a small part of the overall effort. Although several DoD facilities were evaluated, no viable military options were identified during my approximately nine months on the TF.

Capitalizing on my deployment history and rare PRT experience, my supervisors assigned me to represent SF on the working group that was updating Irregular Warfare (IW), Agile Combat Support (ACS), Stability Operations, and COIN doctrine and policy documents within the DoD, followed by the AF supporting documents.

I was also asked to be a key speaker in a meeting with a delegation from South Korea. We discussed in-depth the concept and purpose of the PRTs, operating techniques, and lessons learned. In the end, Korea decided to accept the coalition's invitation to establish a PRT in one of the few Afghan provinces that still shared a PRT with another province.

It was exciting to have a position at the Pentagon where I could use my background in SF, HUMROs, and my two deployments in Afghanistan to contribute to policy improvement that not only impacted the AF and entire DoD but also overseas contingency operations with our coalition partners.

* * * * *

I finally found a quiet café in Ventas de Narón where I could do the day 27 study while enjoying yet another café con leche.

Referencing 1 Thessalonians 3:11–13, the lesson pointed out that everyone appreciates encouraging comments. Whether from your boss, a friend, or a relative, it warms our heart to know we are appreciated. But no earthly encouragement can compare to what we will feel when our Savior welcomes us to heaven and says, "Well done, good and faithful servant!" However, it is vital that we understand that nothing that we do in and of ourselves can earn us those wonderful words. Because of our sinful nature, it is only through our personal acceptance of God's salvation made possible through the crucifixion of Christ that we can have the heart of service that can lead to those wonderful words. When we willfully and faithfully follow Christ's leading, the outcomes are not the important thing; those are God's responsibility. Rather, for us, our obedience, motivation, and intentions behind the acts are what are important. We must faithfully let God work through us.[55]

The AF does a good job of showing its appreciation for the work of airmen. We have the opportunity to face and conquer numerous challenges. Successful completion is often enough reward. Knowing that you can overcome your fears or even merely accomplish a difficult task can fill a person with pride and self-worth. There is no internal feeling quite like accomplishing something you did not believe you could do. The AF offers many accolades for working hard and going above and beyond the minimum expectations: an extra day off, a letter of appreciation presented in front of your peers, quarterly or annual awards, medals and ribbons for display on formal uniforms, and promotions to name a few. Even now, plaques and other

---

[55] Fryar, p. 56–57.

mementos attesting to my accomplishments decorate my "I love me" walls upstairs in my retirement home. When I put on my uniform in the performance of ALO duties, I stand much straighter and taller than when in civilian clothing.

If wearing the uniform and reminiscing while looking at my plaques can make me feel so good, I can hardly imagine how I will feel when my Savior says, "Well done, my good and faithful servant!"

Before setting out again into the wild jungle, I decided it would be prudent to make a reservation for a place to stay. With these crowds and so many making reservations, it was best not to take a chance.

I still had a few more kilometers in me for the day, so I found a guidebook reference to a small private albergue in a tiny hamlet about six clicks away. It only had eight beds, so I was confident it would not be crowded. I called the number provided and reserved a bunk.

Relieved that was set, I hit the trail.

I hadn't intended to stop again, but as I passed a bar in Ligonde, Joy got my attention. I decided to stop and have a drink with her. I had a bed arranged, so I was no longer any hurry.

She was with another American that I had not met.

"I started in St. Jean but had to stop in Pamplona because I got tendinitis," the American explained. "While I healed, I did a lot of touring by bus. I started walking again in Sarria. I plan to take it easy from here out and only do about 10 km a day."

"Good idea," I said. "The main thing is to walk into Santiago. It doesn't matter when."

After enjoying a glass of wine with them, I bid them "Buen Camino" and set out for the day's final stretch.

\* \* \* \* \*

Late one afternoon, I was working on answering yet another tasker dealing with the vehicle registration issue when my phone rang. Word of my PRT command experience had worked its way to the Office of the Secretary of Defense's (OSD) Training Readiness and

Strategy directorate. An action officer there was looking for some-body with PRT experience to represent the DoD as an instructor during field training for interagency personnel preparing to deploy to Afghanistan. Some students would be assigned to PRTs, others to either a regional headquarters or the national-level International Security Assistance Force (ISAF) Headquarters. The training would last a week, and I would have to leave within a few days.

My heart leaped. I was becoming weary of staff work at the puzzle palace. Since I was still convinced the PRTs were critical to stabilizing Afghanistan, I could really sink my teeth into such a pro-gram. Besides, I had always enjoyed FTXs, and participating in the role of an instructor would have a major impact.

My boss was a little hesitant to approve it, but eventually I talked him into letting me go since they didn't have much time to find someone else.

It was an incredible week. The course was run by the Department of State's Foreign Service Institute (FSI). The students came from nine different federal agencies—including State, Agriculture, USAID, FBI, Homeland Security, Treasury, and Health and Human Services, to name a few. There were a few military students who were there to learn about the agencies they would be working with in-country. The first couple of weeks of the course, the students had been in the classroom at the FSI campus in Washington, DC. The field exer-cise was conducted at the Army National Guard's Muscatatuk Urban Training Center (MUTC) in Indiana.

The students were divided into a few interagency teams, each playing the role of a PRT. The week started out with an in-depth briefing about the political, economic, social, and insurgent situa-tion in Kunar Province, an actual province in eastern Afghanistan. By selecting an actual province for the scenario, FSI could use "real-world" historical and situational data instead of having to create a hypothetical framework for the exercise. The goal was to introduce the students to actual cultural issues and situational complexities.

Once familiar with the battle space, each team was given a series of scenarios around which to plan missions and then convoy out and meet with Afghans to address an issue. An Army National Guard team planned and executed the actual convoys and security operations as part of their annual two-week training requirement. Afghans who had immigrated to the United States played the roles of Afghan government officials, villagers, and interpreters, adding immeasurably to the realism.

I was in heaven. Being in the field was an incredible stress relief, and I felt extremely useful. I was blessed to have another opportunity to put my experiences in Afghanistan to use helping prepare others for their assignments. Through our students, our mentorship had major impacts at all levels throughout the country. Far more impact than any one of us could've had individually in-country. Apparently, FSI and OSD were happy with my contributions. They invited me to come back the following month to help with another class.

Participating in this exercise changed my trajectory at the Pentagon.

\* \* \* \* \*

I limped into the albergue A Paso de Formiga in Portos just before 1600 hours. Today's trail had been a mostly wide dirt trail, with the occasional skinny footpath along the edge of a lightly traveled paved road. We passed through wooded areas and farmlands and crossed the couple of rivers. The variety was enjoyable.

After making my bed and arranging my gear, I conducted mission planning in the common area. I figured 28 km would be a good distance. This would set up a midday arrival in Santiago on Friday. There was a small village about that distance away with an albergue and a casa rural. The hospitalero spoke pretty good English and offered to call and make reservations for me. To my dismay, both were already booked.

Loved this warning sign in a private yard.

The next opportunity after that was over three clicks further. Twenty-eight was pushing it; thirty-one busted the envelope. I would have to stop earlier. There were two lodging options 2.2 km closer in a hamlet called Boente. This is where Mom, Ria, and I had stayed. My notes in the guidebook prominently reminded me about the negative experience we had had at one of the private albergues, "Os Albergues."

We had planned to stop at Os. The guidebook gave very little information about either albergue, so we had just chosen one and arranged for Ria's pack to be shipped there with the intent of checking out both places before deciding which one to stay at.

We had a very bad feeling about the place as soon as we stepped through the door. It was a dimly lit, somewhat grungy bar. In the far-right corner, the TV was turned to an overly sexy show. With no words needed, we found Ria's pack next to the left wall, grabbed it, and started for the door. The hospitalero emerged from a back room and called out to us. We indicated that we had decided not to stay there, and his manner turned very ugly.

He insisted that shipping the pack there constituted making a reservation and we were obligated to stay there. No choice. Of course, I argued that that had not been the policy at any albergue we had shipped the pack to previously and we had changed our minds on several occasions without a problem. He didn't care. He stuck to his guns and insisted if we didn't stay there, we still owed him payment for the night. Mom and I refused and walked out, but for some reason, Ria held back to discuss it with him further. We went to the other albergue, signed in, and grabbed our beds. When Ria did not join us, we went back looking for her.

The hospitalero was still talking to her harshly and had managed to get her to give him her passport. Suddenly he was having trouble understanding English. I turned on my angry voice so he would be sure to understand, pointed at the passport, and indicated I wanted him to give it back to Ria. He angrily refused, referring again to our "reservación."

"Telephono policía," I said, adding an authoritarian aspect to my voice.

This just made him angrier. We went back and forth with me trying to convey my disagreement to him in my very limited Spanish. At this point he was pretending he knew no English at all. I knew better since he had addressed us in broken English initially. Seeing that I was making no progress, I took Ria by the hand and hotfooted it out the door. As we headed back to the other albergue, he came out on the street and continued yelling at us.

Safely inside the café portion of the other albergue, I approached the hospitalero and explained the situation to him.

"He still has her passport and refuses to give it back. Can you call the police for us?"

He spoke fairly good English and understood clearly what I was saying. However, he suggested that he try calling the other proprietor and see if he could fix it for us. He dialed the phone and had a fairly long and sometimes-tense discussion. Finally he hung up.

"He has agreed to give you the passport back. You can go back and get it now."

"I'll get it for you, Ria," I offered as Mom suggested she get her bed set up.

A little nervous, I returned to the other albergue and approached the man at the bar counter.

Extending my hand, I simply said, "Pasaporte."

Still obviously angry, he handed it to me while chewing me out once again in Spanish. I ignored him and rejoined my team. We did not leave the albergue again until we were ready to go the next morning.

With this memory clearly etched in my mind, I asked the helpful hospitalero to try to make reservations for me to stay at the Casa A Calzada again. Fortunately, they still had a lower bunk available.

With that taken care of, I ordered a drink and started talking to three peregrinos at the next table. They explained to me that the two men were brothers from Colorado and the lady was the wife of one of them.

"We wanted to stay here, but they are full," one of the brothers explained.

"We are waiting for a cab to take us into Palas de Rei. It is a large city with plenty of options to stay. We've had a long day and are not interested in walking another 5.5 km."

In my mind, I patted myself on the back for making a reservation! A large city at the end of stage 30 meant a crowded nightmare!

We discussed our experience so far. The single brother explained that he had done part of the Camino last year but had stopped in Sarria.

"I came back to finish it, and my brother and sister-in-law decided to come along. We intend to go all the way to Finesterre."

"I'm sure you will enjoy that. We took a bus last time because it was pouring down rain. But it was great to walk the last 3 km to the lighthouse and look over the ocean at the end of the earth," I replied. "However, five hundred miles to Santiago is far enough for me."

The cab arrived, and they offered the obligatory Buen Camino as they grabbed their packs and headed out.

# CHAPTER 36

Portos to Boente, 25.8 Kilometers
30 Sep 2015
D+32

Checking e-mail over breakfast, I was excited to find one from Mark, my former interpreter from Afghanistan. I had not heard from him since I dropped him off at the airport in early August. He had returned to his home country on a mission to help his wife get a visa to join him in the United States. He felt it was essential for him to be there in person because she needed a male relative to take her to the embassy for the interview and medical screening. I did not understand why, but he did not think her father would do it, and he did not trust her brother. Besides, she had disowned him because of his religious conversion and informed his brothers of his "grave sin," which earned him a brutal beating. By accompanying her to the interview, he hoped to demonstrate that they had reconciled. The incident was documented in his immigration package as proof of the danger he faced not only from the Taliban but also from his family.

It had been almost two months since he flew to Kabul. As was typical in that country, I had seen numerous news reports of terrorist attacks in the capital; occasionally they happened near the US embassy. Each time I prayed for his safety and frequently wondered if it was possible that I had not heard from him because he had been killed or injured in one of the attacks. I knew I was being paranoid, but I could not help myself. Now I knew he was safe, at least for the time being.

Unfortunately, they had made no progress with the immigration request. The paperwork was submitted about a month before he left for Afghanistan. Other interpreters had told him that their wives' paperwork had taken about thirty days to process before they were scheduled for the interview and medical exam. This information drove the timing of his trip. However, two months after the thirty-day point, they were still waiting for the embassy to contact them for the medical exam and interview. Mark had tried to follow up with them a couple times, but the embassy told him he just needed to wait until they contacted him. Basically, "Quit calling us, we'll call you—eventually."

I hit the trail at 0820 and used the first few minutes of the day's hike to pray for Mark's and his wife's safety and the speedy processing of the application.

At first I had a lot of privacy. Most people from the albergue left about fifteen minutes earlier. The solitude ended after a mere 5.5 km when I entered a good-sized city at the end of stage 30. To my dismay, a full load of adult day hikers dismounted a bus about one hundred meters ahead of me at the outskirts of town. Two empty buses sat next to theirs, having already sent their loads on their way. My heart sank. It would be another tough day of crowded trail.

\* \* \* \* \*

Spending three weeks at the Pentagon and the other week in Indiana each month became SOP.

The MUTC was an interesting place. Fifty or sixty years ago, it started as an institution to house mentally unstable and delinquent boys. This was back when the prevailing way to deal with insanity was to institutionalize the person. They weren't politically correct back then, and the facility was often referred to as a "home for wayward boys." Today it is occupied by an Indiana Army National Guard unit.

"So not much has changed," joked the unit's operations officer as he gave me a tour of the place during my first visit.

Many of the original buildings remained. Although in need of refurbishment, several were being used as offices, dormitories, classrooms, and training facilities. A new section had been constructed that simulated an Afghan village street—complete with Arabic graffiti on some walls. Because the facility was also used for training by military and civilian domestic crisis response teams, other structures were built to simulate bombed-out buildings. There was even a building designed as a collapsed parking garage, complete with a few crushed cars. It was actually an incredible place.

Students and role-players follow the direction of their Army National Guard security team during an ambush on a simulated Afghan street.

Over time, I became entrenched in the course. I updated the introductory intelligence briefing the students received on the first day and started providing it to my "new interagency staff" while playing the role of PRT commander. I spent the rest of the week as a mentor to one of the student "PRTs," usually ten to twelve students. Since we used the same scenarios month after month, I soon had my discussion points and typical after-action review (AAR) comments memorized. Between FTX weeks, I carved out some time from my SF duties to work with OSD and FSI to locate and arrange for former PRT commanders, XOs, and other key military personnel to participate occasionally as team mentors.

Eventually, the division chief I worked for in the SF directorate received orders to PCS and assume command of a large Security Forces Group. Based on the scenario envisioned by my mentor, I should have moved into his position. However, I was still struggling with the anxiety issues and the division was the lead for numerous issues that had intense four-star, OSD, and even presidential and congressional interest. The new general and I came to a mutual agreement that I was not the best person to take over the high-stress, high-visibility position.

By this time, I had been a colonel for about a year, so we also agreed that continuing as the deputy division chief was not ideal for somebody of my grade. Brainstorming other opportunities, it occurred to me that I could work the interagency training course full-time. I discussed it with both the FSI course management and the contractor that led the field training exercise, and we all agreed that it was worth pursuing. I pitched the proposal to the general, and he agreed to allow me to work out the details and get the appropriate approvals. After a couple of weeks, we had the approval of the FSI leadership and the director of OSD/TRS who would be my new TACON boss. It was decided that I would move into an office at FSI and be the liaison between OSD and the course managers at FSI. Since I was not moving to an authorized position, I would remain on the SF directorate's books as an overage, and the general would still be my official supervisor.

* * * * *

Countless streams of pseudo-peregrinos swarmed past me in groups of five to ten, talking and laughing loudly. The kids demonstrated their endless energy by skipping, running, and sword-fighting with sticks, seemingly oblivious to the presence of anyone else on the trail. In fact, no one seemed to have any regard for how close they came when passing. Many came within inches as they snuck by; others actually rubbed up against me with either their arms or equipment. I was on red alert all day.

Some satisfaction was achieved when I passed late starters who were obviously battling blister and muscle problems. It was about time they started paying their dues!

Stopping for a break at an old European-style albergue and café called Casa Domingo, I was distraught to find the place filled with an extremely large

My favorite way-marker on the side of a house.

adult tour group. I considered going to the next one, but it was at least a kilometer away, and I needed to use the restroom. The establishment had one unisex bathroom with an endless line. Standing in line with people who had no concept of personal space did not appeal to me, so I decided to order a coffee and wait for the group to depart. I found a seat in the far-back corner where I was at least away from all of the movement and could monitor the line. It seemed as if every time one person entered the bathroom, two more got in line. When I finished my coffee, I decided I was just going to have to bite the bullet and stand in line or I would be there all day.

After the café experience, I was relieved to be back on the trail. At least here there was some break between the passing groups and I could step off the trail and just wait for them to pass.

The Way had lost most of its appeal . . . but I had not come this far to quit two days out. I must put up with the new conditions, make the most of it, and finish!

\* \* \* \* \*

While mentoring the interagency classes full-time over the next year, there were a few major themes that I hit hard with each group of students.

I emphasized looking at the big picture when deciding what projects to pursue and how to address destabilizing issues in the communities. In the middle of the "battle," it is easy to get caught up in the emotion of passionate individual requests and the points of view of the latest people you talk to. Too often the local's perspective revolved around personal, family, or tribal dynamics without regard for the overall impact on the greater community, let alone Afghanistan in general. Especially outside the major cities, Afghans are focused on their daily tasks and the needs of their family and tribe. For many, this is all they know. Some do not even understand the concept of being Afghan. International actors must understand this dynamic.

The most important lesson from the "school of hard knocks" I wanted to relay was the importance of closely examining all relevant aspects of each potential COA and making decisions based on what I came to call the "So What Factor." In other words, is the action being considered actually going to do anything to solve the problem it is meant to address, or improve the quality of life and self-sufficiency of the people you are serving in a long-term, tangible, and sustainable way? Or alternatively, could it result in additional destabilizing problems (unintended consequences) such as feeding corruption, creating a culture of dependency, or undermining social norms that were beneficial to the community?

It was not important that a building was constructed. What was important was the long-term impact of that construction on the community. What exactly were we trying to achieve? What were the root causes of the problem being addressed? Would the project *actually* positively impact the root causes? Would the project solve the problem, or at least improve the situation, or just put a Band-Aid on a symptom?

Sometimes I wondered if the focus was far too much on improving statistics rather than making a real tangible difference. We measured success based on how many projects were approved, how much money was spent "helping" the communities, how many people completed classes that we taught, etc. We were never really able to figure out a good way to measure if anything we were doing was having a beneficial, long-term impact. A major problem was the requirement for us to report on our progress and impact on a monthly, quarterly, and annual basis. How do you measure the impact of the new school each month? Annual team rotations made the long-term view impossible to grasp. Our goal was to do as much as we could with the short time we had.

Understanding this with twenty-twenty hindsight, I explained to the students that when planning what to do about a problem, they needed to ask "why?" at least five times, digging deeper toward root causes of the problem with each successive answer. Once the underlining causes of the situation were known, potential solutions could be evaluated.

Just as important as drilling down—or "peeling back the onion," as it was often described—to find the root cause of an issue was analyzing forward and anticipating the second, third, and fourth order of effects our actions would have on the community.

One of the projects my PRT started was building a hydroelectric generator on a small river in order to give power for the first time ever to 1,500 businesses and homes in a nearby village. We were really excited about this project and worked hard on the surveying, planning, and coordinating with the affected village and the district and provincial government officials for the greater part of our year in-country. Just before my team rotated out, we received funding approval for the project.

The PRT that replaced us got the project started but ran into numerous problems. First, the local contractors that were hired for the construction used poor techniques and materials and really didn't know what they were doing. Second, when a nearby village found out their neighbors were getting power, they became desperate to get in on the deal. Knowing that the system would not have enough capacity for the other village, the PRT commander offered to build them a school instead, and that project was initiated. Although they were more than happy to get the school, this did not resolve their desire for electricity and all the capabilities that brought. Without the knowledge of the PRT, the elders convinced (bribed) the contractor to extend the power-distribution infrastructure to their village.

Between poor-quality construction and the extension of the grid far past capacity, the hydroelectric system failed. They never got it to work. The result was that no one got electricity and there was a lot of frustration and anger because the promised benefit was never achieved, even for the first village. Instead of helping improve the lives of the villagers and increasing their support of the coalition and Afghan government, the project turned into a counterproductive nightmare.

Another prime example of figuring out the complexities and root causes of a circumstance that needs to be improved was a USAID project to train thirty women to be midwives. The issue of women's health care was very complex. Due to cultural norms, clinics had to have a separate area for female patients, to include a separate entrance through the security wall so they could get in without men seeing them. But this was not enough to ensure that they had access to health care because women were not allowed to be examined by male doctors. Since Sharia law did not allow women to be educated or work in a professional capacity, there were no women doctors to treat women patients.

To at least address the high child mortality rate, USAID implemented a project to train thirty women as midwives in Paktia province so they could work out of the women's section of the clinics. By working there, they could serve women from several surrounding villages. They all graduated, but only one actually went to work at a clinic. Although their husbands allowed them go to the training, they would not let them travel to and work at the clinics. "So what" good had the training done?

A key factor that did not seem to have been considered was that women were not allowed to leave their house without being in the company of a male relative. Not only did this apply to the patients but also the midwives. After further consideration and some discussion with friends working for international aid organizations, I concluded a better approach would have been to focus on training one or two women in each village that could either work out of their own homes or go to the pregnant woman's home.

There was another major problem dealing with the clinics, schools, and other government infrastructure the coalition was building—operability and sustainability. Physical buildings did not ensure public benefit. This required the hiring and payment of staff, recurring funding for equipment, supplies (books, paper, writing utensils, medicines, rubber gloves, etc.), and facility maintenance and upkeep. The problem was that the Afghan government did not have a tax system to generate funds to operate all the government-service programs we were helping them set up. They were completely dependent on contributions from the international community. Besides this making the country as a whole dependent on the rest of the world, each contributing country established strict guidelines and limitations concerning what the funds they contributed could be used for. It was very frustrating to know about massive pots of money flowing into the country that could not be tapped into because of all the caveats.

The struggles of the Afghan National Police (ANP) provided a good example. We purchased and delivered vehicles for them to use for patrolling and emergency response, but there was little funding available for gas and maintenance.

Another problem that plagued the police (and all government employees, for that matter) was that the nation's banking system was archaic. To pay their wages, money had to be physically driven to each provincial and district capital for dispersement to individual policemen who stood in line for hours on payday. Because of rampant corruption, percentages were skimmed off every step of the way, so the actual policeman would get a fraction of his monthly pay. Staff members at the national ANP headquarters, drivers, provincial and district governors, and chiefs of police all took their cut and got rich.

We provided the governors with computers for them and their staff to use, but they only had electricity in Gardez and Puli-Alam for about four hours a day. To address this, we started putting solar power systems in schools and other government buildings. Even though the contracts included initial training for the local staff, the knowledge was not adequately ingrained in them, and nothing was available to train their replacements. This was essential because of the high turnover rate.

None of this was sustainable—and really, how long could the international community be expected to take care of all of this for them? First, there was only so much money and commitment the world would be willing to make for one country. The other major issue was, what good would it be if we fostered a culture of dependency and created a welfare state where people counted on the government to provide everything and the government counted on the rest of the world so they could provide the services to their people?

*So what* had we really achieved with all these good-intentioned efforts?

Hence, another teaching theme—the absolute necessity of designing projects with Afghan self-sustainability in mind. We needed to help the Afghans establish processes whereby they could do these things on their own, to include training future generations. We needed to work our way out of a job by creating the conditions to achieve a realistic and viable "end-state" that allowed the coalition to leave the country and for the Afghans to assume responsibility for a successful and prosperous society.

Of course, if there were obvious and easy ways of achieving this end-state, we would not still be there after fifteen years of hard work.

Connecting the Afghan people to their government was another complex mission objective. To be successful, we first needed to convince the population to *trust* the government. There were two major obstacles to achieving this: government corruption and incompetence.

There were plenty of blatantly obvious examples of government corruption the population was well aware of. The skimming of funds meant to pay the wages of government employees such as the ANP was foremost. Complicating this issue was the individual policeman's method of trying to get enough money to live on and support his family in light of the skimming: they frequently set up illegal checkpoints and demanded "taxes" from passing drivers.

Another example was the previously discussed MoI skimming of provincial operating funds. Governor Rahmat asked for assistance from the Afghan president, and I asked my chain of command if the coalition headquarters could exert pressure to resolve the problem. All to no effect. The officer who replaced me as PRT commander in Gardez came to MUTC a few times as a mentor. He told me that the governor had been relieved of his position because of ineffectiveness and corruption. Could it be that he never gave in and therefore could not operate his government? After his personal savings ran out, did he have to resort to corruption to fund provincial activities without a budget? Or did the minister fabricate some charges to have him removed because of his continual refusal to pay? Or did he finally start paying the bribe and then eventually jumped on the corruption bandwagon himself? I doubt I will ever know. One thing was for sure: he was in a no-win situation.

A major part the corruption was a cultural expectation to take care of your family and tribe as your top priority. Therefore, if we left it to government officials to decide which projects to request funding for and what contractors to hire, their decision would always benefit their family and tribe, leading to major heartburn for other elements of the population who felt sidelined, overlooked, and discriminated against.

One of the strongest examples of the problem caused by an inept government revolved around the ANP. My team visited a village in a dangerous area where the Taliban were dominant. We expected hostility from the elders. Instead, the team was warmly welcomed. Discussions revealed that the village elders wanted peace and projects to improve their standard of living; they even said they would enthusiastically welcome a girl's school. My XO, the mission commander, was shocked. Education for girls was the last thing he expected this village to want. The elders went on to explain that they wanted to support the government, but they were afraid. Their perception of the ANP and ANA was that most of them were corrupt, and even if that had not been the case, there were not enough of them, and they did not have the resources or adequate training and experience to actually protect the village from the ever-present Taliban. Between the two security agencies, the government could not patrol the village 24-7. There was no question: if the villagers supported the government and opposed the Taliban, they would be killed as soon as the security forces moved on to check out another village.

The major question the village elders had that my team could not answer was, "Why should we risk our lives and the lives of our families to support a government that is corrupt and incapable of providing effective security and other services?"

What a dilemma for us. We found it very difficult to mentor officials away from the culture of corruption and tribal allegiance that was separating them from their people, and

Interagency students meet with "Afghan village leaders" while training at MUTC.

how do you quickly build competence in a mostly uneducated and illiterate workforce?

Another aspect of this dilemma was the importance of us demonstrating through our actions that the government was in charge and we were in a supporting and assisting capacity, not occupiers pulling the strings of our local puppets. Whenever we went to meetings with the public, I made it a point to stay in the background to ensure that the governor was out front showing his leadership. The problem with this CoA was that if the people perceived their government officials as corrupt and incompetent, and they saw us supporting them, then we were by extension also corrupt and incompetent.

My position as the DoD's liaison to the predeployment training program gave me the opportunity to exchange war stories with other former PRT personnel, both military and civilian. I also closely monitored what was going on in-country and read as many analytical reports as I could get my hands on. Over time, it became clear we were not achieving our objectives; in fact, in many ways our well-intentioned efforts were actually counterproductive.

For instance, the theory was that if we completed projects that enhanced security and improved economic opportunity, health, and education, the people would have hope for a secure and prosperous future for them and their children. With this positive outlook, they would be motivated to stop supporting insurgents and join with the government in a constant improvement effort. Violence should decrease drastically. Instead, what the data showed was that the more projects and money that were allocated to a specific area, the more unstable it got. Exactly opposite of our objective. Our money and efforts seemed to be feeding instability and corruption.

By the time I left my position due to a deployment tasking to Iraq, I was completely disillusioned about our entire effort in Afghanistan.

Our government was sending people over to do a job they didn't have the experience nor near-enough training to do. They were hiring civilians for thirteen-month stints (one month of processing and training, followed by twelve months in-country) who offered only limited experience that had some relevance to the general mission of the agency in question. After three weeks of very general training that had nothing to do with their specific role, they were sent to the front lines to work on their own from a functional perspective at the village, district, and province level (normally, there was only one person from each agency assigned to each interagency team at each level below the national).

The message sent to all of us other unqualified people on the frontline was that anybody from State could do any type of governance capacity building; the Ag rep could do anything DA-oriented; and the USAID temp hire knew everything about international development. They were no more experts in their jobs than I, as an AF SF officer, was as a PRT commander. To make matters worse, the career agency employees were given the high-level positions in cubicles in the Kabul embassy, at ISAF HQ, or at the lowest level—a regional command HQ. Not that they would have been much more effective on the front lines since their mission in Afghanistan was not really part of the core missions of their agencies—i.e., governance capacity building is not a mission of the State Department.

We were not passing the "so what" test. All of our good intentions, and our human and financial sacrifices, were not having a long-term, positive impact in stabilizing the country. I became convinced that we were wasting our time, money, and lives.

While running all this through my mind, it occurred to me that it would be really great if our politicians would learn from and factor these lessons into their decision-making processes here in the United States.

Every time something devastating happens here, there is a knee-jerk reaction to do something to address it. But normally, the action taken is not well-thought-out or planned and does not in any way address the actual underlying root causes of the devastating incident or situation currently in the limelight of the media. The politicians just want to say they did something—whether that "something" actually solves, or even addresses, the actual problem is irrelevant. Then the message is sent through our media that anyone who disagrees with the action does not care about solving the problem. In reality, the people that don't support the action often care deeply about solving the problem, but they understand that the proposed action will do nothing to resolve the problem and is therefore a waste of time and money.

Furthermore, the identification and evaluation of potentially effective COAs is constantly hampered by our new culture of political correctness and the media's propagation of emotionally charged, biased, and deceptive political rhetoric and propaganda. The media has become the fourth and, dare I say, most powerful arm of our government. Public opinion is shaped by short, politically biased sound bites designed to elicit strong emotional responses but contain no substantive depth or discussion of the actual causes of problems, let alone the likely unintended third and fourth order of effects of the proposed "solutions."

I have always loved my country and considered it an honor to serve in the military in the old patriotic traditions of our ancestors. We are the best country in the world, and our freedoms allow everybody the opportunity to succeed if they apply themselves and work hard to achieve their goals. But our politicians have no clue what they are doing either domestically or internationally. They just pursue their ideological, biased agendas; most of which have no relevance to reality. Tragically, they do not care about what is best for America. They only care about implementing their naively idealistic agenda, bringing as much money as they can to their state or district, and getting reelected regardless of the damage done to the country as a whole. It seems to be all about their power and personal wealth.

I hate to admit it, but when I get wrapped around the axil about this, I am actually glad that I am no longer serving in uniform.

\* \* \* \* \*

The ever-present crowds were not my only irritant for the day. The path closely paralleled a busy road called N547. Occasionally, the trail would veer away from the side of the road, but seldom more than a hundred meters and never really out of earshot of the endless flow of passing cars and trucks. Passing through the industrial city of Melide with its population of 7,500 did not help. All in all, I was very stressed out by the time I arrived at the albergue where I had reservations just before 1600 hours.

In excited anticipation of a restful night, I passed through the doorway only to find the restaurant area practically bursting at its seams with a large group of rowdy teenagers (again!). Any spot that did not contain a loudly chattering kid was filled with one of their packs. I could hardly get through the door and across the room to the counter to check in. It was an anxiety-spawning obstacle course!

I certainly wasn't going to switch to the other albergue in town—not with that sex-obsessed, hostile, and overbearing proprietor. I was stuck!

But God was looking out for me. By the time I finished my shower and returned to the main floor, the kids and all their gear were gone. After a quick prayer of thanksgiving, I opened my service study for the day.

Day 28's message revolved around Matthew 25:34–40. Basically, every time we do a good deed here on earth that benefits another person, as long as we do it with a pure heart of service, it is the same as doing that deed for God Himself.[56]

Considering this in relation to my earlier "so what" reflections, I thought of my work at His Pantry. On the one hand, we are serving the poor as God tells us to. But does it make sense from a "so what" perspective? By giving them food each week, were we enabling them to remain dependent, thus preventing them from seeking to improve themselves so they could get a job that would propel them to self-sufficiency? I often wondered about this, primarily in regards to our working-age, able-bodied clients.

Our outreach pastor addressed this concern occasionally by saying that while some were abusing our generosity, we must remember that we were serving the Lord and that many of the people that came really needed the help. Our willingness to help and the car-

---

[56] Fryar, p. 58–59.

ing demeanor of the volunteers often opened the door for spiritual encouragement that occasionally led to salvation and eternal life, which was far more important than the meager amount of food we distributed.

One gentleman had had several strokes, was bound to a wheel-chair, and had the use of only one hand. Another was a ninetysome-thing World War II pilot struggling to make it on a tiny social security payout. Others used it as a bridge to take care of their families for a few months between jobs.

Although it could be stressful, especially when we handed out Thanksgiving and Christmas meal packages (when our client numbers could easily double), it was overall a very positive experience. Similarly, working with high-quality high school students interested in pursuing a career as an officer through attendance at the academy garnered immense self-satisfaction when I got the pleasure of watching two or three students each year achieve their goal and set off on a path that would lead to exceptional service opportunities and personal success.

The position at the American Legion was another story. I often finished the day extremely stressed out and frustrated from banging my head against the VA wall and dealing with personality conflicts and poor leadership in the Legion chain of command. Anxiety attacks were frequent, and I often felt overwhelmed with the never-ending phone calls and streams of clients coming in, many who would not bother to make appointments. It didn't help when clients took their frustrations with the VA out on us.

Additionally, my arthritic hands weren't helping. It was becoming harder and harder to type the forms for our clients. Dictation software would not work in the office environment because verbal interaction was necessary between me and the client. The voices of my partner and her client at the next desk didn't help.

Generally, I went home from the Legion completely stressed out and exhausted. It was common for me to experience the tightness and pain in my chest that I had to come to understand to be a physical manifestation of complete and utter exhaustion and anxiety, when my body was trying to tell me I needed significant rest.

Although I was retired, this volunteer position had caused my physical and mental state to return to where they were when I decided to retire to avoid potentially joining my contemporaries who had worked themselves to death. I was irritable, physically and mentally exhausted, easily overwhelmed, became frustrated at the smallest things, and even lost motivation to do many activities because all I really wanted to do was rest. Even my parents had noticed that I was struggling.

All this and I wasn't getting paid a dime for my sacrifice. At least while I was in the service, I was compensated for putting up with stress and bad bosses with a very nice monthly paycheck and good benefits.

I enjoyed helping the veterans, but was it really worth sacrificing my health?

I also had concerns with the Legion in general. They claimed to represent the views of veterans but made no effort to solicit input from members. When we tried to provide input regarding our opinion on general veteran issues and proposed organizational changes, the response from department leadership was always a negative article in the monthly organizational newspaper forcefully explaining why all the opposing views were wrong and why their views were correct. They would then take their opinions to Washington, DC, and sell them as the opinions of all veterans in the organization. Additionally, selections for office positions revolved around the good-old-boy system with the leaders just exchanging chairs every year or two.

Why was I destroying my physical and mental health to volunteer for such an organization? The self-satisfaction I got when a deserving veteran finally got the benefits he or she deserved after sometimes years of fighting with the VA is what motivated me to continue as long as I had. But after two and a half years, was it time to say "Enough"?

In the month that I had been walking The Way, I had felt my body slowly recovering from exhaustion, even though I was averaging twelve to fifteen miles a day. I had slowly become mentally relaxed. It wasn't until the last couple of days when the end was in sight and the crowds had become overwhelming that my condition had started deteriorating again. This would be over soon, and I would be back into the middle of the rat race. I dreaded going back to my duties at the Legion.

Considering the situation half a world away, it was clear that the correct intellectual decision was to resign from the SO position. This prospect excited me because it meant that I would have more time to serve in a Christian manner.

Because being an ALO for USAFA was such a positive experience, kept me connected with my military career, and allowed me to use my vast experience to benefit others—I definitely wanted to continue doing that.

I would also continue working at His Pantry. Even if some of the clients were abusing our kindness, many others really needed the help, and we were providing more than just food. Because we were working out of the chapel, we demonstrated God's love to both believers and nonbelievers. Occasionally, one of them got saved. This was the Pantry's "so what factor." From an eternal spiritual perspective, this was definitely a worthwhile volunteer position.

The logical decision was clear. When I returned, I would resign from the Legion, put more time into ALO duties, and seek other opportunities for Christian service. Maybe I would even go on a mission trip to Haiti as our mission's pastor had been encouraging me to do for several years.

With this decision, I felt a heavy burden lifted off of my back. This was exceptional evidence of the truth of God's Word:

> Come to Me, all you who labor and are heavy laden, and I will give you rest. Take My yoke upon you and learn from Me, for I am gentle and lowly in heart, and you will find rest for your souls. For My yoke is easy and My burden is light. (Mathew 11:28–30)

# CHAPTER 37

### Boente to A Rúa, 26.3 Kilometers
### 1 Oct 2015
### D+33

To my surprise, it was mostly a quite morning walking along a dirt path through the woods. I encountered just a handful of peregrinos, spread out in small groups or as individuals. A couple of biking pilgrims glided by.

To protect myself from the potential of a large crowd, before I hit the trail, I made reservations for a private room at a casa rural in a small hamlet called A Rúa a couple of kilometers before the end of stage 32. The guidebook described it as having a restful bar and an extensive garden. It sure sounded peaceful, and I thought it would be a wonderful way to spend my last night before entering the immense city of Santiago. A quick check of my funds revealed that I would need to find an ATM before arriving. Arzúa, a town of about 6,300, was about 8.5 km away. It would be my best shot for that.

The peaceful morning gave me ample time to reflect on the months leading up to my deployment to Iraq.

\* \* \* \* \*

The routine of the interagency training program was far less stressful than working high-visibility taskers at the puzzle palace. As the months passed, I started feeling more relaxed and able to focus. I was having a significant impact on the Afghan war effort and was happy that my past experiences could benefit others.

Even as I became more confident in my contributions, my regrets regarding the struggles at the end of my PRT deployment and the resulting years of emotional turmoil continued to eat at my soul. The better I felt, the more I wanted to prove to myself that I could successfully complete a combat deployment and return home with my head held high. I did not want the regrets and failures of my last deployment to forever define my career memories. I wanted to—no, I *needed* to go out on a positive note.

Be careful what you ask for! Before long I had deployment orders to Joint Security Station (JSS) Shield in Baghdad, Iraq, to fill the position of chief of staff (CoS) for the Iraqi Training and Advising Mission to the Ministry of Interior (ITAM-MoI). The unit's mission was to assist the general staff at the national Iraqi Police (IP) headquarters develop the building blocks for an effective national police force.

As the CoS, I would be the second-in-command with my primary duties being to manage the workflow and provide guidance and support to our various sections who directly mentored their Iraqi functional counterparts. We had teams advising on human resource management, logistics, infrastructure development, operations and maintenance, communications, and even Inspector General functions. I would not be in an advising role as I had been on the PRT. My boss, the ITAM-MoI director, was the adviser to the top generals, and our subordinates advised leaders of the different functional areas. My role would be internal unit orchestration, and because of my background, I anticipated being the mentor of the mentors.

Before deploying I had to attend a ten-day combat skills refresher course. Fortunately, this time it was run by the AF. I did not have to put up with the Army training mentality. Everyone in the course was going to different positions and varied in rank from airman first class to colonel, so there was no job specific training. The focus was basic, mostly defensive combat skills. The intent was to ensure that airmen whose primary jobs did not normally take them outside the wire or involve them in combat operations would at least be able to react and defend their comrades during potential attack situations.

Although I had plenty of experience with these basic skills throughout my career, I was happy for the refresher since I had been in staff positions for several years and was arguably rather rusty.

During our first session in the classroom, the instructor attempted to get everybody in the right mind-set.

"You should expect to work twelve-hour days." His intent was to explain to airmen who were used to eight-hour days in an office environment that more would be expected of them in-country.

Since I had to work fifteen- to eighteen-hour days during both of my deployments to Afghanistan, I could not help but think "Only twelve-hour days? This is going to be a cakewalk!"

The other vivid memory I have from training occurred during a convoy training exercise. I was in command. We were following the approved convoy route when we entered a mock village. Everything about it screamed "Ambush." No one was in the streets. There were numerous large barrels and other solid items strategically located along the street to hide the aggressors. Ominous second-floor windows were perfect high points for the enemy to rain bullets or RPGs down on us. I tensed and went on high alert. To my surprise, we made it through the town without incident.

Relief was short-lived. About a hundred meters on the other side of town, our lead vehicle noticed an IED on the side of the road ahead. The SOP for such a situation was to stop and back the convoy away from the threatening device. Once at a safe distance, we would set up security and call for an EOD team to remove the device so it would not pose further danger to either other coalition convoys or the local villagers. The problem was, to get far enough away to be safe, we would have to back into ambush alley. Not only would we have to reenter the village, but SOP would have had us in there for an extended period.

During classroom training, the instructors explained the enemy knew this SOP. Recently they had been implementing a new tactic where they would set out obvious IEDs they were sure we would notice. Expecting us to fall back to a safe distance, they would be waiting there to launch an ambush or set off a string of explosive devices.

Between the blatant obviousness of the IED and the ominous village, I was certain we were being set up. As we retreated from the device, I noticed a dirt road heading off to our left.

"Tell the convoy to go down this side road for fifty meters and set up security there," I ordered my radio operator.

When we made the turn, the instructors demanded we follow SOP and go straight back into the village. I refused.

"The village has ambush written all over it," I responded and then authoritatively directed the team to follow my orders.

The instructors were not happy. For several minutes, we had a battle over the radio with my troops caught in the middle. They were obviously torn between following the orders of the commander or the instructors. Eventually, they did as I told them. The instructors proceeded to give me a scathing critique during the AAR.

I believe they were just upset because I had perceived their setup and avoided the ambush. There were likely some learning objectives they were trying execute by ambushing us, and my refusal to comply had ruined their training scenario. Oh well, I stood my ground. I had made the decision to protect my troops.

Back in the dormitory, my team met to discuss the scenario without the instructors being present. To my surprise, many were angry that I had not followed SOP and defied the instructors.

I used the opportunity as a teaching moment to explain that rigidly following SOP could get you killed.

"SOPs are only a starting point to deviate from as the situation and conditions develop. The more units adhere to rigid SOPs, the quicker the enemy will figure them out, and the easier it will be for them to take advantage of this knowledge and attack with catastrophic lethality."

"Remember Murphy's laws," I continued. "The first casualty of war is the plan, no plan survives contact with the enemy, and the enemy gets a vote. You can't just blindly follow SOP. You must continually assess the situation and modify your plan as new information dictates and the situation develops."

I think some understood; others just couldn't get over the fact that I had refused to do what the instructors wanted us to do. I didn't let it bug me. I knew I had done the right thing for the safety of my troops.

The main thing I learned during the ten-day course was that the arthritis in my thumbs and toes and my back problems had progressed to the point where basic combat maneuvers, especially when wearing heavy protective gear, had become both difficult and painful. The pain and instability in the lower two joints of both thumbs was a major problem on the weapons' firing range. It was very difficult to effectively aim and fire, especially the handgun, which was an officer's primary weapon and the one I would be carrying on a daily basis.

It occurred to me that my physical limitations could put other members of my team at risk if I were to venture outside of the wire. A doctor could medically disqualify me because of these issues. But CoS was a staff position, and I would be flying a desk in the relative safety of a base. The chances of me being caught in an ambush or firefight against the enemy was remote.

By this time, my mind-set was that I needed to go. The prospect of being disqualified actually scared me. This was my chance to prove to myself that I was able to handle a deployment, that I was not a failure. Besides, I had been tasked to take the position, and I needed to stand tall and do my duty as an officer.

Since I did not believe that my medical conditions would prevent me from doing the actual tasks associated with the job, I decided it would be wrong to pursue a medical disqualification. I did my best to convince my doctors I could handle it. I guess I made a good sell because they signed off on my medical clearance form. God had not closed the door.

\* \* \* \* \*

I was almost through Arzúa without locating an ATM. I decided to depart the marked route and check out the busy parallel streets. I found an ATM within two blocks and then took a break at a nice café that not only served coffee and OJ but also bacon and eggs!

As I enjoyed my late breakfast, I logged into the Wi-Fi and found the website for an organization called Global Radio Outreach and sent them a donation of $400 as part of my tithe for receiving back pay from the VA. I became aware of the organization through my friendship with Mark. The man who led the organization had connections with a Seattle-based group that ministered to Muslim immigrants who had converted to Christianity. His Internet ministry reached out to Muslims around the world who were interested in exploring the Gospel. As part of my new commitment to focus more of my time and resources on Christian endeavors, I decided to start supporting his ministry with monthly contributions. This initial large sum was a good way to use part of my recent claim settlement in a way that I was confident would have an eternal impact in a violent and struggling part of the world.

As I set out once again, I decided to reflect more on my general experiences with ITAM MOI rather than the stressful relationship I had with the dictator—I mean, *director.*

* * * * *

The first things I noticed as I climbed out of the military cargo plane that brought us to the sprawling Camp Victory in Baghdad was the blistering June heat, extremely bright sun, and a haze in the air. Within seconds of stepping off the plane and onto the flight line in full combat gear, I was covered in flowing sweat.

I was met by an officer from my unit's logistics section. He and several other members of ITAM-MoI worked out of an office near the flight line. Their job was to receive cargo coming in on strategic airlift for the unit and arrange for it to be transported across town to JSS Shield. While we waited for my new boss to finish up meetings with the command staff, the lieutenant took me to the team's office for a tour and orientation to their operation.

It was during this first hour that I discovered that it was not a haze in the air after all. Rather, it was fine dirt particles, and a lot of it. At first I theorized that there must've been a windstorm earlier in the day that kicked it all up. But this was not the case. It was there all day, every day. Frequently, the dirt in the air was so thick that you could not even tell it was a sunny day. As a result, everything was always covered with a layer of fine dirt; there was no way to keep anything clean. This proved to be a major problem with technology such as computers, copy machines, and other office machines. I could not help but wonder what the long-term effects of breathing this air would be on our lungs.

I got a hearty laugh one day when I observed a friend from the State Department on the porch in front of his office connex sweeping the dirt off a case of bottled water. I couldn't help myself; I had to take a picture and give him a hard time.

Sweeping water

Since I only ended up being in Baghdad from June through August, extreme heat was a constant companion. Fortunately, our living and office connexes had air-conditioning, but of course, that did little good when we had to go outside to get to another office, the chow hall, gym, or during my obligatory daily trek to the Green Bean coffee shop. On a particularly hot day in August, I was astounded to see a thermometer with the mercury level so high I thought it was about ready to burst through the top.

Our water tanks also illustrated the effects of the extreme heat. As a colonel, I was fortunate to have a wet containerized housing unit (CHU). This meant that I had running water, enabling the luxury of a tiny indoor bathroom and shower. The water tank was on top of the CHU with the direct blistering sun beating down on it all day. It only took me one mistake to learn to take my shower in the morning when the water temperature was tolerable. By midafternoon, it was scalding hot.

JSS Shield was unique in one very positive way, at least from the perspective of those of us stationed there. Whereas the international Green Zone (often referred to as the IZ), Camp Victory, and smaller military outposts throughout Baghdad were frequently targeted by indirect fire, such as rockets and mortars, Shield experienced no such attacks during my three months there. While our counterparts around the city—and around the country, for that matter—raced for protective bunkers several nights a week, we slept with relative confidence that we were safe. The reason for our good fortune was, we were located next to the country's major prison.

A few months before I arrived, the base was targeted by indirect fire. Since the insurgents did not have precision targeting, they aimed their shots in the general direction of their target and hoped to hit something important or at least kill a lot of people. Apparently, this particular group were worse shots than most. They hit the prison instead and killed quite a few of their own guys. Except for the precisely positioned IED attack aimed at State Department personnel and police at the prison admin offices, Shield was not targeted again.

The showdown with my boss in mid-August ended my good fortune. I remained at Shield for a few days but then moved to our HQ in the IZ once the generals decided it would not be in anybody's best interest for me to remain as second-in-command of ITAM-MoI.

Extra-tall T-Walls between double-stacked CHUs in the IZ.

The indirect fire warning sirens went off many times while I was there. Because twenty- to thirty-foot-tall concrete T-walls were positioned between the CHUs where I was staying, we just put on our protective gear and lay on the floor until the all clear sounded. After being scared to death the first couple of times, it became a tense routine. I soon decided that the extra foot and a half between the floor and my mattress would make no difference; after all my CHU was stacked on top of another, so my floor was about fifteen feet off the ground anyway. I quit getting on the floor. There were several nights when I was nervous enough that I slept with my IBA laid over me like a blanket and my helmet next to my pillow. Even so, I knew intellectually that none of this would make any difference. With the tall T-walls all around, the only blast danger would be if the rocket landed directly on top of my CHU or at least was in the approximately twenty-by-fifty-foot area within the closest walls. If that happened, I doubt my IBA and helmet would have done any good.

Rocket attacks also plagued us the nights I spent at Camp Victory for the mental health eval after the deterioration of my relationship with the boss, as well as during my short stay at the in-country R&R facility (how does one rest and recreate under the constant threat of rocket attacks?). In fact, the alarms went off three times the last week I was in-country: once just before I left the IZ, again at Camp Victory the night before I flew out, and finally while I sat in the passenger terminal waiting to be called to load the plane.

Crunched down in the bunker just outside the passenger terminal, I looked at the guy next to me and said, "That's it! I've had it. I'm getting on the next plane out of here!"

Before my departure from Shield, I was honored to be invited to a baptism ceremony for about twenty members of the base's security force who were deployed from Sierra Leone. One by one they climbed into a large metal barrel that the chaplain had filled with water, and he baptized them. Afterward, they held a praise-and-worship music service to celebrate. The singing was overflowing with life to a very engaging beat. Everyone in attendance  swayed back and forth and clapped their hands to the beat for a good forty-five minutes. The service was so amazing to me, not only because of the fun energy, but the ironic fact that this was happening in the middle of the capital city of a Muslim country where converting to Christianity meant a death sentence for Muslims.

Another incredible memory dealt with how far communication had come since my first overseas tour. During my year at Pirinclik AS, Turkey, everyone had to sign up for a time slot for a monthly fifteen-minute call over the base's one line dedicated to morale calls. The operator would connect us to a military base closest to where we wanted to call. We would then ask that military phone operator to connect us to an off-base commercial line. If the number we wanted to call was long-distance from the base, we needed to use a calling card to pay the charges. Everyone really looked forward to their monthly morale call!

During my tours in Afghanistan, the morale tent had a whole bank of phones that people could use. We did not sign up in advance but went when we had time, signed in, and then waited for a phone to open. Calls were limited in duration if there were people waiting. If not, you could talk as long as you wanted. Some service members bought cell phones and local SIM cards at the BX and used them to call home from a more private location.

By the time I got to Iraq, Wi-Fi was available at MWR facilities and contracted commercial food services locations such as Green Bean Coffee. This meant anyone could call home anytime they wanted to using any device with Internet capability. While at the R&R facility at Camp Victory, I got a real kick out of holding up my iPad and turning on the camera so my parents could see the man-made lake and one of the palaces that had belonged to the former dictator Saddam Hussein. At the time, it was being used as a part of the headquarters for the international military coalition. In the background, they could hear the sounds of aircraft coming and going from the nearby flight line and even watched a couple of helicopters fly over the lake.

The evolution of communication was impressive.

\* \* \* \* \*

I still battled arthritis pain in my toes, but the excruciating pain in the balls of my feet had subsided considerably. I could almost hike without a limp today and was able to pick up the pace. Still, I needed to be very careful to limit the length of my strides. Even with the metal plates in my shoes, the toes tended to bend some if I took too big of steps.

I started closing in on a coed student group. I heard them long before I saw them. I tried slowing down to avoid catching up with them. This seemed to be working for a few minutes, but then the group suddenly stopped midtrail. When I got within about fifteen meters, they started walking again.

Crap! Looks like I needed to implement plan B. I sped up to pass them, but there were about twenty of them walking close together and blocking the entire trail. One by one I worked my way past each until I reached a middle-aged woman that appeared to be their leader. Somehow I managed to greet her with a friendly smile and Buen Camino. She returned the greeting and then instructed the students to clear a path for me to get through. I was very thankful! Although it hurt, I sped up in order to pull ahead of them far enough that they were not crowding my six.

After a couple more clicks, I saw a sign advertising a café off trail. Thinking this might be the one I was watching for, I went to investigate. But that meant the kids would close in on me again. After a leery few minutes, the side trip did not look promising, so I headed back to the trail, cringing at the thought of having to deal with the kids again. Not to worry, they stopped at the intersection, regrouped, and headed in the direction where I had just gone.

Relieved, I found a café about five minutes later. In accordance with the new norm, it was packed with peregrinos. There must have been twenty at the bar fighting to place their order. Nope, not eating here. I continued through town and finally saw two more cafés. The one on the trail side of the road appeared packed (there was a tour bus parked next to it), but the one across the street was empty. I had a welcomed, peaceful lunch. Only a little more than 7 km remained before the paradise that awaited me at the pension.

Leaving the café in Salceda, I realized the crowd in the place across the street was another high school group. They were just getting underway. Kids and noise were everywhere. I got so flustered that I missed an arrow and headed off in the wrong direction. After about ten minutes, I got to an intersection where it was obvious I needed to make a decision which way to go. There was no arrow to guide me. This was a sure sign I had made a mistake. I tried retracing my steps, but finally had to ask a local to point me back to the Camino.

Lesson learned—focusing too much on what frustrates you and causes anxiety only results in losing your way!

I couldn't help but ponder on how totally different the Camino experience was to these groups. They had absolutely no flexibility, no solitude. They started walking when they were told, ate where and what was prearranged, distances and lodging were predetermined, and they met few people besides the others in their group. They did not interact and make friends with people from every corner of the world like true pilgrims did. Were they just doing it to say that they did it? To get a Compestella? If they were trying to get the peregrino experience, why were they transported so much by bus?

As I left the village, I was able to separate myself from the groups. As the trail veered slightly away from the busy highway, it became a peaceful walk through the woods. Although there were always other peregrinos in sight, they were spread out enough not to be a major issue. As we passed, we happily greeted each other with Buen Camino. Now this is what the trail should be like.

\* \* \* \* \*

I had not been in Iraq long before I noticed some similarities to Afghanistan, tempered by some distinct differences. One of the most striking differences was Iraq had money, and plenty of it. Contrasting what many who opposed intervention in Iraq claim, the United States and coalition were not there to steal oil from the Iraqis. Far from it. In fact, we used US taxpayer money to help them rebuild and develop their oil infrastructure and businesses. The resulting profits went to the Iraqi government and into the country's economic system.

Not only were we not stealing the oil or the proceeds, but just as in Afghanistan, we were pouring money into the country via various forms of assistance. And just as in Afghanistan, our money and efforts were fueling a culture of dependency.

For instance, we were paying to build and equip security coordination centers. Not only were we providing US taxpayer–funded television screens, computers, and copy machines, but even little things like pens and paper. It confounded me that we were utilizing our funds for such little things when they had more than enough resources to provide for themselves. Of course, the Iraqis were not refusing our assistance.

Whenever I had the opportunity to give my opinion during multifunctional project planning meetings, I always strongly expressed my disapproval of such "projects." I emphasized that we should focus our funding and assistance resources on strategic projects with substantial US interests and big-ticket items that the Iraqis might not be able to do for themselves. I also expressed my opinion that maybe Iraq should be contributing to the costs of the military and development efforts the international community was helping the Iraqi government with. This would not constitute us stealing their oil resources; the money would be used to secure, stabilize, and develop Iraq itself. To me this only made sense.

Many others, both military and State Department civilians, seemed to be slaves to the "good idea fairy." They looked for gaps and what they perceived as shortfalls and then proposed a project to fund a solution, instead of mentoring and assisting the Iraqis to use their own manpower, funding, and resources to fix the problem. I saw this as a major problem. Our intended end-state was a self-sufficient, effective, and efficiently operating Iraqi government and economy. All of our efforts should have been designed to reach this objective.

Another similarity with Afghanistan was the apparent inability for government officials to understand the basic principles of good governance, strategic planning for their society, and basic operations for an effective organization. In Afghanistan, much of the problem was due to a lack of education and on-the-job experience, not to mention the impact that thirty years of war had had on the country's infrastructure, economy, and general public mind-set. In light of the terrible brutality of the Soviet occupation followed by Taliban oppression, not to mention all the fighting involved in both, I often wondered if the entire country's population had PTSD.

Iraq was different. Although they had endured many years of rule by a brutal dictator, the population was educated, and they had a functional economy, extensive national infrastructure, and of course, oil and plenty of it. Some of the current problems had resulted from the removal of Saddam loyalists in the government and military. This left a major experience void that would take some time to overcome. Even so, they could not seem to understand the basics of administrative and operational planning nor efficiencies.

For example, we struggled with ineffective logistics planning throughout the IP. After some mentoring, the logistics leaders were convinced to stock vehicle parts at their bases with the idea that they could conduct maintenance on-site instead of having to send the vehicles back to Baghdad to be fixed. The problem was that they sent parts to bases seemingly at random. The parts sent were not necessarily based on the vehicles in operation at the base. They just sent parts, so even though they had a significant stock, they still couldn't fix the vehicles. This type of illogical thinking was rampant throughout the organization. Their lack of common sense never ceased to boggle our minds.

Contrary to anti-war media reports in the Western world, coalition military presence was not causing an escalation in violence in either country. Rather, the coalitions were separating warring factions and were bringing at least some semblance of security. In Afghanistan, it was keeping tribes from fighting each other and trying to protect the public from the Taliban. In Iraq, the coalition was working hard to keep the Sunni, Shia, Kurds, and other factions of Islam from killing each other while trying to foster a combined government that represented all people groups. With deep historical hatred, distrust, and violent fighting against each other, this was not an easy task.

As a testament to the level of effectiveness the coalition had in bringing some stability, the day after the last of our forces pulled out in December 2011, the Iraqi vice president was declared a war criminal and an arrest warrant was issued. He had to flee for his life. Bloody factional fighting and terrorist attacks erupted all over the country within days. Some of this violence had plagued the country while the coalition was there trying to assist the new government, but the frequency and brutality drastically increased as soon our forces left.

Our military leaders had warned our national leadership countless times that this would happen, but they pulled us out anyway.

It was very disheartening to see that all of our goodwill, efforts, resources, and the lives of our dead and wounded had been wasted as everything crumbled before the exhaust of our departing planes and convoys had dissipated from the dirty, stagnate Iraqi air.

It was even more frustrating watching the news over the following years as ISIS rose to fill the void left by the coalition, going so far as to commandeer and use the weapons, vehicles, and other military equipment that we had left for our Iraqi allies to use to protect their population. Instead, our equipment was being used by terrorists to slaughter and oppress the population.

\* \* \* \* \*

After about 5 km, I approached the handful of buildings known as Santa Irene where we had spent our second to last night on the trail in 2013 at a wonderful, rustic casa rural. My memories were of a quiet, comfortable evening where we met a tour group of people who were ecstatic to meet real peregrinos. Today's experience was the opposite. Instead of peace, I quickly closed in on yet another large group of schoolkids. Complete pandemonium prevailed once again. Fortunately, the trail went straight through the hamlet, so I did not have to worry about missing a turn. I did my best to pass the group and get out of town as quickly as possible.

\* \* \* \* \*

As I tried to deal with the increasing tension between me and my boss while running interference to protect the rest of the unit from our self-absorbed, careless, and sadistic director, I tried to focus the work of our various functional sections on closing out as many aspects of their program as possible. Initiatives that needed to continue had to be prepared for transition to the company contracted by DoS to take over the police development mission.

The boss convinced himself that the contractors were not capable of taking over the mission and found as many ways as he could to obstruct progress. I believe his resistance was due to the fact that the

DoS and the contractors didn't see the need for the position he had created for his girlfriend. They had no intention of continuing her contract. As a result, there was no love lost between the boss and the contractors. It was left to me to work with them as best as possible to prepare for the transition.

By the time the boss and I had our blowout, the contractors had decided that they would just focus on their own future planning, stay out of the boss's way, and just wait until he was gone. They refused to attend staff meetings where we were discussing the transition, which completely infuriated the boss.

Since the boss did not leave until around November and I left in late August, I often wondered how the transition progressed once I was out of the picture. I will likely never know.

* * * * *

I was excited to reach the pension where I reserved a room by 1600. The hospitalero escorted me across a beautiful grassy secluded courtyard to my private room under the shade of a lush tree. It was a basic room inside, but I was thrilled to have a private bathroom, sheets on the bed, and large, soft towels. Pure luxury!

As happy as I was for the solitude, I was looking forward to the potential of meeting other pilgrims at dinner. This would be the best of both worlds.

Once I got my shoes off, I realized that my feet were not doing as good as I had perceived all day. Don't get me wrong; the orthotics and metal plates were still doing wonders. But when I tried to walk in my socks or sandals, the pain in the balls of my feet was almost crippling. Even the tops of my feet hurt at the base of my toes. The persistent blister on my left heel also hurt more without the protection of my shoe.

Over 760 km were behind me, with about twenty-one remaining until I arrived at my final objective. As far as my feet were concerned, I could not obtain "mission complete" status quick enough.

I stacked my pillows about two-thirds of the way down my bed and elevated my feet while opening my service study to day 29.

Today's message encouraged the reader to consider these words: "No matter how hard we try, it's impossible to imagine the joy that will belong to us forever! We serve now in joy, to be sure. But frustration, grief, sin, and even persecution often mark that service, too. Eternity's joy, though, will be unadulterated." We were then asked to reflect on what it will be like the first moments we stand in heaven, absorbing the unimaginable wonders and greeting long-lost friends and loved ones, forever to share with them an eternity of peace.

"How does it inspire you to serve with all your heart today?" the author concludes.[57]

With my elevated feet throbbing, I could not help but draw a parallel between that day and the joy I would feel walking into the courtyard in front of the Santiago de Compostela Cathedral tomorrow afternoon. Yes, it would pale in comparison to my first day in heaven, but the feeling will be as close as I can get on earth!

With no need to conduct mission planning for tomorrow, I took a short nap, then a shower, and headed to the restaurant in hope of sharing my last evening on The Way with other pilgrims.

To my surprise, there was no pilgrims' dinner, and only one other couple was in the restaurant when dinner was served just before 1900. It turns out that they were Americans from Indianapolis. We exchanged pleasantries and a few war stories, and then each retired to our respective rooms to contemplate the events that awaited us in the morning.

My thought of entering the huge metropolis generated anxiety. I needed to get in the right mind-set. As I recalled, the first 15 km or so passed through peaceful wooden areas and skirted around the end the Santiago's international airport. About 5 km out, I would enter the hustle and bustle of the Camino's largest city. Hordes of peregrinos would merge with normal city crowds and traffic. I hoped that the excitement of satisfying my damaged ego would temper the anxiety of the crowds.

---

[57] Fryar, p. 60–61.

It occurred to me that the crowded last five stages could possibly be the Camino's way of helping us deal with the pending end of our journey that would inevitably lead to the feeling of "now what?" that you get after accomplishing a goal and defeating a challenge that had been your focus for several years.

# CHAPTER 38

A Rúa to Santiago de Compostela, 21.6 Kilometers
2 Oct 2015
D+34
Mission Complete

I took my time getting ready for my final day on The Way. I had taken the Compeed off my blisters last night, and everything was dried out fairly well. I decided to go without any protective covering. If they started hurting, I could always stop and put new Compeed on. Too easy.

However, per SOP, I applied Vaseline on the high-risk areas of each foot and put new lamb's wool in the heels of each shoe. I also spread the anti-inflammatory and pain creams on the balls, toes, and the tops of my feet. Finally I put my hiking shoes on. More than anything else, this final, simple act took about 70 percent of the pain away.

While enjoying a light breakfast at the pension restaurant, I spoke briefly with the couple from Indianapolis.

"I guess we don't have to ask how far you intend to go today," the wife joked in anticipation.

"Nope," I smiled in return. "Santiago or bust!"

The path started out on a wonderful, smooth earthen trail through the woods. I could hear the traffic in the distance, but it was not too distracting. Similar to the early hours of yesterday's trek, I encountered only a small number of hikers that were spread out pretty well in small clusters of one to three people.

I knew it wouldn't last, but I relished the tranquility as long as it endured.

\* \* \* \* \*

The final adventure of my career turned out to be the best deployment I could wish for. After the fall out with my boss in Baghdad, I was in search of a new position. With the drawdown, there were not a lot of colonel slots available in Iraq. In fact, they were working hard to determine who would go home and when.

I was not ready to go back to the Pentagon. All my household goods went into storage a mere three months earlier. Since I had been renting a house, the contract had ended when I moved out, so I had no place to go back to. Besides, I had deployed with the mind-set of being gone for a year.

I was intrigued by an e-mail announcement for an O-6 chief staff officer position at Camp Lemonier, Djibouti (CLDJ). Djibouti is located at the north end of the Horn of Africa at the mouth of the Red Sea. Yemen is across the sea to the north; Somalia is to the east; and other countries in the area are Ethiopia, Kenya, and Eritrea.

Although the words were in a different order, it sounded like the job was similar to what I had been doing at JSS Shield. The unit's mission was obviously going to be different, but orchestrating staff functions would be similar regardless of what the mission objective was. They were looking for someone to fill a six-month deployment. That sounded just about right. It would get me back about ten months after I left, and then I could process for retirement. Of course, the other advantage of going to Djibouti would be that it's not in the middle of a combat zone, so I probably would not have to worry about rockets, mortars, IEDs, nor other types of attacks on the base or convoys! I sent an e-mail to the point of contact (POC) and provided the requested information for consideration. A couple days later, I was informed that I was selected.

I went to the United States for two weeks of leave and then mission orientation on the East Coast before forward deploying to Djibouti. While visiting my parents, we spent a lot of time searching for a house for me to buy. I had decided that I wanted to retire to the general area where they lived. This way we would be able to do things together while they were still young and healthy enough to be active. It would be much better than getting a six-figure job, traveling all over the world for the next twenty years, and then finally settling down when I could go visit them in a nursing home on Sunday afternoons. Besides, my sister and her family of seven kids lived in the same general area. My brother had also moved to the Seattle area a couple of years earlier. It seemed like a no-brainer that northwest Washington would be the best place to retire. On my last day of leave, I found my dream home: a log cabin in the woods, on an island, across the street from a lake. I immediately put an offer on it and started the purchase process while conducting predeployment orientation with the unit I would be working with. After two weeks there, I flew to Djibouti and was introduced to the men and women of the Joint Special Operations Task Force with whom I would be working.

It is really not my place to tell the story of the unit that I was assigned to support. I was merely in a supporting role in what they called an individual augmentee (IA) position. Even though I was the ranking person in our camp (a subsection of the overall base), I had no authority over the operations of the unit. My job was to run our compound and supervise logistics, supply, communications, and administrative support for those executing the mission.

African safari military style. Hippos viewed through NVGs.

I can say this: the unit was made up of people from multiple services, and they had a dynamic mission. They were professional and dedicated to serving their country. They were doing a critical and sometimes-dangerous mission to keep Americans and the free world safe. They did this mission in complete humility and shied away from any recognition or fanfare. I was extremely honored to have the opportunity to work with this professional organization as the last hoorah of my career. I was blessed to be welcomed into their fold for a precious few months even though their mission was way outside of anything I had ever done in the military before. I could not fathom a better way to end my career than by contributing my small part in support of this outstanding unit and their incredible mission. I want to thank everyone involved for giving me that opportunity.

I hope someday their story will be told, but if left up to them, it probably won't be. For them, every incredible thing they do is just another day at the office.

\* \* \* \* \*

The relative bliss only lasted an hour before the first large group of excited young twentysomethings closed in on my six. I slowed down significantly and moved off to the right side of the trail so they could move ahead of me quickly. A short while later, they joined just about all the other peregrinos at a crowded café. Passing the café

Drowned rats take a break from the rain in 2013.

without even slowing down, I reaped another forty-five minutes of peace.

My first objective for the day was a café just shy of halfway at the end of the airport runway. Dripping wet and cold, we had sought relief from the rain here in 2013, as had virtually everybody else on this section of The Way. Wet packs had lined both sides of the hallway leading to the restrooms. Normally the packs would've been left outside, but not in a downpour. The floor of the restaurant was slick with water, and it was difficult to find a place to sit. It seemed that none of the drowned rats were in a big hurry to get back out into the rain.

Today the packs were lined up along the wall outside the café, and the inside was dry, but it was just as crowded and noisy. I had to stand in three different long lines: first for the bathroom, then to get my stamp, and then to order coffee. It was complete craziness!

With all these people, you would think that I would see some-body that I knew. But I did not. Everyone I had met were so spread out that I began to wonder if I would ever see any of them again. Crowds of strangers seemed to be the norm now.

Checking my e-mail while drinking my coffee, I discovered Eunice and Marty had completed their journey two days ago. I replied with my congratulations and an update on my progress and then set out to conquer another segment. The day's second objective was just under 6 km away. The book showed a café at a road inter-section in an area called Camping San Marcos. My intent was to eat lunch there before entering the city.

\* \* \* \* \*

Djibouti was a poverty-stricken country with hardly a hint of green foliage, littered with garbage as far as the eye could see in any direction. It did not take me long to realize why it was such a waste-land. Basically, it boiled down to a complete lack of motivation to succeed or concern for their living conditions.

As a predominantly a Muslim country, the role of women in business was limited to selling food or crafts on the side of a street.

Regardless of the time of day I went off-base, I witnessed men apparently wandering around aimlessly, talking with other men, or just sitting somewhere watching the activity around them. Little work was being done.

In the afternoon, all men I observed had at least one bulging, fat cheek. A friend explained they were chewing the leaves of a plant called Kot. This drug was grown in Kenya and other places in the area and exported to countries all over the region. After a lazy morning of minimal work, the men spent the afternoon stuffing their cheeks and sucking on the leaves to get high. Some protruded outward two to three inches. Years of use must have stretched their cheeks. The admiral who was in charge of CLDJ explained one day that a high-level government official downtown had told him that chewing Kot was a critical sign of manhood, and they took it very seriously.

The dismal Djiboutian work ethic was a critical issue when it came to the air traffic controllers at the airport, whose runway we shared. Their complete lack of concern for doing a quality job resulted in numerous near misses between aircraft. After long negotiations with the government, whose pride caused them to strongly resist, the base's AF element assigned their own controllers to the tower, officially as observers but ready to step in if they saw a dangerous situation developing. The Djiboutian controllers were very offended, refused to admit their shortcomings, and did all they could to prevent the Americans from "interfering" with their duties. They insisted they had no need for American assistance, training, equipment, or counsel. After finding out about the extent of this problem, I became very nervous every time I had to fly in or out of the base or civilian airport.

An obvious sign of their minimalist culture was the garbage that covered almost every inch of ground throughout Djibouti (not only the name of their country, but also their major city near our base). The admiral explained that he had tried to get the local Djiboutian government leader to clean up the road leading to the base. The official refused, insisting that they did not care about the garbage and if the United States wanted it cleaned up, they would have to do it themselves. Of course, for an absurdly high amount, he would be happy to find a contractor to do the work. As it was, between the rent that the United States paid to use the base and the local economic impact of supplies, contracts, and base operations, Camp Lemonier accounted for 50 percent of the country's economy. Even so, they wanted to raise the rent significantly! I guess they were at least smart enough to know that they had a gold mine due to the base's strategic location.

These observations, combined with my growing frustrations with what I had learned about Afghanistan and Iraq's problems, further convinced me that international assistance, missionary trips, and development efforts are a complete waste of time, effort, and money. Decades of international government, NGO, and missionary efforts had made little progress anywhere in the third world because nothing will change until the people themselves, their culture, and their work ethic change. Educating children will get you nowhere if they just follow the ways of their parents or their corrupt society impedes their efforts to succeed and become self-sufficient or even profitable. As long as the fabric of the country is based on corruption, poor work ethic, dependency, and just a general lack of concern for personal or national success, nothing that we do—no matter how well intentioned—will ever have a true, lasting positive impact. The "so what factor" analysis concludes with "Don't bother."

One bright spot of my tour was that I was blessed to observe at least one country in the region where the locals were trying to change their trajectory. When I went to a meeting in Nairobi, Kenya, I saw billboards encouraging people to get behind and assist with the country's development plan. They called it Kenya 2020. The vision was to improve the standard of living and develop a thriving economy for their country. The people seemed fully behind their government's vision. I saw a man walking on the side of the road at five o'clock in the morning. My local driver explained that it was common for poor men who could not afford a bicycle to walk ten miles to work in the morning and then, of course, walk back at night—only to do it all over again the next day. Now, this was motivation. This country was heading somewhere. If their motivation continues, this could be a huge success story for the continent of Africa.

But it would help the entire region if Kenya would quit growing and exporting Kot. I saw no sign that they were using it themselves, but they were definitely profiting from the addiction of the rest of the region! If this was what was fueling their progress, maybe it wasn't such a bright spot after all!

* * * * *

The café at Camping San Marcos turned out to be another location where we had stopped in 2013—an ad hoc, temporary-looking building but functional. As I ate my half loaf of bread with thin slices of chorizo to give it flavor, I decided this was one thing I would not miss about the Camino. Lunches with substance were beginning to seem like a luxury.

Six point 6 km to the cathedral in Santiago!

\* \* \* \* \*

Although I really enjoyed my work with the task force, I clearly remember walking across our compound late one evening feeling completely exhausted. The tightness in my chest was a vivid reminder that I needed to slow down. I had done my part. I had had enough. It was time to rest.

A friend recommended I give myself at least three months to process for retirement after returning from deployment. Factoring that in, plus about ninety days for terminal leave, I formally submitted my retirement request in early 2012, requesting an effective date of 1 November 2012.

Once I had my retirement orders in hand, I made arrangements for my household goods to be delivered to my new log home in Washington. I planned to take a few days leave in May to receive the shipment, then return to DC to complete out-processing, and hold the formal retirement ceremony near the end of July.

Since I had not been working with the SF staff for almost two years and was only going to be there for three months, it made no sense for them to give me any real responsibility or put me in charge of a division. So I completed odd taskers for the general and spent most of my time at medical appointments, attending transition training courses, copying my medical records, and working with a VFW service officer at their DC office to submit the disability claim for my various service-connected issues. I was surprised that retirement processing could actually be a full-time job for almost three months. For most, these activities could be spread out over a year and balanced with continuing to do one's primary duties. Since I had been deployed, I did not have that luxury.

I had a small retirement ceremony in the Pentagon's Hall of Heroes in late July. I was honored to be able to have the ceremony in such a prestigious location. My direct AF bosses from my Afghanistan deployments (both retired now) and the AF general who had saved my career at the end of my second AFG tour (now a three-star stationed at the Pentagon) honored me with their attendance. The deputy commander I worked with while deployed to Djibouti played an active role by pinning on the Defense Meritorious Service Medal I had been awarded for my accomplishments while supporting the TF. I could not have asked for a greater honor at my retirement ceremony and will forever be in his debt for agreeing to come! My boss from OSD when I was working in interagency predeployment training was the primary presiding officer. A couple of people who had been on my PRT and a former US ambassador and several others with whom I had worked during field training in Indiana were also able to attend.

Besides military friends, former bosses, mentors, and coworkers—my parents, two sisters, a niece, my cousin's daughter, and the neighbor with whom I was staying joined the festivities. They all got a real kick out of seeing the inside of the Pentagon.

There was probably less than thirty people there because I did not make a big deal about advertising the event, but the people who really counted were there.

Afterward, my parents and I spent two weeks driving my car from DC to my cabin. We did a lot of sightseeing along the way, but by the time we got to Montana, I wanted nothing more than to get home and escape from the world for at least a month or so.

I just wanted to rest.

* * * * *

My soul leaped with excitement as I caught my first glimpse of the ancient cathedral spires towering over the tops of Santiago's modern buildings. The final forty-five-minute walk through the congested city was difficult, but the anticipation of completing my mission propelled me through the crowded streets at a rapid clip. I would soon have more than enough rest.

Beggars manned their posts along The Way, hoping to benefit from the excitement of the jubilant pilgrims. The density of the crowds sharply increased, and souvenir shops were plentiful, offering every imaginable Camino novelty. Yep, I had entered a tourist trap!

None of that mattered as I strolled into the city square in front of the cathedral.

Mission accomplished! Time hack: 1400 hours, 2 Oct 2015.

Victory pose in front of the cathedral. Too bad it was under renovation!

A sea of peregrinos occupied the plaza staring at the inspiring cathedral while resting their tired bodies. Others were enthusiastically greeting their Camino family in joyous spontaneous reunions.

As I glared at the cathedral, relishing the moment and absorbing the incredible scene around me, I heard someone call out my name. Turning to my right, I saw Tara and Al moving quickly in my direction, smiling from ear to ear!

"We did it!" we exclaimed in unison as we embraced in a three-way hug, each reminiscing about the physical pain and numerous temptations to quit that we had overcome.

"How long have you been here?" I asked.

"Only about thirty minutes," Al said. "We decided to hang out here for a while and watch for people we know."

"Would you mind taking a picture of the three of us?" I asked a pilgrim standing nearby.

"Of course," she said as I handed her my phone.

Within minutes another beaming couple approached us. They were friends of Tara and Al from Bend, Oregon. Another round of hugging and picture-taking ensued; this time I was the official photographer.

"The incense will swing at the service at seven tonight," I explained to the group. "It's the only time during the week that you can be sure they will do it. Why don't we meet here at six fifteen and go in together. It will be very crowded, and we want to get seats on the crossbar so we can see the full swing, so we better go early."

Everyone agreed.

"I'm going to head over to the Pilgrims Office and get my Compostela," I continued as I picked up my pack and poles.

"Sounds good," Tara said. "See you tonight."

Since I had been here before, it only took me a few minutes to get reoriented and find the office. It was hard to miss once I got to the correct street. There was a very long line.

"It's taking about an hour and forty minutes to get to the front," someone told me. "I think I will come back later on tonight or in the morning when there aren't so many people."

As he headed down the street, Jacque emerged from the crowd and greeted me. I could tell she had been here for a while. She was cleaned up, wearing clothes I would not consider "hiking clothes," and of course, the telltale sandals.

"I've been here since last night," she explained. "Do you know where you are staying tonight?"

"No, I just got in about twenty minutes ago," I replied.

"I stayed in an albergue last night. I'm done with that. I'm going to catch a train to Madrid at ten in the morning. Are you interested in joining me in a nice hotel? We can share the cost and have a really nice place tonight."

"Sure, sounds great!" I agreed. "After I get done here, I'm going to see if I can get to the travel office and make plane arrangements. I could end up on the train with you in the morning."

"Awesome. I'll come back in about an hour and a half and take you to the hotel to get settled in. We can meet at the bar across the street." With that she was off in search of other friends.

I noticed that the train ticket office was right next door; that will be the next line that I stand in.

As I settled into line, Eunice and Marty walked up. This set off another round of photos and more excited small talk. We agreed to meet at the fountain in front of the cathedral at 1700 to share a drinks before I met Tara and Al for the service.

It took about forty minutes, but finally I entered the courtyard outside the Pilgrims Office. A few minutes later the German couple I had become friends with exited the Pilgrims Office proudly raising their certificates in victory. After hugs and greetings, they posed for a picture, holding their prize.

There were short garden walls along the edges of the courtyard that we could sit on as we waited for the line in front of us to move forward. Since I had about a half hour more to wait, I grabbed my service study booklet from my pack and used the time to do the final lesson.

Lesson 30 encouraged the reader to make two lists. The first should contain the names of people, events, and opportunities that bring joy during our service for Jesus and His people. The second should list all of the temptations, roadblocks, and challenges that frustrate our service. The author then asks us to imagine how our joys will be multiplied and frustrations eliminated once we reach our eternal home.[58]

It didn't take much effort to draw distinct parallels to my feelings and experiences on the Camino.

As I slowly neared the office door, I began to worry that I would not have time to complete everything. If nothing else, I should at least try to get the train ticket from the office next door before going with Jacque to the hotel.

Once at the counter, I handed over my pilgrims' credentials so the volunteer could log my start point and nationality. A summary of this information for everyone who finished today would be announced at the pilgrims' service at the cathedral tonight. He then wrote my name on a preprinted certificate and sold me a protective tube to put it in so it would not be damaged on the trip home. I now had my proof of success, proof that I was still able to overcome physical obstacles to obtain a goal. My damaged ego was healed!

I had about fifteen minutes before I needed to meet Jacque, so I went to the train office. From the second I entered the door, it

---

[58] Fryar, p. 62–63.

was obvious the line was far too long for me to get through before I needed to start meeting all the obligations I had arranged with my friends. I decided that trying to leave tomorrow was pushing it and wasn't really necessary. There was no reason I couldn't wait until tomorrow morning to make my travel arrangements. What was the hurry? After all I had been through, why shouldn't I just relax and enjoy the time with my friends?

Somehow I got into a conversation with a lady in the ticket office who spoke English.

"How was your Camino?" I asked.

I was shocked by her reply. "I had the worst Camino ever!" she said, almost in tears.

"Oh no," I said. "What happened?"

"My friend John and I were doing it together. We had been friends for many years. A couple weeks ago, he had a heart attack and died. I have been wearing his fleece vest ever since. I don't believe in God, but I'll wear the vest to the service tonight to honor his memory. It's the least I can do for him."

I was shocked. We had passed several memorials that had been erected over the years for peregrinos who had met their fate on The Way, but I had heard no discussion about anyone dying so recently.

Jacque was not at the café/bar we had agreed to meet at, so I grabbed an outside table, ordered a glass of wine, and commenced in an activity that I called "peregrino watching." Mom and I had developed the basics of this activity two years ago. The idea was to sit at an outside café, enjoy some wine, and watch all the people go by. Since Santiago was a major tourist location, pilgrims were not the only ones wandering the streets. Our job was to pick the hikers out of the crowd. It wasn't a difficult task. We were looking for hiking pants, hiking shirts, sandals, and the telltale limp of somebody struggling with blisters on both feet. Once you get good at it, you can pick out a pilgrim from a mile away!

After about ten minutes, Jacque arrived, and we headed to the hotel to complete registration and drop off my pack. I was shocked when my share of the bill came out over sixty dollars. I guess I should have asked more questions before agreeing to share the room. Oh well, I had just completed five hundred miles and redeemed myself for my failure two years ago. This was a big deal. I deserved a night in a high-scale hotel!

After showering, I headed out to meet Eunice and Marty. We enjoyed wine and tapas while exchanging Camino stories.

"We are taking the train to Barcelona tonight," Eunice revealed. "We'll spend a few days there before heading home."

"Sounds great. Me, I've had all I can take of crowds and tourist traps." I shook my head. "There is a travel agency a couple of blocks from the cathedral. I'll go there early in the morning and make flight arrangements. I've tried buying a ticket on the Internet, but with all the people logging in, it was too slow. Besides, I get a little nervous about paying by credit card over the public Wi-Fi. If all goes well, I could leave the day after tomorrow."

After bidding farewell to my friends, I went to the designated rendezvous point to meet Al and Tara. I waited about fifteen minutes and then got nervous that I would

not be able to find a good place to sit, so I went into the cathedral alone. I was somewhat bummed because I was looking forward to spending time with this wonderful couple. I proceeded to search for seating on the crossbar and was fortunate enough to be invited to join another friend.

To be clear, what I mean by "crossbar" refers to the design of European cathedrals. The structure is constructed around the basic design of a cross with the altar at the intersection of what would be the long "vertical" pole and the shorter horizontal crossbar. Sitting in the crossbar provided a clear view of the entire arc of the swinging incense. My friend offered me a perfect seat.

This service, with the guarantee of the swinging incense, was the grand finale of the entire trip. Although the service was in Spanish, it was a thrill to be present and observe the world-renowned ceremony. Since I was raised Catholic, it was not difficult to follow along and understand the general progress of the service.

Once again, the presiding priest informed everyone that photography was not authorized during the service. But just like last time, the pilgrims ignored this instruction. Every cell phone was out taking either still shots or a movie of the event, including mine.

After the service I returned to the hotel room and got a wonderful night's sleep.

On the third, I settled into an albergue where I could stay a couple of nights until it was time to go to Madrid to catch my flight home. In the cramped solitude of a bed cubicle reminiscent of what I would expect in a Navy ship at sea, I composed the following final update to family and friends who had been tracking my progress.

### Subject: Mission Accomplished

I arrived at the Cathedral in Santiago de Compestella about 2pm yesterday! Throughout the afternoon and evening I ran into people I had met along the Way. Great reunions and fellowship. In the evening I attended the Pilgrim's Mass and saw the incense swing. I bet there was over a 1,000 people in there!

The last few days on the trail were a little frustrating. We never seemed to be too far from a busy highway. Additionally, there was a large adult tour group and at least three large groups of teenagers. All very loud and resulted in the trail, cafes, etc. being very crowded. Plus, since

Sarria is the last place you can start and still get the completion certificate, there were hundreds of others that started there.

One thing is for sure, God is not calling me to be a tour guide or work in a youth ministry!

Maybe these crowds are the Camino's way of making us more comfortable with ending our journey. Completing it has mixed feelings. You are excited to have accomplished your goal, but sad to see the experience end and have to say goodbye to your friends.

I was finally able to get my arrangements completed to travel home. Flying out today or tomorrow would cost $2.500+ . . . So I am here for a couple days. Monday I take a train to Madrid and fly out of there on Tues. This saves me over $1,200 minus the cost of lodging and food for the next two days (the train and Madrid hotel is included in travel costs). I am staying at an albergue for the next couple nights to keep the cost down. I have a lower bunk, so I am fine with this.

Looking forward to seeing everyone soon!

# REFERENCES

Rodney Atkins, *If You're Going Through Hell*

*Atlas Response / Silent Promise*, http://www.globalsecurity.org/military/ops/silent_promise.htm

Gregory Ball, *OPERATION ALLIED FORCE*, Posted 8/23/2012, Air Force Historical Studies Office, Joint Base Anacostia Bolling, DC., http://www.afhso.af.mil/topics/factsheets/factsheet.asp?id=18652

Bible references are from the New King James Version of the Holy Bible

John Brierley, *A Pilgrim's Guide to the Camino de Santiago: St. Jean - Roncesvalles - Santiago,* 12ᵗʰ edition, Published by Camino Guides, 2015, 117-121 High Street, Forres IV36 1AB, Scotland.

Historical facts from Comiso were validated at the following website: https://en.wikipedia.org/wiki/Comiso_Airport

*Contrails*, Volume 29, 1983, United States Air Force Academy, Colorado.

Emilio Estevez, *The Way,* Produced by Filmax Entertainment, Icon Entertainment International, Elixir Films, 2010.

Jane L. Fryar, *Shaping Hearts, Changing Lives: 30 Days to Grow in Service*, Published by CTA Incorporated, 2014, www.CTAinc.com. 1625 Larkin Williams Rd., Fenton, MO 63026.

Luke AFB facts validated at: https://en.wikipedia.org/wiki/Luke_Air_Force_Base, 1 Sep 2016.

Pirinclik facts validated at: https://en.wikipedia.org/wiki/Pirinçlik_Air_Base

*Seeking Allah, Finding Jesus, A Devout Muslim Encounters Christianity* by Nabeel Qureshi. Copyright © 2014 by Nabeel A. Qureshi. Used by permission of Zondervan.

Douglas Day Stewart, *An Officer and a Gentleman*, produced by Lorimar Film Entertainment, Paramount Pictures, 1982

Tom Wolfe, *The Right Stuff* (Farrar, Straus and Giroux: 1979).

# ACRONYMS

| | |
|---|---|
| 1SGT | first sergeant |
| 24/7/365 | 24 hours a day; 7 days a week; 365 days a year |
| 3AF | Third Air Force |
| AAR | after-action review |
| ABGD | Air Base Ground Defense |
| AB | Air Base |
| ABS | Air Base Squadron |
| ACS | Agile Combat Support |
| ADCON | Administrative Control |
| AETC | Air Education and Training Command |
| AEW | Air Expeditionary Wing |
| AFFOR | Air Force Forces |
| AFPC | Air Force Personnel Center |
| AFSFC | Air Force Security Forces Center |
| ALO | admissions liaison officer |
| AMC | Air Mobility Command |
| ANA | Afghan National Army |
| ANDS | Afghan National Development Strategy |
| ANP | Afghan National Police |
| ANSF | Afghan National Security Forces |
| AO | area of operations |
| AO | action officers |
| AOR | area of responsibility |
| AS | Air Station |
| ASAP | as soon as possible |

| | |
|---|---|
| AT | antiterrorism |
| AT/FP | Antiterrorism/Force Protection |
| ATOC | Alternate Tactical Operations Center |
| BAF | Bagram Airfield |
| BCT | Basic Cadet Training |
| BDOC | Base Defense Operations Center |
| BDU | battle dress uniform |
| BOLO | be on the lookout |
| BTZ | below-the-zone |
| BX | base exchange |
| C2 | Command and Control |
| CA | civil affairs |
| CAPT | Navy's way of abbreviating captain, their equivalent to a colonel |
| CAS | Close Air Support |
| CATM | combat arms training and maintenance |
| CE | civil engineering |
| CENTCOM | Central Command |
| CG | commanding general |
| CHU | containerized housing unit |
| CINC | Commander-in-Chief |
| CJTF | Combined Joint Task Force (i.e., multinational and multi-service) |
| CLDJ | Camp Lemonier, Djibouti |
| CMSgt | chief master sergeant |
| CoA | course of action |
| COCOM | Combatant Command |
| COIN | Counterinsurgency |
| CONOP | Concept of Operation |
| CoP | chief of police |
| CoS | chief of staff |

| | |
|---|---|
| CP | Command Post |
| CRC | contingency response cell |
| CS | cadet squadron |
| CSO | chief staff officer |
| CV | critical vehicle |
| CVAMP | Core Vulnerability Assessment Management Program |
| DCU | desert camouflage uniform |
| DFAC | dining facility (chow hall) |
| DFC | defense force commander |
| DFP | defensive fight position |
| DG | distinguished graduate |
| DoD | Department of Defense |
| DUI | driving under the influence |
| EAL | entry authority list |
| EC | entry controller |
| ECP | entry control point |
| EMSG | Expeditionary Mission Support Group |
| EOD | explosive ordnance disposal |
| EUCOM | European Command |
| FD | fire department |
| FOA | Field Operating Agency |
| FOB | Forward Operating Base |
| FP | Force Protection |
| FSI | Foreign Service Institute |
| FSO | flight security officer |
| FSS | flight security supervisor |
| FTX | field training exercise |
| GAL | global address Listing |
| GCRES | Ground Combat Readiness Evaluation Squadron |
| GLCM | Ground Launched Cruise Missile |
| GO1 | General Order 1 |

| | |
|---|---|
| GoA | Government of Afghanistan |
| GPS | Global Positioning Satellite |
| GSU | geographically separated unit |
| GWOT | Global War on Terrorism |
| HAF | Headquarters Air Force |
| HQ | headquarters |
| HMMWV | highly mobile multi-wheeled vehicle |
| HVT | high-value target |
| HUMRO | Humanitarian Relief Operation |
| IA | individual augmentation |
| IAG | Interagency Action Group |
| IAW | in accordance with |
| IBA | Interceptor Body Armor |
| ID | identification |
| IED | improvised explosive device |
| IG | Inspector General |
| INF | Intermediate-ranged Nuclear Forces |
| IO | information operations |
| IOT | in order to |
| ISAF | International Security Assistance Force |
| ISB | Intermediate Staging Base |
| ISO | in support of |
| IT | Information Technology |
| ITAM-MoI | Iraqi Training and Advising Mission to the Ministry of Interior |
| IW | Irregular Warfare |
| JDOC | Joint Defense Operations Center |
| JRTC | Joint Readiness Training Center |
| JS | Joint Staff |
| JSF | Joint Security Forces |
| JSO | Joint Security Office |

| | |
|---|---|
| JSS | Joint Security Station |
| JTF | Joint Task Force (multiple US military services) |
| JTF-SH | Joint Task Force SHINING HOPE |
| JTF-B | Joint Task Force–Bravo |
| KIA | killed in action |
| LCC | Launch Control Center |
| LE | law enforcement |
| LED | Law Enforcement Desk |
| LN | local national |
| LNO | liaison officer |
| LOC | letter of counseling |
| LoC | Lines of Communication |
| LOR | letter of reprimand |
| LPC | Leadership Planning Conference |
| LT | the Navy's and Army's way of abbreviating lieutenant |
| Lt | the AF's way of abbreviating lieutenant |
| LTC | the Army's way of abbreviating lieutenant colonel (O-5) |
| LtCol | the AF's way of abbreviating lieutenant colonel (O-5) |
| LZ | landing zone |
| MAC | Mobility Airlift Command |
| MAJCOM | Major Command |
| MDS | Missile Defense Squadron |
| MEDEVAC | medical evacuation |
| MEDOP | medical operation |
| MEU | Marine Expeditionary Unit |
| MoI | Ministry of Interior |
| MOS | military occupational specialty |
| MP | military police (Army version of the AF's SF) |
| MPA | military performance average |

| | |
|---|---|
| MSG | Mission Support Group |
| MUTC | Muscatatuk Urban Training Center |
| MWD | military working dog |
| MWR | Morale, Welfare, and Recreation |
| NAF | Numbered Air Force |
| NATO | North Atlantic Treaty Organization |
| NCO | noncommissioned officer |
| NCOIC | noncommissioned officer in charge |
| NGO | nongovernmental organization |
| NVG | night vision goggles |
| OAF | Operation ALLIED FORCE |
| O/C | observer/controller |
| OCF | Officers' Christian Fellowship |
| OIC | officer in charge |
| OP | observation point |
| OPC | Operation PROVIDE COMFORT |
| OPCON | Operational Control |
| OPORD | operations order |
| OPFOR | opposition forces |
| OPR | officer performance report |
| OSD | Office of the Secretary of Defense |
| OSI | Office of Special Investigation |
| PA | physician's assistant |
| PA | public affairs |
| PCC | Provincial Control Center |
| PCM | primary care manager |
| PCS | permanent change of station |
| PDC | Provincial Development Council |
| PDP | Provincial Development Plan |
| PFT | physical fitness test |
| PKK | Kurdistan Workers' Party |

| | |
|---|---|
| PM | provost marshal |
| PME | Professional Military Education |
| POC | point of contact |
| POI | point of impact |
| POO | point of origin |
| POW | prisoner of war |
| PRF | promotion recommendation form |
| PRT | Provincial Reconstruction Team |
| PT | physical training |
| PTAT | Police Training and Advisory Team |
| PTO | protected time off |
| PTSD | post-traumatic stress disorder |
| QA/QC | quality assurance /quality control (CE/project inspections) |
| QC | quality control |
| QRF | quick-response force |
| RC-E | Regional Command–East |
| RAF | Royal Air Force |
| ROE | Rules of Engagement |
| RON | remain overnight |
| RPG | rocket-propelled grenade |
| R&R | rest and relaxation |
| R&S | Reconnaissance and Surveillance |
| RTB | return to base |
| RTO | radio telephone operator |
| RV | recovery vehicle |
| SA | situational awareness |
| SAC | Strategic Air Command |
| SAM | surface-to-air missile |
| SAMI | Saturday morning inspection |
| SEA | senior enlisted adviser |

| | |
|---|---|
| SECFOR | security force |
| SED | simulated explosive device |
| SERE | Survival Evasion Resistance and Escape |
| SES | senior executive service |
| SF | security forces |
| SFS | Security Forces Squadron |
| SGM | sergeant major |
| SITREP | situation report |
| SIV | Special Immigration Visa |
| SO | service officer |
| SOCOM | Special Operations Command |
| SOP | Standard Operating Procedure |
| SP | security police |
| SPS | Security Police Squadron |
| SSgt | staff sergeant (AF-style abbreviation) |
| SWA | Southwest Asia |
| TACON | Tactical Control |
| TALCE | Tactical Airlift Control Element |
| TB | tuberculosis |
| THREATCON | Threat Condition |
| TEL | transporter erector launcher |
| TFW | Tactical Fighter Wing |
| TOC | Tactical Operations Center |
| TTP | Tactics, Techniques, and Procedures |
| UCMJ | Uniform Code of Military Justice |
| UIF | unfavorable information file |
| UN | United Nations |
| UNAMA | United Nations Assistance Mission – Afghanistan |
| USAFA | United States Air Force Academy |
| USAFE | United States Air Forces Europe |
| USAID | United States Agency for International Development |

| | |
|---|---|
| USDA | United States Department of Agriculture |
| USG | United States government |
| USSR | Union of Soviet Socialist Republics |
| VA | vulnerability assessment |
| VAMP | Vulnerability Assessment Management Program |
| VIP | very important person |
| VOQ | visiting officers' quarters |
| WIA | wounded in action |
| WSA | weapons storage area |

# ABOUT THE AUTHOR

Colonel Tracey Meck was born in Bozeman, Montana. After spending her early life moving every couple of years around Montana and Minnesota, her family settled in Anchorage, Alaska, in 1976. After high school, she reported to the United States Air Force Academy. Graduating in 1987, she earned a bachelor's degree and a commission as a second lieutenant. She served the majority of her career in her primary field, security forces (SF). In 2006, she took a one-year career-broadening deployment as the commander of Provincial Reconstruction Team (PRT) Gardez in Afghanistan. For the remainder of her AF career, she rotated between SF and Stability Operations assignments at the Headquarters Central Command and Pentagon levels. Her other contingency deployments included serving as the provost marshal for Joint Task Force (JTF) SHINING HOPE (supporting Kosovar refugees fleeing to Albania) and JTF ATLAS RESPONSE (a flood relief operation in southern Africa); the deputy commander for the 455th Expeditionary Mission Support Group at Bagram Airfield, Afghanistan; the chief of staff for the Iraqi Training and Advisory Mission to the Ministry of Interior in Baghdad, Iraq; and as the chief staff officer for a Joint Special Operations Task Force in Djibouti, Africa. She retired in 2012 at the rank of colonel and settled on Camano Island, Washington.

Col Meck is spending her retirement as a "professional volunteer.". She serves as a volunteer admissions liaison officer for USAFA, diligently working with students from over forty high schools in Northwest Washington. Additionally, she is active in her local church, Camano Chapel, where she volunteers at the food bank, His Pantry, and with the His Veterans Ministry. In early 2017, she deployed as a member of a short-term mission trip to Haiti.

CPSIA information can be obtained
at www.ICGtesting.com
Printed in the USA
FSHW022259141118
53652FS